"The EU political system has become difficult to m[...]
manifold reforms and a profound transformation of [...]
and expanded text provides an exhaustive analysis [...]
of its operation. Analytically sharp, and backed up by scientific literature, it is
highly recommended to readers who want a thorough understanding of how
the EU responds to the challenges it faces."

Renaud Dehousse, *President, European University Institute, Italy*

"Olivier Costa and Nathalie Brack's remarkable book may be the very best
place to look for those who need to understand the European Union in all of its
complexity. European integration, nearly seventy years old, has helped achieve
European peace, built an open and dynamic European market, bolstered existing national democracies and nurtured new ones, and contributed significantly
to international solidarity. All this has all happened, however, despite EU institutions that ordinary Europeans have rarely understood and often disapproved.
Recently the EU has experienced repeated crisis and its national members growing uncertainty. Today's EU sits on shaky economic, political, and international
grounds, therefore. Costa and Brack eschewing hyperbole and pulling no
punches, provide a very rewarding read. They understand what the EU's future
might if be things turn out well and they also give us what we will need if things
do not."

George Ross, *Université de Montréal, Canada*

"This is an excellent text for teaching students how the European Union (EU)
operates. It draws on much of the scholarly literature on the EU, explaining it
clearly for those who have not studied the integration process or the EU's institutions before. The coverage of theories, institutions and policy-making in one
volume makes this a highly effective textbook."

Richard Whitaker, *Leicester University, UK*

How the EU Really Works

The European Union is facing a profound crisis and is confronted with multiple challenges. Over the last two decades, it has experienced a series of dramatic changes to its powers, its institutional design, its constitutional framework and its borders. The current political, economic and financial crisis puts the EU's legitimacy further under pressure and creates the impression of a turning point.

This book provides a concise analysis of the EU and its dynamics by paying particular attention to its day-to-day operation. It aims to help students and scholars understand its evolution, its institutions, its decision-making and the interactions between the EU and various actors. Avoiding abstract theorizing, the authors propose an easy to read analysis of how the Union works while recognizing the complexity of the situation. Throughout the book, the key issues of European integration are addressed: democratic deficit, politicization, the role of member states, institutional crisis and citizen involvement.

This edition has been fully updated to include:

- Brexit, the migration crisis as well as the consequences of the 2014 EP elections for all the EU institutions;
- An in-depth analysis of the 2014 EU elections;
- More empirical data across the board;
- New developments in EU decision-making such as the trialogues, and differentiated integration;
- More in-depth discussion of the role of interest groups in EU policy-making.

This text is of key interest to students, scholars and readers interested in European Union politics and studies.

Olivier Costa is CNRS Research Professor at the Institute of Political Studies of Bordeaux, France. He is also Director of European Political and Governance Studies at the College of Europe in Bruges, Belgium, and co-director of the Jean Monnet European Centre of Excellence of Aquitaine in Bordeaux, France. He is associate-editor of the *Journal of European Integration*, and member of the editorial board of the *Journal of Legislative Studies* and the *Italian Political Science Review*.

Nathalie Brack is Assistant Professor in the Department of Political Science and at the Institute for European Studies of the Université libre de Bruxelles (Cevipol), Belgium. She is also Visiting Professor and Coordinator of the European General Studies Programme at the College of Europe (Bruges). Her research has been published in *JCMS*, the *Journal of European Integration* and the *International Political Science Review* among others.

How the EU Really Works

Second Edition

OLIVIER COSTA AND NATHALIE BRACK

Routledge
Taylor & Francis Group

LONDON AND NEW YORK

Second edition published 2019
by Routledge
2 Park Square, Milton Park, Abingdon, Oxon OX14 4RN

and by Routledge
711 Third Avenue, New York, NY 10017

Routledge is an imprint of the Taylor & Francis Group, an informa business

© 2019 Olivier Costa and Nathalie Brack

First edition published by Ashgate Publishing 2014; Routledge 2016
English translation of *Le fonctionnement de l'Union européenne*, by Olivier Costa
and Nathalie Brack
© 2011, 2014, 2017 by Editions de l'Université de Bruxelles.
All rights reserved including the right of reproduction in whole or part in any
form.
This edition published by arrangement with the original publisher Editions
de l'Université de Bruxelles, Brussels.

British Library Cataloguing-in-Publication Data
A catalogue record for this book is available from the British Library

Library of Congress Cataloging-in-Publication Data
Names: Costa, Olivier author. | Brack, Nathalie, 1984- author.
Title: How the EU really works / Olivier Costa and Nathalie Brack.
Description: Second edition. | New York: Routledge, 2018. |
"English translation of Le fonctionnement de l'Union européenne,
by Olivier Costa and Nathalie Brack " 2011, 2014, 2017
by Editions de l'Université de Bruxelles"–T.p. verso. | "This edition published
by arrangement with the original publisher Editions de l'Université de
Bruxelles, Brussels"–T.p. verso. | Includes bibliographical references
and index.
Identifiers: LCCN 2018005522 | ISBN 9780815370437 (hardback) |
ISBN 9780815370475 (paperback) | ISBN 9781351249232 (ebook)
Subjects: LCSH: European Union. | European Union–Decision making. |
Administrative agencies–European Union countries. | Legislative bodies–
European Union countries. | European Union countries–Politics and
government.
Classification: LCC JN30.C665 2018 | DDC 341.242/2–dc23
LC record available at https://lccn.loc.gov/2018005522

ISBN: 978-0-8153-7043-7 (hbk)
ISBN: 978-0-8153-7047-5 (pbk)
ISBN: 978-1-351-24923-2 (ebk)

Typeset in Avenir and Dante
by Sunrise Setting Ltd., Brixham, UK

MIX
Paper from
responsible sources
FSC
www.fsc.org   FSC® C013056

Printed and bound in Great Britain by
TJ International Ltd, Padstow, Cornwall

Contents

Figures

Tables

Boxes

Acknowledgements

This book is the result of years of both research on various aspects of the inner working of the EU and of teaching on the EU's institutions and decision-making processes in different universities across Europe and the USA. It greatly benefited from numerous discussions with colleagues, EU practitioners and students, whom we thank for that.

We would also like to warmly thank Katya Long and Alice May Candy who contributed to the translation and proofreading of the manuscript.

This book is dedicated to our families (Karel, Hélène, Cécile and Anne) who supported us with patience during the research and writing process.

Nathalie Brack and Olivier Costa

Introduction

One faces the threat of banality when writing the introductory chapter of a book on the European Union (EU). We are indeed constrained to acknowledge the success of this form of regional integration, unprecedented in both scale and intensity, and yet also admit the limitations and shortcomings of this process. It is especially so since the Brexit vote in June 2016, which highlighted even more the risk of regression of the integration process and underlined the extent to which the EU's legitimacy is questioned amongst the population. Despite its lack of originality, both paths – the success and limitations of European integration – will be explored in succession.

1 An original construction, an undeniable success

European integration is an unprecedented and unparalleled success. However, the history of Europe is ambivalent. On the one hand, the true concept of Europe has emerged since the shared values of ancient Greece that provoked continued reflection on the conditions, opportunity and virtues of regional integration. On the other hand, Europe's history has been punctuated by countless conflicts that have seen nations exhaust themselves in endless wars. European countries contributed to global unrest twice in the twentieth century. Nonetheless, the Community experience has succeeded in rapidly and completely pacifying relations between Member States. Even though its leaders still experience friction and national sentiments endure, the EU has had no internal diplomatic crises or any form of economic, symbolic or armed conflict amongst its members. While citizens do not necessarily demonstrate strong affiliation to the EU, they no longer imagine going to war with their neighbours. Until the Brexit vote, it was also considered unthinkable that they could lose the benefits of free movement or the protection of their human rights. European citizens' support for the EU institutions, its actors and its policies is limited, but the European integration project is most often not disputed. Moreover, opinion polls show that the Brexit vote has acted as an electroshock, and has sparked a renewed commitment to European integration in all Member States, including the United Kingdom.[1] From an economic perspective, even if the current crisis creates mixed assessments as to the pertinence of its policies, it is clear that European integration allowed national economies to recover after the war or, for the more recent Member States, to have a rapid transition to a market economy. Today, the EU is the world's largest economy and by far the leading aid donor to developing countries. Despite the essentially 'civil' nature of its power, it is also a key player in international relations and, as such, the EU contributes to the promotion of peace, democracy, human rights and multilateralism at the global level, and plays a central role in issues such as the fight against global warming.[2] Even though the EU is often described as being 'in crisis', it remains a strong magnet for its neighbours. Of the approximately 200 existing regional integration organizations, the EU is the most advanced in every way (integration, institutions and policies) and is also the largest in terms of wealth, population, territory and number of Member States.

It is the only organization that has seen the emergence of independent supranational institutions endowed with authority, which involves citizens directly in its actions and which has developed a full repertoire of values, goals and government standards.[3] After more than 65 years of European integration, we must acknowledge the undeniable success of this singular experience. This being the case, no one can ignore the difficulties the European Union faces today. Euroscepticism has become a stable component of political life in most Member States and European integration now seems to lack any plan or direction. Moreover, for the first time in EU history, there is a fear that certain policies will be dismantled, or even that one or more Member States will leave. How can this be explained?

2 An integration experience faced with a crisis of trust and growth

Generally, since the early 1990s, developments in European integration no longer seem to fit a coherent project. Instead they seem to reflect partial reactions towards a series of unforeseen crises. Thus, the integration process appears to be more reactive than proactive. It seems that institutions deploy all their energy in reacting to current events and crises rather than defining a medium- and long-term strategy. While the innovations contained in the Single European Act emerged from a long evolution and a widespread desire to revive an integration process that had lost its momentum, more recent innovations (Maastricht, Amsterdam, Nice, draft European Constitutional treaty and the Lisbon treaty) have been directly dictated by two kinds of constraints.[4]

Reform was primarily driven by the need to address the upheaval in Central and Eastern Europe. The collapse of the Soviet bloc in the early 1990s forced EU officials and heads of state to consider the prospect of extending European integration to the entire continent much earlier than expected. After some uncertainty, they agreed on a strategy of simultaneously deepening and broadening the EU (European Council of Copenhagen, June 1993). The goal was, first, to rapidly deepen European integration in order to provide the EU with the ability to respond to events in the East (through the establishment of a common foreign and security policy and cooperation on justice and home affairs) and to anticipate the likely difficulties of treaty reform in an enlarged Europe (through the institution of the Euro, expansion of Community jurisdiction and institutional reform). Meanwhile, the decision was made to open negotiations without delay for the integration of Central and Eastern European countries so as to stabilize the region as soon as possible, end a senseless East–West divide and support the transition of these candidate countries towards democracy and a market economy.

Second, Community reform since the early 1990s has been motivated by growing concerns in the general public over European construction. After a long period of relative indifference towards this process (rather hastily described as a 'permissive consensus'),[5] successive reforms of various treaties provoked strong reactions in national politics and public opinion.[6] Upon ratification of the Maastricht Treaty (1992–1993), many people discovered the extent of European integration and the constraints it imposed on Member State governments. Many politicians, opinion leaders, civil society actors and ordinary citizens stated their strong opposition to European integration even while this treaty sought to establish a link between the EU and its citizens in order to better justify the extension of its powers (European citizenship, strengthened powers of the European Parliament, creation of the European ombudsman, etc.). These protests have varied over time depending on the period and the individual Member States but different forms of resistance to Europe have become stable components of EU political life and now form the major forces in many states.[7] In their attempt to resolve these difficulties, treaty negotiators have opened Pandora's Box: they have attracted attention from both political leaders and citizens on issues such as the democratic deficit or European citizenship and have gradually made the functioning of the Union and its institutional reform important political issues. This contributed to repeated treaty revisions born from the desire to better reflect citizens' expectations in matters of public policy and pursue the 'democratization' of European construction, a process that goes back to the decision, in 1976, to elect the European Parliament by direct universal suffrage.[8] In the early

2000s, this concern for democracy even generated an entirely new process at the supranational level, with the institution of the Convention on the future of Europe, which drafted a constitutional treaty for the EU. However, the constraints of intergovernmental negotiation have limited the ability of Member State representatives to achieve their goals. Successive treaties have thus suffered a great deal of criticism and have faced more pronounced difficulties in ratification.

The entry into force of the Treaty of Lisbon put an end to all wide-ranging reforms by providing two clear texts: the Treaty on the European Union (TEU) and the Treaty on the Functioning of the European Union (TFEU). The European sovereign debt crisis that started at the end of 2008 has since led to the negotiation of new texts (the Stability and Growth Pact, the Twopack, the Sixpack) and to the Fiscal Compact – formally, the Treaty on Stability, Coordination and Governance in the Economic and Monetary Union. This new intergovernmental treaty has been signed, in March 2012, by only 25 Member States but the discussions on the coordination of national fiscal and budgetary policies have also reactivated the reflexions on the opportunity to build a Federal Union, for instance, during the European Council of June 2012. However, no concrete initiative has been taken and the extreme tensions arising from the debates over the multiannual budgetary perspective (2014–2020) have shown that national leaders are reluctant to make further sacrifices of sovereignty to the EU.

In June 2016, the decision of the citizens of the United Kingdom to demand the exit of their State from the European Union, through the activation of Article 50 of the Treaty on European Union, led to an unprecedented confidence crisis and raised strong questions about the fate of Europe. National leaders have been slow to come up with solutions to overcome this crisis, but they are also slow to take initiatives to challenge the nature of European integration. The EU therefore remains functional but failing, a construction in which all the most recent elements are relatively adequate answers to pressing issues but which struggle to form a legible and coherent whole.

The Treaty of Lisbon thus remains the main frame of the EU political system. Despite its weaknesses, it provides answers to a number of outstanding issues that have arisen since the Maastricht Treaty. It introduces a simpler system of majority voting in the Council (in application since the 1st of November 2014), which is also better adapted to future enlargements as it generalizes the use of the co-decision procedure (now called 'ordinary legislative procedure') and of qualified majority voting within the Council. It also merges the three 'pillars' introduced by the Maastricht Treaty and gives the EU a single legal status. It establishes a permanent President of the European Council and clarifies, to a certain extent, the division of powers between the national and European levels. The Treaty opens the door to the theorization of a European regime by devoting a chapter to the issue of democracy. It also defines the limits of integration. However, far from the ambitious goals of the Constitutional Treaty, the Lisbon

Treaty confirms the hybrid character of the EU, at the crossroads between inter-governmental and federal perspectives. This is mirrored by how, through the Council and the European Council, Member States not only remain significant but even gain importance. The treaty also regulates the European institutions' use of their powers through the principles of attribution, subsidiarity and pro-portionality. It finally opens, for the very first time, the possibility for a Member State to leave the EU. While some considered it to be a symbolic concession to the most Eurosceptic national officials, intended to compensate the expansion of EU powers and the strengthening of its supranational aspect, with the Brexit, it will lead to a regression of European integration. The first decisions taken after the entry into force of the new Treaty, particularly regarding the choice of the Presidents of the Commission, the European Council and the High Repre-sentative for Foreign Policy, reinforced the sense of a sustainable balance between intergovernmental and supranational logic.

The page has been turned on institutional reforms, which had proved partic-ularly laborious. Today, it is hard to see where an effective revival of the federal project could come from, apart from declarations of good intentions and initia-tives that have no lasting benefits. The strategy of constitutionalizing the EU, launched in the 2000s, has demonstrated its limits and perverse effects: it sought to address citizens' concerns, but has increased the reluctance of many of them towards European integration.[9] After a very long sequence of institutional reforms, the EU must once again demonstrate its utility by focusing on policies. This is the course of action followed under Jean-Claude Juncker, President of the Commission since 2014, who intends to reduce the number of legislative initia-tives but focus on themes that are at the heart of citizens' concerns, i.e. growth, employment, global warming, security.

The sovereign debt crisis did not serve as a demonstration of that, since it was mainly managed in an intergovernmental way by the European Council and the Eurogroup – i.e. the meeting of the finance ministers of the Eurozone. As noted by Copsey, the Eurozone crisis has confirmed the 'powerlessness of the EU's collective leadership' and should not hide the fact that the EU still faces signifi-cant challenges that need to be addressed.[10] Similarly, the refugee crisis in 2015 highlighted the shortcomings of the free movement of persons, which was not designed to deal with such a possibility, and made the EU a priority target for populist and extremist movements opposed to migrants. For if, more than ever, the legitimacy of the unusual system of the EU has been called into question, opinion polls (including Eurobarometer surveys) demonstrate that people remain committed to the principle of European integration: a survey of December 2016 shows that the citizens of any Member State – including the United Kingdom – are not willing to leave the EU.[11] On the other hand, European citizens expect the EU to be particularly enterprising regarding issues related to globalization such as off-shoring, climate change, social dumping, migration, international security issues, energy supply, regulation of capitalism and of financial system, etc. Indeed, recent surveys also show that citizens feel the EU should focus on their concerns regarding the economy, unemployment and immigration as well as on tackling poverty and social exclusion.[12]

The European integration crisis is not unique: it is only the most visible and most evident aspect of a crisis affecting contemporary democracies – in Europe and elsewhere. It is a multiple crisis: economic, social, environmental, political. Contemporary states are undermined by autonomist or independent movements (as evidenced by renewed regionalist claims in Scotland and Catalonia), by phenomena of political dislocation, and by frontal oppositions within society. Societies are increasingly divided according to territories, religions, lifestyles, ethnic origins . . . There is a general decline in the citizens' loyalty towards institutions and parties as well as a rejection of elites which are not specific to the European Union, but are even more acute and visible at that level.

3 A political system under constraints

Under the present circumstances, and pending a potential revival of European integration through public policy (or in-depth reforms as promoted recently by several scholars),[13] the functioning of the EU is strongly dependent on a series of tensions and difficulties. Methodologically speaking, it is crucial to analyse its progress within the global context. The European integration process has long been studied mainly by focusing on EU's capitals (Brussels, Luxembourg, Strasbourg) and, at best, taking into account the influence of national permanent missions to the EU. It is, however, advisable to emphasize the interactions that currently exist between European institutions and society in general, and to propose a more encompassing view. The issue of public opinion, which, in the 1980s, did not yet really impact the EU, now weighs significantly on the determination of its agenda and decision-making.[14]

Three paradoxes specific to the EU stem from this situation.

1   First, one must recognize that even if the EU is usually seemingly absent from national public arenas and even if it seems remote to citizens, the EU is now an inescapable reality. The relative weakness of EU media coverage does not preclude an actual awareness of citizens of the importance of European integration issues. Henceforth, the debate in this matter becomes complex. It is not that much about the need to continue and deepen European integration or not, but rather about its direction, about the nature of the EU's political development and the virtues and shortcomings of its institutional system. Thus, Eurosceptics no longer include only those opposed to the principle of supranational European integration. The category has

expanded to include citizens and political actors who are not opposed to the European project as such but challenge the choices made, whether they concern economic policies, institutional structure or values.[15] This is particularly the case in the current context of economic, financial and migration crisis, where European issues are becoming increasingly salient in domestic political life. The scope of the positions of politicians and citizens on European issues such as solidarity, austerity measures and economic governance has widened considerably. However, the quality of this debate is poor as the protagonists are largely unaware of the realities of European construction and their arguments are often more in an emotional register (fear of decommissioning and decline, the rejection of foreigners or the establishment, the glorification of the nation, nostalgia of a golden past) than a rational one. The Greek crisis has democratized the European Union in the worst possible way: citizens have begun to talk about Europe in their homes, but about a Europe that compels and punishes, or a Europe that is powerless, and dominated by Germany. On the other hand, citizens are ill-informed about what European standards can offer them in terms of protection of consumers, workers or citizens, and are no longer aware of the progress that free movement has allowed.

2 Second, the paradoxical nature of citizens' and policy-makers' attitudes vis-à-vis the EU should be noted. Few would dispute the overall results of European integration. It has created lasting peace on the continent, assured reconstruction and prosperity and achieved the age-old goal of European unification. In the 1980s, European integration contributed significantly to the transition to democracy for Greece, Spain and Portugal. More recently, integration allowed the continent to overcome the division imposed on it by the Cold War and to support former Soviet-bloc countries in their transition to democracy and market economy. Today, despite the institutional and financial crises, the EU's appeal remains strong for most of its neighbouring countries[16] and beyond and is still the model of integration that is spontaneously opposed to free-trade zones.

Despite its overall success, European integration garners few favourable comments from citizens, opinion leaders and national policy makers. Integration is presented alternately as a Trojan horse of liberalism, an invisible foreign power that challenges social benefits and Member States' societal models and imposes austerity on the masses to save banks and relocate migrants or, on the other hand, as an overzealous, bureaucratic leviathan that curbs the initiatives of economic actors and handicaps them when competing outside of Europe. It is true that European integration, as an essentially economic construction from the beginning ('common market', later the 'single market', now complemented by Economic and Monetary Union) was an accelerator of economic and social reforms. Its impact has been crucial to labour-market deregulation, public-service reform, reviews of social-protection mechanisms, the dismantling of monopolies and so on. More recently, public opinion has been affected by the Commission's desire to multiply global free-trade agreements, particularly with the United States and Canada, and have perceived its action as a desire to accelerate globalization and challenge European social and environmental standards. Historically, the EU has indeed shown itself to be better able to deregulate – with all its effects on Europeans, as workers, service users and consumers – than to regulate. When the EU has been a regulator, the need for uniform standards has often conflicted with the general public. One will recall the controversies surrounding the 'ban' on raw-milk cheeses, open-season dates for hunting migratory birds and even market-stall refrigeration.

The sovereign debt crisis has led to new initiatives and even to a new treaty (2012). But the situation is contrasted. On the one hand, the negotiations proved that national leaders are not very enthusiastic about increasing the powers of the EU in the field of macro-economic regulation. Many even consider that the European institutions are responsible for the economic and social crisis and accuse them of imposing a policy of fiscal austerity without reason. When the Commission, under the new regulatory mechanisms, adopted specific recommendations to certain Member States concerning their budget and their choice of public expenditure and social policy, the protests picked up. In 2017, in more than half of the Member States, some political parties propose to leave the EU or the eurozone. But, on the other hand, the EU institutions (Commission, ECB) have acquired new powers to supervise and control the decisions of national leaders regarding their budgetary and fiscal policies. The sovereign debt crisis has made it possible to correct some of the most obvious shortcomings of EMU and to transfer new macroeconomic skills to the EU, which had seemed totally impossible before.[17]

The difficulties of legitimation experienced by the EU are amplified by its weak structural capacity to satisfy its citizenry. Even today, its powers are largely oriented towards liberalization and regulation of the European market and recently towards the imposition of austerity policies on nation states. The EU has little means to meet the population's most pressing demands, such as employment, security, social protection and macroeconomic regulation. Member State officials have jealously maintained control over social benefits (health, family, unemployment, disability, grants, etc.), the budget and taxation, which are instruments commonly used by governments to ensure their popularity with voters.[18]

The EU does have some capacity for limited redistribution, specifically the Common Agricultural Policy and regional policy. However, it is not a welfare state and its overall budget is capped at 1 per cent of Member States' GNP (with a theoretical maximum of 1.27 per cent) as opposed to the 20 per cent to 30 per cent budget for a 'classic' federal state[19] such as the USA, Canada, Brazil or Germany and the 40 per cent to 60 per cent of GNP for its Member States (all levels of government and social security combined). Even if citizenship cannot be considered as a purely clientelist relationship between voters and governments, it is clear that the EU has little capacity to meet the immediate needs of European citizens when its power of redistribution is limited to very specific groups of people such as farmers, local elected officials, researchers and students. Regulatory policies are another tool policy makers can use to improve citizens' satisfaction. Their effect is less evident however, both from an individual point of view – citizens are unconcerned with industry standards and may not even be aware of their existence and effects – and collectively – standards often only produce effects in the medium to long term. In the case of the EU, we must also reckon with the system's weak ability to communicate its actions to the public.[20]

In recent years, the resentment of public opinions towards the EU has also been fuelled by the feeling that it was unable to contribute to their security or even that it actually put them in harms' way. The coincidence of Islamist terrorist attacks in several EU countries and of the refugee crisis triggered by the conflict in Syria has made it possible for populists and right-wing movements to denounce both the EU's passivity when facing these phenomena, and the fact that the principle of free movement of persons favours, in their views, the activities of terrorists and the arrival of migrants.

The EU institutional system is also the subject of harsh criticisms. These include its lack of transparency, its overly bureaucratic nature and lack of respect for the principles that form the basis of Member States' political systems, including separation of powers, the primacy of elections, the potential for partisan change, parliamentary sovereignty, political responsibility and media coverage. Since the early 1990s, reforms have introduced many procedures, institutions and norms intended to strengthen the democratic character of the EU. The original system has not been radically changed, however, and its current architecture is hybrid, complex and impossible to explain simply. Thus, any gains in terms of legitimacy resulting from the successive reforms of the European institutional framework have been partially nullified by decreased clarity.[21] Indeed, it is no longer possible to stress the sui generis ('one of its kind') nature of the EU in order to justify its specific characteristics, in particular the fact that it does not fully respect the democratic standards in force at the national level (such as the separation of powers, representation of the citizens and political accountability of leaders).

The attitude of national political leaders has done nothing to improve this situation. Many are adept at the practice of doublespeak: often demanding reforms favourable to them or that seem necessary behind closed doors in Brussels, but later appearing to be hostile to the actions of European institutions when it comes to their implementation. The example of the Stability Pact is particularly telling. The same politicians who demanded that a principle framing national fiscal policies be enshrined in the treaties, adopted unanimously, to protect the eurozone from individual states' lack of rigour also pursued costly policies and then denounced the Commission's 'interferences' when it called them out. Even more recently, they have condemned the lack of budgetary safeguards, but have simultaneously criticized the comments made by the Commission about various national situations. The EU appears convenient scapegoat on two fronts. First, it conducts unpopular reforms for which national leaders are unwilling to take responsibility at home and, second, it is accused of opposing the fulfilment of their electoral commitments. To the extent that EU institutions have no perceptible voice within Member States and currently enjoy limited support, this discourse is deployed with no tangible obstacles.

3   Finally, beyond the misunderstandings surrounding its institutional system, one must recognize that the EU suffers from a real tension between the intensity of its influence on almost all aspects of public action on the one hand and the opacity of its decision-making system and the anonymity of its institutional actors on the other. Citizens are unaware of the identity of their leaders, whether it be the Commission, the Council, the European Parliament or the European Central Bank.[22] The institution of a President of the European Council by the Treaty of Lisbon seems unlikely to remedy this situation. The first holders of this office, Herman Van Rompuy (2010–2014) and Donald Tusk (2014–), were indeed unknown outside of their own countries. It is also unclear how their jurisdiction is supposed to be linked with those of the President of the Commission, the High Representative for Foreign Policy and the six-month rotating presidencies of the Council. Moreover, the media is quite indifferent to the present activities of European institutions and seems only to be interested in cases of scandal, crisis or conflict.[23] The decision of the five main European parties to organize the 2014 European elections around their respective candidates to the Presidency of the European Commission, using the German 'Spitzenkandidaten' system, has 'dramatized' a campaign that is usually dull and focused on national issues. The fact that the candidate of the European People's Party, J. C. Juncker, was named President of the Commission after his party's victory underlines the growing impact of the European elections on the functioning of the EU system. However, this new process remains informal for the moment, it did not generate much media coverage and, above all, did not trigger electoral participation of the same order of magnitude as for national elections.

4 The importance of taking Euroscepticism seriously

These three paradoxes must be underscored. They create a strained relationship between citizens and the EU and thereby strongly determine the work of EU institutions as well as reflections on treaty reform. It is important to be wary of the attitude of certain actors, such as Europhile enthusiasts, derisive experts and backward-looking lawyers who brush aside the concerns and reluctance of the population towards European integration with the wave of a hand on the grounds that they are unfounded and result from a lack of understanding and information. In the 1990s, many analysts considered opposition to the Maastricht treaty as a phenomenon that was the product of obscurantism, incompetence or the unfounded scepticism of the masses. We must challenge this interpretation for at least two reasons. First, it should be noted that the 'Eurosceptics' category is not homogenous: citizens may object to the EU for many reasons other than a lack of information or an attachment to the nation. Euroscepticism can come from the left and the right and may alternatively be directed towards the European project, its institutions, its policies or its actors.[24] Moreover, what is often called Euroscepticism refers to a broader rejection of politics and distrust towards institutions and political parties, at both the national and supranational level. Thus, many Eurosceptic parties are first and foremost populist and develop a rudimentary anti-European discourse, which is merely the continuation of the anti-establishment discourse they develop mainly on a national scale. Second, one must note that the question of the EU's legitimacy can no longer be considered without referring to the analytical framework of democracy. The original European construction, like any classic international organization, has legitimized itself in a rational–legal mode (the expertise of institutional actors and respect for treaties and the law), can no longer do so. More in-depth analysis of the EU is justified given the continued expansion of its competences and the introduction of multiple standards, procedures and bodies inspired by national regimes and even of explicit references to representative democracy (Article 10 TEU), into the treaties. In a democratic regime, the representations and opinions of citizens must be considered to be legitimate and be addressed. The democratic character of the system is not assessed only on the basis of objective criteria determined by institutional actors and experts: it also depends on the perceptions of citizens. In other words, democracy is also in the eyes of citizens. Condemning the 'ignorance of the people' in Europe is to question democracy itself by denying voters the ability to make appropriate choices.[25] This is the whole point of a political analysis of the functioning of the Union which should explain the reservations raised by this political system – underscoring the role played by the lack of information and cultural openness of citizens,[26] among other factors – while being careful not to stigmatize them.

5 The pitfalls of a political analysis of the European Union

One must avoid three analytical and methodological pitfalls in the study of the EU.

The first is the teleological approach, which presupposes that the developments of European integration were either understood by political analysts or foreseen by the EU's founding fathers. This is not the case. No one knows what will happen to the EU, even in the medium term. There is no 'genetic code' hardwired into the treaties that would push it inexorably towards a specific model, federal or otherwise, especially since the Treaty of Lisbon included provisions allowing a State to leave the EU and authorizing the 'renationalization' of certain policies. Social sciences are poorly equipped to predict the future on European matters as well as on all other subjects. While there has been a constant validation of the *'acquis communautaire'* (i.e. the total body of EU legislation) in the jurisprudence of the Court of Justice and successive treaty reform, the EU is not immune to stagnation, regression or rupture. This is demonstrated by Brexit or by the proposals to leave the EU, the Eurozone or the Schengen area put forward by some political parties in almost all Member States. Similarly, we must be careful not to describe *a posteriori* European integration as a linear process, and remember instead that it was largely shaped by historical events, the political situation in Member States and international, economic and social constraints which do not form a continuum. Its history since the turn of the century proves this, alternating between moments of enthusiasm and severe crisis. Among the former we can mention the Convention on the Future of the Union (2002–2003), the adoption of the Constitutional treaty (October 2004), the treaty of Lisbon (December 2007) and the Fiscal Compact (January 2012), or the nomination of Jean-Claude Juncker as the new President of the Commission (June 2014) in line with the expectations of the European Parliament. There have also been many moments of crisis, including clashes at the Nice Summit (December 2000), the statement of disagreement on the Constitutional treaty (December 2003), its rejection by France and the Netherlands (May–June 2004), Irish voters' refusal to ratify the Lisbon Treaty (June 2008), the many fruitless meetings of the European Council since the beginning of the sovereign debt crisis at the end of 2008, not forgetting the refugee crisis, the Brexit vote in 2016 or the 'illiberal' drifts that are currently affecting several EU member states (Poland and Hungary in particular).

The alternation of moments of crisis and recovery allows European integration to progress, despite everything. The Eurozone crisis and its management confirm the resilience of the integration process: while often presented as a deep existential crisis similar to the Eurosclerosis of the 1970s, integration has continued to take steps forwards. Even though the pace of integration is slow, the budgetary treaty (2012) or the new Permanent Structured Cooperation (PESCO) in the area of defence security and policy (2017) brought forward institutional developments to deal with crucial issues which were unthinkable a few years ago. But they do not reflect the 'ideal' of an 'ever closer Union' and rather refer to an intergovernmental logic, not even involving all the Member States, and not to the Community method. The federal perspective is therefore resistible; other options may emerge. From now on, and for the first time in the history of the EU, it is no longer unimaginable that the degree of integration will be significantly reduced. Several national leaders are openly Eurosceptic, pessimism reigns within the institutions, and no tangible initiative seems to emerge to get the EU out of its torpor. Moreover, the European Union is now seen by some as a structure to be fought, both in Russia and in the United States.

The second hazard of EU analysis is the illusion of partisan neutrality. European integration poorly reflects the traditional divide between left and right; commentators are often perceived to be neutral and objective – as being situated above the left/right divide – even if they take a stand in favour of or against European integration. A significant part of European studies literature has long been marked by methodological bias with many authors displaying openly militant pro-European opinions or explicitly prescribing solutions to hasten or improve the integration process. More recently, more critical work on EU policies and institutions has been emerging, grounded on a rejection of the principle of European integration, on a refusal of its policies (macro-economy, migrations, security, etc.), or on the questioning of the supranational level as a framework for political life and public action. However, the study of the European system, like any political system, requires a clear distinction between the analytical and normative registers. One may be led to take a position in a debate based on available evidence and objective arguments, but one must be careful not to do so in the name of an ideal vision of Europe or metaphysical or ideological choices.

EU analysis poses a final challenge that stems from its hybrid nature. Being neither a federal state nor a typical international organization, we must be cautious in the use of concepts, theories and categories developed by comparative politics, constitutional law or international relations.[27] One should therefore beware of two extreme positions, both open to criticism. The first is the sterile invocation of the *sui generis* nature ('one of its kind') of the EU which implies that one would not be able to compare it to any other political system or organization. Given the centrality of comparative methodology in the social sciences, this would limit the study of the EU to an esoteric description of its institutions, decision-making procedures and policies and would exclude any consideration of its legitimacy. This position is untenable since the many changes that have affected the communities since the early 1980s have been largely inspired by the parliamentary system, the federal model and the desire to resolve the 'democratic deficit'. Similarly, the forms of regional integration that have multiplied on every continent since the 1960s are an invitation to a comparison with the EU, which is a model for some.[28]

Nevertheless, one should also be cautious in the use of concepts and theories forged in other contexts and use comparison wisely. Regarding concepts, one must pay attention to the risks of nominalism: it is not because an EU institution is called the 'European Parliament' that it can be studied, without prior discussion, with the tools of legislative studies. Similarly, theories must be handled properly. They are forged as a function of a specific context and are then empirically validated in a particular case; applying them to another political and institutional system requires precaution. The idea, for example, that the primary purpose of a member of parliament is to be re-elected should be considered with some circumspection in the case of MEPs. The logic of a political career and the selection of candidates is not the same at the European level as at the national level. In short, it is necessary to keep the EU's characteristics in mind including its unique institutional structure, the absence of separation of the executive, legislative and judicial powers, the specific nature of the EU's powers and policies, the limited role of partisan logic in its operation, the robustness of nation states, etc. The comparative tool should be used sparingly, making sure – as far as possible – to respect the principle dear to John Stuart Mill of 'all things being equal' and using, when necessary, specific or specifically defined concepts.

In order to comprehensively analyse the functioning of the EU, this book is organized in nine chapters. The first one outlines the history of European integration, as a mirror of the complexity of its institutional system and its operating procedures. The goal here is not to trace the chronology of European integration as such but to demonstrate that the original political system of the EU as well as the various decision logics driving it are, in large part, the product of a turbulent history of multiple crises, successes and compromises. This perspective is, therefore, essential to understand the EU. In the second chapter, we propose an overview of the theories of European integration that account for this complex reality and of the various trends in contemporary EU studies. We also address the multifaceted topic of Europeanization.

We then systematically review all the institutional and non-institutional actors that contribute to EU operations. Chapter 3 deals with the EU executive power, i.e. the European Council and the Commission. Chapter 4 is devoted to the legislative power, namely the Council and the European Parliament. In Chapter 5, we present the numerous organs that ensure law enforcement and control at the EU level. The other European organs (consultative bodies, financial organs, agencies) are presented in Chapter 6; which also analyses the growing role of national Parliaments in the EU policy making.

Finally, we examine the methods of European decision-making with particular emphasis on the more practical and informal aspects of the EU legislative process. Chapter 7 presents the various competences of the EU and the main procedures of decision-making. Chapter 8 proposes a typology of four models of decision-making within the EU. The last chapter analyses this decision-making process from a public policy network perspective and underlines its specificities. The concluding chapter discusses issues related to the EU's legitimacy, the integration process in times of crisis and the balance of power between the supranational and national levels.

Notes

1 Eurobarometer November 2016.
2 Mario Telo, *Europe: A Civilian Power? European Union, Global Governance, World Order* (Houndmills: Palgrave MacMillan, 2007).
3 Olivier Costa and François Foret, 'The European consociation, an exportable model? Institutional design and relations between politics and religion,' *European Foreign Affairs Review* 10(4) (2005): 501–516.
4 See the Special Issue of the *Journal of European Integration* 'The Maastricht Treaty: second thoughts after 20 years,' 34(7) (2012).
5 Leon N. Lindberg and Stuart A. Scheingold, *Europe's Would-Be Polity. Patterns of Change in the European Community* (New Jersey: Prentice Hall, 1991). For a discussion, see Virgnie Van Ingelgom, *Integrating Indifference. A Comparative, Qualitative and Quantitative Approach to the Legitimacy of European Integration* (ECPR press, 2014).
6 Ian Down and Carole J. Wilson, 'From "Permissive Consensus" to "Constraining Dissensus": a polarizing union?' *Acta Politica* 43(1) (2008): 26–49.
7 Justine Lacroix and Ramona Coman, eds, *Les résistances à l'Europe: cultures nationales, idéologies et strategies d'acteurs* (Brussels: Éditions de l'Université de Bruxelles, 2007); Richard C. Eichenberg and Russell J. Dalton, 'Post-Maastricht blues: The transformation of citizen support for European integration, 1973–2004,' *Acta Politica* 42(2–3) (2007): 128–152; Mark Franklin, Michael Marsh, and Lauren McLaren, 'Uncorking the bottle: popular opposition to European unification in the wake of Maastricht,' *Journal of Common Market Studies* 32(4) (1994): 455–472; Robert Harmsen and Menno Ewout Spiering, eds, *Euroscepticism: Party Politics, National Identity and European Integration* (Amsterdam: Rodopi, 2004); Olivier Costa, Antoine Roger and Sabine Saurugger, eds, *Les remises en cause de l'intégration européenne,* Special issue of the *Revue internationale de politique comparée* 15(4) (2008).
8 Olivier Costa, '*The history of European electoral reform and the Electoral Act 1976: issues of democratisation and political legitimacy*' (Historical Archives of the European Parliament, European Parliament Research Service, European Union History Series, 2015, 44).
9 Hans-Jörg Trenz and Pieter de Wilde, *Denouncing European integration: Euroscepticism as a reactive identity formation* (RECON Online Working Papers Series, no. 10, 2009).
10 Nathaniel Copsey, *Rethinking the European Union* (London: Palgrave, 2015).
11 Survey conducted from 25 November to 7 December 2016 by the Win Gallup Institute. See for example: www.lecho.be/dossier/brexit/Les_Belges_ont_davantage_confiance_dans_l_Europe.9847071-8048.art.

12 Eurobarometer EB 82, Autumn 2014 and the European Parliament Eurobarometer, 'One year to go to the 2014 European elections,' EP/EB 79.5.

13 Nathaniel Copsey, op.cit.; Giandomenico Majone, *Rethinking the Union of Europe Post-Crisis: Has Integration Gone Too Far?* (Cambridge: Cambridge University Press 2014); John Peet and Anton La Guardia, *Unhappy Union: How the Euro Crisis—and Europe—Can be Fixed* (London: Economist Books, 2014); Antoine Vauchez, *Democratizing Europe* (Palgrave, 2016).

14 Liesbet Hooghe and Gary Marks, 'A postfunctionalist theory of European integration: from permissive consensus to constraining dissensus,' *British Journal of Political Science* 39(1) (2009): 1–23.

15 Michael Bruter, 'Legitimacy, Euroscepticism & identity in the European Union—problems of measurement, modeling and paradoxical patterns of influence,' *Journal of Contemporary European Research* 4(4) (2008): 273–285; Nathalie Brack and Olivier Costa, 'Introduction: beyond the pro/anti- Europe divide: diverging views of Europe within EU institutions,' in *Euroscepticism within the EU Institutions. Diverging views of Europe*, eds Nathalie Brack and Olivier Costa (London: Routledge, 2012), 1–12; Amandine Crespy and Nicolas Verschueren, 'From Euroscepticism to resistance to European integration: an interdisciplinary perspective,' *Perspectives on European Politics and Society* 10(3) (2009): 377–393; Henry Milner, '"YES to the Europe I want; no to this one". Some reflections on France's rejection of the EU Constitution,' *Political Science and Politics* 39(2) (2006): 257–260.

16 For a recent discussion, see Heather Grabbe, 'Six lessons of enlargement ten years on: the EU's transformative power in retrospect and prospect,' *Journal of Common Market Studies* 52(Annual Review) (2014): 40–56.

17 R. Vilpišauskas, op.cit.

18 Andrew Moravcsik, 'Federalism in the European Union: rhetoric and reality,' in *The Federal Vision: Legitimacy and Levels of Governance in the United States and the European Union*, eds Kalypso Nicolaïdis and Robert Howse (Oxford: Oxford University Press, 2001), 161–190.

19 The US federal budget is approximately $3,000 billion (2008), with a GNP of just over $10,000 billion or 30%. Of course state and local authorities have their own budgets.

20 Ana Isabel Martinsa, Sophie Lecheler and Claes H. De vreese, 'Information flow and communication deficit: perceptions of Brussels-based correspondents and EU officials,' *Journal of European Integration* 34(4) (2012): 305–322.

21 O. Rozenberg, 'L'influence du Parlement européen et l'indifférence de ses électeurs: une corrélation fallacieuse?' *Politique européenne* 28 (2009): 7–36.

22 According to recent surveys, more than a third of Europeans are unable to name any European institution while only 11% could name the Council, 24% the Commission and 27% the European Central Bank. Similarly, 27% of Europeans feel that they know nothing at all about EU leaders and 46% know a little about the people who run the EU institutions. Finally, a majority of Europeans (56%) are not interested in EU affairs. See the European Parliament Eurobarometer 'Two years to go to the 2014 European elections', EB/EP 77.4, 2012 as well as 'One year to go to the 2014 European elections,' EB/EP 79.5, 2013.

23 Jochen Peter and Claes H. de Vreese, 'In search of Europe: a cross-national comparative study of the European Union in national television news,' *The Harvard International Journal of Press/Politics* 9(4) (2004): 3–24.

24 Pieter de Wilde, Hans-Jörg Trenz and Asimina Michailidou, *Contesting EU Legitimacy; The prominence, content and justification of Euroscepticism during 2009 EP election campaigns* (Arena Working paper, no. 14, 2010); Petr Kopecký and Cas Mudde, 'The two sides of Euroscepticism. Party positions on European integration in East Central Europe,' *European Union Politics* 3(3) (2002): 297–326; André Krouwel and Koen Abts, 'Varieties of Euroscepticism and populist mobilization: transforming attitudes from mild Euroscepticism to harsh Eurocynicism,' *Acta Politica* 42(2/3) (2007): 252–270; Bernhard Wessels, 'Discontent and European identity: three types of Euroscepticism,' *Acta Politica* 42(2/3) (2007): 287–306.

25 Gérard Duprat, ed., *L'ignorance du peuple: essai sur la démocratie* (Paris: Presses universitaires de France, 1998).

26 Olivier Costa, Antoine Roger and Sabine Saurugger, eds, *Les remises en cause de l'intégration européenne.*

27 See the debate between S. Hix and A. Hurrell and A. Menon: Andrew Hurrell and Anand Menon, 'Politics like any other? Comparative politics, international relations and the study of the EU,' *West European Politics* 19(2) (1996): 386–402; Simon Hix, 'Comparative politics, international relations and the European Union! A rejoinder to Hurrell and Menon,' *West European Politics* 19(4) (1996): 802–804.

28 Olivier Costa, Clarissa Dri and Stelios Stavridis, eds, *Parliamentary Dimensions of Regionalization and Globalization. The Role of Inter-Parliamentary Institutions* (Palgrave MacMillan, 2013).

A political system forged by history

1

The history of social phenomena is always of interest when studying a political system,[1] even more so with the EU, whose institutions, competences and geography are continuously changing and where institutional and national balances have largely been determined by a succession of events and crises. Thus, it is important to pay attention to the historic dimension of European integration, to emphasize its incremental nature and manifold inspirations in order to understand, not only the essence of its political system and its institutional architecture but also the division of powers between the national and European levels, the specificities of European decision-making and the difficulties of its legitimation.[2] In summary, we need to consider the EU as the result of a Darwinian evolutionary process and not of intelligent design.

The many unification projects that have marked the history of the continent from ancient Rome to Denis de Rougemont[3] will not be discussed here. Let us simply remind our readers that the idea of a structured European cooperation is very old. Already in 1620, the Duke of Sully imagined 'a body politic of all European states that could produce a permanent peace and perpetual trade amongst its members'.[4] In the nineteenth century, Victor Hugo wrote:

> A day will come when we will see these two vast groups, the United States of America and the United States of Europe, located across from each other, reaching out over the sea to exchange their products, their business, their industry.[5]

However, it is only after the Second World War that the idea of a voluntarily united Europe was translated into concrete achievements.

1.1 Motivations for European integration: returning to an old idea

To understand the institutional architecture of the EU and discussions over its reform and future, we must first review the initial motivations for European integration. Even if this approach may seem trivial, it allows us to understand both the EU's current operational difficulties as well as the problem of its legitimation.

Treaty negotiations for the European Coal and Steel Community (ECSC) and the European Economic Community (EEC) were motivated by three main objectives: peace, prosperity and the idea of Europe.

1.1.1 Peace

At the end of the Second World War, European states were anxious to find a way to avoid the outbreak of new conflicts. Different attempts towards European integration endeavoured to address this concern. The ECSC, the first stage of EU integration, sought to deprive its first six Member States (West Germany, Belgium, France, Italy, Luxembourg and the Netherlands) of the means to go to war by merging their coal and steel markets. Subsequently, the Euratom Treaty did the same for civilian nuclear energy. In both cases, the rationale was to integrate the resources necessary to the manufacture of arms in a structure that prevented their use for military purposes, promoted cooperation between the elites and thus the peaceful coexistence of European nations. The goal was to create tangible solidarities between Europeans beyond mere diplomatic dialogue and economic exchanges. This is why European Communities institutions were endowed from the beginning with responsibilities that are exactly the contrary of those of a federation. Instead of intervening in domains of state sovereignty (defence, justice, political, currency, foreign affairs, etc.), which national leaders kept jealously and whose integration could have generated resistance within the population, European institutions served at a very practical level by ensuring the integration of European economies and developing specific policies (a customs union, the free movement of workers and goods, a common agricultural policy, transportation). This strategy was intended to foster exchanges both between the political, administrative, social and economic elites and between groups of Europeans such as workers, students and consumers. The socialization of these actors and the emergence of common interests averted the spectre of new conflicts.

1.1.2 Prosperity

Second, the European construction addressed the desire to promote reconstruction and economic development. In economic matters the inspiration was twofold: state interventionism and liberalism. The arbitration between these two visions reflected the national circumstances of the time. Germany and the Benelux countries were more favourable to Anglo-Saxon free trade while France was partial to state intervention in the economy. The French prevailed with the Common Agricultural Policy (CAP) which stemmed both from the need for self-sufficient food production in the European Community and to protect farmers from overly radical reforms. The CAP necessitated a high degree of centralized decision-making, extensive market regulation, imposing new agricultural practices and establishing redistribution mechanisms. Liberalism – or more specifically German 'ordo-liberalism'[6] – prevailed in the domestic market however. The goal was a laissez-faire economy by simply ensuring the proper functioning of the market through the removal of trade barriers, the dismantling of monopolies, the monitoring of mergers and acquisitions, the control of state assistance, etc.[7] Over time, this second motivation for integration has become increasingly important. Community institutions have proven to be much more comfortable with deregulation than regulation, for reasons that are both functional and ideological. In the Community, deregulation is relatively easy. Decisions are made most often by a qualified majority within the Council and this approach has the support of reformers and liberals as well as of the business community, at both the national and European level. In regard to regulation, decisions often require unanimity (although the treaties of Nice and Lisbon did increase the use of qualified majority in this area) and the proposed standards often cause strong reactions at the national level when they disrupt habits and traditions. Moreover, Member States have a tendency to promote European standards that are as similar as possible to their own ('goodness of fit') thus providing themselves with a competitive edge over their partners.[8]

1.1.3 Europe

Finally, the ECSC and EEC were intended to realize the long-term dream of European integration. Though it seems evident, the objective of 'Europe for Europe' is often overlooked. It was a strong incentive for integration. The Community project was largely shaped by the meeting of national interests in a specific political and economic context but the fact remains that the European ideal foresaw the reconciliation of European states at the end of the war and began an ambitious process of unification.[9] If the EU remains unique in the world by the extent of its integration, it is because other regional integration experiences are not based on factors of reconciliation such as European identity and the ideal of Europe.[10]

It should nevertheless be emphasized that Member States have always had mixed perceptions of the European project, its purposes, its methods and its boundaries.[11] As European integration progresses and specifying its nature becomes a necessity, these divergences appear more clearly.[12] Deep divisions exist in most Member States regarding the desirable outline of an integrated Europe as demonstrated by the referendum campaigns on European treaties in the 1990s and 2000s. Citizens, politicians and economic actors have diverse expectations and conceptions of integration.[13] Regarding the degree of integration, expectations vary from simple intergovernmental cooperation to a full-fledged federation. Now, some politicians are even promoting a step backwards. The White Paper on the future of Europe presented by the President of the Commission in March 2017 even reopens this debate, including a 'focusing on the market' and a 'do less but more effectively' approach. Meanwhile, since 2016, in 18 of the 28 Member States, there have been parties in favour of leaving the EU. As for its operating rules, different models are also in competition: the 'Community method', the classic international organization, the parliamentary system, the agency system, etc. Similarly, the scope of the EU's responsibilities provokes diverging assessments: a simple free trade area for some, for others a space of financial solidarity between territories and people, a superpower able to make its voice heard in the international arena, a welfare state or even an organization whose responsibilities are limited to some highly integrated policies. Discussions also rage over what unites the Member States: a commitment to limited core values such as a market economy, democracy and human rights or more elaborate values such as sustainable development, social progress, social and territorial cohesion. Similarly, the assessment of the criteria for joining the Union is mixed. Some believe that any state (ultimately even non-EU countries) committed to the values and rules of the EU should be able to join while others feel that only European states can aspire to be candidates. Finally, others, the so-called 'Christian club' would prevent states such as Turkey and Bosnia from joining the EU.

There is even a geographic uncertainty: the European Union with its 28 (27 after Brexit in 2019) Member States can be compared to the Council of Europe with its 47 Member States, which include the Russian Federation, Azerbaijan and Georgia. Indeed, Europe is not a continent, but the Western peninsula of the Asian continent – along with the Northern peninsula in the case of the Council of Europe. Therefore, the delimitation of the Union's eastern border cannot be based on unquestionable geographical factors, but must be determined politically – which means, in particular, deciding the long-term destiny of countries such as Belarus or Ukraine.

Positions also differ as to the principles that should guide the EU's action: economic liberalism, social protection, sustainable development, territorial cohesion, etc. Finally, the nature of its relationship with other international organizations (NATO, UN, Council of Europe) and certain outside countries (USA, Russia) also creates deep divisions between Member States and political families.

Successive enlargements, from six to 28 Member States from 1973 to 2013, have steadily broadened the spectrum of national preferences and complicated the definition of its objectives, priorities and operating procedures. While a certain consensus existed amongst the original six Member States on the objectives and methods of European integration, the positions are now much more diverse. The use of such vague and consensual terms as 'Europe', 'integration', 'Community' and 'Union' no longer hides these differences. It is necessary to take into account the multiplicity of visions and definitions of Europe that exist and fluctuate according to interests, historical events and crises in order to understand the EU's institutional structure, the nature of its powers, its operations and debates on its reform.[14] In political debates, the word 'Europe' is often used without great precision. It is difficult to know if it means the EU, Europe in the geographical sense or the Europe of the Council of Europe. Even when speaking specifically about the EU, it is sometimes to signify only the supranational institutions and sometimes the group they form with Member States and all levels of government mixed together. As we have already mentioned, from a geographical perspective, Europe is an abstract concept: it is the European peninsula of Asia with uncertain Eastern borders. Their delineation thus depends on political judgement, values and cultural elements. The concept of Europe is underpinned by both a perception of things – a product of belief, culture, history and experience and by strategic choices – driven by economic, geostrategic or electoral considerations.

The EU we know today is the result of more than 65 years of adjustments to expectations by the representatives of the States, of European institutions and of various interest groups and civil society organizations. Besides this, three phenomena have also helped to shape the EU.

First is the process of 'spill over'. The phenomenon was theorized by neofunctionalist authors in the 1960s.[15] This was to account for the tendency of the European Commission to systematically infringe upon the Member States' powers in the name of the efficient and plenary exercise of its powers bestowed by the treaties. This pretention was not openly challenged by the Member States until de Gaulle's 'empty chair' crisis was created (1965–1966). Before this, the States favoured the 'effectiveness' of European public action and relied on the Commission to fulfil the objectives defined by the treaties of Paris and Rome.

The second important phenomenon is the legal formalism that guides the actions of treaty negotiators and the players in European construction. The allure of a simple and systematic construction explains the continued expansion of certain practices and procedures. This has notably contributed to the merger of the executives of the Communities (1965) and of the three pillars of the Maastricht Treaty (as a result of the Lisbon Treaty in 2009), or to the generalization of the co-decision procedure (called today 'ordinary legislative procedure') and qualified majority voting within the Council. The quest for a certain degree of judicial elegance has always contributed to the strengthening of European integration. Indeed, the modalities of treaty negotiations prevent back-tracking since the most pro-integration national representatives have a veto right. Harmonization has thus always happened from the top, through the generalization of the most integrated procedures. Moreover, in the day-to-day functioning of institutions, the Court seeks to ensure the *'acquis communautaire'* and prevent any regression.

The theme of the 'democratic deficit' has also contributed to the continued strengthening of European integration. It could be otherwise: according to its definition, the democratic deficit could be resolved by re-nationalizing certain policies, increasing of the powers of the Council, effectively strengthening the role of national parliaments in the functioning of the EU or empowering judicial and control organs. The theme of democratic deficit has mostly benefited the European Parliament due to the strong mobilization of its members and the tendency of treaty negotiators, socialized in the national parliamentary systems, to systematically favour institutional solutions, resulting in a strengthening of the European Parliament's powers.[16] The slow process of 'parliamentarization' that has affected the EU since the 1970s has thus contributed to the degree of integration and the supranational dimension of decision-making processes.

1.2 A reasoned chronology of European integration

The dynamic of European integration has not been indisputable and unambiguous. It is a complex process, the result of many influences and marked by a high level of contingency.[17]

The history of the Community and then of the EU has been shaped by the meeting of national interests, by external political and economic pressures, by the strategies specific to supranational institutions and by the ideas and ideals relative to Europe and European construction. However, one can distinguish relatively homogeneous and lengthy periods, marked by dominant concerns, which have contributed, each in their own way, to define what the EU has become today. Thus, we propose to break down the period from 1946 to 2017 into six periods of roughly a decade.[18]

1.2.1 1946–1958: in search of a method of integration

After the Second World War, many initiatives sought to pacify Europe by means of its integration. In 1946, Winston Churchill called for 'the United States of Europe' – without British participation.[19] In 1948, The Hague Congress brought together a thousand delegates from 20 European countries to discuss the potential for cooperation among states at the European level in order to maintain peace and national sovereignty. The Council of Europe was created in 1949 as an outcome of this Congress. However, it was a poorly integrated international organization which disappointed the expectations of the federalists. The idea of a truly political union based on the integration of states stumbled, particularly as a result of the desire of the United Kingdom to maintain its sovereignty. In the context of the reorganization of the global order driven by the Cold War, other organizations for European cooperation emerged along the lines of traditional international organizations.[20] As for military cooperation, the Western Union was founded in 1948 (Brussels Treaty) and became the Western European Union (WEU) in 1954. On the economic front, the Organization for European Economic Cooperation (OEEC) was created in 1948 to allocate funds from the Marshall Plan and became the Organization for Economic Cooperation and Development (OECD) in 1961. On 9 May 1950, Robert Schuman, French Minister of Foreign Affairs, proposed – at the suggestion of Jean Monnet and his collaborators – the creation of a European Coal and Steel Community (ECSC), a Franco-German initiative open to other European countries. In 1951, six countries (France, West Germany, Belgium, Italy, Luxembourg and The Netherlands) signed the Treaty of Paris establishing the ECSC for a period of 50 years.

As mentioned earlier, the option of the ECSC marked a strategic shift: the idea was to first build an economic base likely to allow for possible political cooperation in the medium term and to make reconciliation between the Second World War adversaries irreversible by placing the production and management of resources for the arms industry under a common authority. Within the logic of integration 'by sector', the objective was to progressively apply the model of the ECSC to other sectors of the economy and society to create economic, judicial, social and, finally, political solidarity.

> 'Europe will not be made all at once, or according to a single plan. It will be built through concrete achievements which first create a de facto solidarity'.[21]

The goal was that citizens from different Member States would ultimately experience the desire to share the same interests and to form a single community so as to prevent the resurgence of national conflicts and enable political integration.

The ECSC was organized around four bodies. The High Authority was a supranational institution independent of the Member States which exercised most executive, legislative and coordination responsibilities. The Council of Ministers, introduced at the request of 'small' Member States for fear that the High Authority was too heavily dominated by France and Germany, was responsible for validating the legislative proposals of the latter. The Assembly of the

ECSC had only very limited powers and was primarily symbolic. The Court of Justice was charged with resolving conflicts between ECSC institutions, between Member States and between the ECSC institutions and Member States. The ECSC offered a blueprint of a federal state in a limited sector in which integrated institutions enjoyed considerable autonomy vis-à-vis Member States. It was the antithesis of the Council of Europe, whereas the latter proposes little cooperation on broad subjects, the ECSC is putting in place a formally limited cooperation but which is endowed with significant resources.[22]

In 1954 Member States of the ECSC negotiated a new treaty to address the issue of West Germany's rearmament within the context of increased tensions between the two blocs of the Cold War and the eruption of the Korean War. The European Defence Community (EDC – Pleven Plan) extended the path taken by the ECSC to European defence and, in the medium term, planned the creation of strongly integrated political institutions. This treaty, however, was rejected by the French National Assembly, despite having already been ratified by all other states. This challenged the federalist-inspired sectoral integration strategy, the implementation of which seemed overly cumbersome and uncertain, and therefore unfit to allow European integration to progress at the right pace.

Various initiatives attempted to overcome this failure. In 1955, during the Messina Conference, the representatives of six countries decided to abandon 'sectoral' integration and extend integration to the whole economy. They charged an intergovernmental committee to make proposals in this regard.[23] French diplomacy had lost its credibility with the rejection of the EDC; therefore, the renewal came from Belgium and its Foreign Minister, Paul-Henri Spaak, who chaired the committee.

On 25 March 1957, the six states of the ECSC adopted the committee's proposals and signed the treaties of Rome establishing the European Economic Community (EEC) and the European Atomic Energy Community (EAEC or Euratom). The idea of sectoral integration still inspired the EAEC, created at the request of France, but was partly abandoned in favour of the establishment of a common market. This implied a lesser degree of intervention and centralization than that of the ECSC but the establishment of institutions that had some freedom to develop new policies based on general objectives. The goal was to fully but gradually integrate the European economy without undermining the sovereign powers of states. To do so, the Six adopted a framework treaty which defined certain policies and granted autonomy to the integrated institutions to establish others.

The treaties of Rome entered into force on 1 January 1958, six months before the return of General de Gaulle to power in France. He disagreed with full market integration and the federal essence of the project, but instead of preventing any progress from the outset, he first took advantage of European integration to boost French industry and provide opportunities for the agricultural sector.

1.2.2 1958–1966: the triumphant start

This period is one of success. The established institutional structure kept its promises. The Commission increased its initiatives and rapidly advanced the implementation of the common market. The 'functional motor' worked: in accordance with the *spillover* effect, the structure (Commission) always generated more functions (policies), which in turn justified the strengthening of the structure. National leaders, satisfied with the efficient pursuit of the objectives defined in the treaties and aware of their own problems, allowed them to move forward.

The Common Agricultural Policy (CAP) came into force in 1962 and a Treaty merging the executives of the three Communities was signed in 1965. A single Council and Commission replaced the bodies of the ECSC, EEC and Euratom. The Parliamentary Assembly and the Court of Justice were already shared.

The first crisis of European integration took place in the second half of 1965. Charles De Gaulle decided to practice 'empty chair' politics and asked his ministers to refrain from sitting in the Council. He wanted to express his opposition to the federal nature of the EEC which became more evident with the end of the transition to qualified majority voting within the Council in certain areas (10 years after the entry into force of the Treaty) from unanimity, which had previously given the Council an essentially intergovernmental mode of functioning. It also marked his irritation with the federalist tropism of the Commission, then headed by Walter Hallstein, who suggested replacing national contributions to the Community budget with its own resources, thereby increasing the independence of the Commission and the power of the parliamentary assembly. The empty chair crisis paralyzed the Council for seven months. On 29 January 1966, the Luxembourg Compromise was reached. This text, a simple political agreement with no legal authority, allows a Member State to request the postponement of a vote by qualified majority within the Council and the pursuit of further discussions on a draft EU decision when it affects 'very important national interest(s)'. In addition to the oil crisis, this plunged the Community into a long period of stagnation which continued until 1984 and profoundly changed the balance of EU institutions.[24]

The Council, which exercised formal control over the legislative branch and which had previously operated in a fairly integrated way despite the requirement of unanimity, gradually saw its power increase and established itself as an intergovernmental body. State representatives thoroughly examined the Commission's proposals seeking provisions that might affect an individual country's 'very important interests'. The scope of the agreement was uncertain: De Gaulle saw it as a guarantee of his right to veto, while the most federalist leaders considered it to be a symbolic concession with no future, and which did not call into question the logic of Community integration. Despite the letter of the treaties, the Council no longer voted passed votes and the slightest provocation invoked the Luxembourg Compromise.

1.2.3 1966–1974: the return of intergovernmentalism

The decade following the empty chair crisis was a period of stagnation in which the intergovernmental nature of the Council increasingly asserted itself. Individual states sent a growing number of officials and diplomats to monitor Council activities and to dissect Commission proposals. The latter incorporated this constraint by limiting its initiatives and by proposing routine and unambitious texts. The institutional development of the European Parliament, including its involvement in determining the Community budget, came to a standstill. Despite this dismal context, which some feared marked the end of the integration process, three positive events took place. In July 1968, the customs union between the six Member States was formed 18 months ahead of schedule. Second, the election of Georges Pompidou as President of France in June 1969 removed a number of obstacles. In 1970, the Luxembourg Treaty provided the Community with its own resources and awarded the European Parliament some responsibility for adopting and implementing the budget. The same year, the Council of Ministers adopted the Davignon Report on political cooperation and established a mechanism for information exchange and consultation on foreign policy issues. Finally, the first enlargement of the Community took place on 1 January 1973 with the accession of Denmark, the United Kingdom and Ireland. After a negative referendum, Norway refused to accede. This first enlargement was made possible by De Gaulle's departure as he had strongly opposed the accession of the United Kingdom. Contrary to what is often said, this enlargement did not hinder the integration process. In some ways, it even facilitated its resurgence by generating new expectations vis-à-vis the common market.[25] The three new Member States, which never hid their reluctance regarding federal integration, were interested in continuing the project of opening national markets and contributed to the revival of community initiatives.

1.2.4 1974–1986: Europe in search of a second wind

The first enlargement initiated a transition period marked by an atmosphere conducive to increased – if yet slow – European integration. In 1974, in line with the Davignon Report and under the leadership of Valery Giscard d'Estaing, heads of state or government decided to meet as the European Council three times a year to determine broad guidelines for European policy and initiate political cooperation. The creation of this new body can be interpreted as a powerful sign of the return of intergovernmentalism and loss of leadership for the Commission.[26] More optimistically, this might also be considered as evidence that the 'de facto' solidarity between the Europeans was a reality and that economic integration may be completed as a result of burgeoning political integration. The latter interpretation is substantiated by the willingness of Member States to have the Community play a role in the international arena, as seen by the signing of the Lomé Convention in 1975 involving the Community and 46 African, Caribbean and Pacific (ACP) states. The same year, the creation of the ERDF (European Regional Development Fund) highlighted the fact that the Community was not only a market but also an area of financial solidarity between Member States and regions.

At the Bremen Summit in July 1978 France and West Germany proposed the revival of monetary cooperation through the creation of the European Monetary System (EMS). Established in 1979, the EMS was meant to ensure the stability of European currencies so that the single market remained functional. It created the ECU (European Currency Unit) as the accounting currency of the Community. The first elections of the European Parliament (EP) through direct universal suffrage were also held in 1979. Following a 1976 decision, Europeans elected 410 MEPs for the first time. On 1 January 1981, the Community recorded its second enlargement with the accession of Greece.

In 1984 and under the aegis of Italian MEP Altiero Spinelli, the European Parliament adopted an ambitious draft Treaty on the European Union. Even if the text had no legal value and did not wield direct results, it has inspired the negotiators of new treaties including members of the Convention on the Future of the Union. For the first time, the Spinelli project merged two seemingly divergent strategies: that of integration and that of political cooperation.

In 1985, based on a Franco-German proposal, the European Council launched a reflection on a revision of the Treaty of Rome with a view to the achievement of the internal market and a codification of the political cooperation that existed in the margins of treaties, particularly as a result of EU summits.[27] This initiative was favoured by the combination of several factors. First, the draft Treaty of Union proposed by the Parliament and, more broadly, the strong mobilization of MEPs in favour of deepening European integration helped the recovery process. It also benefited from the arrival of Jacques Delors as President of the Commission in 1985. Third, the impact of the success of the neo-liberal doctrine in Europe – notably under the influence of Margaret Thatcher – must be underscored. Neo-liberalism thinks the state to be obsolete and a source of rigidity and considers that it should give more powers to the EEC to achieve the common market and to undertake reforms which cannot be carried out at the national level. The definition of new goals for integration, including that of the single market, finally enjoyed renewed mobilization from transnational economic actors (multinationals, banking groups, European employers, etc.) towards European construction.

Moreover, 1986 is the year of Spain and Portugal's entry into the EEC and the signature of a new treaty, the Single European Act (SEA). It is named the Single European Act because of the inclusion within the text of a revision to the EEC Treaty (in particular the establishment of the internal market by 31 December 1992) and a codification of political cooperation outside the formal framework of the EEC Treaty. In any case, the Single Act is fairly modest in its ambitions, particularly compared to the Spinelli project, and does not address the wishes of the EP or of federalists.

1.2.5 1986–1995: deepening European integration

The period following the Single European Act was marked by the preparations for the entry into force of the internal market which required the adoption of 310 European norms to replace national standards. The *White Paper on the Single Market* of the European Commission listed these norms and established a kind of legislative agenda for the period 1987 to 1992. In fact, the strategy to adopt European standards in order to organize all aspects of the domestic market was ultimately overly restrictive as a result of the uncertainties of decision making. It was gradually phased out in favour of the 'mutual recognition' of standards. According to a precedent set by the Cassis de Dijon decision (ECJ 120/78), Member States were therefore committed to accept the validity of their partners' standards. Today, this principle still ensures the free movement of goods throughout the Community without requiring the harmonization of national legislations. A product manufactured in a Member State in accordance with its national standards cannot be banned from sale in another Member State even if it does not meet that state's technical and/or quality standards.

The prospect of the entry into force of the single market and the collapse of the Soviet Union in late 1989 precipitated events. Member States were encouraged to take the next step in the direction of integration and to move beyond the single market to an economic and political union. On 9 December 1989, the European Council, meeting in Strasbourg, decided that an intergovernmental conference on the final stages of the economic and monetary union would meet before the end of 1990. On this occasion, 11 Member States (the United Kingdom opted out) adopted the Community Charter of Fundamental Social Rights of Workers, which is recorded as the 'social policy protocol' in the Maastricht Treaty. This was later integrated into the Treaty of Nice (2000) after the Labour Party takeover of British government which no longer opposed the text. In 1990, under the pressure of events in Eastern Europe, the European Council, acting on a Franco-German proposal, convened two intergovernmental conferences to prepare treaties for an economic and monetary union and for a political union. The objective was to 'achieve' economic integration and accompany it with political integration. This objective of deepening integration was presented as a prerequisite for Eastern enlargement and as a way of anticipating the effects of democratic and economic transition in countries freed from Soviet domination. However, others saw it as a way to delay the accession of Central and Eastern European countries, increasing to excess the level of 'community acquis' to be respected by candidate countries. The Schengen Agreement was signed in June 1990; it abolished border controls between Member States of the Community.

In December 1991, the two intergovernmental conferences were successful in the adoption of the 'Treaty on the European Union', or the Maastricht Treaty, by the European Council – it was signed by Foreign Ministers in February 1992.[28] This text has a rather baroque architecture as Member States were not able to agree on introducing new goals (foreign policy, defence, domestic affairs, justice) into the framework of the EEC, but also wanted to preserve the appearance of overall unity. They agreed to 'ascribe' new forms of integration to Community institutions. The treaty's structure has three 'pillars': the European Community (minus the term 'economic'), the Common Foreign and Security Policy (CFSP) and the Justice and Home Affairs Cooperation (JHA). The Maastricht Treaty also introduced the Economic and Monetary Union (EMU), which was included in the EC pillar, anticipating the establishment of a single currency and the coordination of the Member State's macroeconomic policies.[29] It extended the powers of the European Parliament and established European citizenship. Thus one can see a dual 'politicization' of European integration through, on the one hand, the exercise of supranational sovereign powers hitherto reserved to Member States (foreign policy, defence, justice, police, currency, etc.) and, on the other hand, the affirmation of the political nature of the functioning of the Union (co-decision procedure, recognition of the role of European political parties, European citizenship, the principle of transparency, etc.).[30]

In 1993, the Single Market and the Maastricht Treaty (after a difficult ratification process)[31] entered into force on 1 January and 1 November, respectively. By establishing the European Union and transferring many competencies to the supranational level, this treaty has sparked many tensions and fears within public opinion and is undoubtedly a 'critical turning point' when it comes to integration.

The European Council of Copenhagen (1993) recognized the vocation of Central and East European countries to join the EU, but imposed economic conditions and specific policies on them that exceed the letter of the treaties (the so-called 'Copenhagen criteria'). On 1 January 1995, the EU included three new Member States: Austria, Finland and Sweden, while Norwegian citizens again refused membership of the EU.

1.2.6 1996–2009: the unification of the continent and the constitutional process

Since the mid 1990s, the EU has undergone a period of intensive reforms related to its territorial expansion, the extension of its competences and the improvement of the effectiveness and legitimacy of its institutions. Despite the warmth of the majority of Member States, the prospect of the accession of 10 new members made it essential to further reform the treaties, at least to simplify decision-making and adapt institutions to a Europe of 25 or 30 Member States.[32]

The Amsterdam Treaty was adopted in 1997. It granted new powers to the EU, simplified the decision-making process and initiated the 'communitarization' of cooperation in matters of justice and domestic affairs. This treaty, however, did not carry any political project and did not implement the necessary reforms concerning the composition of the Commission (which threatened to be massive with a potential enlargement) and qualified majority voting in the Council (which promised to be increasingly difficult).[33] Once again, institutional reforms were postponed: a protocol was attached to the treaty stipulating that at least one year before the EU enlarged to more than 20 Member States another intergovernmental conference would be convened. In March 1998, negotiations for the accession of Central and East European countries officially opened.

In January 1999, 11 Member Countries moved to a single currency – the euro – and from this point forward the European Central Bank (ECB) was responsible for the monetary policy of the Member States in the eurozone. In March of the same year, the European Commission, chaired by Jacques Santer, collectively resigned as a result of its mismanagement of the 'mad cow disease' crisis and other various dysfunctions. At the European Council meeting in Berlin, the heads of state and government asked Romano Prodi to form a new European Commission. They also decided on the financial framework for the development and enlargement of the EU for the years 2000 to 2006 involving deep reforms of the CAP and of regional policy ('Agenda 2000'[34]). The Amsterdam Treaty came into force in May 1999. In December, the European Council (Helsinki) on enlargement confirmed the negotiation process with the countries of Central and Eastern Europe as well as Malta and Cyprus and acknowledged Turkey as a candidate country.

The Charter of Fundamental Rights of the European Union, elaborated by an *ad hoc* convention chaired by Roman Herzog, was announced in December 2000. In the same year, a new intergovernmental conference was convened, mainly to adapt the institutions to a massive enlargement of the EU. The Treaty of Nice was signed in February 2001 and came into force in February 2003. This new text extended the co-decision procedure to new areas, strengthened the CFSP and reformed EU institutions with a view to enlargement. The reform was however *a minima*, in conditions of extreme intergovernmental tensions, especially during the European Council in Nice in December 2000 as there were deep division between small and large Member States concerning voting weight in the Council and the Commission. There was a consensus to record the relative failure of this treaty and call for new institutional reform before the enlargement.[35]

As a consequence, a 'Convention on the Future of the Union' was convened in December 2001 by the European Council to propose elements of a treaty reform, especially regarding the institutions. It was composed of representatives of governments and parliaments of the Member States, the European Parliament and the Commission and included observers from candidate countries. In June and July 2003, at the end of its deliberations, it delivered a full draft of a European Constitution to the European Council, exceeding its original mandate.

In 2002, the single currency had been implemented in 12 states, with Greece joining the eurozone in 2001.

The Brussels Summit on the adoption of the Constitution in December 2003 failed mainly due to the refusal of Spanish and Polish Prime Ministers to abandon the voting arrangements in the Council provided by the Treaty of Nice and which were particularly favourable to them. On 1 May 2004, the EU underwent its biggest enlargement with the accession of 10 states although the functioning of its institutions had not been fundamentally reformed. The first European elections in the EU of 25 were held in June 2004. They were followed by the start of the procedure for the nomination of a new Commission.

The European Council finally managed to adopt the slightly altered draft European Constitution as a result of lengthy negotiations and a change of majority in Spain. Signed in Rome on 29 October 2004, the Constitutional Treaty consolidated, enriched and clarified the founding treaties and integrated the 'Charter of Fundamental Rights'. The ratification process for this new treaty then began. Nine states held referendums, some of which were advisory. On 22 November 2004 the Barroso Commission took office after a reorganization of the prospective college under pressure from the Parliament. On 16 and 17 December 2004, the European Council decided to open accession negotiations with Croatia and Turkey in 2005, subject to certain criteria. On 25 April 2005, accession treaties for Bulgaria and Romania were signed in Luxembourg.

The rejection of the European Constitution by referendum in France (29 May 2005) and the Netherlands (1 June 2005) opened a long period of uncertainty over the EU's future. The main institutions launched initiatives to stall for time, to understand the reasons for the rejection of the Constitution by citizens and to define their expectations of European integration.

On 1 January 2007 Bulgaria and Romania entered the EU and the eurozone extended to Slovenia. On 23 June 2007 in Lisbon, the 27 Member States reached an agreement on a draft treaty containing a large part of the Constitution but which left out all federalist or constitutional provisions. The Lisbon Treaty was signed on 13 December 2007. It changed the Treaty on the European Union and transformed the EC Treaty into the Treaty on the Functioning of the European Union (TFEU).

On 1 January 2008, Cyprus and Malta adopted the euro, bringing the number of members of the eurozone up to 15. On 13 June 2008, the Irish referendum on the Lisbon Treaty failed and the hopes of having a new treaty to organize the European elections in June 2009 were dashed. The Irish Prime Minister agreed to hold a second referendum on the treaty before November 2009 at the European Council of 11 and 12 December 2008 in exchange for some concessions, notably on the composition of the Commission.[36]

On 1 January 2009, Slovakia adopted the euro as its official currency. The seventh European elections were held from 4 to 7 June 2009, 30 years after the first ballot was cast. In September 2009, the Parliament re-elected José Manuel Barroso as the head of the Commission after the proposal of the European Council. On 2 October, the ratification of the Lisbon Treaty was the subject of a second referendum in Ireland, this time with positive results. The treaty entered into force on 1 December 2009. In January 2010, the European Parliament conducted the audition of the Commissioner candidates of the Barroso Commission II (2009–2014), who then took office in February 2010.

1.2.7 2009–2018: facing crises and new institutional developments

While the period of constitutional and institutional problems seems to have come to an end, the EU is facing a new round of difficulties related to the stability of the eurozone. In 2008 and 2009, against the backdrop of the worsening US financial crisis, European states were disorganized in their reaction to assist their banks. This caused a deterioration of the public finances in many eurozone countries and a serious erosion of market confidence in the solvency of some states such as Ireland and Greece. In the fall of 2009, the new Greek government announced that the country had lied for years about the extent of its deficits. In late 2009, the 'debt crisis' erupted in several states, threatening the credibility and continuity of the eurozone.

This issue, and more broadly, the issue of the EU's macroeconomic policies and eurozone regulation mobilized European institutions throughout the first half of 2010. In February 2010, a special European Council meeting examined the financial situation of Greece, which had been placed under surveillance by the Commission. In May, a joint aid package of 110 billion euros from countries in the eurozone and the International Monetary Fund was awarded to Greece with the condition that it implement a set of fiscal austerity measures. EU finance ministers approved a parallel rescue package to ensure Europe's financial viability and stability through the creation of the European Financial Stability Fund. This was a temporary tool, perceived as a solution to stop a possible contagion of the crisis and as a testimony that eurozone leaders stood behind the common currency.[37] In October 2010, the European Council agreed on the need for a permanent mechanism for crisis management in the eurozone (for the period post-2013) while the following month, Ireland also called for European assistance. The image of the EU's reaction to this crisis was one of confusion as the Member States were struggling to provide a unified response, contributing at the same time to the volatility of the financial markets.[38]

While the eurozone expanded with the entry of Estonia in January 2011, the financial crisis remained the priority of European institutions, despite divisions and tensions among Member States. The decision to marginally change the Lisbon Treaty (TFEU) in order to establish the European Stability Mechanism was formally adopted in March and serves now as a permanent rescue fund.[39] It was coupled with a strengthening of fiscal discipline with the adoption of the 'Euro Plus Pact',[40] echoing the Franco-German idea of an agreement intended to ensure the competitiveness and convergence of economies in the eurozone. This was Germany's condition to join the compromise of financial assistance to troubled countries. The pact's mechanism strictly limited Member States' public debt and enhanced the coordination of national policies in areas critical to the competitiveness of the eurozone. However, this pact is non-binding and is managed by the heads of state and government. The Commission's role is limited to advising on the commitments of participating countries.

Concerns about refinancing the Greek debt reappeared in May 2011 but Member States did not seem to be able to adopt a concerted response and interstate negotiations demonstrated the limits of the European system for the coordination of financial policies. Meanwhile the risk had spread as Portugal, Italy, Spain and Cyprus were also being targeted by the financial markets. Four months later, in Greece, the possibility of bankruptcy and an exit from the euro zone (Grexit) was seriously considered. On 27 October, the leaders of the 17 eurozone states reached an agreement on an ambitious three-part-plan: strengthening the EFSF to the cost of a trillion euros; recapitalizing banks for 106 billion; bailing out Greece for 100 billion. On 9 December 2011, representatives from the Eurozone countries, joined by those from the other EU countries except the United Kingdom and Hungary, agreed on an increased centralization of their budgets and on automatic sanction mechanisms for the states that do not respect common standards on public deficits. The end of 2011 was also marked by the adoption of a set of legislative measures, called 'Six Pack', aimed at reforming European economic governance.[41]

Despite these decisions, in January 2012, the rating agency Standard & Poor's downgraded nine eurozone countries, blaming the failure of their leaders to deal efficiently with the debt crisis.

This lasting distrust of the markets encouraged the European Council to pursue negotiations. On 2 March 2012, the Fiscal Compact (namely the 'Treaty on Stability, Coordination and Governance in the EMU', or 'Fiscal Stability Treaty') was signed by all EU Member States, except the Czech Republic and the UK. To avoid the difficulties of the ratification process (in October 2011, the Slovakian Parliament was unable to ratify the text reinforcing the EFSF), for the very first time it was foreseen that a treaty would enter into force even if it is not ratified by all the Member States. Indeed, the treaty provides that it would become effective for every country which has ratified it on the first day of the month following its ratification by the twelfth eurozone member; if this would have happened after 1 January 2013, the treaty would have retrospectively entered into force by this date. This was not necessary, since 12 eurozone states were able to ratify by December 2012.

In 2012, the situation continued to be very confused in Greece. In March, the eurozone members decided to back a second Greek bailout of 130 billion euros, but in May, Greek citizens voted in the general election for parties that rejected the country's bailout agreement with the EU. New elections in June led to a three-party coalition favourable to the agreement with the EU and the IMF. Meanwhile, also in June, a report on the future of Europe was published by the Presidents of the European Council, the Commission, the ECB and the Eurogroup – MM. Van Rompuy, Barroso, Draghi and Juncker. This document advocated for a federal option, in which EU institutions would be more democratic but would enjoy the ability to interfere in the conduct of budgetary and fiscal matters at the national level.[42]

The European Council of 29–30 June 2012 happened to be an unpredicted success after 19 meetings with little results. The European Council and the Eurogroup agreed on a deal allowing banks to receive aid directly from the permanent bailout fund, the European Stability Mechanism.

As planned, the Fiscal Compact came into force on 1 January 2013 for the 16 states who had completed its ratification. These Member States were required to enact laws demanding that their national budgets be in balance or in surplus and providing for a self-correcting mechanism. The treaty also contains a mechanism of 'debt brake' (inspired by the Stability and Growth Pact) that defines at which rate debt-to-GDP levels above 60 per cent of GDP should decrease to a level below that limit. Still in January 2013, J. Dijsselbloem was appointed President of the Eurogroup. He had the difficult task of dealing with the continuing financial crisis. Two months after his appointment, Cyprus's banking system needed rescuing and the country asked for a bailout. Greece, Spain, Portugal and Ireland still faced difficulties. In May 2013, the 'Two-Pack reform' package entered into force in all eurozone countries: it was intended to further strengthen the European monitoring of budgetary cycles and improve economic governance. In October 2013, the EU institutions adopted rules creating a single supervisory mechanism for the oversight of banks and other credit institutions, establishing the first 'pillar' of a European banking union. It was completed in April 2014, with the adoption by the EP of rulebooks on dealing with banks in crisis without using public money. The year 2013 ended on a relatively positive note as Ireland exited its bailout package, giving some breathing space for the eurozone after several years of turmoil. In May 2014, Portugal exited its bailout package. And in November 2014, a 'Single Supervisory Mechanism' came into force which allows the European Central Bank to oversee banks in the Eurozone to ensure that they operate safely and thus prevent the weaknesses that triggered the economic crisis in 2008.

If the efforts of the European institutions and the adoption of a new treaty have allowed the eurozone to overcome the crisis, the issue of sovereign debt remains at the heart of the European agenda. Member States are facing difficult economic and social situations, with little growth, high unemployment and a high level of deficit and debt. Governments are constrained by their European commitments to pursue a policy of austerity and are therefore facing the growing dissatisfaction of citizens at home and feeding Euroscepticism and populism. EU institutions are now more criticized than ever. With the unpopular bailouts and austerity policies, the EU has become a particularly salient issue among public opinions. The measures it promotes directly affect citizens who blame it, more than in the past: in 2014, 63 per cent of citizens considered the EU to be responsible for austerity.[43]

Facing political crisis

European institutions struggle to cope with this confidence crisis. They do not have enough legitimacy to interfere in Member States' fiscal, budgetary and social policies. Moreover, Member States have very contrasted visions of the EU's future and policies, and are increasingly developing individual strategies. As shown by the negotiations over the 2014–2020 multiannual financial framework there are strong cleavages between Member States and between the EU institutions there is no EU dynamic whatsoever.

This situation of mistrust, combined with austerity policies, led to the election of a large number of Eurosceptic MEPs during the May 2014 European elections and to the rise of Eurosceptic parties at the national level in many Member states.[44] The EP has never counted so many Eurosceptic members as it does in the 8th Parliament. In some Member States, such as France, the United Kingdom and Denmark, populist and Eurosceptic parties won the 2014 European elections, while in others, new Eurosceptic parties emerged and gained seats in the EP such as in Germany (Alternative für Deutschland and NDP), Greece (Golden Dawn) and Spain (Podemos). But the alarmist claim of a Eurosceptic earthquake or storm should be nuanced.[45] They account for roughly one third of the European assembly and remain scattered across the ideological spectrum, from the extreme left to the far right, and are incapable of developing concerted actions on a large scale.[46] The success of Eurosceptic parties and the type of Euroscepticism vary a lot from country to country: radical and right-wing Eurosceptics did very well in Western Europe particularly in the net contributing countries to the European budget (France, Denmark, the UK and Finland), the radical left was more successful in Southern Europe strongly affected by the crisis (Spain, Portugal, Greece). The number of elected Eurosceptics declined in other Member States, especially in Central and Eastern Europe. However, it is important to highlight that the most striking change is the increasing success of Eurosceptic parties in national and local elections. While, for long, they were mainly or even exclusively successful in EP elections, they are now doing well in other elections. They have benefited from the growing popular discontent about austerity and the integration process and have gained legitimacy and credibility due to their long-term representation in the EP. Their success contributes to shaping the agenda on European issues and indirectly influences the activities of national leaders, at the domestic and European levels. Thus, recent studies show that the impact of Eurosceptic parties is twofold. Their growing success leads, on the one hand, to a 'normalization' of Eurosceptic attitudes and positions: for a long time confined to the margins of political life, Euroscepticism is gradually becoming mainstream. On the other hand, traditional parties seem to be under pressure and tend to hide their pro-EU positioning, and even to hold increasingly critical speeches against the EU.

The rise of Euroscepticism has recently taken on a new dimension in Greece, with the success of the left wing and Eurosceptic party Syriza in general elections on 27 January 2015, and the appointment of Alexis Tsipras as Prime Minister. Greek citizens, by voting massively for Syriza, have tried to put an end to the austerity policy conducted by Greek leaders to comply with their European commitments. We are witnessing the emergence of a two-level game, in which citizens use national elections in order to impact EU governance. We are also observing the growing influence of European politics on domestic politics, since Alexis Tsipras was the candidate of the European party GUE (European United Left) for the Presidency of the Commission during the May 2014 elections (see below). If he was already a popular political leader in Greece before that, his prominent role in the European campaign increased his notoriety and credibility.

Today, the EU is facing a paradox. On the one hand, most national leaders agree that more common policies are needed to efficiently address the financial and economic crisis, but also other challenges such as unemployment, migration, global warming, peace and energy security. On the other hand, national leaders are more and more critical of European integration as anti-EU rhetoric is becoming increasingly common among mainstream media and parties[47]; their impact on the functioning of the EU is also growing, since a process of 'renationalization' is underway through the institutionalization and the reinforcement of the European Council, which soon became the agenda-setter of the EU.[48]

Despite these difficulties, or maybe thanks to them, EU institutions have continued to evolve, at least from an informal point of view. Hence, on 28 April 2014, in the perspective of European elections, the five main European political parties nominated their candidates for the Presidency of the Commission. The aim was to personalize the European elections in a logic similar to the German political practice by appointing 'leading candidates' (*Spitzenkandidaten*), so that the leader of the party that won the elections was appointed to head the European Commission. During the campaign, these candidates took part in several 'presidential debates' that attracted significant media coverage – at least compared to the previous European elections campaigns.

In May 2014, the EPP 'won' the European elections – despite a decrease in its number of seats. As a consequence, the three main political groups (the Christian democrats of the EPP, the socialists of the S&D, and the liberals from the ALDE) appointed Jean-Claude Juncker as the official candidate of the EP for the Presidency of the Commission. At first, several national leaders strongly criticized this initiative, arguing that it was contrary to the spirit of the treaties, but Juncker was finally appointed by the European Council, and then 'elected' by the EP on 15 July 2014. Martin Schulz, who was the forerunner of the European socialist party, was re-elected President of the EP for a second term; in a logic of political equilibrium, the conservative Antonio Tajani (PPE) succeeded him in December 2016. In October 2014, Donald Tusk (former Prime Minister of Poland) was appointed President of the European Council, and Federica Mogherini (S&D), the Italian Foreign Minister, EU High Representative for Foreign Affairs and Security Policy. On 22 October 2014, the EP approved the composition of the new Commission, after hearings of the candidates-designate. As an answer to the concerns over the efficiency of austerity measures, which had led to the significant success of Eurosceptics in several Member States and in exchange for socialists' support, one of J. C. Juncker's first proposals was the creation of a European Fund for Strategic Investments (EFSI), capable of mobilizing €315 billion in new investments between 2015 and 2017 and aimed at boosting growth in Europe. The European Council backed this initiative. On 1 November 2014, as stipulated in the Treaty of Lisbon, new rules came into force regarding voting in the Council. The main decisions must now obtain a majority of both Member States (55 per cent) and population (65 per cent). This does not fundamentally change the functioning of the Council, but makes decision-making a little easier and will simplify further enlargements.

Despite the complex crisis that the European project has faced, the process of enlargement of the EU has continued. In June 2013, the European Council decided to open accession negotiations with Serbia and, on 1 July, Croatia joined the EU, becoming the 28th Member State. The Ukrainian issue – especially after the annexation of Crimea by Russia – became central to EU foreign policy and in March 2014 the European Council decided to enforce sanctions against Russia. Despite these tensions, however, the association agreements between the EU and Georgia, Moldova and Ukraine were confirmed in January 2015. The Ukrainian crisis has highlighted the limits and failures of the European Neighbourhood Policy, but also its continued attractiveness for neighbouring countries.

Facing Brexit

The political crisis of the EU took an existential turn in 2016 with Brexit. Although it is not the only cause, the success of UKIP is essential to understanding the decision by British Prime Minister David Cameron in January 2013 to hold an in–out referendum on EU membership before 2017, after renegotiating the EU–UK relationship, and if the Conservative Party won the 2015 general election.[49] For the first time in the history of European integration, a national leader openly evoked the possibility of a withdrawal from the EU albeit for the purpose of domestic policy and pressuring his partners. The window for such an eventuality, which had never happened (if we ignore the 'technical' cases of Algeria, Greenland and Saint Barthélemy), was now opened by the Lisbon treaty and its article 50 TEU. In 2015, the Conservative Party won the legislative elections and the British government initiated discussions with EU counterparts to negotiate adjustments to the European treaties in favour of the UK, in particular in relation to the free movement of persons. The subsequent deal was considered weak and unconvincing in the UK. After a campaign barely longer than three months, David Cameron failed to convince his fellow citizens and the Brexit option won with 51.9 per cent of the vote in the referendum held 23 June 2016. Following this result, David Cameron resigned and was replaced by Theresa May, who promoted a radical approach to the exit from the EU, illustrated by her words 'Brexit means Brexit'. After strained negotiations with the British Parliament over its role, the Prime Minister initiated the UK exit procedure under Article 50 on 29 March 2017.

The implementation of Brexit is very complicated, and remains quite uncertain because of the doubts and oppositions it raises. The difficulties are threefold. They are primarily constitutional and political: the House of Lords does not support Mrs May's approach, and a large majority of Scottish and Northern Ireland citizens voted to remain in the EU. Through the Joint Ministerial Committee on EU Negotiations, the British government intends to involve the Scottish Parliament as well as the assemblies of Wales and Northern Ireland in the negotiations. However, many individuals in these regions are vocal in their opposition to a hard Brexit from the EU and feel that it would disregard their rights. In March 2017,

Nicola Sturgeon, the Prime Minister of Scotland, announced her wish to organize a new referendum on Scottish independence following Brexit. Another obstacle is the prospect of recreating a physical border to prevent illegal immigration between the Republic of Ireland, which is of course a member of the EU, and Northern Ireland, an option that was excluded by the first agreement between the Commission and UK authorities on 8 December 2017.

A second area of concern is the attitude of the leaders of the European institutions and of the other Member States. All of them adopted very cautious and even hostile positions on Brexit, refusing in particular to open any negotiations before the activation of Article 50 TEU. They also widely asserted that the UK could only retain access to the single market if it accepted the principle of freedom of movement of goods, capital, services and persons – which seems to have been ruled out by Downing Street. While the European states have remained relatively united so far, it is highly likely that this front will shatter once negotiations begin, given the issues and the different relations between each country and the United Kingdom. Finally, the situation facing nationals of other EU Member States who are residents in the UK is a matter of great concern in many capitals.[50]

The last major issue of Brexit is its consequences for the EU. The United Kingdom is the second-largest economic power in the Union, the third most populous Member State, and the second-largest contributor to the European budget. From a military point of view, it is, with France, the main power, with a permanent seat on the UN Security Council. In the event of its departure from the EU and in the absence of a free trade or partnership agreement, trade between the EU and the United Kingdom will be subject to the general customs tariff. It is only 2.4 per cent on average, but it is higher on some key products, such as cars (9.7 per cent). More generally, Brexit will encourage protectionism and contribute to exacerbating tensions within the Union between leaders who have different approaches to European integration. On the other hand, the domino effect dreaded or predicted by some has not happened. While national policy-makers remain relatively critical of the UE, Brexit has not encouraged other initiatives aimed at the withdrawal or exit from certain policies – such as the Schengen area or the euro. It is true that most states are much more dependent on the Union than the United Kingdom, and that the smaller states would have difficulties dealing with an exit from the Union from an economic perspective. Brexit may, however, reinforce Euroscepticism in many states, especially if the British economy improves after leaving. The implications for the legitimacy of the European project are also likely to be considerable.

Facing the migratory crisis

The refugee crisis is the second unprecedented event in the history of the Union. In 2015, an increasing number of illegal immigrants began to arrive in various

EU countries via South-East Europe and the Mediterranean Sea. Most of the immigrants were fleeing conflict and war zones (Syria, Libya, Afghanistan, Iraq, etc.), but some also came from various countries in the Middle East, South Asia, North Africa, Sub-Saharan Africa and the Western Balkans. These migrants therefore include persons applying for refugee status and/or asylum, but also economic migrants. Public opinion was suddenly sensitized to this dramatic situation in April 2015, when five boats carrying migrants sank, resulting in the death of more than 1,200 people. In total, more than 1,200,000 asylum applications were introduced in 2015, mainly in Germany, Hungary, Sweden and Austria.

The EU, which never confronted a migratory influx of this magnitude, did not have the specific, legal or logistical means to deal with such a phenomenon. In addition, it quickly appeared that the concept of the Schengen area, which allows the unimpeded movement of citizens between states, was being challenged by this situation. Since 2015, the EU institutions have been struggling with this crisis and have taken many decisions that include: increased funding for patrol operations in the Mediterranean; an anti-smuggling programme; a new quota system to 'relocate' asylum seekers in Member States as well as agreements with Turkey and Libya to control the flow of migrants. Several Member States have reintroduced temporary checks at the borders, and tensions have arisen between countries favouring asylum seekers and those seeking to discourage them from entering their national territory.

Everywhere in Europe, populist and extreme right-wing parties are developing a virulent anti-refugee discourse, particularly by spreading amalgams concerning the terrorist attacks that have hit several states since 2015. These parties have criticized the EU's actions, and accused it both of being unable to stem the influx of migrants and of creating hosting obligations for Member States. Hungary, after having built a wall along its border with Serbia, organized a referendum on the plan for the relocation of migrants proposed by the Commission. Although the government of V. Orban failed to mobilize enough citizens, it was clear that the rhetoric used frequent amalgams between immigration, terrorism and the EU. The refugee issue also played a key role in the referendum campaign on Brexit in 2016, even though the United Kingdom is not a member of the Schengen area and is not confronted with the influx of migrants contrarily to the countries of Southern and Central Europe. It finally contributed to weakening the position of Angela Merkel in Germany, through the unprecedented score of AfD, a nationalist party, at general elections (September 2017).

*

The institutional, economic, political, budgetary and migratory crises that have marked EU history since the early 2000s show the extent to which European integration, far from being linear and predictable, has been a succession of phases of enthusiasm, stagnation and crisis, punctuated by unexpected events. As noted by G. Ross, the integration process has never been easy and the EU is 'crisis prone'.[51] Recent EU chronology attests that any prediction, even in the short term, is doomed to failure, as the parameters that control EU operations and its progress towards integration are numerous and complex. The process of European integration remains eminently sensitive to the developments in national political life, and is even more so as European issues have become central at a national level. The traditional political divide between the left and the right, or progressives and conservatives, has been replaced by a divide between the supporters of closure, protectionism and the economic, social and cultural refusal of globalization,[52] and those who support openness, European integration and controlled globalization. This second divide, between the 'winners' and the 'losers' of globalization, has created deep divisions within the different political families, and has disrupted Member States' party systems. In the present state of affairs, and despite regular initiatives by the proponents of European integration, the sceptics' movement is in full swing. Indeed, both the economic and migration crisis have reinforced this division and the challenge for political leaders, both at a national and a European level, is to find a way to address the concerns of those citizens who feel left out or do not feel like they are benefiting from free movement and free trade and who see the European project and immigration as a threat to their identity and culture.[53]

The initial European integration project based on the progressive inclusion of new sectors and a method of 'baby steps' in the economic field has not, contrary to neo-functionalist expectations, led to the creation of a federal state across the continent. Since 2012, several initiatives have been taken at the highest level of the Union's institutions with the aim of promoting a federal revival, or a formalization of a multi-speed Europe around a main core of states that have the desire to push integration further. According to some economists, the debt crisis and instability in the eurozone calls for an overly extensive federalism at the European level.[54] But there remain diverging opinions between the Member States and the mechanisms chosen, which are largely inspired by the intergovernmental method.[55] The federal perspective is also challenged by the strong resistance shown by some national leaders – starting with the Germans – to equipping the eurozone with financial solidarity mechanisms. Indeed, the Commission's role since the beginning of the crisis in 2010, has been minor, 'most of the major responses to the eurozone crisis have been intergovernmental'[56] and it is likely to remain this way.[57]

This new phase of crisis has highlighted the fundamental tensions that affect the European integration project. Most actors and observers of the EU recognize that the current challenges call for urgent action at the supranational level in order to stabilize the eurozone and avoid putting the single currency at risk.

Also, the main European parties have succeeded in their strategy to appoint the President of the Commission as a result of European elections, in order to improve his legitimacy and to tighten the links between the European Parliament and the Commission. However, at the national level, political leaders appear to be in no hurry to reinforce European integration, especially to pledge their resolve in front of their respective public opinions that are increasingly eurosceptic (what is commonly referred to as 'constraining dissensus').[58] The political will to implement effective policies and responsive regulation mechanisms is coupled with a paradoxical refusal to do so on a federal basis and a willingness to act by way of intergovernmentalism. By definition this implies the search for unanimity and is thus not conducive to rapid decision-making or to radical reforms.

The turbulent and ambivalent evolution of European construction – under the combined effects of the clash of national egos, of mediation and initiatives by supranational institutions and the dissemination of European ideals – has led to the construction of an original and complex political regime. It is based on the subtle balance between European institutions (supranational and intergovernmental), Member States with contrasting expectations and representatives from various private- and public-interest groups.

More than 65 years after its first steps, the Union is a very powerful political system: it unites half-a-billion citizens and has the largest GDP in the world. Its institutions are in charge of numerous policies and have a more diffuse influence – through the process of Europeanization – on nearly all sectors of public action. However, the EU still suffers from a disconnection between polity, policies and politics. Since there was no consensus after the Second World War to undertake political integration, European Communities focused on establishing a common market and common policies.[59] Law and expertise became substitutes for the absence of polity[60] and for the reluctance of national government to create sovereign institutions. The founding fathers were, in a way, expecting the progressive emergence of a European polity from economic integration. This did not happen since national institutions proved to be more robust than expected and the public spaces remained mainly national and regional. Although today we can detect some Europeanization of political life within Member States and a politicization of European issues, this has not led to deeper integration, as the neo-functionalist would have hoped for. On the contrary, this happened mainly through the consolidation of a more or less radical eurosceptic discourse and a growing objection towards European policies.

The Maastricht Treaty was a first attempt to induce the emergence of a European public space and of EU politics, by creating a European citizenship, acknowledging the role of European parties and empowering the EP in many ways (legislation, budget, control, appointment). However, despite those efforts and many other reforms, the EU remains a two-level game in which the national level is predominant: national politics are still central for citizens and have a deep impact on EU activities, whereas European elections and European parties do not attract much attention from electors and the media. Also, the decision-making style of the EU remains driven by intergovernmental logics for key-decisions, and technocratic procedures for the routine ones. At the EU level, politics only play a secondary role, even within the EP. Citizens thus have the feeling that the EU is developing important and compelling policies, but without a polity and politics (i.e. contradictory and public debates) to legitimize them.[61]

The EU is today at a crossroads. Some believe it is fighting for its survival as it faces multiple crises.[62] On the one hand, there is a tangible risk of dismantlement with Brexit, the success of eurosceptic and populist movements in European and national elections, and the incapacity of national leaders to define a clear and coherent vision of the EU's future. The eurozone crisis is still causing turmoil and, predating it, the EU is still struggling with a legitimacy and democratic deficit as well as a crisis of leadership. On the other hand, the hypothesis of a federal Europe has been reactivated by the 'Spitzenkandidaten' procedure during the 2014 European elections and by several recent proposals, aimed in particular at creating a multispeed Europe because of the United Kingdom's exit from the EU. And it seems that the federal perspective of Europe is still implicitly embedded in the discourses of many European leaders and of such influent national leaders as Merkel and Macron but that the 'F-word' remains taboo since the failure of the Constitution.[63]

Notes

1 Wolfram Kaiser, 'History meets politics. Overcoming interdisciplinary Volapük in research on the EU,' *Journal of European Public Policy* 15(2) (2008): 300–313; Paul Pierson, *Politics in Time. History, Institutions and Social Analysis* (Princeton: Princeton University Press, 2004).

2 Craig Parsons, *A Certain Idea of Europe* (Ithaca: Cornell University Press, 2003); Paul Pierson, 'The path to European integration: a historical institutionalist analysis,' *Comparative Political Studies* 29(2) (1996): 123–163.

3 Denis de Rougemont, *Vingt-huit Siècles d'Europe: la conscience européenne à travers les textes: d'Hésiode à nos jours* (Paris: Payot, 1961); Gerard Delanty, *Inventing Europe: Idea, Identity, Reality* (London: Palgrave Macmillan, 1995).

4 Maximilien de Béthune and Duc de Sully, *Mémoires du Duc de Sully* (1620).

5 Victor Hugo, Congrès de la Paix, Paris, 1849.

6 Peter Koslowski, *The Theory of Capitalism in the German Economic Tradition: Historism, Ordo-Liberalism, Critical Theory, Solidarism* (Berlin/Heidelberg: Springer Verlag, 2000).

7 John Gillingham, *European Integration, 1950–2003: Superstate or New Market Economy?* (Cambridge: Cambridge University Press, 2003); René Leboutte, *Histoire économique et sociale de la construction européenne* (Brussels: Peter Lang, 2008).

8 Maria Green Cowles, James Caporaso and Thomas Risse-Kappen, eds, *Transforming Europe: Europeanization and Domestic Change* (Ithaca: Cornell University Press, 2001), 1–20.

9 Stanley Hoffman, 'Obstinate or obsolete? The case of the Nation-state and the case of Western Europe,' *Daedalus* 95(3) (1966): 862–915; Andrew Moravcsik, 'European integration in retrospect,' in *The European Union*, ed. Simon Usherwood (London: Routledge, 2011), 393–425.

10 Olivier Costa and François Foret, 'The European consociation, an exportable model? Institutional design and relations between politics and religion,' *European Foreign Affairs Review* 10(4) (2005): 501–516.

11 Amandine Crespy and Nicolas Verschueren, 'From euroscepticism to resistance to European integration: an interdisciplinary perspective,' *Perspectives on European Politics and Society* 10(3) (2009): 382.

12 Liesbet Hooghe and Gary Marks, 'The making of a polity: the struggle over European integration,' *European Integration Online Papers* 1(004) (1997); George Ross, *The European Union and Its Crisis. Through the Eyes of the Brussels' Elite* (Basingstoke: Palgrave McMillan, 2011).

13 Nathalie Brack and Olivier Costa, eds, *Diverging Views of Europe. Euroscepticism Within EU Institutions* (London: Routledge, 2012).

14 Du Réau, *L'idée d'Europe au XXᵉ siècle: des mythes aux réalités*; Edgar Morin, *Penser l'Europe* (Paris: Gallimard, 1990).

15 For an overview of the main theories of integration see Chapter 2 as well as: Ben Rosamond, *Theories of European Integration* (Basingstoke/New York: Macmillan/St. Martin's Press, 2000); Sabine Saurugger, *Theoretical Approaches to European Integration* (Basingstoke: Palgrave, 2013); Antje Wiener and Thomas Diez, eds, *European Integration Theory* (Oxford: Oxford University Press, 2004).

16 Olivier Costa and Nathalie Brack, 'The role of the European Parliament in Europe's integration and parliamentarization,' in *Parliamentary Dimensions of Regionalization and Globalization. The Role of Inter-Parliamentary Institutions*, eds Olivier Costa, Clarissa Dri and Stelios Stavridis (Palgrave MacMillan, 2013); Berthold Rittberger, *Building Europe's Parliament: Democratic Representation Beyond the Nation State* (Oxford: Oxford University Press, 2005).

17 Brigid Laffan and Sonia Mazey, 'The European Union—reaching an equilibrium?' in *European Union: Power and Policy-making*, ed. Jeremy J. Richardson (Abingdon/New York: Routledge, coll. 'Routledge Research in European Public Policy,' 3rd ed., 2006), 31–54.

18 For a more profound analysis of the history of European integration, we suggest the following works: Marie-Thérèse Bitsch, *Histoire de la construction européenne de 1945 à nos jours* (Paris: Éd. Complexe, new ed., 2004); Desmond Dinan, ed., *Origins and Evolution of the European Union* (Oxford: Oxford University Press, 2006); Desmond Dinan, *Europe Recast: A History of European Union* (Basingstoke: Palgrave MacMillan, 2004); Gillingham, *European Integration, 1950–2003;* Alan S. Milward, *The European Rescue of the Nation-State* (London: Routledge, 1st ed., 1992); Bino Olivi and Alessandro Giacone, *L'Europe difficile: histoire politique de la construction européenne* (Paris: Gallimard, 3rd ed., 2007).

19 Winston Churchill's speech, University of Zurich, 19 September 1946.

20 Several organizations were also born in the same period, notably the United Nations (UN–1945), the North Atlantic Treaty Organization (NATO–1949), the International Bank for Reconstruction and Development (IBRD—1944, World Bank), the International Monetary Fund (IMF–1944).

21 Schuman Declaration, 9 May 1950.

22 Desmond Dinan, ed., *Origins and Evolution of the European Union;* Gillingham, *European Integration, 1950–2003.*

23 Bitsch, *Histoire de la construction européenne de 1945 à nos jours;* Olivi and Giacone, *L'Europe difficile: histoire politique de la construction européenne.*

24 Olivi and Giacone, *L'Europe difficile: histoire politique de la construction européenne.*

25 Desmond Dinan, *Europe Recast: A History of European Union.*

26 Emmanuel Mourlon-Druol, 'Filling the EEC leadership vacuum? The creation of the European Council in 1974,' *Cold War History* 10(3) (2010): 315–339; John Young, ''The Summit is dead. long live the European Council': Britain and the Question of Regular Leaders' Meetings in the European Community, 1973–1975,' *The Hague Journal of Diplomacy* 4(3) (2009): 319–338.

27 Reform proposals came from the ambitious Dooge Report which calls not only for economic but also political recovery, supplemented by the Adonnino Committee report of the creation of a 'Europe of citizens'. See in particular Olivi and Giacone, *L'Europe difficile: histoire politique de la construction européenne.*

28 Each European Treaty refers to three dates: that of the European Council which concluded the intergovernmental conference and conducted the final arbitration; that of its formal signature, several weeks later, by the representatives of the Member States after the legal review; and that of its entry into force, after parliamentary vote or referendum vote in the Member States that may take a year or two.

29 Thomas Christiansen, Simon Duke and Emil Kirchner, 'Understanding and assessing the Maastricht treaty,' *Journal of European Integration* 34(7) (2012): 685–698.

30 Desmond Dinan, ed., *Origins and Evolution of the European Union;* Gillingham, European Integration, 1950–2003; Olivi and Giacone, *L'Europe difficile: histoire politique de la construction européenne.*

31 The French ratified the treaty by referendum but with a narrow approval as only 51% voted in favour of the treaty while in June 1992, the Danes rejected the Maastricht Treaty with 50.7% against during the referendum and it's only after Denmark obtained several opt-outs from treaty obligations that the Danes ratified the treaty during a second referendum in May 1993. Desmond Dinan, 'The Arc of institutional reform in Post-Maastricht treaty change,' *Journal of European Integration* 34(7) (2012): 846–847.

32 Desmond Dinan, 'The arc of institutional reform in post-Maastricht treaty change,' 843–858.

33 Ibidem.

34 Agenda 2000 is a 1997 communication of the Commission calling for a reform of the CAP, regional policy and structural funds to limit the impact of enlargement on the EU budget.

35 Bitsch, *Histoire de la construction européenne de 1945 à nos jours.*

36 John FitzGibbon, 'Referendum briefing. The second referendum on the Treaty of Lisbon in Ireland,' *Representation* 46(2) (2010): 227–239; John O'Brennan, 'Ireland and the Lisbon treaty: quo vadis?,' *Ceps Policy Brief* 176 (2008).

37 Ledina Gocaj and Sophie Meunier, 'Time will tell: the EFSF, the ESM and the Euro crisis,' *Journal of European Integration* 35(3) (2013): 239–253.

38 Gocaj and Meunier, 'Time will tell,' in *A European Mechanism for Sovereign Debt Crisis Resolution: A Proposal*, eds François Gianviti, Anne O. Krueger, Jean Pisani-Ferry, André Sapir and Jürgen Von Hagen (Bruegel Blueprint Series, vol. 10, 2010).

39 Desmond Dinan, 'Governance and institutions: impact of the escalating crisis,' *Journal of Common Market Studies* 50 (Supplement 2 Annual review) (2012): 85–98.

40 This pact includes the states of the eurozone plus Bulgaria, Romania, Lithuania, Poland and Denmark (hence the name 'Euro Plus Pact').

41 Michele Chang, 'Fiscal policy coordination and the future of the community method,' *Journal of European Integration* 35(3) (2013): 255–269.

42 'Towards a genuine economic and monetary union' (2012), accessed 27 June 2013, www.consilium.europa.eu/uedocs/cms_Data/docs/pressdata/en/ec/134069.pdf.

43 Eurobarometer 82, Autumn 2014.

44 Nathalie Brack, 'Populist and radical right parties at the 2014 EP elections: much ado about nothing?' in C. Fasone, D. Fromage and Z. Lefkofridi, *Parliaments, Public Opinion and Parliamentary Elections in Europe*, EUI Working Papers, MWP 2015/18, http://cadmus.eui.eu/bitstream/handle/1814/37462/MWP_WP_2015_18.pdf?sequence=1&isAllowed=y; Sara B. Hobolt, 'The 2014 European parliament elections: divided in unity?,' *Journal of Common Market Studies*, 53 (2015): 6–21. DOI: 10.1111/jcms.12264.

45 Nathalie Brack, op.cit.

46 Nicholas Startin and Nathalie Brack, 'To cooperate or not to cooperate? The European radical right and Pan-European cooperation,' in *Euroscepticism as a Transnational and Pan-European Phenomenon*, eds FitzGibbon, Leruth and Startin (Abdingdon: Routledge, 2016).

47 Nathalie Brack and Nicholas Startin, 'Euroscepticism: from the margins to the mainstream,' Special Issue *International Political Science Review* 36(3) (June 2015).

48 Uwe Puetter, *The European Council and the Council: New Intergovernmentalism and Institutional Change*, (Oxford: Oxford University Press, 2014); Dermot Hodson, Chris Bickerton and Uwe Puetter, *The New Intergovernmentalism: States and Supranational Actors in the Post-Maastricht Era* (Oxford: Oxford University Press, 2015).

49 See Harold D. Clarke, Matthew Goodwin and Paul Whiteley, *Brexit. Why Britain voted to leave the European Union* (Cambridge: Cambridge University Press, 2017).

50 On the negotiation process on Brexit: see the project 'Negotiating Brexit: national governments, EU institutions and the UK,' http://ukandeu.ac.uk/brexitresearch/negotiating-brexit-national-governments-eu-institutions-and-the-uk/.

51 George Ross, *The European Union and its Crisis*; Pierson Paul, *The Path to European Integration: A Historical Institutionalist Analysis*.

52 Hanspeter Kriesi, Restructuration of partisan politics and the emergence of a new cleavage based on values. *West European Politics* 33(3) (2010): 673–685; Hanspeter Kriesi, Edgar Grande, Romain Lachat, Martin Dolezal, Simon Bornschier and Timotheos Frey, *West European Politics in the Age of Globalization* (Cambridge: Cambridge University Press, 2008), 154–182.

53 Sara B. Hobolt, 'The Brexit vote: a divided nation, a divided continent,' *Journal of European Public Policy*, 23(9) (2016): 1259–1277.

54 See especially the interview with Jean-François Robin, *'Le marché veut le fédéralisme,'* accessed 27 June 2013, www.euractiv.fr/jean-francois-robin-marche-veut-federalisme-interview.

55 While French President Nicholas Sarkozy spoke of the start of a European Monetary Fund with the enhanced role of the European Financial Stability Fund, some government leaders refused to use that term and German Chancellor Angela Merkel has been particularly reluctant to provide financial assistance to countries in difficulty if the conditions on aid and fiscal discipline have not been reinforced.

56 Desmond Dinan, 'Governance and institutions: impact of the escalating crisis,' 91.

57 Ledina Gocaj and Sophie Meunier, 'Time will tell'.

58 Liesbet Hooghe and Gary Marks, 'A postfunctionalist theory of European integration: From permissive consensus to constraining dissensus,' *British Journal of Political Science* 39(01) (2009): 1–23.

59 Nicolas Jabko, *Playing the Market: A Political Strategy for Uniting Europe, 1985–2005.* (New York: Cornell University Press, 2006).

60 Mikael Rask Madsen and Antoine Vauchez (2005). 'European constitutionalism at the cradle. Law and lawyers in the construction of a European political order (1920–1960), in *In Lawyers' Circles. Lawyers and European Legal Integration*, eds Alexander Jettinghoff and Harm Schepel (The Hague: Elsevier Reed, 2004), 15–34.

61 Vivien A. Schmidt, *Democracy in Europe: the EU and National Polities* (Oxford: Oxford University Press, 2006).

62 David Phinnemore, 'Crisis-ridden, battered and bruised: time to give up on the EU?,' *Journal of Common Market Studies* 53 (2015): 61–74. DOI: 10.1111/jcms.12267

63 Arthur Borriello and Amandine Crespy, 'How not to speak the F-word. Federalism between mirage and imperative in the eurocrisis,' *European Journal of Political Research*, 54(3) (2015): 502–524.

The main theoretical approaches in EU studies

As is the case for many phenomena in political sciences, the development of EU studies[1] has been directly influenced by the progress of the European integration process itself. In the 1950s and 1960s, it was mostly International Relations scholars who were interested in European construction. They sought to understand the reasons for such cooperation between nation-states and developed 'grand theories' to explain the integration process, with strong debates between neo-functionalists and intergovernmentalists. After the 'empty chair' crisis and with the recession in the 1970s, supranational integration slowed down and there was no major theoretical development in EU studies for some time, most of the work being rather descriptive.[2] Keeler refers to this as the doldrums or 'dark ages' of EU studies.[3] This came to an end in the late 1980s, with the 'renaissance' of EU studies. Since then, there has been an explosion of work related to the European Union. There was a revival of the debates between the grand theories[4] but more importantly, EU studies entered the sphere of 'normal' political science as comparatists mobilized theoretical and methodological tools generally used to study domestic political systems to examine the EU. They are/ were not much interested in explaining the integration process itself but rather in analysing its results – the EU as a political system – and how it works. Since then, 'the bulk of research occupies itself with lower-order problems tackled through middle-range theories, most often drawing on (or at least consonant with) broader political science literatures. Debates seem increasingly pragmatic rather than paradigmatic.'[5] However, with the eurozone crisis and the rise of Euroscepticism, debates between (renewed) grand theories have been revived. With the increased politicization of the EU, scholars proposed new theories such as post-functionalism or new intergovernmentalism to understand the integration process, while a burgeoning literature has emerged on the perspective of resistance to integration and disintegration.[6]

Mapping the mosaic of EU theories is increasingly difficult as EU studies have evolved 'from boutique to boom field', especially since the 1990s, entailing a diversification and an expansion of the EU scholarly community as well as a proliferation of new topical subfields.[7] Given the space constraint within this book, it will not be possible to deepen each theoretical approach or to explain the details of the controversies and debates that ensued.[8] However, this chapter will give the reader a concise overview of the main theories in order to gain a better understanding of how the EU works.

We will proceed in four steps. A first section is dedicated to the 'grand theories', which focus on explaining the process of European integration. It describes neo-functionalism, intergovernmentalism and federalism. We shall also briefly present the development of these meta theories during the post-Maastricht era, in particular post-functionalism and new intergovernmentalism. A second section deals with the so-called 'normalization' of the EU in political science, by describing the various approaches and middle-range theories drawing on broader political science literatures to analyse the EU as a political system. It briefly introduces the reader to new institutionalism, constructivism, to sociological and governance approaches in European studies but also to recent theoretical developments in International Relations. A third section focuses on the topic of Europeanization as one particular strand of research that examines the impact of the EU on its Member States and vice-versa. Finally, we will discuss the best way to present and analyse the EU political system taking all these elements into account.

2.1 The grand theories of European integration: neo-functionalism, intergovernmentalism and federalism

For years, European studies have focused on the analysis of the integration process. Early research on the ECSC and the European Communities originated from the field of International Relations and primarily sought to explain the process of integration and the rationale behind state cooperation in this regional organization. This first era of European studies was marked by the debate between two grand theories: neo-functionalism and intergovernmentalism.

2.1.1 Neo-functionalism

Neo-functionalism is, historically, the first theory that sought to explain the cooperation between Member States within the European regional organization. The authors of this trend[9] wanted to create a general theory of regional integration and stressed the originality of this process in the European case.

Contrary to intergovernmentalists, neo-functionalists are interested in the process itself and do not solely look at isolated events.[10] They felt that the socio-economic problems confronting European societies could no longer be resolved at the national level and that the integration of technical and non-political domains within the European Community was the product of a functional necessity. The theory insisted particularly on two phenomena: the spillover effect and the role of interest groups. According to neo-functionalists, the initial decision to place a sector under the authority of a supranational institution generated pressure to extend the authority of that institution to other sectors that Haas describes as an expansive logic of sector integration.[11] Thus, the integration process was designed to expand gradually to an increasing number of sectors, first economic then political (the spillover phenomenon). According to neo-functionalists, sectorial economic integration produced de facto solidarities between states, solidarities that required in return a more significant supranational regulatory capacity and, ultimately, political integration.[12] European integration was thus a phenomenon that was intended to deepen automatically, under a cyclical strengthening of the structure (the institutions) and functions (the policies). The more powerful the structure (formal powers, human resources, budget), the more functions it can carry out, and conversely, the more extended and dense the functions, the more they are eligible for structural reinforcement. But according to neo-functionalists, support for the integration process among economic and political elites was also very important. Indeed, this process was, in theory, facilitated by national interest groups operating in the related sectors: benefiting from the process of integration and the support of the High Authority (and later the Commission), they were thought to lobby their national governments to promote and deepen the European project. National elites would come to perceive that some problems could not be effectively addressed at the domestic level and therefore should be dealt with at the supranational level. Finally, neo-functionalists tend to consider that a further impetus for regional integration would come from supranational institutions and more particularly, the European Commission, which would gradually act so as to increase its mandate.[13]

This approach has been particularly conducive to the study of early European integration and the Community method in areas such as the CAP and the customs union but faced severe criticism. Its grand theoretical pretensions have been strongly critiqued, as it could not explain regional integration in all settings. The automaticity of the spillover phenomenon has also been questioned and the lack of attention of neo-functionalists to domestic political processes and structures has led to strong criticism.[14] But more importantly, this theory was particularly unable to explain the 'empty chair' crisis and, more broadly, the policy of obstruction led by de Gaulle in the Council in the 1960s. Moreover, in the 1970s, the intergovernmental aspects of the Community were reinforced with the creation of the European Council and Ernst Haas came to the drastic conclusion of the obsolescence of regional integration theory.[15]

2.1.2 Intergovernmentalism

The troubled period of European integration at the end of the 1960s facilitated the emergence of a competing theory: intergovernmentalism, which stems from the realism International Relations. Although proponents of this theory have developed multiple approaches to Community construction and have focused on various explanatory factors (external and internal environment, the role of key political figures), they agree on the central role of sovereign states, which they see as rational actors seeking to promote and maximize their interests. While neo-functionalists underscore the weakening of national sovereignty in favour of the Community, intergovernmentalists believe that nation states, far from being obsolete, are strengthened by an integration process they want and control.[16] According to them, European cooperation is explained by the rational strategy of national leaders who, in a context of growing economic interdependence, intend to better manage specific problems through the sharing of limited aspects of their sovereignty. Thus, the process remains managed by national interests, which hinders the emergence of a truly supranational polity, and is only the result of negotiations between Member States (interstate bargaining). The Commission, far from being the great organizer of this process, is considered to be a simple secretariat and the supranational institutions in general are seen simply as tools in the hands of nation states.[17] This view is supported by the work of historians such as Alan Milward who showed that it is the Member States, not supranational organizations, that are the central actors in the historical development of the European project.[18]

Andrew Moravcsik reinvigorated this approach by offering his own interpretation of the European integration process, called 'liberal intergovernmentalism'.[19] He advanced a model that explains the European integration process in three stages. First, by starting with a liberal theory of the formation of national preferences, he believes that government leaders aggregate the interests of their respective nations and articulate them into a national position. Each state then defends its national position at the negotiating table at the European level where the agreements reflect the relative power of each Member State. Supranational institutions only play a marginal role: the decisions are determined by the states' bargaining power, package deals (global agreements) and side-payments. Finally, Moravcsik relies on rational choice to explain the decision of states to delegate powers or to share their sovereignty within a supranational institution. The states choose the institutional arrangement that facilitates collective action by reducing costs and increasing mutual benefit, while ensuring the respect of commitments by the partners. States are described as actors who want to reduce transaction costs in a context of an open economy. European integration is seen as a strategy for these actors to maximize their gains, which have no inherent autonomy or inertia.[20] The European Union is best understood, according to Moravcsik, as 'an international regime for policy coordination'.[21]

These two grand theories are often presented as radically opposed and intrinsically incompatible. Their supporters are quick to caricature their own positions to reaffirm the centrality of the debate between them. However, as noted by Puchala in his famous metaphor, scholars have been studying the EU like blind men touching an elephant to discover the nature of the beast who each feeling a different part, described a very different animal.[22] Neo-functionalists and inter-governmentalists have been looking at different dimensions of the integration process, leading to various controversies as to the nature of the phenomenon. But recent studies show that the two theories can be complementary by providing insight on different phases of the integration process, on different types of decisions and different players.[23]

2.1.3 Federalism

A third way, among others, was put forward by the theory of federalism.[24] Proponents of an analytical (not normative) federalist approach study both national and regional integration systematically and seek to explain their results. In the case of the EU, they oppose the intergovernmentalists by assigning a crucial role to the supranational level as the true decision-making centre, but at the same time, they refute neo-functionalist theories by estimating that there are no spillover effects between public sectors as the interest and willingness of Member States remain fundamental to the progress of the integration process. In brief, these scholars consider that the EU is best understood as a form of cooperative federalism, with joined decision-making and shared executive and legislative powers.[25]

2.1.4 Grand theories of European integration and the post-Maastricht era

After a period of relative theoretical stagnation, the transformation of the Communities into the European Union resulted in a renewal of debates between the grand theories of European integration. This burgeoning literature, which has grown in importance since 2010, considers that the post-Maastricht period is peculiar and that renewed theoretical frameworks are needed to grasp the new dynamics of the integration process.[26]

Based on insights from neo-functionalism and the multilevel governance approach (see infra), L. Hooghe and G. Marks developed a post-functionalist framework.[27] They consider that one should look beyond the economic interest of interest groups and that national and supranational politics are more tightly coupled in the post-Maastricht era. The main difference is that European integration has been politicized, resulting in higher levels of engagement of the mass public especially through political entrepreneurs (typically Eurosceptic parties). The main problems of the Union are now being further challenged at the national level and the issue of identity is at the heart of EU debates. While the neo-functionalists postulate that this politicization will lead to a citizen mobilization against national elites that are in favour of European integration, the post-functionalist approach shows that it is rather the opposite and that a gap is widening between elites and the public opinions who are reluctant towards European integration. This politicization and the existence of strong cleavages at the national level concerning European issues now constrain the course of the EU and its policies as the governments' margin for manoeuvre is more limited. After the long period of 'permissive consensus', the post-Maastricht context is characterized as a time of 'constraining dissensus': the hands of national governments are now tied when dealing with European issues as they need to account for more and more Eurosceptic public opinions.[28] The Eurocrisis could then be considered to be a post-functionalist moment: with the bailouts and austerity measures, the EU has become increasingly salient. Not only does the EU take measures that affect citizens directly but they are also attributable to the EU, hence lowering public support for the EU and leading to mass protests in some countries such as Greece or Spain. The constraining dissensus can hence lead to blocked decision-making, setbacks in the integration process (such as Brexit) or increased differentiated integration,[29] presented as the solution to European apathy.[30]

New intergovernmentalism, developed by Chris Bickerton, Uwe Puetter and Dermot Hodson,[31] also starts from the idea that the post-Maastricht period is different from the others, this treaty having constituted a critical juncture.[32] According to them, supranational institutions remain important but their relative significance in determining the nature and direction of the integration process has diminished. In a context of growing disenchantment with representative democracy in Europe, the theoreticians of neo-intergovernmentalism argue that we are falling back on decentralized and informal modes of decision- and policy-making, with the complicity of supranational institutions that are no longer engines of integration. Intergovernmental institutions, in particular the European Council, have become the focal point of the EU because of the salience of the policies involved (economic governance, foreign policy and internal affairs).[33]

With the crises and the rise of Euroscepticism, there has also been a renewed interest in federalism, as well as reflections on disintegration.[34] Scholars have argued that the latest developments in the EU and more particularly in European economic governance have opened a new era for federalism, with a deepening of the integration process but also the emergence of a more coercive form of federalism. For instance, A. Borriello and A. Crespy's recent study shows that although the notion of federalism has become taboo for EU leaders after the debacle of the Constitution, the deepening of functional federalism to cope with increased economic interdependence nevertheless justifies moving towards an ever-closer union.[35] The responses to the economic and financial crisis have therefore transformed the EU into a post-democratic and executive federal polity.[36]

2.2 A 'normalization' of EU studies

From the late 1980s and the 1990s, there has been what some have called a 'normalization' of European studies.[37] Since then, the European level has ceased to be regarded solely as a dependent variable and there has been a shift of focus towards comparative politics, as scholars became interested in the EU itself, how it works and what it does. The EU is now understood as a political system, a decision space that can be studied with the same methods, tools and theories that are used in the studies of national political systems.[38] Researchers have shown increasing interest in European decision-making, inter-institutional relations, the development and evolution of the polity and of public policies and have mobilized a variety of approaches and trends from general political science. We have seen the development of conceptual frameworks or middle-range theories seeking to account for the functioning of the European political system, its evolution and its impact on national systems.[39]

2.2.1 New institutionalism and the EU

Following the work of March and Olsen[40] and Hall and Taylor,[41] neo-institutionalists have begun to penetrate the field of European studies. Given the density of its institutional system and the increasing importance of its rules, the EU has provided an interesting laboratory for institutionalist scholars, who draw on literature from comparative politics to examine the work of the EU's institutions. They have greatly contributed to our understanding of legislative, judicial and executive politics in the EU by focusing on decision-making within the Council and the Parliament, the role of the Court and its relations to the Member States, the nature of the Commission and of the various executive agencies.[42] They have also focused on the effect of institutions over time and on how these institutions constrain or influence the margin of manoeuvre of those who created them.[43] They have convincingly approached the process of integration as being path-dependent, exposing the stickiness of EU institutions and how they can shape historical trajectories over time.[44] The proliferation of institutions at the European level means this theoretical approach has gradually become dominant. Neo-institutionalism quickly gave rise to different variants (historical, sociological, discursive, rational choice institutionalism, etc.), which have a more or less formalized vision of institutions. All neo-institutionalists, however, agree on the importance of institutions (*institutions matter*) and believe that they influence the political process and the EU's public policy and consequently confirm their impact on the European integration process in the long term.[45]

2.2.2 Sociological approaches to European integration

Since the end of the 1990s, other trends have emerged in EU studies.

Sociological approaches to integration place actors at the centre of the analysis. This is a very disparate body of work, both methodologically (from qualitative ethnographic research to quantitative demographic work, not forgetting prosopography) and by the subjects studied. One might rather speak of a sociological research agenda than of a theoretical approach as such.[46] Authors are interested in the sociology of public action, the questions of legitimacy and power games, the transformation of national and transnational corporations, or even individuals and their interactions with institutions.[47] They emphasize the importance of studying the social dimension of the EU and the links between EU institutions and European society. Some scholars have proposed a political sociology of EU politics, consisting in the analysis of the behaviours, social characteristics and views of actors involved in EU politics (i.e. EU professionals) to understand broader EU dynamics.[48] Within sociological studies, critical and post-positivist approaches are particularly popular among French researchers.[49] A variety of researches have drawn on the theoretical and methodological tools developed by the sociologist Pierre Bourdieu to understand the development of a distinct European political arena (or 'field'), with specific types of resources (or 'forms of capital') and potentially influencing the 'habitus' of the actors involved. They have mostly focused on the careers and strategies of EU professionals and used ethnographic methods to go inside EU institutions and understand underlying power struggles and how European careers are built.[50]

2.2.3 The constructivist turn in EU studies

Another equally diverse body of work relies on constructivist approaches and also emphasizes the socially constructed aspect of 'reality'. In European studies, as in other disciplines, Constructivism is less a theory than an analytical orientation which branches into multiple trends (conventional, interpretive, critical, radical, etc.).[51] It complements other approaches by emphasizing the fact that human agents do not exist independently of their social environment and shared value systems. Actors do not have fixed preferences but adjust their behaviour to each socially constructed situation. Proponents of these approaches are particularly interested in the nature of European identity, in socialization processes and the dissemination of standards in the EU's political system.[52] They also study the communicative practices and meanings of Europe to determine how the EU is discursively constructed and to what extent a European public sphere is emerging.[53] They attempt to demonstrate that European institutions shape the behaviours, preferences and identities of individuals and governments.[54] The increased parliamentarization of the European political system and the assertion of democratic principles as the basis of the functioning of the EU in the Lisbon Treaty have reinvigorated the studies on democracy and political representation, including a 'turning point' in European studies.[55]

2.2.4 The governance approach

Originating from both international relations and comparative politics, the 'governance approach' aims to consider the EU's socioeconomic and political system as a non-hierarchical articulation between different levels and sources of power.[56] Governance is defined as 'a polycentric configuration in which patterns of horizontal coordination among social subsystems prevail at the expense of notions of political authority and sovereignty, which only occupies one place among others'.[57] These approaches, which rely on various concepts and models (multilevel governance, governance networks, new forms of governance), do not see the European regime as a traditional international organization nor as a classic political system, but rather as a new system of governance without a government. From this point of view, political authority was not simply transferred from national governments to the EU, but was gradually dispersed among a multitude of actors, public and private, acting at numerous different levels (European, national, regional, local and global). The focus is then on the articulation between these different levels of government and on policy-making within the EU.[58] The multilevel governance model has been developed largely in reference to the EU and to stress the fact that EU institutions and Member States are not monolithic but consist of various actors.[59] This model considers that regional governments also play an increasingly important role, alongside European institutions and national governments. It then focuses to a large extent on territorial politics in the European governance and on the shift of authority towards sub-national and supranational actors.[60] The network governance approach centres on the interactions between private and public actors in various policy sectors as well as on the resources, strategies, interests and constraints of these actors.[61] It seeks to understand how networks influence the preferences of actors and how they manage to put some issues on the agenda of the EU institutions.[62] Again, governance approaches are not so much a theory as a conceptual framework or a cluster of related theories emphasizing common themes, allowing for an understanding of the EU as a group of non-hierarchical networks including a multiplicity of private and public actors.[63] This literature addresses questions related to policy-making, the governance capacity of the EU and its democratic legitimacy as well as the emergence of new modes of governance such as the Open Method of Coordination and more recently, the potential of deliberative democracy to solve the legitimacy challenges faced by the EU.[64]

2.2.5 Others' approaches: sociology of international relations and new regionalism

Alongside comparatists, international relations scholars have also developed new theoretical tools to study the EU. For example, sociological approaches stress the changing role of the nation state. Although it remains a key actor, the state faces competition from other types of actors with the internationalization of the economy and the emergence of transnational relations among social movements.[65] Various scholars have then studied the emergence of these new social movements, the transfer of values and ideas but also the cultural and religious flows across European borders.[66] Others have developed interesting reflections and conceptualizations of the notion of power in the case of the EU. They have showed that the power of a Member State, for instance in the European institutions, depends on a variety of factors and not only on its size or military capacities.[67] They have also developed notions such as 'civilian power' and 'normative power' to characterize the influence of EU norms and values in the world.[68]

Finally, regionalism has attracted renewed interest recently, under the name 'new regionalism'.[69] Scholars have sought to understand why nation states cooperate within international organizations and, more particularly, how to explain the increasing number of regional cooperation institutions worldwide (Mercosur, Asean, etc.) and to determine if comparison can be a useful tool to study the different cases of regional integration.[70] Some scholars have highlighted the link between globalization and regionalism[71] while others have analysed the influence of the relevant international institutions on the relations between participating members in regional integration as well as the development of a collective identity within such regional institutions.[72]

2.3 Europeanization

2.3.1 A vast trend in EU studies

The theoretical and empirical literature on Europeanization has been a major trend in European studies since the early 1990s. It has progressively become a catch-all label for investigating the transformations of a variety of objects (institutions, organizations, policies, paradigms, ideas, perceptions, actors, etc.) brought about by the economic, social, legal and political unification of Europe.[73]

At first, Europeanization referred to the very general process of convergence of Member States towards a European polity. More precisely, the seminal researches focused on the implementation of EU norms and policies. Other works then analysed how national governments manage EU affairs, be it their involvement in EU negotiations or in the implementation of EU decisions. Studies have also focused on national parliaments, political parties, interest groups and local authorities.

The inflation of literature on this topic was the result of researchers' disaffection for major theories, and especially the endless and ultimately quite sterile debates between neo-functionalists and intergovernmentalists. Also, the Maastricht Treaty (which entered into force in November 1993) mobilized or remobilized numerous scholars around the European integration process. This was thanks to the reinforcement and creation of several policies, as well as to new references to national parliaments, European political parties, local authorities and European citizens. As a consequence, researchers multiplied the projects to measure the impact of European integration on domestic political, social and economic systems.

2.3.2 Four approaches of Europeanization

Despite the emergence of Europeanization as a kind of sub-discipline of EU studies, the concept has been defined in several ways. In this very vast and sophisticated literature, we can distinguish four main views of the concept.

1   The first to appear was the 'top-down' or 'downloading' approach. It considers that change emanates from the impact of the Union onto the national policy: the states are viewed as re-active towards changes occurring at the EU level, and more particularly towards developments in treaties and secondary legislation. Robert Ladrech proposed one of the earliest conceptualizations of Europeanization as 'an incremental process of re-orienting the direction and shape of politics to the extent that EC political and economic dynamics become part of the organisational logic of national politics

and policy making'.[74] The top-down approach is privileged by researchers who study institutional and legal processes. Policy-making analysts have criticized this definition because it assumes a passive role of Member States; conversely, they consider states to be not only 'takers' of European norms, models or instructions, but also active 'shapers' of these within EU institutions.

2   From a 'bottom-up' or 'uploading' approach, Europeanization occurs when states begin to affect the policy of the EU in a given area.[75] Studies thus insist on national input in EU policy-making. They first only considered state institutions (governments, diplomats, central administrations, parliaments, etc.) but soon also took into account other actors: companies, trade-unions, regional governments, parties, civil society organizations, media, etc. Many studies described the way these were 'Europeanized', i.e. mobilized towards EU institutions, organs and policies. The difficulty with this approach is that Europeanization tends to be confused with European integration itself.

3   Some authors have also defined a 'horizontal' approach to Europeanization. It focuses on the transfer of politics, policies and policy-making between Member States in the context of European integration, but in the absence of constraining EU norms. The trans-national transfer is based on non-constraining mechanisms, such as the identification of 'best practices' and the mutual recognition of national norms. These studies stress that national policy-makers no longer plan to undertake reforms without examining those carried out in the other Member States or without reflecting on the reforms' impact on the competitiveness of their country in a European context.

4   More recently, researchers have tried to offer a more nuanced and inclusive approach to Europeanization that takes into account both the downloading, uploading and horizontal phenomena.[76] In this case, Europeanization is the result of constant interactions between the national and the European level, or even of horizontal diffusion processes. Scholars insist on the fact that EU policies in fact constrain national ones, but also modify resources and preferences among actors as well as condition their capacity to weigh on the EU policy-making process. Most authors refer to a broader definition, proposed by Claudio Radaelli, who describes Europeanization as:

> a process of (a) construction, (b) diffusion, and (c) institutionalization of formal and informal rules, procedures, policy paradigms, styles, 'ways of doing things', and shared beliefs and norms which are first defined and consolidated in the making of EU public policy and politics and then incorporated in the logic of domestic discourse, identities, political structures, and public policies.[77]

More simply, Vink and Graziano define Europeanization as a process of 'domestic adaptation to European regional integration'.[78] Those definitions encompass the different means of influence described by Europeanization literature by referring to both construction and diffusion and to all areas of influence. In this context, Europeanization should be understood in the broadest possible sense, whereby institutions can also refer to non-material concepts such as norms, ideas and beliefs.

2.3.3 Europeanization and theoretical debates

Europeanization played an important role in the developing of EU studies in the 1990s, since it involves scholars coming from various disciplines (political science, law, anthropology, sociology, history, etc.) and sub-disciplines that aim at studying the process of change induced by European integration in many fields and in various ways. Europeanization studies have widened their field of investigation: today they are no longer limited to EU impact on politics and policy-making, but they also analyse its effects on processes, policies and institutions (policy, polity and politics), and more generally on the whole of society.[79] Europeanization has thus become a concept used to study a wide range of phenomena and transformations.

These evolutions are quite interesting, but they have led to a substantively blurred epistemological debate, where the distinction between cause and effect, between the independent and the dependent variable tends to disappear.

As a reaction to this, the question of causality is once more central to the discussions. Scholars consider that Europeanization should be distinguished from convergence, harmonization or political integration,[80] and that speaking of Europeanization implies demonstrating that European integration has indeed caused the domestic change, and that this is not just a result of other phenomena like modernity, globalization or the economic crisis.[81] Methodological problems are thus becoming central to the agenda of Europeanization studies.[82]

Since the beginning of the 2000s, the development of Europeanization works has revitalized theoretical debates. The priority nowadays is on explaining the observed phenomenon, and not only on measuring and describing it because of the need to distinguish Europeanization from other potential causes. As a consequence, like the other branches of EU studies, Europeanization studies have incorporated concepts and theories from comparative politics, public policy and sociology.

Recently, the main challenge for Europeanization specialists has been to understand why it often differs so much across policy sectors and across countries.[83] To explain these variations, they refer to existing models (such as new institutionalism) or specific concepts.

A first notion is the 'goodness of fit'.[84] A 'misfit' between the national situation and what is promoted at the European level is considered to be a necessary condition for domestic change and an explanatory factor of its degree: as long as there is no policy or institutional misfit, there will be no pressure for change.[85] In this model, Europeanization has five different outcomes depending on the degree of misfit in a given country: 'inertia' or the lack of change, 'retrenchment' or increasing misfit; 'absorption' or the incorporation of the EU's influence without substantial national change; 'accommodation' or national change at the margin; and 'transformation' or the full replacement of policies and institutions.[86] The misfit approach is useful to analyse situations where there is a clear EU template that has to be 'downloaded' and where the supranational institutions have a considerable amount of power delegated to them. It is less convincing when Europeanization appears as a more diffuse phenomenon.[87]

Authors thus insist on the importance of 'mediating factors'. To explain Europeanization's variations, Risse, Cowles and Caporaso underline the role played by veto points, formal institutions, political and organizational cultures, differential empowerment of actors, and learning.[88]

Falkner et al. have developed an alternative approach to differential degrees of Europeanization that is more sensitive to context and national cultures.[89] They consider Member States belonging to various 'worlds of compliance': a world of law compliance, a world of domestic politics, a world of transposition neglects, and a world of dead letters.

2.3.4 Recent developments

Recently, several studies have underlined the fact that Europeanization specialists tend to overstate the phenomenon and to disregard resistances because of a confirmation bias.[90]

Brouard, Costa and König have, for instance, reactivated the downloading approach, in order to measure the effective degree of law-Europeanization at the domestic level.[91] The study, based on a systematic analysis of laws in nine domestic cases, concludes that the Europeanization of law-making is much more limited than assumed in the literature and public debate: depending on the country it varies from 10 to 30 per cent of laws, far less than the 80 per cent supposedly predicted by Jacques Delors in the late 1980s and mentioned daily by medias and public opinion leaders to demonstrate the EU domination of Member States. The research also shows that the impact of Europeanization on the balance of power between governments and parliaments is distorted. Consequently, these authors call for a reappraisal of Europeanization that would focus on effective outcomes in a systematic way rather than on institutional rules or single case analysis.

In another recent study, Coman, Kostera and Tomini also argue that the literature on Europeanization tends to overestimate the impact of the EU and its capacity to steer change at the national level.[92] They consider that the main reason for this is methodological, since scholars have focused on institutional adjustments and not on structural transformations. Coman et al. underline the need to take into account the duality of the processes and outcomes of Europeanization: one gradual, incremental and cumulative, and another more intense, when incremental Europeanization is rapidly interrupted or reshaped. In other words, they suggest paying more attention to the relationship between Europeanization and European integration. They insist on the limitations of the legal and political European integration that, combined with structural domestic factors, are both a cause and a consequence of the incremental and limited change induced by the EU.

2.3.5 Europeanization and the study of EU functioning

Fundamentally, this book's aim is not the study of Europeanization, but the analysis of the functioning of the EU political system. It is, however, a phenomenon to take into account for three reasons.

First, the main task of EU institutions, organs, and actors is to design and implement policies that have a deep impact at the national level on all kinds of actors, pertaining to both the public and private sector. The EU thus pays much attention to the expectations and reactions of these stakeholders, in order to legitimize its decisions as much as possible and to promote their proper implementation.

Second, as demonstrated by the 'uploading' approach of Europeanization, these actors are not passive but are aware of the impact of EU policies and are strongly mobilized towards its institutions in order to influence them. This can happen in many ways. Member States officials are directly represented in the European Council and the Council, appoint many EU actors, and can try to influence them as well as their MEPs. Local authorities and socio-economic forces are represented in the Committee of Regions and in the Economic and Social Committee. Citizens are directly represented in the European Parliament. Interest groups and civil society organizations are very active in the European microcosm.

Finally, we must underline the importance of resistances to European integration. They are expressed through elections and in political life, with the rise of Eurosceptic parties in many Member States, but also in a less visible way, through a reluctance to take into account European norms and policies or even strategies to avoid or contest them. More recently, the crisis of the eurozone has given rise to uninhibited protests against EU constraints on governmental action. Brexit is another event that demonstrates the importance of these protests and mobilization.

Today, more than ever, EU institutions are encouraged to pay heed to the reactions provoked by Europeanization. They closely follow the evolutions of public opinions expressed in the media and in the public sphere, and as measured by instruments such as Eurobarometer and Parlemeter.[93] They develop multiple strategies in order to combat the idea that EU institutions and actors are disconnected from the citizens and societies.

For all these reasons, the functioning of the EU political system should be analysed by taking into account Europeanization and the constant interaction between different levels of government. Even if we focus on the EU headquarters, our study should be sensitive to the many dimensions of Europeanization and to their impact on actors' behaviour, strategies and choices.

2.4 How can we theorize the EU institutional system?

European integration and the resulting institutional system are largely marked by a functional logic, advancing technical solutions without normative impact. If the signatories of the Treaty of Rome said they were 'Determined to lay the foundations of an ever closer union among the peoples of Europe' it was not to build a European state but to promote peace and prosperity through intergovernmental cooperation between a limited number of states characterized by a long history of conflict and significant political and economic contrasts. The treaties did not create a coherent constitution and are infused with strong pragmatism. Successive reforms have not fundamentally altered this initial situation. They responded more to the need to adapt the institutions and decision-making procedures of the Communities, to extend their powers or address specific concerns and events (including the so-called 'democratic deficit'), than to a desire to overhaul the system. Treaty reform was essentially intended to react to criticisms, to reassess the role of the Member States in the institutional framework, to review inter-institutional relations, streamline EU functioning and clarify its objectives and values.

However, an evolution happened over time. Indeed, one can discern a process of 'parliamentarization', spread over the EU institutional architecture, which takes the form of an assertion, since the Maastricht Treaty, of the political nature of European integration.[94] The strengthening of the EU's parliamentary logic, which could have been understood as a one-shot measure mimicking parliamentary systems, can no longer be seen that way. From now on, one must see this development, not as the result of institutional engineering favouring more effective and proven modes of governance, but as a more comprehensive, though chaotic, process of confirmation of the European Union as a political regime.

Over time, the Court has gradually extracted a number of fundamental rights and general principles from the treaties and the derived law, which the Treaty on the EU recognized by referencing the European Convention for the Protection of Human Rights, signed in Rome in 1950. The adoption of the Charter of Fundamental Rights of the European Union, whose legal status was recognized by the Treaty of Lisbon, continued this trend.[95] Treaties adopted since the early 1990s have also provided the EU with some symbolic attributes of a normative political system by establishing European citizenship and increasing references to European political parties, democracy and human rights.

Since the Maastricht Treaty, we see a shift towards a more political institutional operation, with the investiture of the Commission by the European Parliament, increased powers for the latter, the institutionalization of European parties and the involvement of national parliaments in EU governance. The parliamentary model has been an implicit structuring element of treaty reform.[96] The Lisbon Treaty, which entered into force on 1 December 2009, confirms this trend by devoting a title to 'democratic principles'. Article 10 of the Treaty on the European Union now provides that 'the functioning of the Union shall be founded on representative democracy' and establishes the principle of the dual representation of citizens:

> 'Citizens are directly represented at Union level, the European Parliament. Member States are represented in the European Council by their Heads of State or Government and in the Council by their governments, themselves democratically accountable either to their national Parliaments, or to their citizens.'

This clause – which allowed the leaders of the five main European parties to impose the logic of 'Spitzenkandidaten' in 2014 – substantiates a parliamentarist interpretation of the EU. However, this is tempered by a reaffirmation of intergovernmentalism and a reference to the mechanisms of participatory democracy. The first is illustrated in both the nature of the Council and the European Council as well as the reassessment of the role of national parliaments which creates a two-tier parliamentary system.[97] Participatory democracy is in turn the subject of a specific reference in Article 10.3 which provides that 'Every citizen has the right to participate in the democratic life of the Union' and that 'Decisions shall be taken as openly and as closely as possible to the citizens'. Additionally, the procedure of European Citizens' Initiative allows one million citizens to call directly on the Commission to propose a legal act.

Even if the Lisbon Treaty does not provide a specific principle of legitimation of the EU, references to the democratic model and to representation tend to rule out alternative forms of legitimation that have been put forward to date – with reference to notions of agency, governance, government of experts, pluralism, neo-corporatism or a strictly intergovernmental rationale.[98] In more general terms, the Treaty of Lisbon increases references to democracy which becomes simultaneously an operating principle of the EU, one of its core values and an objective in both its domestic and external action.

Today, the EU's institutional framework is marked by a dual pragmatic and political logic. It remains guided by the pursuit of efficiency and the balance of multiple interests through decentralized decision-making and a dispersal of authority. Nevertheless, it tries to provide assurances to its detractors regarding the 'democratic deficit' and to affirm the EU as a fully committed political system which directly involves citizens. The Lisbon Treaty has simplified its decision-making procedures and clarified its principles of legitimation but the institutional system remains complicated and unusual and still combines the Community method with intergovernmental cooperation.

It is thus difficult to summarize the EU's institutional framework. The original pragmatism created a novel and convoluted institutional framework. Decision-making is the result of the shifting arrangements of diverse levels of interdependent power. European institutions are involved to varying degrees and with differentiated modalities depending on the division of powers between different levels of government. The belated 'parliamentarization' of these arrangements has not always helped improve their clarity.

*

Within the framework of this book, we strongly endorse the goal of the 'normalization' of European studies. Our ambition is not to explain the creation of the European Communities, to define the motor of European integration or to qualify the political system that resulted from this process, but to describe and analyse the actual functioning of the EU. To do so, we will mobilize the concepts and tools developed by comparative politics and public policy analysis. This approach, which was applied to the EU in the 1980s, has the advantage of reporting on the activities of a political system without having to resolve beforehand a series of – supposedly fundamental, but often trivial and unnecessary – debates on its purpose, nature and future. It is also a way of avoiding any normative statement regarding the way the EU should be or should function, or concerning desirable treaty reforms. Our only objective is to study the mechanisms and logics of EU decision-making, paying particular attention to its practical and informal aspects. This pragmatic outlook leads us to focus on the actors who effectively participate in decision-making and implementation of European policies – including non-institutional actors – to assess their respective influence, and to identify the concrete dynamics underlying EU public action.

To do so we will use categories and concepts from comparative politics and public-policy analysis, even if the specificities of the European institutional system should be kept in mind. We faced them as we tried to design the structure of this book, since the separation of powers is not really respected in the European Union.[99]

Notes

1 One should talk about 'EC studies' before the entry into force of the Maastricht Treaty but, by convention, we will use the expression 'EU studies' all through this book.

2 Amber K. Curtis and Joseph Jupille, 'The European Union,' in *International Encyclopedia of Political Science*, ed. George Thomas Kurian (Washington, DC: CQ Press, 2011), accessed 28 June 2013, www.sobek.colorado.edu/~jupille/research/research.htm.

3 John T. S. Keeler, 'Mapping EU studies: the evolution from boutique to boom field 1960–2001,' *Journal of Common Market Studies* 43(3) (2005): 557.

4 With new debates between neo-functionalists and liberal intergovernmentalists and the emergence of 'governance approaches'. See for instance: Gary Marks, 'Structural policy and multilevel governance in the EC,' in *The State of the European Community, The Maastricht Debates and Beyond*, eds Alan W. Cafruny and Glenda G. Rosenthal (Boulder: Lynne Rienner, 1993), 391–422; Andrew Moravcsik, 'Negotiating the Single European Act: national interests and conventional statecraft in the European Community,' *International Organization* 45(1): 19–56; Wayne Sandholtz and John Zysman, '1992: recasting the European bargain,' *World Politics* 42(1) (1989): 95–128.

5 Curtis and Jupille, 'The European Union,' op. cit.

6 Cf. Stefan Auer, 'European disintegration—A Blind Spot of Integration Theory?' 22nd International Conference of Europeanists (CES), July 2015; Benjamin Leruth, Nicholas Startin and Simon Usherwood, eds, *Handbook of Euroscepticism* (London: Routledge, 2017); Hans Vollaard, 'Explaining European disintegration,' *Journal of Common Market Studies* 52(5) (2014): 1142–1159.

7 Keeler, 'Mapping EU studies: the evolution from boutique to boom field 1960–2001,' op. cit., 551–582.

8 For an excellent book introducing the various approaches of integration theory, see Antje Wiener and Thomas Diez, *European Integration Theory* (Oxford: Oxford University Press, 2nd ed., 2009). We also recommend Knud Erik Jørgensen, Mark Pollack and Ben J. Rosamond, eds, *Handbook of European Union Politics* (London: Sage, 2007).

9 Of which the most important are E. Haas, L. Lindberg and S. Scheingold, then later Ph. Schmitter, A. Stone Sweet and W. Sandholz.

10 Arne Niemann and Philippe C. Schmitter, 'Neofunctionnalism,' in *European Integration Theory*, eds Antje Wiener and Thomas Diez (Oxford: Oxford University Press, 2nd ed., 2009), 47.

11 Ernst B. Haas, *The Uniting of Europe: Political, Social and Economic Forces, 1950–1957* (London: Stevens, 1958), 383.

12 Mark A. Pollack, 'Theorizing EU policy-making,' in Helen Wallace, Mark A. Pollack and Alasdair R. Young, *Policy-Making in the European Union* (Oxford: Oxford University Press, 6th ed., 2010), 15–42; Sabine Saurugger, *Théories et concepts de l'intégration européenne* (Paris: Presses de Sciences Po, 2010), 67–92. On the theories and approaches of European integration, see also: Ben Rosamond, *Theories of the European Integration* (Basingstoke: Palgrave, 2000).

13 Arne Niemann and Philippe C. Schmitter, 'Neofunctionalism,' in *European Integration Theory*, eds Antje Wiener and Thomas Diez (Oxford: Oxford University Press, 2nd ed., 2009), 45–66.

14 Andrew Moravcsik, 'Preferences and power in the European community: a liberal intergovernmentalist approach,' *Journal of Common Market Studies* 31 (1993): 473–524; Robert O. Keohane and Joseph S. Nye, 'International interdependence and integration,' in *Handbook of Political Science*, eds Fred I. Greenstein and Nelson W. Polsby (Reading: Addison-Wesley, 1975), 363–377.

15 Ernst B. Haas, 'Turbulent fields and the theory of regional integration,' *International Organization* 30(2) (1976): 173–212 cited in Niemann and Schmitter, 'Neofunctionalism,' 51–53; Mark A. Pollack, 'Theorizing the European Union. International organization, domestic polity or experiment in new governance?' in *The European Union*, ed. Simon Usherwood (London: Routledge), 63–108.

16 Stanley Hoffman, 'Obstinate or obsolete? The fate of the nation-state and the case of Western Europe,' *Daedalus* 95 (1966): 862–915.

17 Thomas Diez and Antje Wiener, 'Introducing the mosaic of integration theory,' in *European Integration Theory*, eds Antje Wiener and Thomas Diez (Oxford: Oxford University Press, 2nd ed., 2009), 7–8.

18 Alan Milward, *The European Rescue of the Nation-State* (Berkeley: University of California Press, 1992).

19 Andrew Moravcsik, *The Choice for Europe. Social Purpose and State Power from Messina to Maastricht* (Ithaca/London: Cornell University Press/Routledge, 1998).

20 Pollack, '*Theorizing EU Policy-Making*,' 15–42; Frank Schimmelfenning, '*Liberal Intergovernmentalism In European Integration Theory*', eds Antke Wiener and Thomas Diez (Oxford: Oxford University Press, 2004), 75–94.

21 Moravcsik, 'Preferences and power in the European Community,' 480.

22 Donald J. Puchala, 'Of blind men, elephants and international integration,' *Journal of Common Market Studies* 10(3) (1971): 267–284.

23 Bruno Palier and Yves Surel, *L'Europe en action. L'européanisation dans une perspective comparée* (Paris: L'Harmattan, 2007); Antje Wiener and Thomas Diez, 'Taking stock of integration theory,' in *European Integration Theory*, eds Antje Wiener and Thomas Diez (Oxford: Oxford University Press, 2nd ed., 2009), 241–252.

24 See especially Olivier Beaud, *Théorie de la fédération* (Paris: PUF, 2007); Michael Burgess, ed., 'Federalism and the European Union,' *Publius, the Journal of Federalism* 26(4, special issue) (1996): 1–162; Michael Burgess, 'Federalism,' in *European Integration Theory*, eds Antje Wiener and Thomas Diez (Oxford: Oxford University Press, 2nd ed., 2009), 25–44; Maurice Croisat and Jean-Louis Quermonne, *L'Europe et le fédéralisme* (Paris: Montchrestien, 1999).

25 Tanja A. Bürzel and Madeleine O. Hosli, 'Brussels between Bern and Berlin: comparative federalism meets the European Union,' *Governance*, 16(2) (2003): 179–202.

26 See the special issue of the *Journal of European Public Policy* 'European integration in times of crisis: theoretical perspectives,' 22(2) (2015).

27 Liesbet Hooghe and Gary Marks, 'A postfunctionalist theory of European integration: from permissive consensus to constraining dissensus,' *British Journal of Political Science* 39(1) (2008): 1–23.

28 Ian Down and Carole J Wilson, 'From "Permissive Consensus" to "Constraining Dissensus": a polarizing union?' *Acta Politica* 43 (2008): 26–49.

29 Frank Schimmelfennig, 'European integration in the Eurocrisis: the limits of postfunctionalism,' *Journal of European Integration* 36(3) (2014): 321–337.

30 The idea of differentiated integration has been mentioned since the mid-1990s, but has recently seen a great deal of renewed interest, particularly in the 'Rome Declaration' adopted by the European Council on the 60-year anniversary of the Treaty of Rome (25 March 2017).

31 See the debates on new intergovernmentalism: Bickerton Christopher J., Dermot Hodson and Uwe Puetter,' 'The new intergovernmentalism: European integration in the post-Maastricht era,' *Journal of Common Market Studies* 53(4) (2015): 703–722; Frank Schimmelfennig, 'What's the news in "New Intergovernmentalism"? A critique of Bickerton, Hodson and Puetter,' *Journal of Common Market Studies* 53(4) (2015): 723–730; Bickerton Christopher J., Dermot Hodson and Uwe Puetter, 'Something new: a rejoinder to Frank Schimmelfennig on the new intergovernmentalism,' *Journal of Common Market Studies* 53(4) (2015): 731–736; Bickerton Christopher J., Dermot Hodson and Uwe Puetter, eds, *The New Intergovernmentalism: States and Supranational Actors in the Post-Maastricht Era* (Oxford: Oxford University Press, 2015).

32 Bickerton Christopher J., Dermot Hodson and Uwe Puetter, *The New Intergovernmentalism* (Oxford: Oxford University Press, 2015).

33 Fabbrini Sergio and Uwe Puetter, 'Integration without supranationalisation: studying the lead roles of the European Council and the council in Post-Lisbon EU politic,' *Journal of European Integration* 38(5) (2016): 481–495.

34 See particularly John Erik Fossum and Markus Jachtenfuchs, 'Federal challenges and challenges to federalism. Insights from the EU and federal states,' *Journal of European Public Policy* 24(4) (2017): 467–485; Michael Keating, 'Europe as a multilevel federation,' *Journal of European Public Policy*, 24(4) (2017): 615–632.

35 Arthur Borriello and Amandine Crespy, 'How not to speak the F-word. Federalism between mirage and imperative in the Eurocrisis,' *European Journal of Political Research* 54(3) (2015): 502–524.

36 Ben Crum, 'Saving the Euro at the cost of democracy?' *Journal of Common Market Studies* 52(4) (2013): 614–630.

37 Curtis and Jupille, 'The European Union,' op. cit.; Liesbet Hooghe and Gary Marks, 'European Union?' *West European Politics* 31(1/2) (2008): 108–129.

38 Simon Hix, *The Political System of the European Union* (Basingstoke/Hampshire: Macmillan Press, 1999).

39 Pollack, 'Theorizing EU policy-making.'

40 James G. March and Johan P. Olsen, 'The new institutionalism: organizational factors in political life,' *American Political Science Review* 78(3) (1984): 734–749; James G. March and Johan P. Olsen, *Rediscovering Institutions: The Organizational basis of Politics* (New York: The Free Press, 1989).

41 Peter A. Hall and Rosemary C. R. Taylor, 'Political Science and the three new institutionalisms,' *Political Studies* 44(5) (1996): 936–957.

42 Karen J. Alter, *Establishing the Supremacy of European Law: The Making of an International Rule of Law in Europe* (New York: Oxford University Press, 2001); Simon Hix, 'The study of the European community: the challenge to comparative politics,' *West European Politics* (17) (1994): 1–30; Joseph Jupille and James Caporaso, 'Institutionalism and the European Union: beyond international relations and comparative politics,' *Annual Review of Political Science* 2 (1999): 429–444; Paul Pierson, *Politics in Time: History, Institutions and Social Analysis* (Princeton: Princeton University Press, 2004);

Mark A. Pollack, *The Engines of European Integration: Delegation, Agency and Agenda Setting in the EU* (New York: Oxford University Press, 2003); Antje M. Pollack, 'The new institutionalisms and European integration,' in *European Integration Theory*, eds Antje Wiener and Thomas Diez (Oxford: Oxford University Press, 2nd ed., 2009), 125–143; Alec Stone Sweet and James A. Caporaso, 'From free trade to supranational polity: the European Court and integration,' in *European Integration and Supranational Governance*, eds Wayne Sandholtz and Alec Stone Sweet (New York: Oxford University Press, 1998), 92–133; Jonas Tallberg, 'The anatomy of autonomy: an institutional account of variation in supranational influence,' *Journal of Common Market Studies* 38 (2000): 843–864; Georges Tsebelis and Geoffrey Garrett, 'Legislative politics in the European Union,' *European Union Politics* 1 (2000): 9–36.

43 Kathleen Thelen, 'Historical Institutionalism in Comparative Politics,' *Annual Review of Political Science* 2 (1999); Sven Steinmo, Kathleen Thelen and Frank Longstreth, eds, *Structuring Politics: Historical Institutionalism in Comparative Politics* (New York: Cambridge University Press, 1992).

44 Paul Pierson, 'The path to European integration: a historical institutionalist analysis,' *Comparative Political Studies* 29 (1996): 123–163; Fritz W. Scharpf, 'The joint decision trap: lessons from German Federalism and European integration,' *Public Administration* 66 (1988): 239–278.

45 Saurugger, *Théories et concepts de l'intégration européenne*, op. cit., 193–225.

46 For an overview, see Adrian Favell and Virginie Guiraudon, eds, *Sociology of the European Union* (Houndmills: Palgrave MacMillan, 2011) and Sabine Saurugger and Frédéric Merand, eds, 'Mainstreaming Sociology in EU Studies,' *Comparative European Politics* 8 (1, special issue) (2010).

47 Neil Fligstein, *Euroclash, the EU, European Identity and the Future of Europe* (Oxford: Oxford University Press, 2008); Niilo Kauppi, *Democracy, Social Resources and Political Power in the European Union* (Manchester: Manchester University Press, 2005); Chris Rumford, *The European Union: A Political Sociology* (London: Blackwell, 2002); Chris Shore, *Building Europe: The Cultural Politics of European Integration* (London: Routledge, 2000).

48 Jay Rowell and Michel Mangenot, *Political Sociology of the European Union* (Manchester University Press, 2016).

49 See Adrian Favell, 'The sociology of EU politics,' in *The Handbook of EU politics*, eds Knud Erik Jørgensen, Mark Pollack and Ben J. Rosamond (London: Sage, 2007), 122–137; Didier Georgakakis, 'The historical and political sociology of the European Union: a uniquely French methodological approach?' *French Politics* 7 (2009): 437–455.

50 Olivier Baisnée, 'En être ou pas. Les logiques de l'entre soi à Bruxelles,' *Actes de la recherche en sciences sociales* 166(7) (2007): 110–121; Irène Bellier and Thomas M. Wilson, eds, *An Anthropology of the European Union: Building, Imagining, Experiencing Europe* (Oxford: Berg, 2000); Willy Beauvallet and Sébastien Michon, 'Professionalization and socialization of the members of the European Parliament,' *French Politics* 8(2) (2010); Didier Georgakakis, 'Tensions within Eurocracy? A socio-morphological view,' *French Politics* 8 (2010), 116–144; Virginie Guiraudon, 'The constitution of a European immigration policy domain: a political sociology approach,' *Journal of European Public Policy* 10(2) (2003): 263–282; George Ross, 'What do "Europeans" think? Analyses of the European Union's current crisis by European elites,' *Journal of Common Market Studies* 46(2) (2008): 389–412.

51 See Jeffrey T. Checkel, 'Social constructivism in global and European politics: a review essay,' *Review of International Studies* 30(2) (2004): 230–231. See also the special issue of the *Journal of European Public Policy*, 6(4) (1999) on the Social Construction of Europe.

52 Jeffrey T. Checkel, ed., 'International institutions and socialization in Europe,' *International Organization* 59(4, special issue) (2005); Jeffrey T. Checkel, *International Institutions and Socialization in Europe* (Cambridge: Cambridge University Press, 2007); Niilo Kauppi, 'European Union institutions and French political careers,' *Scandinavian Political Studies* 19(1) (1996): 1–24; Jan Beyers, 'Conceptual and methodological challenges in the study of European socialization,' *Journal of European Public Policy* 17(6) (2010): 909–920.

53 Thomas Diez, 'Speaking "Europe": the politics of integration discourse,' *Journal of European Public Policy* 6(4) (1999): 598–613; Thomas Risse, 'Let's argue! Communicative action and world politics,' *International organization* 54 (2000): 1–39; Ben Rosamond, 'Discourses of globalization and the social construction of European identities,' *Journal of European Public Policy* 6(4) (1999): 652–668.

54 Thomas Christiansen, Knud Erik Jørgensen, and Antje Wiener, *The Social Construction of Europe* (London: Sage, 2001); Thomas Risse, 'Social constructivism and European integration,' in *European Integration Theory*, eds Antje Wiener and Thomas Diez (Oxford: Oxford University Press, 2nd ed., 2009), 144–160; Antje Wiener, 'Constructivism and sociological institutionalism,' in *Palgrave Advances in European Union Studies*, eds Michelle Cini and Angela K. Bourne (Basingstoke: MacMillan, 2006), 35–55.

55 Francis Cheneval and Frank Schimmelfennig, 'The case for demoicracy in the European Union,' *Journal of Common Market Studies* 51(2) (2013): 334–350; Sandra Kröger and Dawid Friedrich, eds, *The Representative Turn in EU Studies* (London: Routledge, 2016); Sandra Kröger and Dawid Friedrich, 'Democratic representation in the EU: two kinds of subjectivity,' *Journal of European Public Policy* 20(2) (2013): 171–189; Christopher Lord and Johannes Pollak, 'The EU's many representative modes: colliding? Cohering?' *Journal of European Public Policy* 17(1) (2010): 117–136; Kalypso Nicolaïdis, 'European democracy and its crisis,' *Journal of Common Market Studies* 51(2) (2013): 351–369; Kalypso Nicolaïdis and Richard Youngs, 'Europe's democracy trilemma,' *International Affairs* 90(6) (2014): 1403–1419.

56 Guy Peters and John Pierre J., 'Governance approaches,' in *European Integration Theory*, eds Antje Wiener and Thomas Diez (Oxford: Oxford University Press, 2nd ed., 2009), 91–104; Rod A. W. Rhodes, 'The new governance. Governing without government,' *Political Studies* 44 (1996): 652–657.

57 Saurugger, *Théories et concepts de l'intégration européenne*, 227.

58 Simon J. Bulmer, 'The governance of the European Union: a new institutionalist approach,' *Journal of European Public Policy* 13(4) (1994): 351–380.

59 Beate Kohler-Koch and Rainer Eising, *The Transformation of Governance in the European Union* (London: Routledge, 1999).

60 Liesbet Hooghe, ed., *Cohesion Policy and European Integration: Building Multi-Level Governance* (New York: Oxford University Press, 1996); Liesbet Hooghe and Gary Marks, *Multilevel Governance and European Integration* (Lanham: Rowman & Littlefield, 2001).

61 Thomas Christiansen and Simona Piattoni, ed., *Informal Governance in the European Union* (Cheltenham: Edward Elgar, 2003); Rod A. W. Rhodes, Ian Bache and Stephen

George, 'Policy networks and policy making in the European Union: a critical appraisal,' in *Cohesion Policy and European Integration: Building Multilevel Governance*, ed. Liesbet Hooghe (Oxford: Clarendon Press, 1996).

62 For more details on network analysis, see Chapter 9.

63 Markus Jachtenfuchs, 'The governance approach to European Integration,' *Journal of Common Market Studies* 39(2) (2001): 245–264; Saurugger, *Théories et concepts de l'intégration européenne*, 227–254.

64 The recent emphasis on deliberative democracy or deliberative supranationalism refers to the 'deliberative turn' in EU studies. It also overlaps with constructivist approaches and discourse analysis. See Christian Joerges and Jürgen Neyer, 'From intergovernmental bargaining to deliberative political process: the constitutionalization of comitology,' *European Law Journal* 3 (1997): 273–299; Dermot Hodson and Imelda Maher, 'The open method of coordination as a new mode of governance: the case of soft economic policy co-ordination,' *Journal of Common Market Studies* 39 (2001): 719–746; Paul Magnette, 'Deliberation or bargaining? Coping with constitutional conflicts in the convention on the future of Europe,' in *Developing a Constitution for Europe*, eds Erik Oddvar Eriksen, John Erik Fossum, and Agustín José Menéndez (London: Routledge, 2004), 207–225.

65 Robert O. Keohane and Joseph S. Nye, ed., 'Transnational relations and world politics: an introduction,' *International Organization* 25(3) (1971): 329–349; Saurugger, *Théories et concepts de l'intégration européenne*, 349–375.

66 Virginie Guiraudon and Gallya Lahav, 'A reappraisal of the state sovereignty debate,' *Comparative Political Studies* 33(2) (2000): 163–195; Sidney Tarrow, *The New Transnational Activism* (Cambridge: Cambridge University Press, 2005).

67 Joseph S. Nye, *Soft Power: The Means to Success in World Politics* (New York: Public Affairs, 2005).

68 François Duchêne, 'The European Community and the uncertainties of interdependance,' in *A Nation Writ Large? Foreign Policy Problems Before the European Community*, eds Max Kohnstamm and Wolfgang Hager (Basingstoke: MacMillan, 1973), 1–21; Zaki Laïdi, *Norms Over Force. The Enigma of European Power*, trans. Cynthia Schoch (Basingstoke: Palgrave Macmillan, 2008); Sonia Lucarelli and Ian Manners, eds, *Values and Principles in European Union Foreign Policy* (London: Routledge, 2006); Jan Orbie, 'Civilian power Europe. review of the original and current debates,' *Cooperation and Conflict* 41(1) (2006): 123–128; Mario Telò, *Europe: A Civilian Power? European Union, Global Governance, World Order* (Basingstoke: Palgrave Macmillan, 2006).

69 Saurugger, *Théories et concepts de l'intégration européenne*, 377–397; Fredrik Söderbaum and Timothy M. Shaw, eds, *Theories of New Regionalism. A Palgrave Reader* (Basingstoke: Palgrave Macmillan, 2003).

70 Andrew Hurrell, 'The regional dimension in international relations theory,' in *Global Politics of Regionalism. Theory and Practice*, eds Mary Farrell, Bjorn Hettne and Luk Van Langenhove (London: Pluto Press, 2005), 38–53; Peter J. Katzenstein, 'Regionalism in comparative perspective,' *Cooperation and Conflict* 31(2) (1996), 123–159; Finn Laursen, ed., *Comparative Regional Integration: Theoretical Approaches* (Aldershot: Ashgate, 2003); Alex Warleigh Lack and Luk Van Langenhove, 'Introduction. Rethinking EU studies: the contribution of comparative regionalism,' *Journal of European Integration* 32(6) (2010): 541–562.

71 Bjorn Hettne, Andras Inotai and Osvaldo Sunkel, *Globalism and New Regionalism* (Basingstoke: Palgrave Macmillan, 1999); Mario Telò, ed., *European Union and New Regionalism. Regional Actors and Global Governance in a Post-Hegemonic Era* (Aldershot: Ashgate, 2007).

72 Olivier Costa, Clarissa Dri and Stelios Stavridis, *Parliamentary Dimensions of Regionalization and Globalization. The Role of Intra-parliamentary Institutions* (Basingstoke: Palgrave Macmillan, 2013); Michael Schulz, Fredrik Söderbaum and Joakim Öjendal, eds, *Regionalisation in a Globalizing World* (London: Zed Books, 2001); Nikki Slocum-Bradley and Luk Van Langenhove, 'Identity and regional integration,' in *Global Politics of Regionalism. Theory and Practice*, eds Mary Farrell, Bjorn Hettne and Luk Van Langenhove (London: Pluto Press, 2005), 137–151.

73 Paolo Graziano and Maarten P. Vink, eds, *Europeanization. New Research Agendas* (Basingstoke: Palgrave Macmillan, 2008); Paolo Graziano and Maarten P. Vink, 'Europeanisation: concept, theory and methods,' in *The Member States of the European Union*, eds Simon Bulmer and Christian Lequesne (Oxford: Oxford University Press, 2013), 31–54; Robert Ladrech, *Europeanization and National Politics* (Basingstoke: Palgrave Macmillan, 2010).

74 Robert Ladrech, 'Europeanization of domestic politics and institutions: the case of France,' *Journal of Common Market Studies* 32(1) (1994): 69–88.

75 Simon Bulmer and Claudio Radaelli, 'The Europeanization of national policy,' in *The Member States of the European Union*, eds Simon Bulmer and Christian Lequesne (Oxford: Oxford University Press, 2005), 340; Thomas Risse, Maria Green Cowles and James Caporaso, 'Europeanization and domestic change: introduction,' in *Transforming Europe: Europeanization and Domestic Change*, eds Maria Green Cowles, James Caporaso and Thomas Risse (Cornell University Press, 2001), 1–20.

76 Trine Flockhart, 'Europeanization or EU-ization? The transfer of European norms across time and space,' *Journal of Common Market Studies* 48(4) (2010): 787–810.

77 Claudio M. Radaelli, 'The Europeanization of public policy,' in *The politics of Europeanization*, eds Kevin Featherstone and Claudio M. Radaelli (Oxford: Oxford University Press, 2003), 30.

78 Maarten P. Vink and Paolo Graziano, 'Challenges of a new research agenda,' in *Europeanization: New Research Agendas*, eds Paolo Graziano and Maarten P. Vink (New York: Palgrave Macmillan, 2007), 7.

79 Tanja Börzel and Thomas Risse, 'Conceptualizing the domestic impact of Europe,' in *The Politics of Europeanization*, eds Kevin Featherstone and Claudio M. Radaelli (Oxford: Oxford University Press, 2003), 60; Theofanis Exadaktylos and Claudio M. Radaelli, eds, *Research Design in European Studies: Establishing Causality in Europeanization* (Basingstoke: Palgrave Macmillan, 2012).

80 Radaelli, *'The Europeanization of Public Policy'*.

81 Sylvain Brouard, Olivier Costa and Thomas König, *The Europeanization of Domestic Legislatures: The Empirical Implications of the Delors' Myth in Nine Countries* (Springer Verlag, 2011).

82 Ian Bache, Simon Bulmer and Defne Gunay, 'Europeanization: a critical realist perspective,' in *Research Design in European Studies. Establishing Causality in Europeanization*, eds Theofanis Exadaktylos and Claudio M. Radaelli (Basingstoke: Palgrave Macmillan, 2012); Bache, Bulmer and Gunay, *'Europeanization: A Critical Realist*

Perspective,' 65; Ramona Coman, Thomas Kostera and Luca Tomini, eds, *Europeaniza-tion and European Integration: From Incremental to Structural Change* (Basingstoke: Palgrave Macmillan, 2013).

83 Annette E. Töller, 'Causality in quantitative approaches,' in *Research Design in Euro-pean Studies. Establishing Causality in Europeanization,* eds Theofanis Exadaktylos and Claudio M. Radaelli (Basingstoke: Palgrave Macmillan, 2012).

84 Risse, Cowles and Caporaso, *'Europeanization and Domestic Change'.*

85 Tania Börzel, 'Europeanization: how the European Union interacts with its member states,' in *The Member States of the European Union,* eds Simon Bulmer and Christian Lequesne (Oxford: Oxford University Press, 2005), 49–60.

86 Börzel, *'Europeanization: How the European Union Interacts with its Member States,'* 58–59.

87 Simon Bulmer, 'Theorizing Europeanization,' in *Europeanization: New Research Agendas,* eds Paolo Graziano and Maarten P. Vink (New York: Palgrave Macmillan, 2007), 52.

88 Risse, Cowles and Caporaso, *'Europeanization and Domestic Change'.*

89 Gerda Falkner, Oliver Treib, Miriam Hartlapp and Simone Leiber, *Complying with Europe: EU Harmonisation and Soft Law in the Member States* (Cambridge: Cambridge University Press, 2005); Gerda Falkner and Oliver Treib, 'Three worlds of compliance or four? The EU 15 compared to new Member States,' *Journal of Common Market Stud-ies* 46(2) (2008): 293–313.

90 Philip E. Tetlock, *Expert Political Judgment: How Good Is It? How Can We Know?* (Princeton, NJ: Princeton University Press, 2005), 125–128.

91 Brouard, Costa and König, *The Europeanization of Domestic Legislatures.*

92 Coman, Kostera and Tomini, *Europeanization and European Integration.*

93 Eurobarometers (EB) are public opinion surveys established in 1973 by the Commis-sion. The Standard EB consists of around 1000 face-to-face interviews in each Member State; it is conducted between 2 and 5 times per year. There are also Special Euroba-rometer reports, based on in-depth thematic studies, Flash Eurobarometer, i.e. tele-phone interviews on a specific topic, and Qualitative Studies, that investigate in-depth the motivations and feelings of some social groups towards a given subject or concept. http://ec.europa.eu/public_opinion/index_en.htm. Parlemeter is a Eurobarometer-style opinion survey conducted for the European Parliament once a year since 2007.

94 Olivier Costa, 'La parlementarisation de l'Union: pour une approche dynamique du régime politique européen,' (Thesis for the Accreditation to supervise PhDs (Habili-tation à Diriger les Recherches), Sciences Po Bordeaux, 2013); Dieter Grimm, 'Treaty or constitution? The legal basis of the EU after Maastricht,' in *Developing a Constitu-tion for Europe,* eds Erik Oddvar Eriksen, John Erik Fossum and Agustín José Menéndez (London: Routledge, 2004), 70–89; Adrienne Héritier, 'Elements of democratic legit-imation in Europe: an alternative perspective,' *Journal of European Public Policy* 6(2) (1999): 269–282; Paul Magnette, *What is the European Union? Nature and Prospects* (Houndmills/Basingstoke/Hampshire/New York: Palgrave Macmillan, 2005); Berthold Rittberger and Frank Schimmelfennig, 'Building Europe's Constitution. The parlia-mentarization and institutionalization of human rights,' in *The State of the European Union,* eds Sophie Meunier and Kathleen R. McNamara (Oxford: Oxford University Press, vol. 8, 2007); Fabien Terpan, *Droit et politique de l'UE* (Paris: Larcier, 2013).

95 Berthold Rittberger and Frank Schimmelfennig, 'Explaining the constitutionalization of the European Union,' *Journal of European Public Policy* 13(8) (2006): 1148–1167.

96 Olivier Costa and Paul Magnette, 'Idéologies et changement institutionnel dans l'Union européenne. Pourquoi les gouvernements ont-ils constamment renforcé le Parlement européen?' *Politique européenne* 1(9) (2003): 49–75.

97 Olivier Costa, 'La parlementarisation inachevée de l'Union européenne: le Parlement européen entre puissance institutionnelle et faiblesse politique,' in *L'Europe prochaine: regards franco-allemands sur l'avenir de l'Union européenne*, eds Martin Koopmann and Stephan Martens (Paris: l'Harmattan, coll. 'Logiques politiques,' 2008), 265–278.

98 Olivier Costa and Paul Magnette, 'Idéologies et changement institutionnel dans l'Union européenne'; Berthold Rittberger, 'Institutionalizing representative democracy in the European Union: the case of the European Parliament,' *Journal of Common Market Studies*. 50th Anniversary Special Issue (2012): 18–37.

99 For different readings on the separation of powers in the EU institutional system, see a.o. Amie Kreppel, 'Looking "Up", "Down" and "Sideways": understanding EU institutions in context,' *West European Politics* 34(1) (2011): 167–179; Sergio Fabbrini, *Which European Union? Europe After the Euro Crisis* (Cambridge: Cambridge University Press, 2015); Richard Corbett, John Peterson and Elizabeth Bomberg, 'The EU's institutions,' in *The European Union, How does it Work?* eds Elizabeth Bomberg, John Peterson and Richard Corbett (Oxford: Oxford University Press, 3rd ed., 2012), 47–73; Richard Corbett, 'Democracy in the European Union,' in *The European Union, How Does it Work?*, eds Elizabeth Bomberg, John Peterson and Richard Corbett (Oxford: Oxford University Press, 3rd ed., 2012), 141–160.

Executive power **3**

For a long time, distinguishing the executive from the legislative power within the EU was quite problematic. The Commission and the Council were involved in both, and the European Parliament held little sway in law-making. The classic typology of powers and the principle of separation of powers were thus irrelevant, or at least misleading to describe the functioning of the EC/EU.

However, due to a process of constant parliamentarization of the EU, and to the creation and then the institutionalization of the European Council, matters became clearer – even if the principle of separation of powers is still not evoked, directly or indirectly, in the treaties. Today, we can describe the EU institutional system as a quadripartite structure. On the one hand, an executive power composed of the European Council and the Commission, that more or less play respectively the role of a collective Head of State (European Council) and a government and central administration (Commission). On the other hand, a legislative power made up of the European Parliament and the Council, which can be assimilated to the low chamber and the high chamber of a bicameral Parliament.

In this chapter, we will focus on the executive power; the legislative one will be the topic of the next chapter.

3.1 The European Council: the impetus

The European Council was not initially created by the treaties, but originated in the summits between Member State Heads of State and government. The first one was held in Paris on 10 and 11 February 1961. The French president at the time, Charles De Gaulle, convened the meeting outside of the Community framework in order to launch the idea of a political union primarily based on intergovernmental cooperation (that would lead to the failed Fouchet Plans of

November 1961 and January 1962). The Heads of State and government of the six Member States met again in 1967 in Rome but for a ceremonial purpose (the 10th anniversary of the Treaty of Rome) and it is only in 1969 that another summit took place in The Hague to discuss completing, widening and deepening the Community. This ad-hoc summit was considered a success.[1] The question of institutionalizing these meetings was raised in 1972 and the practice was formalized in the form of the 'European Council' in 1974, without needing to modify the Community institutional mechanisms.[2] In 1986, the Single European Act formally institutionalized this practice and increased the European Council's influence but it was not until the Treaty of Lisbon that it became legally recognized. Now, as a part of the EU institutional system, the European Council is subject to the same obligations as the other institutions and the European Court of Justice may consider appeals against its actions, except for issues related to the Common Foreign and Security Policy. The European Council is now headquartered in Brussels, within the *Europa* building, next door to the *Berlaymont* (Commission) and the *Justus Lipsius* (Council). The European Council synthesizes the two major tensions underlying European integration – supranationalism and intergovernmentalism. Indeed, with the Lisbon Treaty, the European Council became a supranational institution with a permanent president, but its role is to ensure the visibility and predominance of the most intergovernmental body of the EU.[3]

3.1.1 The role of the European Council

The European Council is similar to an EU 'collective Head of State'. It is first and foremost an institution of impetus and arbitration. The Lisbon Treaty states that the European Council provides the EU

> with *the necessary impetus for its development* and shall define the *general* political directions and *priorities* thereof.[4]

Its role is to discuss key issues and problems arising within the EU's framework by adopting 'history-making decisions'[5] such as treaty reform, EU enlargement or the opening of new policy projects. As noted by Bulmer and Wessels, once established, the European Council became the most politically authoritative institution of the EU and since then most major decisions have been taken in the European Council.[6] It was thus the European Council that took the initiative for cooperation in the fight against crime in the 1970s, opened accession negotiations with Central and East European countries (European Councils of Cologne and Helsinki, 1999) or adopted the draft Constitution for Europe in June 2004. More recently, it was the European Council that took responsibility for the management of the eurozone and the refugee crisis, as well as of Brexit. The European Council also plays an arbitration role with a political authority of appeal in order to release sensitive documents and resolve conflicts that paralyse the Council of Ministers. For example, the 1984 European Council in Fontainebleau found a solution to the recurrent problem of the United Kingdom's contribution to the Community budget.

By virtue of its institutionalization, the Lisbon Treaty assigned the European Council the following tasks: appointment of its permanent president, proposal to the Parliament concerning the name of the Commission's president, appointment of the High Representative for Foreign and Security Policy, establishment of the Council's rotating presidency and the decision to transition from unanimity to qualified majority voting in the Council.[7]

Finally, it plays a central role in foreign policy. According to the Treaty, the European Council

> shall identify the Union's strategic interests, determine the objectives of and define general guidelines for the common foreign and security policy, including for matters with defence implications.[8]

During its meetings, the European Council adopts diplomatic statements to comment on the international political situation or to react to current events. It also meets regularly with the Heads of State of foreign countries. Its president holds a function of representation of the EU in matters related to Common Foreign and Security Policy. He or she is thus the 'political face of Europe' alongside the President of the Commission, the High Representative as well as the President of the European Parliament.

The European Council defines the EU's broad policies and frames the work of the other institutions. The Commission, Council and Parliament are called upon to translate its political conclusions and decisions into legislative acts according to the appropriate procedure. Since 1974 the European Council has exercised the impetus function which originally belonged to the Commission who lost that right due to a lack of sufficient leadership and legitimacy as well as repeated blockages of its proposals in the Council. As many authors point out, the European Council has gradually become the principal initiator of the EU.[9]

3.1.2 The composition of the European Council

The European Council is composed of a permanent president, the Heads of State or government of the EU Member States and the President of the Commission. The High Representative for Foreign and Security Policy is also present and accountable for his actions.[10] This is a significant change introduced by the Treaty of Lisbon. The European Council is institutionally linked to both the Council and the Commission with the presence of the High Representative, who is also the Commissioner for External Relations and presides therefore over meetings of the Foreign Affairs Council. The European Council is attended by the Ministers of Foreign Affairs and a member of the Commission, which varies depending on the subject at hand. Since 1991, the Economic and Finance Affairs Ministers have been invited when issues of economic and monetary union are on the agenda. The European Council's work benefits from the assistance of the Secretary General of the Council, the Secretary General of the Commission and officials from the General Secretariat of the European Council who are responsible for preparing the minutes and providing interpreters.

Since 1974, the aim has been to minimize the number of people present during European Council debates in order to preserve its ability to make policy decisions, to resolve conflicts and negotiate 'package deals' which release several dossiers at once.[11] Officials and national diplomats were deliberately kept out of meetings to avoid conflicts that would divide the Council, the Committee of Permanent Representatives (COREPER) and the Council's working groups. Thus, delegations remain outside the meeting room. Each delegation appoints a 'liaison officer' who provides communication between the delegation and the Head of State or government, referred to as 'Antici' in reference to the Italian diplomat who chaired the group in the late 1970s. The Antici prepares the agenda of the COREPER, has access to European Council chambers and receives reports submitted by officials of the Council's Secretary General. The Antici's reports are then sent to the national delegations which are quickly brought up to speed on the negotiations.[12]

Since the Lisbon Treaty, the European Council has had a stable and full-time president, appointed for a term of two-and-a-half years, renewable once, and incompatible with any national mandate. Until late 2009, the European Council worked under the presidency of the Head of State or government exercising the six-month presidency of the Council.[13] The creation of the post of the President of the European Council was at the centre of the debates during the Convention on the Future of Europe as some wanted this office to be the highest authority in the EU.[14] Then with the outbreak of the economic and financial crisis, more and more voices have called for having a permanent president of the EU in order to give the impetus for a common reaction of the Member States.[15] The creation of this function has been seen as a way to increase the effectiveness of EU decision-making and facilitate reaching agreements among Member States.[16] So far, the rotating presidency was an opportunity for the Member States to put new issues on the agenda and to further their own interests, internally and externally. There was also a great diversity in the capabilities and organizational skills of various Member States during their respective presidencies: some were well prepared and ensured the coherence of European decisions, while others appeared to be less efficient or mobilized.[17] A permanent president would thus ensure greater continuity to the working of the European Council and favour the search for collective responses,[18] as the president does not represent his/her own Member State nor have a government to run and can play the role of an 'honest broker'.[19]

The Belgian former Prime Minister Herman Van Rompuy was chosen in late 2009 and took up his position on 1 January 2010. He was re-elected for a second term by the Heads of State and government in March 2012. Donald Tusk, the former Polish prime minister, was appointed to replace Van Rompuy on 1 December 2014. His term was renewed in March 2017, despite opposition from the Polish authorities, who accused him of interfering in their national politics. The President of the European Council manages the meetings, ensures the preparation and continuity of work and sends a report to the European Parliament after each meeting.[20] Overall, his mission is to promote cohesion and compromise. Known as a consensus-builder, Van Rompuy focused his activities mainly on the economy and the governance of the eurozone, given the serious crisis faced by the EU. He was designated the first President of the Eurozone Summit during the meeting of the European Council in March 2012, for a term of two-and-a-half years. With the ongoing economic crisis, the European Council and its president continue to focus on economic governance, but international developments, and in particular in Ukraine, have led Donald Tusk to devote considerable attention to external relations. Relations with Russia were particularly important, given the significance of the ties between Russia and his country, as well as with Eastern Europe in general. It is too early to assess the style differences between H. Van Rompuy and his successor. However, Donald Tusk seems to have introduced a less conciliatory approach and tends to further stress the EU's external relations, at the expense of economic governance issues in which his predecessor had more expertise.[21]

3.1.3 The activities of the European Council

Currently, the European Council meets in Brussels four to six times a year. Its president plays a key role in the organization of its work: he or she convenes the meetings, announces the agenda, recognizes the speakers, draws conclusions and makes every effort, including 'confessionals' (individual interviews with each country representative), to mediate emerging conflicts. The European Council's decisions are taken only by consensus, which clearly distinguishes it from an assembly, as well as from the Council. Some specific decisions, such as appointments, are exceptions, and are adopted by qualified majority in accordance with the rules of the Council.

The meeting of the European Council usually takes place over two days. The first day opens with a speech by the President of the European Parliament, which is not followed by a debate. This speech that has long attracted little interest from European Council members, now relies on the Parliament's resolutions, which lend more weight to the words of its president. The European Council then reviews the items on the agenda before attending a formal lunch. Work continues throughout the afternoon. In the evening, the Heads of State and government hold a working dinner. This is the opportunity for Member States to engage in bilateral diplomacy.[22] Since the 2004 and 2007 enlargements, most discussions and consultations take place at this moment: negotiations have been moved away from plenary meetings into informal sessions.[23] At the same time, a working dinner is held for the foreign ministers with a separate agenda to discuss the less sensitive matters and to reach agreement at the ministerial level.[24] The President of the European Council then reviews the draft conclusions, which have already been examined by COREPER in the two weeks prior to the meeting. The second day is devoted to the consideration of this draft. It is transmitted to the delegations that must promptly report any changes to their chiefs. The European Council acts by 'negative' consensus whereby silence signifies acceptance.[25] The meeting ends with press conferences: a 'European' conference by the European Council's President and the President of the Commission as well as national press conferences which allow each delegation to present its own version of events. In principle, the Heads of State and government refrain from challenging the conclusions collectively.

The conclusions drawn can be quite variable: sometimes they are long and detailed or they may be very terse especially if no consensus was reached. They focus on four types of dossier:

1 'Community' dossiers: these conclusions contain instructions for the Commission and/or the Council either to overcome obstacles or to undertake new initiatives. In recent years, the European Council's directives have become more precise, particularly regarding the Economic and Monetary Union.
2 Foreign policy: these are either political positions or the articulation of 'strategies', to be implemented by the Council;
3 Budgetary issues: the conclusions are comprised of financial perspectives, especially for long-term budget planning;
4 Treaty reform: these conclusions launch and finalize reforms. It is the European Council that makes the political decision to open negotiations. It convenes an Intergovernmental Conference (IGC) for this purpose, which is composed of diplomats and high-level officials and provides a roadmap. At the end of the IGC's work, a draft treaty is submitted to the European Council. It examines, amends and/or settles any outstanding issue of the draft. If there is a consensus, the European Council adopts the treaty as a political agreement. The draft becomes part of the conclusions. After being translated and reviewed by lawyer-linguists, it is then formally signed by the foreign ministers and submitted for ratification in the various Member States.

The Lisbon Treaty institutionalized and strengthened the European Council, reinforcing the role of the Member States and the intergovernmental logic within the EU. Although some call for a more nuanced interpretation of the post-Lisbon inter-institutional relations, it seems clear that since the outbreak of the European finance and debt crisis, the position of the European Council has been reinforced and that this institution plays a strong leadership role nowadays.[26] However, it should be kept in mind that as any other institution, the European Council is not a monolithic bloc but is rather divided along multiple and complex lines, depending on a Member country's size, its date of accession, its GNP as well as its position as contributor or beneficiary of the EU budget. To this day, there is no majority or clear and stable coalition able to control the Council and influence the European Council.[27]

3.2 The European Commission, a central actor after all?

While the European Council defines the main objectives and general guidelines, it is up to the Commission, the Council and the European Parliament to implement and manage Community policies. This section focuses on the Commission, which is granted legislative, executive and even some judicial powers, but appears today as a kind of government of the EU, acting partly under the European Council's instructions.

Originally, the Commission (and before that, the High Authority of the ECSC) was the central institution of the Community. The creation and institutionalization of the European Council, as well as the rise in power of the Council and the European Parliament, have challenged this centrality, but the Commission retains a key role for several reasons. First, it is the most original element of the EU regime, the *sui generis* institution par excellence, around which the system and the 'Community method' are organized. The Commission also holds a monopoly over legislative initiative in a majority of areas. As such, it plays a significant role in identifying problems, setting the agenda and determining the EU's future. The Commission remains the principle interlocutor of governments and special-interest groups. It also plays an essential role of mediation between Member State positions in European negotiations. Its influence is enhanced by its specific mission to oversee the proper implementation of EU law. The Commission also plays a central role in the implementation of policies and has its own jurisdiction over certain policies, including issues related to competition. It has a prominent function in the supervision of the processes of pre-accession and enlargement and holds a role in international negotiations, including international trade and environmental issues, on behalf of the Council. Finally, it is responsible for the mediation with citizens and civil society organizations and for the EU's communication policy.[28]

For all these reasons, the rise of the European Council and the European Parliament as well as the difficulties encountered by the Commission in the late 1960s and again since the early 1990s, did not generally call into question its centrality but only eroded its ability to lead the process of European integration and to impose its leadership.[29]

3.2.1 The composition of the Commission

The Commission consists of 28 members, one per Member State. Originally, large Member States had two Commissioners but this provision was abolished with the entry into force of the Treaty of Nice to limit somewhat the size of the college. This objective provoked heated debate within the Convention on the Future of the Union and at the Brussels Summit in December 2003. The Convention proposed to limit the size of the Commission to 15 members by establishing a system of rotation between the Member States. This solution was criticized both by the representatives of Member States and by those of the Commission. Even if all Member States agree that a restricted Commission is desirable to ensure policy consistency and reduce the risk of jurisdictional conflicts, Member States remain reluctant to the idea of not systematically having a Commissioner.[30] Members of the Commission, Commissioners and staff alike, are also likely to agree that the institution would be stronger if all Member States are represented.

The Lisbon Treaty provides that from 1 November 2014,

> the Commission shall consist of a number of members, including its President and the High Representative of the Union for Foreign Affairs and Security Policy, corresponding to two thirds of the number of Member States.

Based on a system of equal rotation of the states, the composition of the Commission should reflect the demographic and geographic balance of the EU.[31] States have however reserved the possibility to decide otherwise by unanimity in the European Council, which was decided before the entry into force of the treaty.[32]

The College of Commissioners: the Commission as a political body

The nomination of Commissioners has greatly evolved over time. Originally, the EEC Treaty provided that the Member State governments nominate Commissioners by mutual agreement for four years and with a president chosen from amongst them. In the 1980s, the European Parliament began to approve the appointment of the Commission on the basis of its right to adopt resolutions but without having specific jurisdiction in this regard. The Maastricht Treaty formalized the procedure in the early 1990s by conditioning the investiture of the college to a vote of approval by the European Parliament. It also provided that governments should appoint the President of the Commission first so that he or she participates in the selection of the Commissioners and gains more authority over the college. The treaty also made the Parliament's and the Commission's mandates coincide: since 1994, Commissioners are appointed for five years in the months following the European elections. This harmonization evokes the parliamentary system even though it does not have the same meaning given the absence of the Parliament's direct influence over the selection of Commissioners, the lack of party ties between the two institutions and the fact that election results have no bearing on the choice of candidates. Even though the treaty does not mention it, the EP, inspired by the US presidential system, took the initiative to interview the appointed Commissioners in the relevant parliamentary committees before their collective investiture. The Amsterdam Treaty provides for two separate votes, first on the President of the Commission and the second on the college as a whole, which both echo the policy of certain parliamentary regimes. Since the entry into force of the Treaty of Nice, the President of the Commission is chosen by representatives of the Member States by qualified majority and no longer by unanimity. This way, a candidate with a stronger personality and more likely to ensure leadership can be selected. Additionally, the president is granted increased power in the selection of Commissioners in order to enhance the homogeneity of the Commission as well as improve the management of the college. The president assures the distribution of portfolios, assigns the vice-presidents and may alter his decisions during the term and can force a Commissioner to resign with the support of a simple majority of the Commission.[33] Though this was not yet provided for in the treaties, in 1999, Romano Prodi, then Commission President, asked each Commissioner for an undated, signed letter of resignation.[34] Today, the treaty provides that the President of the Commission may request a Commissioner to resign with no explanation.

The Lisbon Treaty states that the Commission President shall be elected by the Parliament on a proposal from the European Council acting by qualified majority and taking into account the outcome of the European elections:

> Taking into account the elections to the European Parliament and after having held the appropriate consultations, the European Council, acting by a qualified majority, shall propose to the European Parliament a candidate for President of the Commission. This candidate shall be elected by the European Parliament by a majority of its component members.
>
> (Art. 17 par. 7)

If the candidate does not obtain the required majority, the European Council, acting by a qualified majority, shall within one month propose a new candidate who shall be elected by the European Parliament following the same procedure. In practice, members can veto the appointment of the president.

The current appointment procedure, after many reforms from the beginning of the 1990s, has seven stages and must take place within six months of the European elections:

1   The European Council, acting by qualified majority, proposes a candidate for President of the Commission.
2   The candidate is 'elected' by the EP by a majority of its members.
3   The European Council designates, by qualified majority and with the agreement of the president, the other Commissioners on the basis of suggestions made by each Member State.
4   The president freely assigns portfolios and vice-presidencies.
5   The EP auditions candidates within its relevant parliamentary committees.
6   The EP votes on the nomination of the Commission as a body. In fact, it may first comment on the composition of the Commission to obtain adjustments, as it did in 2004 and again in 2009.
7   The European Council, acting by qualified majority, appoints the Commission which takes office for five years. The president remains free to change the distribution of portfolios within the college, especially with the departure of Commissioners during the course of the Commission's mandate.

Since the beginning of the 1980s, MEPs have attempted to maximize their influence over the appointment of the Commission and to go beyond the letter and the spirit of the treaties. Logically, they have tried to take advantage of the new provisions of the Treaty of Lisbon, especially the new obligation for the European Council to take into account the results of the European elections when choosing a candidate for the Presidency of the Commission, and the 'election' of that person by the EP. Their objective was to mimic general elections as organized in some legislative regimes like Germany, in which they have the double purpose to choose a majority in the low chamber and to 'elect' the head of the government. Concretely, the possibility to nominate lead candidates (*Spitzenkandidaten*) for European elections is not new in itself, and could have taken place much earlier. Indeed, it started to be considered and examined in 1999. However, the opportunity to focus EP elections on a competition between the leaders of the main European parties was only seriously discussed in 2009. The promoters of this idea wanted to 'dramatize' and personalize the electoral campaign, raise the stakes of the vote and underline its European dimension and political character and, incidentally, increase the influence of the EP in the choice of the President of the Commission.[35] However, due to delays in the ratification of the Lisbon Treaty, and given the socialists' decision to support J. M. Barroso for a second term, the 2009 campaign was organized in a traditional way, as a collection of national elections weakly interconnected.

With a view on the elections of 2014, the EP voted a resolution on 22 November 2012 urging European parties to nominate candidates for the Presidency of the Commission and to make them central actors of the campaign. The idea was that 'this time, it's different' in the sense that voters would cast a ballot for a list within their constituency, but also for the candidate of a European party to be president of the Commission. The resolution also required that future Commissioners be chosen among the newly elected members of the EP.[36] MEPs were partially supported in their approach by the Commission, which considered that national political parties should clearly display their political affiliation at a European level and inform the voters of their candidacy for the Presidency of the Commission.[37] In response to this resolution, five Europarties (EPP, PES, ALDE, Greens and GUE) nominated their respective candidate (a duo in the case of the Greens) and agreed that the campaign should focus on the competition between these candidates for the Presidency of the Commission. In doing so, they proposed a bold interpretation of Article 17.7, in particular of the phrase 'after appropriate consultations', which was understood as an obligation for the European Council to seek the EP's advice. With the exception of the French president, who had promised to support the candidate nominated by the EP, the Heads of State and government did not share this analysis. However, MEPs had the capacity to veto any other candidate than the leader of the winning party, and seemed to be ready to take on an institutional crisis.

The European parties involved in the process proved their ability to cooperate and the EPP, PES and ALDE agreed to support a single candidate after the elections. Their objective was to avoid a possible conflict between them about the results of the elections, in the case of close results or competing coalitions. The leaders of the main parties thus collectively supported the candidacy of Jean-Claude Juncker at the head of the Commission, and urged the European Council to appoint him.

Within the European Council, views were very much contrasted. Several members openly objected to this new institutional act of force by the EP, and reiterated that the choice of the President of the Commission had to take into account numerous criteria (nationality, gender, age, attitude towards European integration, experience, personality, etc.), and not solely the results of the European elections and the preferences of the EP itself. Within the Commission, the strategy of the EP was also criticized, on the grounds that such evolution would involve a radical change in the nature of their institution and in all interinstitutional relations. After a sequence of great confusion and complex negotiations, the European Council finally decided to appoint Mr Juncker.[38] He was then 'elected' by the EP at the end of October 2014 with a large majority, based on a coalition of three groups: EPP, S&D and ALDE (423 in favour,

209 against and 67 abstentions). For the EP, this success was considered as evidence of the institutions' influence. But it can also be argued that Mr Juncker was an ideal candidate for the European Council: he had extensive experience of European institutions and had a moderate positioning within the EPP, enabling him to obtain the support of the Left. Above all, he was 'one of them', as he was Prime Minister of Luxembourg from 1995 to 2013 and President of the Eurogroup from 2004 to 2013.

It is too early to evaluate the full impact of the procedure of *Spitzenkandidaten*. However, for the first time, the President of the Commission sought the explicit support of a coalition, made up of the PPE, S&D and ALDE groups, called 'The Bloc'. To do this, he had to adapt his programme, and in particular he proposed the idea of a plan to revive growth endowed with 315 billion euros in his speech before the EP, prior to his election. It led the President of the Commission to consult the leaders of the groups that 'elected' him on his key initiatives. Indeed, this modified nomination procedure makes the EP elections comparable to p1mentary elections in national democracies.

After his appointment, J. C. Juncker has merely convened a 'G5' dinner, once or twice a month, composed of the first Vice-President of the Commission, the President of the EP, and the presidents of the groups PPE and S&D. This cenacle allowed him to evoke the Commission's strategy and to ensure the support of the main groups of the EP on important votes. Juncker also possessed a privileged relationship with Mr Schulz, the leading PES candidate, who was re-elected as President of the EP after the elections until December 2016.

The 2014 experience was only a first step and it remains to be seen whether it will be re-conducted (Juncker supported the idea during his state of the Union speech in September 2017 but nothing is certain so far).[39] Voter turnout remained low – although the slow decline initiated in 1979 was interrupted – and the leading candidates remained largely unknown outside their country of origin. For instance, 55 per cent of Luxembourg citizens and 25 per cent of Belgians and Germans could name one of the candidates; but it was the case for only 5 per cent of the Dutch and 1 per cent of the British citizens.[40]

The effect of this new procedure in the medium and long term may also be limited, especially if the European Council continues to be the main principal of the Commission and if J. C. Juncker accepts to act as its agent. Although at first glance, the nomination of Juncker seemed revolutionary and a victory for the EP, it must be recalled that the members of the European Council appointed 'one of their own'.[41]

The interinstitutional negotiations are not only focused on the President of the Commission: they also include the members of the College. In 2009, the appointment of the second Barroso team took more than the usual six months as it was complicated by the uncertainties related to the Irish referendum on the Lisbon Treaty on the one hand and the poor performance of the Bulgarian candidate Commissioner Jeleva during the hearings of the EP on the other hand. The Irish approved the treaty in October 2009 and it was only in early December that the names of all the nominees were known and the portfolios were allocated by J. M. Barroso.

After the 2014 elections, the process of the Commission's nomination was a little quicker although no less difficult. Indeed, the new College of Commissioners started on 1 November 2014 (i.e. less than six months after the elections). But several candidates were strongly criticized during their hearing within the European Parliament. The French candidate, P. Moscovici, did not convince the MEPs and received supplementary written questions. The UK candidate, J. Hill, had to face a second hearing. One of the most controversial candidates was the former Spanish agriculture Minister, M. Cañete, who was criticized for his links with the oil industry and last-minute changes in his statement of financial interest. A manifesto called #stopcanete was launched by the Greens and GUE/NGL groups and an online petition has attracted 600,000 signatures. However, his application was approved at the end of a deal between S&D and the EPP groups. The Slovenian nominee, A. Bratušek was less lucky: after a poor hearing, he was replaced by V. Bulc as the Commissioner for transport. Finally, the EP refused to endorse Hungary's candidate, T. Navrascsic for the portfolio 'Education, culture, Youth and citizenship' because of his links with the Hungarian government. He was appointed, but with lesser responsibilities, which exclude citizenship in particular.

According to the treaties, Commissioners are chosen for their general abilities and not chosen to defend the interests of their state. On the contrary, they are required to be completely independent and not to accept instructions from their respective Member States.[42] However, they often have frequent contacts with their national leaders, and J. C. Juncker has even encouraged this.

Over time, each member of the Commission has become accustomed to having his or her own cabinet, just as the ministers do. Commissioners have been obliged to choose collaborators from countries other than their own to prevent them from serving their Member States. Romano Prodi, Commission President from 1999 to 2004, set a rule that the Commissioner's cabinet may be composed of a maximum of six administrators (except for the cabinet of the president which includes 12 officials) representing at least three nationalities. In addition, a very strict code of conduct defines the incompatibilities which apply to cabinet members, in particular to avoid conflicts of interest and avoid the abuses that occurred under the presidency of Jacques Santer (1995–1999). An ethics committee monitors compliance with this code of conduct.[43]

The Commission as an administrative body

It is important to distinguish the Commission as a political body (a college of 28 Commissioners and their close collaborators) and the Commission as an administrative body. It has over 28,000 permanent staff members and has the largest administrative support among all the EU institutions.[44] It is divided into 52 departments, called 'Directorates-General' (DGs) or 'services'. There are 19 political DGs, 5 foreign affairs DGs, 16 internal services, 6 institutional support DGs, and 6 executive agencies (see Box 3.1). Each DG is in charge of a particular policy area and is managed by a Director General who answers to a Commissioner. The DGs are divided into directorates, and each directorate is further divided into units but the size and organization of each DG and service varies greatly. The individual DGs maintain close ties with various interest groups as well as with national administrations in order to help in the effort of preparing proposals for standards and to facilitate their implementation.

Commission staff are principally located in Brussels and Luxembourg. The Commission also has research and representational staff in numerous European cities (mainly in Ispra, Karlsruhe, Geel, Petten and Seville) and delegations in several other countries outside the EU as well as representing the EU to other international organizations.

Staff fall into three categories:

- officials recruited through competition. For administrators (rank A), national quotas exist. The hierarchical posts are the most important (Directors General, Deputy Directors General) and are excluded from this quota but at the same time are subject to a complex appointment process where state representatives play a key role;
- temporary contractual staff; and
- national experts seconded by their governments of origin.

The Commission's administration is headed by its Secretary General, a key player who is notable by his or her influence, discretion and stability. There have only been six Secretaries-General since 1958; since March 2018, the German Martin Selmayr is in office. He assists the President of the Commission in the preparation of the institution's work and plays a central role in the relations with other EU institutions. He or she is also responsible for interdepartmental coordination within the Commission. The Secretary General must ensure that consultations go smoothly between the DGs and services involved in the same report before its transmission to the College of Commissioners.[45]

The Commission's administration is often described as bloated. It should therefore be clarified that many officials (more than a third) are assigned the tasks of translation and interpretation and that the total number of agents is less than that of a medium-sized national district or of a city such as Paris. On the contrary, the Commission lacks the human resources necessary to enable it to properly manage certain policies, especially foreign policies. Development assistance policy is emblematic of these difficulties. Personnel deficiencies have

Box 3.1 The Directorates-General and services of the European Commission – November 2017

Political DGs

1. Agriculture and Rural Development (AGRI)
2. Climate Action (CLIMA)
3. Communication Networks, Content and Technology (CNECT)
4. Competition (COMP)
5. Economic and Financial Affairs (ECFIN)
6. Education and Culture (EAC)
7. Employment, Social Affairs and Inclusion (EMPL)
8. Energy (ENER)
9. Environment (ENV)
10. Financial Stability, Financial Services and Capital Markets Union (FISMA)
11. Health and Food Safety (SANTE)
12. Internal Market, Industry, Entrepreneurship and SMEs (GROW)
13. Justice and Consumers (JUST)
14. Maritime Affairs and Fisheries (MARE)
15. Migration and Home Affairs (HOME)
16. Mobility and Transport (MOVE)
17. Regional and Urban Policy (REGIO)
18. Research and Innovation (RTD)
19. Taxation and Customs Union (TAXUD)

External relations DGs

1. International Cooperation and Development (DEVCO)
2. Humanitarian Aid and Civil Protection (ECHO)
3. Neighbourhood and Enlargement Negotiations (NEAR)
4. Service for Foreign Policy Instruments (FPI)
5. Trade (TRADE)

Institutional support

1. Budget
2. Joint Research Centre
3. Communication
4. Eurostat – European Statistics
5. Data processing

6. Interpretation
7. Human Resources and Security
8. Translation

Internal service

1. Library and e-Resources Center
2. European Political Strategy Center
3. Data Protection Office
4. Administration and Payment of Individual Entitlements
5. Task-force on the preparation and conduct of negotiations with the United Kingdom (Article 50 TEU)
6. Infrastructure and logistics in Brussels
7. Infrastructure and logistics in Luxembourg
8. Foreign Policy Instruments
9. Publications Office
10. European Anti-Fraud Office
11. European Personnel Selection Office
12. Secretariat-General
13. Structural Reform Support Service
14. Internal Audit Service
15. Historical Archives Service
16. Legal Service

Executive agencies

1. European Research Council Executive Agency
2. Executive Agency for Competitiveness and Innovation
3. Executive Agency for Research
4. Executive Agency for Consumers, Health, Agriculture and Food
5. Education, Audiovisual and Culture Executive Agency
6. Innovation and Network Executive Agency

indeed led the Commission to systematize the use of the Technical Assistance Office (TAO) under conditions that favoured excesses and ultimately contributed to the fall of the Santer Commission in March 1999.

Recurring criticisms concerning the Commission's administration have given rise to several reforms since the mid 1990s, with mixed success. They sought to improve both the operation and the image of the institution, to limit the fragmentation of its services and DGs, to simplify administrative procedures[46] and to address abuse – through the creation of an internal audit service and the strengthening of the Anti-Fraud Office (OLAF).[47]

3.2.2 The powers of the Commission

The Commission enjoys a number of powers, which correspond only partially to those of a national government. Overall, it exercises four main functions.

1   First and foremost, it has the power of **legislative initiative**. The Commission holds a quasi-monopoly in this area and must, as a part of its mission, develop legislative proposals (directives and regulations). This role is crucial. It allows the Commission to set the European agenda and other institutions deliberate primarily on the basis of its proposals, which the Commission may modify or withdraw during the course of the proceedings. In the framework of common policies, its legislative initiative is exclusive, except as provided in the treaty. It develops legislative texts and submits them to the European Parliament and the Council for deliberation. To do so, it has specific expertise and maintains close and permanent contact with the recipients of norms: economic and social actors, national governments, lobby groups, large companies, civil society organizations, etc. The legislative initiative of the Commission is shared with Member States in areas such as Common Foreign and Security Policy, and with the Member States and the European Central Bank regarding the Economic and Monetary Union. In fact, its autonomy over legislative initiative is currently relative: only a limited number of proposals (approximately 5 to 15 per cent)[48] are solely the result of autonomous discussions held within the Commission. In most cases, proposals are the result of legal obligations under international treaties or respond to requests from Member States, the European Parliament or the Council, as well as from guidelines set by the European Council. Indeed, the European Council often downgrades the Commission to a 'subservient position', issuing in its conclusions clear guidelines inviting the Commission to take action.[49] For instance, in 2011, this was the case for 53 per cent of the European Council's conclusions.[50] The Commission's legislative initiative also includes the general EU budget whereby the Commission prepares the draft budget. It is then adopted jointly by the Council and the EP. However, the Commission is again bound by the long-term budget outlook adopted by representatives of the Member States which frames the evolution of the overall volume of the budget and the balance between the main policies.[51]

2   The Commission is also an **executive body** charged by the treaties or by regulations and directives with making decisions. In some cases and domains, the Council may retain executive powers or delegate them to the

Commission subject to specific conditions.[52] This executive function is particularly important in the jurisdictional domains exclusive to the EU, mainly in matters of competition policy. As the executive organ of the EU, it is also responsible for managing and implementing the budget. Even if expenditures are generally managed by national and local authorities, the Commission oversees the entire process and closes the accounts at the end of the fiscal year. It also manages Community funds like the ESF (European Social Fund), the EAGF (European Agricultural Guarantee Fund) or EDF (European Development Fund) and European programmes such as Interreg or Erasmus.

3   The Commission is also the **guardian of the treaties**. It must act in accordance with them and must ensure the application of the treaties and of the EU's secondary legislation by pursuing breaches to Community legislation (especially in Member States) on its own initiative or, most often, by referral. If a breach is discovered, the Commission contacts the organization or institution in question to bring it to an end. If it does not succeed through amicable means, the Commission may take legal action before the Court of Justice.[53]

4   Finally, the Commission is the EU's **external representative** except regarding common foreign and security policy for which there is the High Representative of the Union for Foreign Affairs and Security Policy. It conducts international trade negotiations (trade agreements, association agreements, accession, WTO, etc.) on behalf of the EU and on the basis of a mandate from the Council.[54]

3.2.3 The functioning of the Commission

The Commission operates on the principle of collegiality: important decisions are taken by all members not individually. In theory, the Commission adopts major decisions by a majority vote and the president is considered an equal. Unlike a prime minister, he cannot impose his preference. In fact, recourse to actual voting is rare and the president always seeks a consensus. J. C. Juncker announced that he would not hesitate, unlike his predecessor, to resort to voting, but it was implied that he would do so only to overcome oppositions within his team. Decisions are generally made by 'negative consensus', that is, they are adopted if no member explicitly objects. This approach is less restrictive than unanimity which requires explicit support but nevertheless avoids marginalization of some Commissioners, and thus considers both their sectorial interests and their national susceptibilities. Theoretically, the latter have no place in this process given the principle of the Commissioners' independence and their mission of promoting the general interest. However, Commissioners do not hesitate, to varying degrees, to defend the interests of their state, usually on their own initiative.[55] This explains the resistance of the national governments that arises from the prospect of reducing the number of members to less than the number of Member States enshrined in the treaties. Even in the case of a disputed decision, the minority does not publicly state its differences, as decisions are deemed to be those of the institution as a whole. This practice avoids conflicts between sectors and nationalities but favours a kind of 'conservatism', in that the Commission is unable to make decisions that break with the past or to implement radical reforms.

The president's authority has been progressively strengthened in order to increase his or her capacity to coordinate the Commissioners' actions and to give meaning to the Commission's actions as a whole. Today, the president participates in the selection of the Commissioners, distributes portfolios (sometimes indeed under the lobbying of candidates or of their Member States) and vice-presidencies and may change his or her choices while in office. The treaties also state that the president must outline the framework within which the Commission has to work. The leadership of the president is now significant, and while he or she no longer has the power of impetus as was the case in the 1960s or the late 1980s, the president may have a more or less interventionist style, focusing on certain objectives while setting aside files that he or she does not consider a priority.[56]

The conditions for the appointment of J. C. Juncker in 2014 conferred on him an unprecedented dual democratic and intergovernmental legitimacy: he was successively invested as 'candidate leader' by his party, the EPP; nominated as the EP candidate by the main political groups following the European elections; then chosen by qualified majority by the European Council; and finally, 'elected' by a large majority of MEPs.

The Commission meets on Wednesdays in Brussels or Strasbourg when the EP is in session. Its proceedings are confidential and admit very few witnesses: only the Secretary General, the Director General of the legal service, the Deputy Secretary General, the President's Head of Cabinet and the Commission's spokesperson may attend the college's meetings. The work is prepared in the Commissioners' cabinet-member meetings and then in a meeting of the heads of cabinet, chaired by the Secretary General. This weekly meeting, called the 'hebdo', takes place every Monday, drafts Wednesday's agenda and prepares minor decisions which can be adopted without debate or through a written procedure (A points). On Wednesday, the Commission examines the important files, especially those which could not be agreed upon by the heads of cabinet (B points) and makes its decisions in a collegial manner.

Two other types of formal meetings exist: those of small groups comprised of a limited number of Commissioners appointed by the College to discuss a specific topic, and the so-called 'open' groups in which any Commissioner may participate. Thus, during German reunification, a small group was first convened, including the president and the two Commissioners in charge of Foreign Affairs and the Internal Market, in order to define a coordinated strategy for the Community. In a second phase, an open group was formed under the leadership of the Commissioner responsible for the internal market in order to study the impact and implications of reunification on the Community acquis.[57] J. M. Barroso has innovated by creating thematic 'clusters'; groups of Commissioners working on subjects of common interest.

Upon taking office, J. C. Juncker chose to push this logic further, and to promote the role of vice-president, which had been until then essentially formalistic and honorary. The role has existed since the 1960s, but did not hold specific competences, in order to respect scrupulously the principle of collegiality and equality among Commissioners. To carry out his reform successfully, Juncker drew inspiration from the ideas that were developed in the 1990s and 2000s about how to limit the size of the Commission. One option was to limit the number of Commissioners, an idea that was included in the Nice treaty and adopted again – but not implemented – in the Lisbon Treaty. The other was to distinguish between 'senior' and 'junior' Commissioners, the latter working under the authority of the former, as a secretary of state or a delegated minister under the authority of a full-fledged minister at the national level. This new framework of the Commission (see Figure 3.1), endowed with seven Vice-Presidents (six after the departure of Kristalina Gueorguieva at the end of 2016) with enlarged powers, is clearly evident in the new organizational structure, where they appear in a dominant position with very large portfolios, overlapping those of the other Commissioners. This new structure gives a more political direction to the beginning of the decision-making process during policy debates when the College gives guidance to the administration.[58]

J. C. Juncker completed this system by creating project teams.[59] These include Commissioners and senior officials, who are working on a matter of common interest under the authority of a vice-president (see Tables 3.1 and 3.2). A Commissioner may be a member of several teams, and an associated member of others. Thus, all the Commissioners belong to the project team related to the budget; The one on 'better regulation' only includes two permanent members, but all the other Commissioners are associated. Moreover, these teams are not static and their composition can evolve depending on the needs. The seven project teams match the vice-presidents' portfolios, which also refer to the priorities identified by J. C. Juncker for the new Commission.[60] This new organization has contributed to strengthening the powers of the vice-presidents, but also those of the president.

The Commissioners themselves also have powers of attribution in the areas under their responsibility. They make some decisions personally but they do not enjoy a level of autonomy comparable to that of a minister. However, they have

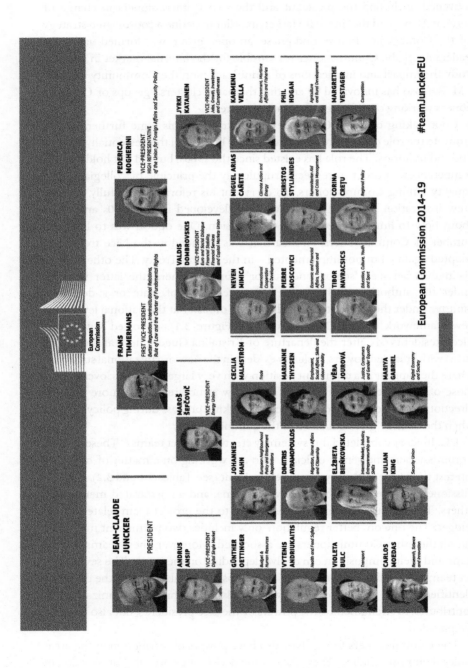

Figure 3.1 New organization of the European Commission (2014–2019)

Source: European Commission (Oct. 2017).

Table 3.1   Commission project teams (2014–2019)

Vice-President	Project team
Frans Timmermans (First VP)	Improving regulation, interinstitutional relations, the rule of law and the Charter of Fundamental Rights
Federica Mogherini	Europe in the World
Günther Oettinger	Budget and Human resources
Andrus Ansip Digital	Digital Single Market
Maroš Šefčovič	Energy Union
Valdis Dombrovskis	Euro and social dialogue, financial stability, financial services and the union of capital markets
Jyrki Katainen	Employment, growth, investment and competitiveness

Source: European Commission (October 2017).

a transversal power, unlike ministers in most countries, since, as a member of the College, they are associated to all major decisions of the Commission and since the president cannot impose his views, contrary to a head of government. From now on, this influence is also exerted within the 'project teams', where they can push their point of view on decisions that are not directly within their competences.

In practice, the DGs design and draft the Commission's legislative proposals (see Box 3.2), but they do not become official until they are adopted by the College. Formal proposals are then forwarded to the Council and the Parliament for consideration.

3.2.4 The uncertain nature of the Commission: government, secretariat or agency?

The question of the Commission's nature remains the subject of recurring debates among both EU practitioners and scholars. Some see it as an embryonic supranational government in a political system affected by an on-going process of 'parliamentarization'. Others defend the idea that it remains an executive body of an essentially administrative and technocratic nature – a kind of Secretariat General implementing decisions adopted by the Parliament and the Council under the aegis of the European Council. Others still continue to refer to the original structure of the Communities, and consider the Commission as an agency, i.e. an autonomous organ responsible for the oversight and administration of specific functions, that should remain completely independent from both Member States and political parties. This issue has indeed never been clarified: the ambivalence of the Commission constitutes a point of equilibrium

Table 3.2 Schedule of meetings under the new organization

Type of meeting	Participants	Frequency
Policy debate	College of Commissioners	4 to 6 times a year
Inter-service Steering Group Meeting	Members of DGs and relevant departments including the Legal Service Chaired by the General Secretariat or the relevant DG	As often as necessary to cover important aspects of the impact-assess-ment process, generally between 5 and 7 meetings per topic
Fixed day	Commissioner and Director General of the respective DG	Weekly
Project team meeting	All relevant DGs and departments	Approximately 1 meeting per month
Strategical fixed day	Vice President, Commissioner and Director General of the respective DG + General Secretariat and Legal Department	Minimum twice a month
Inter-service consultation	All relevant DGs and services	Standard procedure, regularity according to topic and time of the process
Special Meeting of Cabinet Members	Members of Cabinets special-ized in the case discussed	Weekly (usually Thursdays or Fridays)
L'Hebdo	Head of cabinets	Weekly (usually Mondays)
College Meeting	College of Commissioners	Weekly (usually Wednesdays, or Tuesdays in Strasbourg)

Source: Borchardt, M., Notre Europe Policy Paper, 2016.

between the Community method, a parliamentary regime and intergovernmen-tal cooperation.

The Commission combines many functions and must complete multiple tasks in a European decision-making system in which complexity endures and powers continuously increase. This requires many responsibilities: technical expertise in virtually all sectors of public action, close monitoring of the imple-mentation of Community law in the 28 Member States and its integration by candidate countries as well as the ability to manage the conflicting demands of states, institutions, interest groups and its own services. The Commission is, therefore, the victim of a situation of structural administrative overload that

Box 3.2 The Commission's decision-making process

Decision-making within the Commission follows a sequence of six basic steps. They may overlap but each step is unavoidable. This sequence applies to the development of a new legislative proposal, the modification of an existing text or the preparation of an action before the Court of Justice.

1. *Initiation phase*: A DG takes responsibility for the dossier the moment an idea for a proposed standard (or legislative modification or action before the Court) forms in the Commission. In fact, the impetus for a proposal often comes from another institution (European Council, Council, European Parliament, etc.), a Member State or other economic and social actors. The DG in charge of the dossier initiates discussions within the institutional bodies and with representatives of relevant non-institutional actors (interest groups, civil society organizations, representatives of local and regional authorities, etc.). In general, the managing DG sets up an advisory committee of technical experts from academia, interest groups or local and/or national governments.

2. *Writing phase*: The unit officials in charge of the dossier begin writing the proposal including the ideas and perspectives that emerged from the committee of experts. The project then goes back up the hierarchy from the head of unit to the Director General of the DG.

3. *Inter-service coordination*: The inter-service coordination takes place parallel to the writing phase. It is increasingly rare for a DG to be the only one concerned with a proposal. EU institutions have developed a growing number of cross-sectorial policies and actions – that have been reinforced by the project teams. Inter-service coordination is therefore expected and needed under the rules of the Commission and is an essential phase of internal decision-making.[61] The rising importance of this practice, which takes on formal and informal aspects, can be measured by the number of formal inter-service groups overseen by the General Secretariat, from 48 in 1990 to 226 in 2006. Some services are also automatically consulted: the Legal Service controls the legal aspects of the texts (including the choice of the legal basis), while the Budget DG examines any proposal with financial implications. The text is also followed by the Secretary General, which plays a key role in inter-institutional negotiations and ensures that the principles of subsidiarity and proportionality are respected.

4. *Meeting of the members of cabinets*: The text is discussed by the members of the cabinets of the relevant Commissioners. If an agreement is reached, it is forwarded to the heads of cabinet.

5. *Meeting of the heads of cabinet*: The text is discussed at the Monday meeting preceding the College meeting. Heads of cabinet attempt to reach agreement on as many points as possible and then transmit the text to the College of Commissioners.

6. *Meeting of the College of Commissioners*: The proposal is included in the agenda of the next Commission meeting. If a consensus exists or at least 15 of the 28 Commissioners approve the text, the Commission 'adopts' the proposal which must have the unconditional support of all its members under the principle of collegiality. The agreement can be made either through a meeting of the College or through a written procedure. In accordance with the principle of collegiality, the Commission may authorize one or more of its members to take, on its behalf and under its control, clearly defined measures and to adopt the definitive text of an act or proposal for which it defined the content. If no agreement is reached, the text is returned to the relevant cabinet or service.

limits its effectiveness and its ability to legitimize itself through the quality of its actions and European policies, in other words, to enjoy an output-based legitimacy. This situation increases the tension between its political and administrative nature which results both from its organizational duality (College of Commissioners vs. bureaucracy) and the ambiguities of the EU's political system (Commission as a government, agency or General Secretariat).[62] The Commission must be at once a centre of stability, ensuring the smooth functioning of the EU and its policies as well as the 'legal security' of the recipients of European norms, and a place for reflection and innovation, capable of advancing European integration and pursuing the treaties' goals. The antithetical nature of the objectives of impartial service and political leadership refers to the fundamental tension lying in between European integration as a state (the Union) and as a process (integration).[63]

This problem is not new: it dates back to the origins of the Communities. One of the principle concerns of Jean Monnet, visionary of the Community method and the first President of the High Authority of the ECSC, was the need to avoid bureaucratization. He was especially quick to denounce the shortcomings and routine of administration in a parliamentary system. Further, he wanted the High Authority (later the Commission) to be an elite body, composed of experts capable of inventiveness and flexibility to serve the goal of ever-closer integration. However, at the same time, in his opinion, this organization was supposed to ensure the proper operation of the ECSC and to embody a certain stability vis-à-vis the recipients of EU policies.

Walter Hallstein became the first President of the European Commission in 1958 and attempted to give the institutions a more political style. This approach created tensions with some national leaders and led to the 'empty chair' crisis (1965–1966). As a result, the presidents of the Commission were forced to support an apolitical reading of the institution's role until the mid 1980s and to focus on its administrative tasks. Since then, the Commission's role has oscillated between political and administrative conceptions, according to the personality of its president and the political context. Jacques Delors (1985–1995) imposed his leadership and gave the Commission a major political role. Jacques Santer (1995–1999) was faced with a much less favourable context (the rise of Euroscepticism, the EU growth crisis, Commissioner scandals and the Commissions' services). In the face of harsh criticism, he opted for a less political Commission by proposing modest reforms and consolidating existing policies. Romano Prodi (1999–2004) sought to reaffirm the political role of the institution but its excesses and blunders created conflicts with the Parliament and the media which forced him to be more demure. José Manuel Barosso (2004–2014) favoured a more administrative than political institutional interpretation and argued for limiting the role of the Commission, particularly in the legislative domain.[64] However, after what was considered a weak leadership in his first term,[65] he sought to take the lead in some policy areas such as climate change and the eurozone crisis both inside the Commission and vis-à-vis the other institutions.[66] There are mixed opinions concerning the style of J. C. Juncker, President of the Commission since the end of 2014. On the basis of an unprecedented democratic legitimacy, he opted for a less consensual and more political approach to his mandate, aspiring to pursue political leadership.[67] He has already made his marks on the organization of the Commission through the reform of the College. He chose to control the Commissioners more tightly, via his cabinet and a strong secretariat but also, as we have already mentioned, by changing the functions of vice-presidents. And while Barroso developed a 'reasonable working relationship with key players in EU politics', Juncker is a more divisive figure, who has had run-ins with several leaders. He established an unprecedented political tie with the European Parliament, especially when Martin Schulz was president of the EP (until December 2016). He sought and obtained the support of the bloc (EPP, S&D, ALDE) for important decisions. However, some observers note that Mr Juncker has little involvement in the day-to-day functioning of the Commission: he gives the broad guidelines but does not really follow the cases, which gives the Commissioners more autonomy. The central role of its German cabinet director (appointed to the position of General Secretary of the Commission in February 2018, in controversial circumstances), Martin Selmayr, was also criticized: he was presented as the main actor of the Commission, because he imposed his choices without any discussion, and demonstrated authority lacking any legitimacy.[68]

The uncertainties surrounding the nature of the Commission are maintained by the endless divergent demands made by its interlocutors. These are of two kinds. First, it is the EU's 'clearinghouse'; the institution which, by virtue of its powers (monopoly over legislative and budgetary initiatives, policy implementation and supervision of compliance with Community law) is sought out by all types of actors: EU institutions, Member State representatives and their national administrations, interest groups and civil-society organizations, local authorities, businesses, individuals, foreign states, etc. With each one of these having its own objectives, the Commission cannot satisfy everyone and must constantly decide on the points to be added to the agenda and the manner in which to deal with them. It further receives conflicting demands because of the ambiguities surrounding its nature and mission. Some accuse the Commission of being overly bureaucratic and technocratic and of not reflecting current political priorities (unemployment, financial crisis, global warming, counter terrorism, etc.), while at the same time, others accuse it of being overly active and involved in the definition of political priorities (deregulation, reform of social protection, environmental standards, budgetary discipline, etc.) with no democratic legitimacy to do so.

This situation is not specific to the EU: the Commission suffers from an exacerbation of the classic tension between the goals of good governance and reform which affects the executives in all liberal democracies. But, unlike a government, it does not enjoy the necessary legitimacy for the imposition of its views. However, the Commission retains its ability to act: it has always managed to overcome criticism and circumvent the opposition of Member States to propose new initiatives, especially through the development of direct contacts with lobbyists and policy recipients. The Commission is supported by transnational networks of interest groups and civil society organizations in favour of European integration which pressure governments to accept these changes. When it turns out to be impossible to adopt new standards or introduce new policies, the Commission relies on these networks to develop forms of soft law or regulation that define frameworks, practices and specific informal exchanges to structure economic and social interests and to converge national policies without requiring the explicit support of the Member States. These practices have sometimes been codified by the treaties *a posteriori* and were promoted overall through the concept of 'governance'[69] put forward by the Commission in the 1990s.

While the tension between the Commission's political and administrative roles existed from the beginning, a new problem has arisen since the early 1990s: the demand for democracy. Originally, the institution was based on three levels of legitimization: a rational–legal legitimacy, an agency logic and finally on the legitimacy bound to the effectiveness of European policies. The first results from compliance with the treaties and the mobilization of the expert register. The second is based on the Commission's independence and its conception to be a non-majoritarian and supranational institution able to serve the objectives defined by the treaties beyond national and partisan divisions. The third feeds on the satisfaction of the recipients of EU policies (administrative, economic, political and social elites) and its ability to offer creative solutions in response to their requests.

From the early 1990s, the Commission's activities were submitted to increased media attention due to the lassitude caused by its activism regarding the entry into force of the Single Market on 31 December 1992, the difficult ratification of the Maastricht Treaty (1992–1993) and the rising awareness concerning the scope of European integration. Critics have repeatedly questioned the content of its proposals and of the Commission's decisions, judged to be overzealous or excessively liberal, contesting the probity of its members and agents and the overall relevance of its work. More generally, the institution has paid the price for questioning the principle of supranational European integration of which it was the symbol.

The Commission must respond to the following three, somewhat contradictory, demands: good administration; action and reform; and democratic accountability.[70] To deal with this third requirement, which is the newest one, the Commission launched a comprehensive internal reform process, soon to become permanent, promoting the proliferation of forms (access to documents, OLAF, ombudsman, petitions, etc.) and norms (transparency, accountability, subsidiarity, etc.) of participation and control and enhanced the 'parliamentarization' of the EU regime.[71]

Since the early 1990s, successive treaties have continuously strengthened the governmental character of the Commission by increasing the president's role in its composition and current functioning, by reinforcing the EP's powers in its investiture and control and by matching the mandates of both institutions. The Lisbon Treaty confirmed this trend by requiring the European Council to choose the President of the Commission based on European elections results and by describing his or her investiture through the EP as an 'election'. Moreover, the Commission's method of administrative organization increasingly approximates that of a national government. A growing number of Commissioners have prior political experience and aspire to continue through the end of their mandate at the national or European level; Commissioners whose profile is more technocratic often use their experience in the Commission as a transition into politics.[72] All Commissioners of the Barroso II team are affiliated to a political party, 66,6 per cent of them were, at some point in their career, ministers of a national government and more than 40 per cent were party officials.[73] This trend affects the way in which Commissioners perceive their mandate and forces them to focus on reform and communication rather than on administrative work. This has perverse effects. A growing number of defections are evident during or at the end of a term by Commissioners wishing to engage in or return to national politics. The process was particularly marked for the last months of the Barroso II Commission (2009–2014).

The Commission is nevertheless a 'technocratic' body in many ways, deliberately focused on an expert and neutral assessment of possible measures, at the margins of all national and partisan considerations. For instance, the 'concours' to become a European public servant has been deeply reformed recently, so as to favour a logic of bureaucratic effectiveness and to put the emphasis on the competences of the candidates.[74] Also, the Commission's powers are not identical with those of a government. They exceed them in some respects (monopoly over legislative initiative, power to sanction economic operators, guardian of the treaties) but are less than those of a government in other ways (executive powers exercised in part by the Council or under the rules of comitology, absence of power to dissolve the Parliament, inexistence of instruments such as the question of confidence, the blocked vote or the urgency).

Above all, the inter-institutional rationale is not exclusively marked by the partisan factor which, at the national level, structures the relationship between the Parliament, the government and, where appropriate, the Head of State. Thus, despite the growing importance of the Parliament in the Commission's appointment process, despite the *Spitzenkandidaten* process set up in 2014, MEPs are not supposed to choose the President of the Commission (it is not certain that they will be able to impose their choice again in 2019) and have no direct influence on the choice of the other Commissioners. With the exception of its president, the college is also not really designated based on the outcome of European elections: Commissioners almost always carry the political colours of their respective governments, which implies a lack of partisan unity. They also rarely come from the EP, in contrast to what prevails in parliamentary regimes. In general, the Commission does not benefit from stable political support from the Parliament and does not implement a programme of government. Nevertheless, things started to change with the appointment of Jean-Claude Juncker in 2014 and the re-election of Martin Schulz as President of the EP. During the first year of his term, J. C. Juncker received support in principle from the EP in decisive votes, thanks to the agreement between the three groups of the 'bloc': the EPP, the ALDE and the S&D. However, this new approach of the institutional balance is criticized within the EP, in particular by the ALDE and S&D groups, and could easily be called into question, especially with A. Tajani (EPP) being elected as EP President when the S&D Group hoped to keep the presidency. The letter of the treaties does not presuppose the existence of a strong partisan link between the Commission and the EP. 'The election' of the president remains in the hands of the European Council. The approval of the College of Commissioners by the EP is not to reach a political agreement, but to recognize the competence of the Commissioners to exercise their mandate. As for the censorship procedure which allows the EP to bring down the Commission, it is more an instrument of crisis management and of symbolic protest – like that of impeachment in the US – than a tool of political control over the executive by the MEPs. Therefore, it has never been voted. Conversely, we should recall that the Commission (or the Council or the European Council) cannot dissolve the Parliament or use instruments of rationalized parliamentarism.[75] Relations between the Parliament and the Commission therefore have more similarities to those of the US Congress and the executive branch than those of a parliament and a government in a parliamentary regime. Time will tell whether the experience of the *Spitzenkandidaten* is likely to become institutionalized, and/or to strengthen the partisan link between the Commission and the EP.

3.2.5 The crisis of the Commission's growth

Besides the question of its legitimacy, the Commission must also deal with internal stresses stemming from its steady rise in power. As it has been presented and theorized by early analysts of European integration, the Commission is the archetype of a functional institution[76]: its organization emerges directly from its powers and duties; conversely, the latter adjust themselves to its organizational capacities. However, the Commission has had to deal with an increased number of Commissioners resulting from successive enlargements and additional DGs due to the continuous expansion of EU responsibilities.

This process has not been accompanied by a proportional increase in its resources, particularly in terms of personnel. It is both too large and too small. Too large given the initial objective of an efficient and creative agency with limited functions, too large and too powerful for the proponents of an intergovernmental approach to the EU, who see it simply as a Secretariat General. However, it is too small referring to the magnitude of its functions and the ambition of an institution capable of asserting its independence from Member States. It is also too small as compared to national administrations with far greater financial and human resources. This relative weakness prompts its reorientation towards regulatory policies and its mission to defend the four freedoms of the internal market. This tropism is problematic for the development of other policies, of so-called positive integration, essential to the legitimacy and visibility of the Commission. Its lack of resources does not allow it to fully take into account the new objectives that have been gradually assigned to European integration parallel to the creation of the internal market (sustainable development, economic and social progress, democracy, territorial cohesion, etc.) and are recalled in the preamble to the Treaty on European Union.

The Commission further faces important divisions, as a result of the increased number of Commissioners and DGs, contradictions between the objectives of good governance and reform, and rivalries between the proponents of negative integration (through deregulation and opening of the markets) and those of positive integration (through the pursuit of economic, social and territorial cohesion as well as financial solidarity or consumer protection). As a function of their jurisdiction, Commissioners and DG agents have contrasting world-views and divergent objectives. The actors in charge of the environment, agriculture, industry, the internal market or the common commercial policy have, for example, diverging ideas about what constitutes sustainable development and the place it should be given within EU policy.[77] These differences are, as in any bureaucracy, the product of competition among institutional sectors for policy control. Thus, we can describe the Commission as a 'multi-organization'[78] in which different sectors develop their own logic and are stakeholders in independent policy networks. The relations that these sectors maintain with those of other institutions, with the authorities and administrations of Member States and sub-state entities, as well as with interest groups and civil-society organizations contribute to accentuate the divisions. Each DG thus has a special relationship with some working groups in the Council, a Council configuration, a parliamentary committee, an administration in the Member States and a 'sector' of vested interests (lobbyists, economic sector, civil society organizations, independent experts, etc.). One witnesses the development of parallel 'epistemic communities', that is to say, groups of political and administrative leaders, policy recipients, advisors, experts, lobbyists etc., sharing knowledge, values or world views.[79] Within the EU, tensions are often stronger between these different communities than between the institutions that support them. The Union is therefore not only driven by institutional and partisan rationales, but also by these sectoral divisions.

Certain elements, however, moderate the centrifugal effects of this process of segmentation. This includes the mobility of agents within the Commission which are required to regularly change DGs. A second factor is the increased power of its Secretary General, who plays the role of an internal and external coordinator of its activities, particularly through inter-service coordination mechanisms. Finally, the president's strengthened powers and the new project teams improve the dialogue between the Commissioners and the various DGs, increase the cross-sectoral dissemination of new standards and goals such as sustainable development, social cohesion and gender, and impose them on all its constituents as required points of reflection. This coordination takes time and makes the institution unresponsive. However, it is necessary because it maintains the Commission's culture of compromise and the facade of unity, which are key resources in inter-institutional negotiations.

The Lisbon Treaty has affected the role of both the European Council and the Commission but also their relations to each other. There is nothing new in stating that the policy-pioneering days of the Commission are largely over. With the strengthening of the European Council's position, it is more difficult for the Commission to exercise political leadership. In addition to that, the

Commission must now deal with a particular political climate which further hinders a strong supranational approach to European integration based on the Community method in which the Commission has a key role. Indeed, the EU suffered a continuous stream of crises, with the Eurozone crisis starting in 2008, an energy supply crisis in 2009, a 'Schengen crisis' questioning the European *acquis* since 2011, the rise of populism and Euroscepticism in many Member States and, finally, the decision in 2016 of UK citizens to leave the EU. The Commission tried to reassert its leadership during this period but clearly an intergovernmental crisis management has been preferred and the Commission is often demoted to a more managerial role under the authority of the European Council. This is largely due to the transformation of the European agenda and the great political sensitivity of the issues currently being addressed: monetary, economic, foreign affairs, migration, internal and external security, and so on. The impetus and agenda-setting roles are gradually being entrusted to the European Council and its President. Given the controversial nature of the cases, the Commission has increasingly sought the Council's consent and aligned itself with its instructions.[80]

However, the relation between the two institutions is complex and cannot be seen as a purely competitive one. As noted by Höing and Wessels, it 'should not be regarded as a zero-sum game but as a reflection of a growing interconnectedness of national and European interests and decision-making structures'.[81] For instance, the measures to fight the eurozone crisis have reinforced the Commission's role as it is the institution best equipped to supervise the national budgets and financial policy of the Member States. With the crisis of the eurozone, supranational institutions such as the Commission have also seen their prerogatives increase. Although formally confined to a more subordinate role, the Commission has seen its powers and authority strengthened not only by the nature of the crisis but also by the mutual distrust of the Member States. The delegation to the Commission therefore has come across as the best way to depoliticize some of the stakes.[82] In addition, J. C. Juncker's 'election' gave him greater legitimacy to take initiatives and to make his point of view heard. It has also provided him with support within the EP that has allowed him to do so. The current wait-and-see attitude, prompted by an unprecedented crisis of confidence in the EU, does not allow it to take advantage of this new situation, but things could change with the reconfigurations called for by Brexit.

The Commission indeed remains the central institution in the European daily decision-making. It has many assets: its competences, permanence (as compared to the Council whose composition is volatile and whose members have many other activities), its presence at all stages of decision-making, its neutrality (seen as less partisan than the Council, the European Council and the Parliament), its expertise, its links with policy recipients, and its visibility.

Notes

1 Martin Westlake and David Galloway, eds, *The Council of the European Union* (London: John Harper Publishing, 3rd ed., 2004), 171–173.

2 Although several governments (and particularly the Danish one) objected to the term 'European Council', which was therefore not officially used. See Westlake and Galloway, *The Council of the European Union*, 175. See also Jean-Paul Jacqué, *Droit institutionnel de l'Union européenne* (Paris: Dalloz, coll. 'Cours Dalloz, Série Droit public-science politique,' 3rd ed., 2004), 327–335; John Peterson and Michael Shackleton, eds, *The Institutions of the European Union* (Oxford/New York: Oxford University Press, coll. 'The New European Union Series,' 2nd ed., 2006).

3 On these tensions between supranationalism and intergovernmentalism in the institutionalization of the European Council as well as for a long-term overview of the European Council, see Yann-Sven Rittelmeyer, 'L'institutionnalisation de la présidence du Conseil européen: entre dépendance institutionnelle et inflexions franco-allemandes,' *Politique Européenne* 3 (2011): 55–82.

4 Article 15 TEU.

5 John Peterson, 'Decision-making in the European Union: towards a framework for analysis,' *Journal of European Public Policy* 2(1) (1995): 69–93.

6 Simon Bulmer and Wolfgang Wessels, *The European Council: Decision-making in European Politics* (London: Macmillan, 1987), 2.

7 Marianne Dony, *Après la réforme de Lisbonne, les nouveaux traités européens* (Brussels: Éd. de l'Université de Bruxelles, coll. 'Études européennes,' (2008), 19.

8 Article 26 TEU.

9 Philippe De Schoutheete, *The European Council and the community method* (Notre Europe Policy Paper, no. 56, 2012); Sergio Fabbrini, *Which European Union? Europe After the Euro-Crisis* (Cambridge: Cambridge University Press, 2015).

10 Article 15 TEU.

11 Since the start of the European Council, Valery Giscard d'Estaing insisted on having as few officials as possible during the meetings. The London declaration of 1977 stipulates the types of discussion (confidential and informal; discussions leading to specific actions and court of last resort). See Westlake and Galloway, *The Council of the European Union*, 177.

12 Yves Doutriaux and Christian Lequesne, *Les institutions de l'Union européenne* (Paris: La Documentation française, coll. 'Réflexe Europe,' 2007), 31; Helen Wallace, 'An institutional anatomy and five policy-modes,' in *Policy-Making in the European Union*, eds Helen Wallace, Mark A. Pollack and Alasdair R. Young (Oxford: Oxford University Press, 6th ed., 2010), 69–104.

13 See in particular: Peterson, 'Decision-making in the European Union: towards a framework for analysis'; Helen Wallace, William Wallace, and Mark A. Pollack, eds, *Policy-Making in the European Union* (Oxford/New York: Oxford University Press, coll. 'The New European Union Series,' 5th ed., 2005).

14 Olivier Höing and Wolfgang Wessels, 'The European Commission's position in the Post-Lisbon institutional balance. Secretariat or partner to the European Council?,' in *The European Commission in the Post-Lisbon Era of Crises. Between Political Leadership and*

Policy Management, eds Michele Chang and Jörg Monar (Brussels: PIE Peter Lang, 2013), 127–128.

15 François Forêt, 'Introduction. Questions autour des incarnations multiples de l'Union européenne,' in *Les Présidences de l'Union Européenne en Redéfinition: Quelle Légitimité? Quelle Efficacité?*, eds Yann-Sven Rittelmeyer and François Forêt (Les Cahiers du Cevipol, vol. 4, 2008), 3–5.

16 Ben Crum, 'Accountability and personalization of the European Council presidency,' *Journal of European Integration* 31(6) (2009), 685–701.

17 Dinan, D., 'Leadership in the European Council: an assessment of Herman Van Rompuy's presidency,' *Journal of European Integration*, 39(2), (2017): 157–173

18 Spyros Blavoukos, Dimitris Bourantonis and George Pagoulatos, 'A president for the European Union: a new actor in town?' *Journal of Common Market Studies* 45(2) (2007): 231–252; Ben Crum, 'Can a permanent president contribute to the democratic accountability of the European Council?,' in *Les présidences de l'Union Européenne en Redéfinition: Quelle Légitimité? Quelle Efficacité?*, ed. Yann-Sven Rittelmeyer and François Forêt (Les Cahiers du Cevipol, vol. 4, 2008), 5–8; Jonas Tallberg, *Leadership and Negotiation in the European Union* (Cambridge: Cambridge University Press, 2006); Robert Thomson, 'The council presidency in the European Union: responsibility with power,' *Journal of Common Market Studies* 46(3) (2008): 593–617.

19 Concerning the function of a permanent president, see Ingeborg Tömmel, "The permanent president of the European Council: intergovernmental or supranational leadership?' '*Journal of European Integration*, 39(2) 2017: 175–189.

20 Article 15 TEU.

21 Dinan, D., op.cit.

22 Bulmer and Wessels, *The European Council: Decision-Making in European Politics*, 54.

23 Jonas Tallberg, 'Bargaining power in the European Council,' *Journal of Common Market Studies* 46(3) (2008): 685–708.

24 Doutriaux and Lequesne, *Les Institutions de l'Union Européenne*, 33.

25 In March 2017, Donald Tusk was re-appointed despite the opposition of the Polish authorities. Since they could not hinder the nomination, they vetoed the 'conclusions' of the European Council. However, the difficulty was bypassed by a presentation trick. They were called 'Conclusions of the President of the European Council," with the following warning: 'The European Council deliberated on the attached document. It was supported by 27 members of the European Council, but did they not reach a general agreement for reasons unrelated to its content. The references in the attached document to the European Council cannot be considered as a formal approval by the European Council acting as an institution.' Press Release 125/17 of 10 March 2017.

26 Höing and Wessels, 'The European Commission's position in the Post-Lisbon institutional balance,' 123–144; Uwe Puetter, *The European Council and the Council. New Intergovernmentalism and Institutional Change* (Oxford: Oxford University Press, 2014).

27 Simone Bunse, Yann-Sven Rittelmeyer, and Steven Van Hecke, 'The rotating presidency under the Lisbon treaty: from political leader to middle manager?,' in *Readjusting the Council Presidency. Belgian Leadership in the EU*, ed. Peter Bursens and Steven Van Hecke (Brussels: Academic and Scientific Publishers, 2011), 43–63.

28 David L. Coombes, *Politics and Bureaucracy in the European Community: A Portrait of the Commission of the EEC* (London: Allen & Unwin, 1970); Dionyssis G. Dimitrakopoulos, *The Changing European Commission* (Manchester/New York: Manchester University Press, coll. 'Europe in change,' 2004); David Spence and Geoffrey Edwards, eds, *The European Commission* (London: J. Harper Publishing, 3rd ed., 2006).

29 Jörg Monar, 'The post Lisbon European Commission. Between political leadership and policy management,' in *The European Commission in the Post-Lisbon Era of Crises. Between Political Leadership and Policy Management*, eds Michele Chang and Jörg Monar (Brussels: PIE Peter Lang, 2013), 279–295.

30 Neill Nugent, *The European Commission* (Houndmills: Palgrave, coll. 'The European Union Series,' 2001); David Spence, 'The President, the college and the cabinets,' in *The European Commission*, eds David Spence and Geoffrey Edwards (London: J. Harper Publishing, 3rd ed., 2006), 25–74.

31 Article 17 TEU.

32 This provision was challenged by the European Council in 2009 at the request of the Irish government after the failure of the ratification of the Lisbon Treaty by the Irish citizens. The Irish leaders wanted to obtain the support of the Irish Commissioner in the perspective of a new referendum. They also wanted to be able to claim that they had obtained an advantage for the influence of Ireland within the EU in order to convince the citizens to approve the ratification of the treaty. The principle of one Commissioner per Member State has therefore to be maintained.

33 A specific procedure applies to the High Representative, who is dependant both on the Commission and the Council. According to Article 18 TEU, the European Council, acting by a qualified majority and with the agreement of the President of the Commission, may terminate the High Representatives' mandate.

34 Arndt Wonka, 'Technocratic and independent? The appointment of the European Commissioners and its policy implications,' *Journal of European Public Policy* 14(2) (2007): 169–189.

35 Sara Hobolt, 'A vote for the President? The role of Spitzenkandidaten in the 2014 European Parliament elections,' *Journal of European Public Policy*, 21(10) (2014): 1528–1540.

36 The European Parliament, 'Elections 2014: donner aux électeurs européens davantage leur mot à dire,' press release, 22/11/12, www.europarl.europa.eu/news/fr/news-room/content/20121121IPR56164/html/Elections-2014-donner-aux-%C3%A9lecteurs-europ%C3%A9ens-davantage-leur-mot-%C3%A0-dire.

37 The European Commission, 'Élections au Parlement européen de 2014: la Commission recommande la désignation d'un candidat à sa présidence par les partis politiques,' press release, 12 September 2013, http://europa.eu/rapid/press-release_IP-13-215_fr.htm.

38 Hobolt, Sara B. 2014. 'A vote for the President? The role of spitzenkandidaten in the 2014 European Parliament elections,' *Journal of European Public Policy* 21(10): 1528–1540.

39 Julian Priestley and Nereo Penalver Garcia, *The Making of a European President* (Basingstoke: Palgrave, 2015).

40 Sara Hobolt, op.cit.

41 Dermot Hodson, 'Eurozone governance: deflation, grexit 2.0 and the second coming of Jean-Claude Juncker,' *Journal of Common Market Studies*, early view DOI: 10.1111/jcms.12263.

42 Article 17 TEU, Art. 245 Treaty on the Functioning of the EU.

43 Doutriaux and Lequesne, *Les institutions de l'Union européenne*, 67; John Peterson, 'The Santer era: The European Commission in normative, historical and theoretical perspective,' *Journal of European Public Policy* 6(1) (1999): 46–65; Spence and Edwards, *The European Commission*.

44 Richard Corbett, John Peterson and Elizabeth Bomberg, 'The EU's institutions,' in *The European Union, How does it work?*, eds Elizabeth Bomberg, John Peterson and Richard Corbett (Oxford: Oxford University Press, 3rd ed., 2012), 53.

45 The Commission sporadically establishes inter-departmental groups or 'task forces' to regulate specific coordination problems. Doutriaux and Lequesne, *Les Institutions de l'Union européenne*, 70; Maryon McDonald, 'Identities in the European Commission,' in *At the Heart of the Union: Studies of the European Commission*, ed. Neill Nugent (Basingstoke/New York: Macmillan/St Martin's Press, 1st ed., 1997), 51–72; Nugent, *The European Commission*; Anne Stevens and Handley Stevens, *Brussels Bureaucrats?: The Administration of the European Union* (Basingstoke/New York: Palgrave, coll. 'The European Union Series,' 2001).

46 David Spence, 'The directorates general and the services: structures, functions and procedures,' in *The European Commission*, eds David Spence and Geoffrey Edwards (London: J. Harper Publishing, 3rd ed., 2006), 128–155.

47 On the consequences of these reforms: Michael W. Bauer, 'Diffuse anxieties, deprived entrepreneurs. Commission reform and middle management,' *Journal of European Public Policy* 15(5) (2008): 691–707; Antonis Ellinas and Ezra Suleiman, 'Reforming the Commission: between modernization and bureaucratization,' *Journal of European Public Policy* 15(5) (2008): 708–725.

48 Jean-Paul Jacqué, 2004, op. cit.; D. Spence and G. Edwards (eds), 2006, op. cit.; P. Bocquillon and M. Dobbels 'An elephant on the 13th floor of the Berlaymont? European Council and Commission relations in legislative agenda setting,' *Journal of European Public Policy* 21(1) (2014): 20–38.

49 Wolfgang Wessels, *The European Council* (Palgrave Macmillan, 2016).

50 Höing and Wessels, 'The European Commission's position in the Post-Lisbon institutional balance,' 134.

51 For further information on this topic see Chapter 7.

52 For a complete description of the comitology and of its committees, see *infra* the section dedicated to the 'groups' of the Council.

53 Jean-Paul Jacqué, *Droit institutionnel de l'Union européenne*.

54 Spence and Edwards, *The European Commission*.

55 Arndt Wonka, 'Decision-making dynamics in the European Commission: partisan, national or sectoral?' *Journal of European Public Policy*, 15(8) (2008): 1145–1163.

56 Höing and Wessels, 'The European Commission's position in the Post-Lisbon institutional balance,' 138.

57 Spence, 'The directorates general and the services: structures, functions and procedures,' 151.

58 Mark Borchardt, *Une Commission européenne politique grâce à une nouvelle organisation. Cette fois, c'est différent, vraiment?* (Notre Europe policy paper, no. 180, 2016).

59 European Commission, Taking Action – Declaration to the European Parliament, meeting in plenary session, before the vote on the College, SPEECH/14/1525, Strasbourg, 22 October 2014. The College shall consist of the President, Vice-Presidents and

Commissioners of the Commission. There are currently 28 members, so one from each Member State.

60 Since the departure of Vice-President Kristalina Gueorguieva at the end of 2016, the project team 'budget and human resources' is chaired by Commissioner Günther Oettinger, who is not a Vice-President.

61 The growing importance of this practice, which has both formal and informal aspects, can be measured by the number of formalized inter-service groups that are overseen by the General Secretariat: from 48 in 1990 to 226 in 2006.

62 Thomas Christiansen, 'The European Commission: The European executive between continuity and change,' in *European Union: Power and Policy-Making*, ed. Jeremy J. Richardson (New York: Routledge, coll. 'Routledge research in European public policy,' 3rd ed., 2006), 99–119.

63 Janne Haaland-Matlary, 'The role of the commission: A theoretical discussion,' in *At the Heart of the Union: Studies of the European Commission*, ed. Neill Nugent (Basingstoke/New York: Macmillan/St Martin's Press, 1st ed., 1997); Brigid Laffan, 'From policy-entrepreneur to policy-manager: the challenge facing the European Commission,' *Journal of European Public Policy* 4(3) (1997): 422–438.

64 Neill Nugent, 'The leadership capacity of the European Commission,' *Journal of European Public Policy* 2(4) (1995): 603–623; Peterson, 'The Santer era: The European Commission in normative, historical and theoretical perspective'; George Ross, *Jacques Delors and European Integration* (New York: Oxford University Press, coll. 'Europe and the international order,' 1995); Myrto Tsakatika, 'Claims to legitimacy: The European Commission between continuity and change,' *Journal of Common Market Studies* 43(1) (2005): 193–220.

65 Piotr Maciej Kaczyński, *The European Commission 2004-09: a politically weakened institution? Views from the national capitals* (Brussels: EPIN working paper 23, 2009).

66 M. Michele Chang, 'Constructing the Commission's six pack proposals. Political leadership thwarted?' in *The European Commission in the Post-Lisbon Era of Crises. Between Political Leadership and Policy Management*, eds Michele Chang and Jörg Monar (Brussels: PIE Peter Lang, 2013), 147–170; Constance Poiré, 'The creation of a new portfolio on climate action. A strategic political and administrative reform within the European Commission?,' in *The European Commission in the Post-Lisbon Era of Crises. Between Political Leadership and Policy Management*, eds Michele Chang and Jörg Monar (Brussels: PIE Peter Lang, 2013), 67–86.

67 Hussein Kassim, 'What's new? A first appraisal of the Juncker Commission,' *European Political Science* (2016).

68 David Herszenhorn, '"Monster" at the Berlaymont: Martin Selmayr is admired, despised and feared. What's clear: He's the most powerful EU chief of staff ever,' Politico, 17 November 2016. www.politico.eu/article/monster-at-the-berlaymont-martin-selmayr-european-commission-jean-claude-juncker/.

69 See Chapter 2. The term 'governance' refers to a system in which the government is not based on authority, coercion and hierarchy but on negotiation, persuasion and mutual learning. In such a system, the Commission plays a central role as opposed to a more political system of government based on an intergovernmental (Council) and partisan (European Parliament) legitimacy. Burkard Eberlein and Dieter Kerwer, 'Theorising the new modes of European Union governance,' *European Integration*

online Papers 6(5) (2002); Adrienne Héritier, *New modes of governance in Europe: Policy making without legislating?* (Max Planck Institute Collective Goods Preprint, 14, 2001); Adrienne Héritier, 'The White Paper on European Governance: a response to shifting weights in interinstitutional decision-making,' in *Symposium: Responses to the European Commission's White Paper on Governance*, eds Christian Joerges, Yves Meny and Joseph H. H. Weiler (European University Institute, Robert Schuman Centre for Advanced Studies, 2001); Liesbet Hooghe and Gary Marks, *Multi-Level Governance and European Integration* (Lanham: Rowman & Littlefield, coll. 'Governance in Europe,' 2001); Markus Jachtenfuchs, 'The governance approach to European integration,' *Journal of Common Market Studies* 39(2) (2001): 245–264.

70 Giandomenico Majone, 'The European Commission: the limits of centralization and the perils of parliamentarization,' *Governance* 15(3) (2002): 375–392; Tsakatika, 'Claims to legitimacy: the European Commission between continuity and change'.

71 Nicholas Bearfield, 'Reforming the European Commission: driving reform from the grassroots,' *Public Policy and Administration* 19(3) (2004): 13–24; Thomas Christiansen, 'Tensions of European governance: politicized bureaucracy and multiple accountability in the European Commission,' *Journal of European Public Policy* 4(1) (1997): 73–90; Dimitrakopoulos, *The Changing European Commission*; Peterson, 'The Santer era: The European Commission in normative, historical and theoretical perspective'; Martin Westlake, '"Mad cows and Englishmen" – the institutional consequences of the BSE crisis,' *Journal of Common Market Studies* 35 (1997): 11–36.

72 Jean Joana and Andy Smith, *Les Commissaires Européens: Technocrates, Diplomates ou Politiques?* (Paris: Presses de Sciences Po, coll. 'Académique,' 2002).

73 Eviola Prifti, 'The Post-Lisbon treaty Commissioners (2010–2014): experts or politicians?' in *The European Commission in the Post-Lisbon Era of Crises. Between Political Leadership and Policy Management*, ed. Michele Chang and Jörg Monar (Brussels: PIE Peter Lang, 2013), 36–39.

74 Didier Georgakakis, 'Technocracy is dead. Long live bureaucracy! on some recent changes to the civil service and the european commission,' in *The European Commission in the Post-Lisbon Era of Crises. Between Political Leadership and Policy Management*, ed. Michele Chang and Jörg Monar (Brussels: PIE Peter Lang, 2013), 53–64.

75 Haaland-Matlary, 'The role of the commission: a theoretical discussion'; Spence and Edwards, *The European Commission*.

76 Ernst B. Haas, *The Uniting of Europe: Political, Social and Economic Forces, 1950–1957* (London: Stevens & Sons, 1958); Leon N. Lindberg, *The Political Dynamics of European Economic Integration* (Stanford: Stanford University Press, 1963).

77 Michelle Cini, 'Administrative culture in the European Commission: the case of competition and environment,' (European Community Studies Association, 4th Biennial International Conference, Charleston (USA), May 11–14 1995); Liesbet Hooghe, "Serving 'Europe' – political orientations of senior commission officials,' *European Integration online Papers* 1(8) (1997); Liesbet Hooghe, *The European Commission and the Integration of Europe: Images of Governance* (Cambridge: Cambridge University Press, coll. 'Themes in European governance,' 2001); McDonald, 'Identities in the European Commission'; Ulrika Mörth, 'Competing frames in the European Commission – the case of the defence industry and equipment issue,' *Journal of European Public Policy* 7(2) (2000): 173–189.

78 Laura Cram, 'The European Commission as a multi-organisation: social policy and IT policy in the EU,' *Journal of European Public Policy* 1(1) (1994): 195–218.

79 Hugh T. Miller and Charles J. Fox, 'The epistemic community,' *Administration & Society* 32(6) (2001): 668–685.

80 Bickerton, C. et al. (dirs.), *The New Intergovernmentalism*, (Oxford: Oxford University Press, 2015); Renaud Dehousse, 'Why has EU macroeconomic governance become more supranational?' *Journal of European Integration* 38(5) 2016: 617–631.

81 Höing and Wessels, 'The European Commission's position in the Post-Lisbon institutional balance,' 125.

82 Michael W. Bauer and Stefan Becker, 'The unexpected winner of the crisis: the European Commission strengthened role in economic governance,' *Journal of European Integration* 36(3) 2014: 213–229; Dehousse, R., op cit.

The legislative power 4

As mentioned in the beginning of the previous chapter, the evolutions enclosed in the Lisbon Treaty, and confirmed by the 2014 European elections, allow us to describe the EU regime as a quadripartite system, in which the executive power is composed of the European Council and the Commission, and where the legislative power consists of the European Parliament and the Council. Together, these two latter institutions form a kind of bicameral parliament, in which the European Parliament would be the low chamber, representing the citizens through direct elections, and the Council the high chamber, representing the Member States through their ministers. Even if the original treaties did not present things in that way and if the Lisbon Treaty does not explicitly mention such an institutional organization, the numerous evolutions experienced by the EU regime since its creation have led to this model. The executive competences of the Council for example are less important than they used to be, and are today focused on very precise topics. From now on, the treaty makes a clear distinction between its legislative activities, for which the Council meetings are public, and the others, that are still organized behind closed doors. Finally, the generalization of qualified majority as method of decision-making in the Council has restrained the diplomatic logic in its functioning.

4.1 The Council of the Union: between Community and intergovernmental logic

The Council, also called the Council of Ministers or the Council of the European Union, was not included in the first institutional framework of the ECSC. Its creation was demanded later by the states most concerned with preserving their sovereignty against the centralism of the High Authority. The Council validated the most important decisions on the proposition of the Commission and, since

1974, the European Council for intergovernmental matters. Initially, the involvement of the Council was a matter of simple guarantee of principle, but after the crisis of the 'empty chair' (1965–1966), it has become a fastidious legislator and has also developed significant executive powers.

Like the Commission, the Council defies analysis as a result of the paradoxes and vagueness that affect its nature. It is both an executive body, exercising governing functions, and a legislative body, playing a key role in the adoption of EU legislation and budget, whereby it appears more like the high chamber of a European bicameral parliament. The Council, as the case may be, can be intergovernmental (when unanimity is required, when the positions are conflicting or when it debates issues on the sidelines of the legislative procedure) or integrated (when it votes by a simple or qualified majority and exercises more routine executive functions). The Council is a body charged with voicing consensus positions but is also an arena where ministers can freely present their positions guided by national preferences.[1] As a result, the Council is both an engine of European integration and a bulwark against the excesses of this process. It is also distinguished by its dual organizational nature: it is both a permanent institution, recognized by the treaties, equipped with large offices and many staff members, and an ad-hoc (though regular) meeting point between ministers, representatives and officials whose activities take place primarily at the national level. It is also legally unique and multi-functional since it meets in different configurations depending on the issues to be addressed, but they take their decisions on behalf of the Council. Finally, one notes that while the Council has the final say on most policies and is an important factor of their legitimization, its operations are much more obscure than those of the Commission and the EP, with secrecy included at given moments.[2]

4.1.1 Organization of the Council

According to the treaties, the Council is formed by Member State representatives at the ministerial level who are authorized to act for their governments. Federal states such as Belgium or Germany can therefore be represented by a regional minister, provided he or she can speak on behalf of his or her state (Art. 16 TEU). Ministers are sometimes represented by senior officials (chiefly their Permanent Representative to the EU) if meetings are prolonged or when they are not very interested in the day's topic. The Council normally meets in Brussels but takes places in Luxembourg in April, June and October. We can deconstruct the organization into six main components: the Presidency, the High Representative of the Union for Foreign Affairs and Security Policy, the configurations, the General Secretariat, the COREPER and special committees and, finally, the groups and committees.

The Council presidency

In contrast to the European Council, the Council does not have a permanent president. Its presidency has always rotated between each Member State government and lasts for a period of six months. The list of presidents is adopted by the European Council to maintain a smooth succession of states including 'small' and 'big', old and new, North and South, and to allow a state to exercise the presidency alternating between the first and second semesters (see Box 4.1). Since 2007, the presidency is based on the cooperation of the governments of three Member States (troika or trio), which establish an 18-months joint programme. One state formally guarantees the presidency for a semester but all three are involved in setting the agenda and the management of the dossiers for the entire duration. This practice is intended to prevent cracks and inconsistencies which have arisen in past presidential successions where the agendas and styles were mixed and sometimes uncoordinated. The troika system has been formalized in the Lisbon Treaty, which states that the

> Presidency of the Council, with the exception of the Foreign affairs configuration, shall be held by pre-established groups of three Member States for a period of 18 months. These groups shall be made up on a basis of equal rotation among the Member States, taking into account their diversity and geographical balance within the Union.
>
> (Declaration 9 attached to the treaty)

When a state presides over the Council, it performs a dual function and is represented by two delegations. The first one is led by a Minister of Foreign Affairs, or the appropriate minister, who chairs the meetings. The second delegation is led by a minister of any rank or the Secretary of State and represents the Member State itself.

Alongside the European Council, the Council presidency is the second centre of impetus for the EU. The country holding the presidency must mobilize energy and obtain advances from its partners as well as having to propose constructive solutions to overcome obstacles. The presidency convenes the meetings, sets the agenda and runs the various Council configurations (except for the 'Foreign Affairs' configuration chaired by the High Representative). It also organizes and attends meetings of committees and working groups. An active president, taking initiatives and being present, is the indispensable core of making the Council a dynamic institution. The risk of apathy is significant when national leaders, serving as a president, are mobilized by other priorities at their country's level (especially elections), focus excessively on issues that are important only to them or do not have the necessary expertise to deal with the multifaceted tasks attending them (new Member States, states with weak diplomatic services).[3]

Box 4.1 Rotation of Council presidencies, 2015–2030

January – June 2015: Latvia
July – December 2015: Luxembourg
January – June 2016: Netherlands
July – December 2016: Slovakia
January – June 2017: Malta
July – December 2017: Estonia
January – June 2018: Bulgaria
July – December 2018: Austria
January – June 2019: Romania
July – December 2019: Finland
January – June 2020: Croatia
July – December 2020: Germany
January – June 2021: Portugal
July – December 2021: Slovenia
January – June 2022: France
July – December 2022: Czech Republic
January – June 2023: Sweden
July – December 2023: Spain
January – June 2024: Belgium
July – December 2024: Hungary
January – June 2025: Poland
July – December 2025: Denmark
January – June 2026: Cyprus
July – December 2026: Ireland
January – June 2027: Lithuania
July – December 2027: Greece
January – June 2028: Italy
July – December 2028: Latvia
January – June 2029: Luxembourg
July – December 2029: Netherlands
January – June 2030: Slovakia
July – December 2030: Malta

Source: Council Decision 2016/1316 of 26 July 2016 amending Decision 2009/908/
EU laying down implementing measures for the European Council's decision concerning the exercise of the presidency of the Council and the presidency of the preparatory bodies of the Council, Official Journal of the European Union, L. 208/42.
This new list was adopted to take into account Brexit and Croatia's membership.

Moreover, the fact that the presidency regularly rotates can hinder the EU's continuity of action. Not only do priorities shift from presidency to presidency but some presidencies may choose to delay decisions or stall the integration process because of national sensitivities. There are some benefits to the rotating presidency, such as the dispersion of influence, equal opportunity to highlight topics of national importance, and the learning effect of European issues. But overall, it involves a less efficient, potentially longer and less coherent legislative process, which can have adverse consequences, such as the management of the eurozone crisis. The multi-annual programmes adopted for the trio of presidencies can limit the excesses but only give broad guidelines, and might be out of-date by the time a new presidency term starts, leading to a loss in continuity and efficiency.[4]

The High Representative of the Union for Foreign Affairs and Security Policy

The High Representative for Foreign Affairs and Security Policy, established by the Treaty of Lisbon, is appointed by the European Council by qualified majority with the agreement of the President of the Commission. He or she is a member of the Council, of the European Council and the Commission – as Vice President and Commissioner for External Relations – and participates in the European Council's meetings. He or she leads the Common Foreign and Security Policy of the EU and chairs the Foreign Affairs Council. In addition, he or she represents the EU on the international stage for the Common Foreign and Security Policy (CFSP) and is supported by a European External Action Service composed of officials from the Council, the Commission and national diplomatic services. This new position merges functions that were previously provided by the High Representative for the CFSP and the Commissioner for External Relations and European Neighbourhood Policy.[5] It was first occupied (1 December 2009 to 1 November 2014) by Catherine Ashton from the UK,[6] and is currently by Federica Mogherini from Italy (2014–2019).

Council configurations

If the treaties only evoke one institution, the Council, its composition differs depending on the subject. Foreign Affairs ministers are responsible for general questions such as those related to agriculture and the CAP, etc. In the 1970s, Council configurations multiplied and began to operate in an isolated and specialized manner and to converge according to an unpredictable rhythm and with contrasting abilities for action and consensus. The number of configurations – in excess of 20 at one time – was limited at several occasions. In 1999, the European Council of Helsinki adopted a list of 16 configurations and provided that only the General Affairs Council could decide on the creation of any new one. In 2004, the

Council limited the number of specialized configurations to nine: General Affairs and External Relations; Economic and Financial Affairs; Justice and Home Affairs; Employment, Social Policy, Health and Consumer Affairs; Competitiveness (Internal Market, Industry, Research and Space); Transport, Telecommunications and Energy; Agriculture and Fisheries; Environment; Education, Youth, Culture and Sport. The General Affairs and External Relations Council has split as a result of the creation of the High Representative for Foreign and Security Policy position; there are thus 10 configurations today (see Box 4.2). The Lisbon Treaty specifies that the European Council shall adopt the list of Council configurations by a qualified majority with the exception of the General Affairs and External Relations configurations which are subject to specific provisions.[7]

Box 4.2 The Council's principal configurations

- AG (General Affairs): This configuration meets monthly and has jurisdiction over the preparation of the European Council's work (except that pertaining to Economy and Finance or to Foreign Policy and Security) and ensures consistency in the other configurations.
- RELEX (Foreign affairs): Foreign Affairs ministers meet monthly in this configuration which is chaired by the High Representative for Foreign and Security Policy. Its operation is more intergovernmental but, in practice, the difference is barely perceptible due to the phenomena of socialization and institutionalization.
- ECOFIN (Economic and Financial Affairs): The relevant ministers meet monthly for this configuration. It is responsible for the coordination of economic policies, financial aid and long-term budget programming. ECOFIN has become more prominent since the entry into force of the Maastricht Treaty, and even more so since the Eurozone crisis.
- AGRI (Agriculture and Fisheries): This configuration, which meets on a monthly basis, is important as a result of the still considerable weight of the CAP in the EU budget.
- Competitiveness: Generally, European Affairs ministers meet in this configuration but ministers of Research and Industry may also be included. Its activities have declined somewhat since the entry into force of the internal market on 1 January 1993, which explains the extension of its responsibilities to industry, research and space. This configuration meets five or six times per year.
- Other configurations are less active but meet at least once every six months.

Sometimes two Council configurations meet simultaneously (especially AG and AGRI): this is called a 'Jumbo' Council. The Council may also meet informally in the country holding the presidency. These meetings allow for discussion of general topics that do not require immediate decision. Similarly, a decentralized meeting with Foreign Affairs ministers (the 'Gymnich') is usually held each semester. This practice has been a source of confusion when ministers adopt 'decisions' without legal status. These informal meetings cannot result in

Box 4.3 Eurogroup

The Eurogroup is an informal body in which the finance ministers from the eurozone Member States examine issues related to their shared responsibilities concerning the euro. Its goal is to ensure the coordination of the eurozone's economic policies as well as to prepare the meetings of the eurozone summits.

It was created on 13 December 1997 and met for the first time on 4 June 1998 at the Senningen Palace in Luxembourg. In 2004, the Eurogroup decided to adopt a permanent president. J. C. Juncker was elected for a term of office from 1 January 2005 to 31 December 2006 and was then reappointed. The Treaty of Lisbon, in its Protocol No 14, defines the role of the Eurogroup and institutionalizes its permanent presidency. In early 2013, Jeroen Dijsselbloem, Minister of Finance from the Netherlands, took office and was re-elected in 2015. Mário Centeno, from Portugal, will replace him in January 2018.

The Eurogroup meets once a month, the day before 'the Economic and Financial Affairs Council' session. The Commissioner for Economic and Financial Affairs, Taxation and Customs and the President of the European Central Bank also participate in the meetings.

The Eurogroup discusses the following topics:

- The economic situation and prospects in the Eurozone
- The fiscal policies of Eurozone countries
- The macroeconomic situation in the Eurozone
- Structural reforms likely to stimulate growth
- Issues related to the maintenance of financial stability in the Eurozone
- The preparation of international meetings
- The enlargement of the eurozone
- The terms and conditions of financial assistance granted to Eurozone countries experiencing serious financial difficulties.

formal decisions, have no agenda and ministers are accompanied by only one employee. In 1999, the European Council decided to limit this practice to five meetings per presidency (this rule is rarely observed) and to prohibit the adoption of any document in this context.[8]

Secretariat General

The Secretariat General is a little-known body which plays, however, an essential role.[9] The Council is not a purely intergovernmental institution due to several factors: the effects of socialization on its members, the use of qualified majority, the existence of established exchange between its members and of routines of negotiation (such as the Franco-German couple), as well as the existence of a stable secretariat, composed of EU agents concerned with the institution's interest. The Council's institutionalization is due in large part to the existence of the Secretariat General, which counteracts the centrifugal effects of the multiple configurations and of the structurally limited involvement of ministers in the Council's work.

The Council's Secretariat was established by the rules of procedure in order to manage the administrative tasks associated with the meetings: practical organization, drafting of minutes and archiving. Today, its main task remains ensuring the Council's smooth operation. Its officers attend working groups, COREPER and ministerial meetings, prepare reports and conduct the registry work. The Secretariat is also responsible for advising the presidency and plays an even more very important role when the presidency is not well mobilized, equipped or has inadequate experience.

The Secretariat has roughly 3,000 permanent European civil servants (3,048 in 2015), recruited through competition and organized into Director-Generals according to sectoral expertise.[10] It is headed by the Secretary General, a key figure in the institution and the inter-institutional relations. He or she is appointed by the Council by qualified majority, usually for a five-year term, though this is not specified in the texts. The present Secretary-General is Mr Jeppe Tranholm-Mikkelsen from Denmark (2015–2020). It is necessary to highlight the importance of the Secretariat General's legal department. Representatives of the legal department attend all meetings and verify the legal basis of Commission proposals, whereby the choice can have a significant impact on the influence of other institutions (co-decision or a procedure less favourable to the EP or the Commission) and the method of decision within the Council (qualified majority or unanimity). It is also responsible for reviewing the legal validity of Community legislation translations; the texts are legally binding in all 24 official languages, and must thus have the same meaning in each of them. Finally, the Council's legal adviser represents the institution in the event of litigation before the Court of Justice.[11]

COREPER and special committees

COREPER is the Committee of Permanent Representatives (in French: COmité des REprésentants PERmanents). These diplomats represent the Member States in the European institutions. Each state has, in addition to its embassy in Belgium, a permanent representation near the EU, based in Brussels and headed by the Permanent Representative and his deputy. COREPER is responsible for preparing the ministers' work, must confirm agreements negotiated by the working groups and find solutions to problematic issues. For certain policies, specialized committees perform the duties of COREPER in a similar fashion. This is the case of the Special Committee on Agriculture (CSA), established by an intergovernmental decision in 1960. The same is true for the Economic and Financial Affairs Committee, the Employment Committee, the Political and Security Committee, the Social Protection Committee and the Trade Policy Committee (known as the 'Article 207 committee' or former 'Article 133 Committee'), the 'Article 36 Committee' (or CATS – *Comité Article Trente Six*' for Justice and Home Affairs), and the Standing Committee on Operational Cooperation on Internal Security (COSI), all of which were established by the treaties.[12]

COREPER works in three languages: French, English and German. It is organized into two sections: COREPER I is composed of the Deputy Permanent Representatives and COREPER II is made up of Permanent Representatives. The distinction is not hierarchical but rather a division of responsibilities: COREPER II manages the dossiers for ECOFIN, General Affairs, Development, Justice and Home Affairs as well as for Foreign Affairs configuration of the Council, the latter in collaboration with the Political and Security Committee (PSC).[13] COREPER I is responsible for the rest. The two teams work independently.

The COREPER is not the product of a 're-nationalization' of the EC/EU. Its existence has been recognized by the treaties from the beginning:

> The Council shall adopt its rules of procedure.
> These rules of procedure may provide for the establishment of a committee composed of representatives of Member States. The Council shall determine the task and competence of that committee.
> (Article 151 or the EEC Treaty, as signed in 1957)

It is a kind of filter between the Commission and the Council which oversees the quality of legal texts with respect to subsidiarity and Community law and prepares the Council's discussions and decisions.[14] COREPER, as well as the special committees and working groups of the Council (see below), form a network which makes it easier to reach a compromise: these bodies promote a 'club' spirit between diplomats and national officials as well as a sense of collective responsibility.[15]

Groups and Organs of the 'comitology'

Alongside the committees and groups set up by COREPER to deal with very specific issues, there are three types of bodies and groups within the Council.

The **groups of experts** contribute to the preparation of the Commission's legislative proposals by giving an opinion to the Council. This allows the Council to act very early in the legislative process and the Commission to anticipate Member State reactions to its proposals. These groups are composed of officials from the permanent representations and are convened and chaired by a Commission official. They play an increasing role in the co-decision procedures, a result of the frequent use of a 'trialogue' between the Commission, Council and Parliament to promote the adoption of the texts at the first reading, which has become an increasingly common practice in recent years.

Working groups are responsible for preparing the work of COREPER and the Council. They are particularly responsible for building consensus and where possible to facilitate negotiations in the COREPER and the Council. Also composed of officials from the permanent representations, these groups are chaired by a representative of the Member State holding the EU presidency and are convened upon his or her initiative.[16]

Finally, there are several **committees** which play a role in the process of 'comitology' within the Council. Initially, the EC did not take into account the principle of the distribution of powers on which parliamentary and presidential regimes are based usually. The Commission thus enjoys significant executive powers but does not exercise them in their entirety – even if things have evolved under the Lisbon Treaty, as we will discuss further in this book. The Treaty of Rome stated – in its original wording – that the Commission shall 'exercise the competence conferred on it by the Council for the implementation of the rules laid down by the latter'.[17] The Council could also keep them or regulate their delegation to the Commission. The treaties also stated that Member States controlled the exercise of these powers under conditions set by the Parliament and the Council. More often, the Commission was required to consult with 'committees' composed of officials or national experts. Chaired and convened by Commission officials, they advised the Council on proposed implementing measures. In this case, it said that the Commission exercised its power of execution in 'comitology'.

The Commission has always opposed comitology, especially in its most restrictive form. The EP is also motivated to limit the executive influence enjoyed by the Council through comitology and to preserve its own power to control the Commission. Comitology has thus been subject to recurrent conflicts since the

1970s, in particular through appeals to the Court of Justice. The EP has argued that it is impossible to know the committees' number, composition and agenda, which engenders a total opacity of the process. To remedy this situation, the institutions have negotiated a *modus vivendi* (20 December 1994), which included commitment by the Council to inform parliamentary committees on the acts submitted to comitology, a commitment by the latter to rule quickly on the acts if it was urgent, and a commitment by the Commission to account for its opinions. A Council decision on 28 June 1999, also provided that the Parliament may have required the Commission to review a draft submitted to a committee if it had been taken as a result of an instrument adopted by co-decision and if it had believed that the Commission had exceeded its powers of execution.

Until 2011, there were four types of committees: advisory committees, management committees, regulatory committees and regulatory committees with scrutiny. The latter were introduced in July 2006: in matters subject to co-decision, the two branches of the legislative power were placed on an equal footing regarding their ability to control the Commission's use of its conferred powers of enforcement.[18]

Committees were created by legislation according to the degree of attention Council members have upon implementation of the policies in question. In 2011, there were 268 committees primarily concerning the following areas: health and consumer; energy; mobility and transport; environment; enterprise and industry; agriculture; and justice and home affairs.[19]

The Lisbon Treaty has modified this system in several respects. First, it strengthens the Commission's executive role, since Article 17 TEU states that it 'shall perform coordination, enforcement and management functions in accordance with the conditions laid down in the Treaties'. The treaty then makes a distinction between the Commission's traditional implementing powers (Article 291 TFEU) and a new system of 'delegated authority' (see below). Article 291 TFEU provides that states 'shall take all measures of national law necessary for the implementation of legally binding Union acts', but that 'where uniform conditions for the execution of legally binding acts of the Union' Union acts are necessary, they confer implementing powers on the Commission or, in duly justified specific cases and in the cases provided for in Articles 24 and 26 of the Treaty on European Union, to the Council. The Treaty thus clarifies the roles of each entity, reinforces the powers of execution of the Commission, but confirms the principle of their control, specifying that the EP and the Council establish the rules and general principles relative to the control mechanisms the Member States have concerning the exercise of these implementing powers by the Commission (article 291.3 TFEU). These conditions are currently governed by a regulation of 16 February 2011.[20] It is based on the old 'comitology' decision and the lessons learned from its implementation. The text retains the committee structure set out in the previous decision, but simplifies it.

Now, only two procedures are provided[21]:

- the 'advisory procedure' corresponds to the one that already exists. When applied, the committee issues an opinion but the Commission is not obliged to respect it. It is used to address less sensitive measures.
- the 'examination procedure' is a new one that replaces the management and regulatory procedures. It applies to the most sensitive measures of general application but also to cases and to programmes that have significant impact, such as the CAP, environmental protection policies, the common fisheries policy, the protection of health or safety, animals or plants, the common commercial policy and taxation. The Commission must receive a favourable vote by qualified majority in order to adopt the implementing act. If it cannot adopt a proposed implementing act (especially in cases where the committee has voted against it), it may refer the case to the appeal committee, which allows a second debate. Moreover, the EP or the Council may exercise a right to scrutiny at any time by adopting a non-binding resolution if it believes the Commission has exceeded its implementing powers.

One of the major innovations of the Lisbon Treaty, heavily inspired by the 'regulatory procedure with scrutiny' established in 2006, is the 'delegated acts' procedure permitting the EP and the Council to delegate some of their own legislative power to the Commission (Article 290 of the TFEU).[22] The idea is to authorize the latter to amend or supplement elements of a legislative act that are considered non-essential by the legislature. This authorization is inscribed in the basic legislative act. Legal acts adopted as such by the Commission are, in the terminology used by the new treaty, 'delegated acts' (Article 290, paragraph 3).

Failing to introduce a real hierarchy of standards, this new procedure's main objective is to ensure that legislation remains simple. It allows the legislature to focus on the essential elements of the legislation and leaves the Commission to address the more detailed aspects, similar to the national level where parliament passes general laws and leaves the task of adopting regulatory decisions for their implementation to the ministers. The system of delegated acts, however, allows the European legislature to retain its jurisdiction. The EP and the Council must explicitly define the objectives, content, scope and duration of this delegation. In addition, they must establish the conditions to which the delegation is subject.

Since the coming into force of the Lisbon Treaty, the number of delegated acts has strongly increased: from 166 between 2009 and 2014 to 363 between 2014 and 2016 (Figures 4.1 and 4.2). But the number of acts falling under the regulatory comitology procedure with scrutiny remains high as all the measures have not yet been aligned with the new system introduced by the treaty (see Table 4.1).

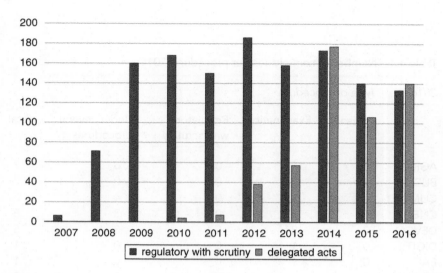

Figure 4.1 Number of measures under the regulatory procedure with scrutiny and delegated acts submitted to the EP each year

Source: European Parliament.

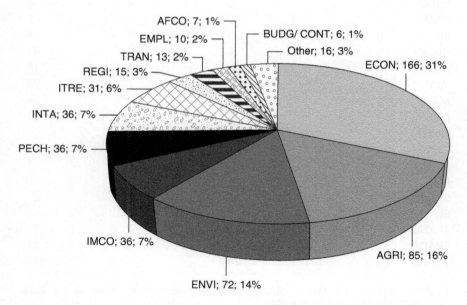

Figure 4.2 Number of delegated acts received by parliamentary committee since 2010

Source: European Parliament.

Table 4.1 Number of committees per procedure (2016)

2016	Type of procedure				
	Advisory	Examination	Regulatory with scrutiny	Under several procedures	Total
AGRI	0	11	0	6	17
BUDG	1	1	0	0	2
CLIMAT	0	1	0	4	5
CNECT	0	3	0	3	6
DEVCO	0	2	0	3	5
DIGIT	0	1	0	0	1
EAC	0	1	0	0	1
ECFIN	0	0	0	1	1
ECHO	0	1	0	1	2
EMPL	0	0	2	3	5
ENER	2	6	3	3	14
ENVI	0	6	5	19	30
ESTAT	0	2	0	4	6
FISMA	0	1	2	5	8
FPI	0	3	0	1	4
GROW	6	9	4	22	41
HOME	2	8	0	3	13
JUST	7	5	4	7	23
MARE	0	2	0	2	4
MOVE	3	8	4	16	31
NEAR	1	1	0	1	3
OLAF	0	1	0	0	1
REGIO	0	0	0	1	1
RTD	0	4	0	1	5
SANTE	0	10	0	11	21
SG	0	2	0	1	3
TAXUD	1	8	0	2	11
TRADE	2	4	0	6	12
TOTAL	25	101	24	127	277

Source: European Commission, report on the working of Committees during 2016, COM(2017) 594 final, 16 October 2017.

The major difference between the process of delegated acts and comitology is the absence of committees and therefore the lack of obligation on the part of Commission to obtain an opinion. This does not mean that it can refrain from conducting consultations, since it is still surrounded by expert committees. The obligations that weighed on the Commission under comitology have been replaced over time by increased control by the EP and the Council, which are both free to choose the mechanisms they prefer.

The first procedure expressly provided for by the treaty is the revocation of legislative delegation by EP or the Council. The treaty does not list the reasons that may lead the EP or the Council to oppose a delegated act: this right is therefore discretionary. In addition, it is provided that the EP or the Council may oppose a delegated act within a time limit set by the basic act. In both cases, the opposition of one of the two branches of the legislative power is sufficient to prevent the entry into force of the delegated act.

In concrete terms, since the coming into force of the Treaty of Lisbon, the Commission can propose and adopt measures of delegated legislation without the involvement of comitology committees. The only control is ex-post evaluation and that is unlikely to occur. This clearly limits the ability of the various actors (national administrations, EP, civil society organizations, lobbies, etc.) to monitor the implementation activities of the Commission. It has therefore set up a number of expert groups and specialized subgroups for certain delegated acts, with a view to consultation.

This initiative has opened up the 'black box' of delegated acts, but it benefits mainly the Member States, since the groups are composed exclusively of national officials. Like the comitology committees, they are chaired by an official of the Commission. The main difference with the comitology groups is that these new ad hoc groups do not vote.

The new system has generated several difficulties. First, the delimitation between implementing acts (to be dealt with by 'comitology') and delegated acts (new procedure under Article 290 TFEU) seemed uncertain and at the centre of interinstitutional tensions. The Court of Justice referred to this difficulty in the *Biocides* case[23] but did not clarify the situation. Second, although new groups of experts have been set up, Member States are only consulted and are thus deprived of the negotiating stage that existed with the Regulatory Procedure with Scrutiny (RPS).[24] They may oppose the proposal, but not formally amend it. Since the entry into force of the Treaty of Lisbon, the EP and the Council have only opposed a limited number of acts. The EP has also expressed its opinion in several resolutions on implementing acts, considering that the Commission was exceeding its powers.[25] Finally, the EP and civil society actors called for greater transparency by proposing the creation of a register of delegated acts and the introduction of consultation procedures. In the system set up by the Commission, MEPs and stakeholders are only involved in the groups if they are invited on an ad hoc basis as experts or observers.[26] In theory, a register of delegated acts has been accepted by the Commission and is supposed to be operational by the end of 2017.

The EP pressured the new Commission, most notably at the hearing of Frans Timmermans, candidate for the first vice-presidency, in charge of improving regulation. On 19 May 2015, the Commission published a new 'Better Lawmaking' programme, which included provisions on delegated legislation. It proposed that all drafts of delegated acts and the most important draft implementing acts be put online on a website open for public comment for four weeks, in parallel with the consultation of Member States in the groups of experts. This new approach allows stakeholders to make their comments known to national experts. In addition, the Commission has decided to publish an indicative list of future actions to facilitate the work of the stakeholders. The details of this new approach to delegated legislation should be included in an interinstitutional agreement.

4.1.2 The powers of the Council

The Council, like the Commission, has a wide range of diverse powers, whose heterogeneity reflects the uncertainties of the institution. It has seven main functions:

1   The Council adopts European legislation proposed by the Commission. Since co-decision has become common law, it now legislates jointly with the EP in most areas.
2   As witnessed, it exercises executive functions that it refuses to delegate to the Commission and often enjoys indirect influence through comitology or delegated acts. It also has specific executive powers regarding the CFSP and in the context of cooperation in criminal matters.
3   The Council approves the EU and its institutions' annual budget together with the EP based on the Commission's proposal.
4   The Council coordinates the Broad Economic Policy Guidelines (BEPGs). Since the Maastricht Treaty, Member States have decided to implement a global economic policy, based on coordination – theoretically limited – of their national economic policies within the Council's ECOFIN configuration; (see also Eurogroup in Box 4.3).
5   The Council is capable of concluding international agreements between the EU and one or more outside countries or international organizations. These agreements, usually negotiated by the Commission on the basis of a mandate from the Council, may cover broad areas (trade, cooperation and development) or more specific questions (fishing, textiles, transport). The Council may also conclude agreements between Member States in areas such as taxation, corporate law or consular protection which do not fall within the EU's powers.

6   The Council defines the EU's Common Foreign and Security Policy on the basis of guidelines set by the European Council. In this area, Member States retain much of their sovereignty. This implies that the EP and the Commission play only a limited role and that the permanent political and military structures were created under the auspices of the Council in order to ensure political control and strategic direction in a crisis.

7   The Council coordinates cooperation between the courts and national police forces in criminal matters within the framework of the Council's 'Justice and Home Affairs' (JHA).[27]

4.1.3 The activities and operations of the Council

The Council's operations vary according to the nature of the powers it implements and the logic (more integrated or more intergovernmental) that animates it. Here we focus on its central activity: the adoption of legislation. This procedure has six main steps.

1   The Commission's proposal submitted to the Council is translated into 24 languages. It is then distributed to the General Secretariat and the Member States' Permanent Representations which solicit instructions from their respective governments and administrations.

2   The proposal is considered by the Council's working groups, which can be one of the existing groups or an ad hoc group created for the occasion. The Commission presents its text through the head of the unit in charge of the dossier, after which the presidency organizes round tables to collect the positions of the various national officials.

3   The General Secretariat prepares a report on the basis of the work of the relevant working group which is transmitted to the relevant configuration of the COREPER or to a special committee.

4   At the COREPER (I or II) or for a special committee meeting, the agenda distinguishes 'I' points for which there is an agreement negotiated by the working group and which are thus examined very quickly, and 'II' points that have been problematic and have to be re-discussed in detail in order to find an arrangement. Round tables are organized by the presidency to try to reconcile national positions.

5   At the end of the meeting (see Box 4.4), the General Secretariat prepares a new report and adopts the agenda from the Council's relevant configuration. 'A' points are those for which an agreement exists and the 'B' points still require negotiation.

6   The Council meets to validate quickly the 'A' points, to debate in detail the 'B' points and eventually to vote afterwards.

Box 4.4 Council meetings

During Council meetings, ministers are assisted and advised by their Permanent Representative or Deputy Permanent Representative, who know the issues. The Presidency is assisted by officials of the Council's Secretariat General, the Secretary General, his deputy and the Council's legal advisor. The Commission also attends the deliberations, unless the Council evokes problems of internal organization.

Including interpreters, 100 officials attend the Council's work; 50 others follow in a listening room. The presidency may decide to limit the number of people in the meeting room and specify if it is a meeting of 'Ministers plus two', 'Ministers plus one' or 'Ministers only'.

Since the entry into force of the Maastricht Treaty, the objective of transparency has led to public being allowed into some legislative debates in the Council. Debates on new legislative proposals or on the programme of the six-month presidency are now televised. Since the entry into force of the Lisbon Treaty, each session consists of two parts: deliberations on EU legislative acts and non-legislative activities. The treaty provides that the Council shall meet in public when it deliberates and votes on a draft legislative act but otherwise meets behind closed doors.

Decision-making: voting procedures and weighted voting

The Council adopts its decisions according to the terms of treaties; they vary according to the relevant domain, and therefore the procedure used. Today, after succeeding reform of the treaties, decisions are taken most often by qualified majority. Unanimity is still required for sensitive issues and only a simple majority is needed for minor or organizational decisions.

The question of a transition from unanimity to qualified majority has been the subject of heated debate between Member State representatives at various times throughout the EU's history. As described in Chapter 1, in 1965 Charles de Gaulle triggered this debate with a violent crisis (the so-called 'empty chair' crisis) within the Council. It was a protest against, among other things, the move to qualified majority voting in some domains which the EEC Treaty provided for the following period of 10 years. The 'Luxembourg compromise', a political agreement that ended a six-month block of the Council, then allowed a Member State to demand further discussion on an issue that would affect 'significant national interests'. In fact, Member States gradually imposed a return to unanimity for the most important decisions, including when a simple majority had been required. With the entry into force of the Single European Act in 1987, the Luxembourg Compromise was officially suspended and the possibility of a qualified majority vote restored. Its scope has since been continuously expanded, becoming the modality for decisions of common law. Even though the Lisbon Treaty has passed many domains from unanimity to qualified majority (96 articles are now concerned, as opposed to 63 prior to the treaty), sensitive areas such as taxation, social security or foreign policy and defence remain subject to unanimity.[28] To the extent that a unanimous decision of the national representatives is required for that qualified majority voting can be applied to a new domain, the opposition of one member is enough to block this process.

The issue of weighting votes in the Council is also a very sensitive subject. It is emblematic of the EU's nature, particularly of the persistent influence of nation states in an otherwise highly integrated system. It is also the issue that causes the most pronounced conflicts and national divisions, one which prevented the European Council from agreeing, first of all, on the draft Constitution (Brussels Summit, December 2003) and which occupied the attention of the Heads of State and government during the final negotiations of the Lisbon Treaty, four years later.

Originally, the weighting system equipped states with a number of voices varying in relation to a vague criterion of 'size'. Luxembourg had one, Belgium and the Netherlands two and France, Germany and Italy respectively four. A decision by qualified majority was possible with 12 votes over 17 (70.5 per cent of voices), including a favourable vote by at least four members for the decisions not based on a proposal of the Commission. This system, which allowed a fine balance between 'small', 'medium' and 'large' states, was designed specially to take into account the various possibilities of blocking minorities.

Intergovernmental tensions prevented a radical reform of this system upon successive enlargements for a long time. It was adapted through an arithmetic extrapolation and by an increase of the global number of voices – large Member States getting 10 voices in the end. It thus progressively lost its virtues of balance. In view of the EU's enlargement to include Central and Eastern European countries, it was agreed to finally reform a system that seemed profoundly unsuitable for a Europe with more than 20 members. National leaders, however, failed to agree on this issue during the negotiation of the Treaties of Maastricht and Amsterdam. The question was therefore referred to the 2000 Intergovernmental Conference. At the conclusion of the Nice Summit (December 2000), the terms of qualified majority voting had been the subject of intense negotiations and open conflict. For the first time in decades, it was indeed a question of changing the respective influence of Member States within the Council (but also in the Commission and Parliament), which has raised nationalist reflexes thought to be outdated. Further, proposals for a radical reform of the Council's voting procedures (including the principle of a double majority of states and the population) have been discarded in favour of a particularly complex compromise. Therefore, the goal of easing requirements for the adoption of a text has not been reached.

Between 2004 and 2014, decisions by qualified majority within the Council were thus governed by the system introduced by the Treaty of Athens (Treaty of Accession of Ten), in reference to the Treaty of Nice. The Council had to gather a double majority:

1 're-weighted' qualified majority, which took state populations more into account in the allocation of votes. Their number varied from 3 for Malta up to 29 for 'large' states; in the EU-28, 260 votes out of 352, or 73.9%, are now necessary to reach a qualified majority (see Box 4.5);
2 simple majority (in some cases, that of two-thirds of the Member States), which was demanded by the 'small' states to offset the effect of re-weighting;
3 a state could have also requested verification of the 'demographic clause' to ensure that a decision was made by states representing at least 62% of the EU's population. This provision was introduced at the request of the 'big' states to avoid 'small' states coalitions. Concretely, the demographic clause is largely symbolic: it opposes the adoption of a decision only in some cases out of the millions of possible combinations to obtain a qualified majority.

Contrary to the objectives which had been assigned to the intergovernmental conference that ended in Nice, achieving a decision was not any easier than before, quite the contrary. It established 70 per cent of the votes according to the old system as opposed to 73.9 per cent of the votes with the new terms and conditions. The goal of a simpler system was not achieved.

Box 4.5 Council voting weights in the EU-28 (Treaty of Athens)

• Germany, France, Italy and the UK	29
• Spain and Poland	27
• Romania	14
• The Netherlands	13
• Belgium, Czech Republic, Greece, Hungary and Portugal	12
• Austria, Sweden and Bulgaria	10
• Denmark, Ireland, Lithuania, Slovakia, Finland and Croatia	7
• Cyprus, Estonia, Latvia, Luxembourg and Slovenia	4
• Malta	3
• TOTAL	352

One of the principle objectives of the Convention on the Future of the Union was to find an alternative to this voting system before EU enlargement to the Central and Eastern European countries. This was not possible as a result of the vicissitudes of the ratification of the Constitutional Treaty. The last two enlargements were implemented according to the rules of the Treaty of Nice, reiterated by the Treaty of Athens. The Lisbon Treaty, which entered into force on 1 December 2009, takes up most of the provisions proposed by the Convention in this context (itself inspired by earlier proposals by the EP) and reviewed by the European Council in June 2004. However, their implementation was once again delayed because of the reluctance of some countries – notably Poland – towards the new system.

The treaty provides that from 1 November 2014, a qualified majority is defined as equal to[29]:

- at least 55% of Council members,
- including at least 15 of them
- and representing Member States comprising at least 65% of the population of the EU.

Moreover, a blocking minority must include at least four Council members representing more than 35 per cent of the EU's population.

In order to rally Poland definitively to the final text, a transitional arrangement (called the 'Ioannina compromise' referring to a similar system negotiated in the context of the 1995 enlargement) was included in the treaty. It provides that if a text arouses significant opposition but less than a blocking minority (one-third of the Member States or 25 per cent of the population), all states commit to find a solution to rally opponents, while reserving the right to vote at any time.[30] However, we should not overestimate the issue of the weighting system since most texts adopted in the Council are not formally voted upon, even when qualified majority voting is required.[31]

In specific domains (mainly under the Common Foreign and Security Policy) and some aspects of the Economic and Monetary Union, decisions are not made according to classic procedures, but by unanimity. These forms of cooperation are similar to the operation of traditional international organizations in that they do not have the supranational character of Community actions. However, they no longer amount to the confrontation of national positions with no possibility for dialogue. Mutual understanding of positions, individual attitudes and interests, routines, alliances, socialization of ministers and national representatives, the 'global' nature of discussions (which may include several texts at a time), fair play and political correctness as well as mediation of Council officers, make clear that, in the EU, intergovernmental negotiations are not diplomatic conferences and zero-sum games.[32] In addition, since 1957, the EEC Treaty states that 'abstentions by members either present or represented shall not prevent the adoption of Council conclusions requiring unanimity' (Art. 148). Unanimous decisions thus do not require the approval of each minister, but as in the European Council, the search for a negative consensus: a decision is considered adopted if none of the national representatives raise an objection or oppose the proposal explicitly.

Since the Maastricht Treaty, the aim has been to ensure greater transparency when it comes to the voting process in the Council to combat the 'democratic deficit'. After the coming into force of the Single European Act, this concept referred primarily to the combined effect of resorting to qualified majority voting (as a result of the evolution of the Treaty and the suspension of the Luxembourg compromise) as well as the secrecy of ballots. Citizens were obliged to respect the standards adopted by the Council, even if they were adopted by qualified majority, and sometimes against the advice of their state. Nevertheless, they had no reliable information on the subject: a minister was free to claim to have opposed a text, even if that was not the case. This lack of transparency prevented national parliaments from controlling their government's European policy and eventually from assuming political responsibility. As for the European Parliament, it was no more able to hold ministers accountable.

Despite the assertion of the principle of transparency in the Council's voting process, the Council has never really met this requirement. The use of a formal vote remains rare, even if the Council is theoretically obliged to do so. The Council's Rules of Procedure provide that a formal vote must be taken whenever it adopts an act under the Treaties (Article 11.2) and that such a vote may also be requested by any member of the Council or by the Commission, and must intervene if the request is approved by a simple majority (Article 11.1). Effectively, the presidency retains a wide-ranging role in this area, and the 'surprise' votes, which could be embarrassing for national representatives, are impossible.[33] In practice, when the presidency considers that a qualified majority is reached, the unwritten rule is that if national representatives wish to vote against or abstain from voting (which also amounts to opposing the adoption of the Act), they must express themselves. Their position is then recorded and made public; if they fail to do so, they shall be deemed to have been in favour of the decision. In practice, once a qualified majority seems to have been acquired, the presidency no longer pays attention to the delegations opposed to the decision.

Ministers prefer to continue negotiating rather than see a disagreement unfold (lack of qualified majority or unanimity, as required), and voting is seen as a last resort when consensus cannot be reached because of a very small number of unyielding opponents.[34] Historically, the protest rates (voting against or abstention) are quite rare and focused on a limited number of public policies. Hosli and his colleagues showed that between 2004 and 2006, the level of protest was particularly low: only 432 of the 33,950 cases studied were voted down by one or more states (i.e. 1.3 per cent).[35] A more recent study by Votewatch shows that between July 2009 and July 2012, of the 309 decisions that could have been adopted by qualified majority, 65 per cent were adopted unanimously, while in 35 per cent of cases, several states abstained or voted against the proposal.[36] And the dispute tends to focus on specific sectors of the Council, especially Internal Market and Agriculture/Fisheries. Hayes Renshaw and her colleagues found that half of the opposition votes are in the latter. A more recent analysis confirms these results (see Figure 4.3).

Dissent at the voting stage thus remains a rare event.[37] Formal voting is avoided in a more general way. It reveals the identity of the opponents of a text and undermines the negotiation process: the vote creates unnecessary tensions and leads to retaliatory measures against representatives who block important negotiations. On the other hand, the ministers prefer not to register their support or opposition to a piece of legislation for fear of being blamed at the national level for not defending the interests of their country. This does not mean that there is no disagreement between national governments but that they are largely outside the requirements of the publicity that is in the treaties.[38] Governments are heavily mobilized by their citizens or by constituents' interests, but by negotiating at Council meetings, they reach a compromise or join the majority when they are afraid of being put in a minority group.[39] National civil servants accustomed to the Council, as well as its employees, are masters in the art of moving the negotiations forward, by means of real or symbolic counterparts, of 'package' deals on a set of texts, orders, exceptions or 'rendezvous' clauses, providing for the subsequent reopening of the negotiations.

More than 60 years after its creation, the Council retains its original ambiguities. As an intergovernmental institution par excellence, it has a more integrated

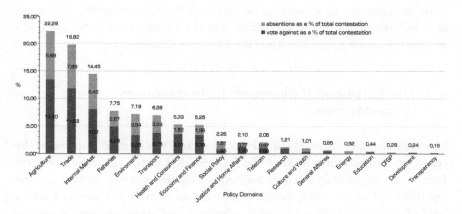

Figure 4.3   Contestation by public policy (1995–2010)

Source: Van Aken, W., 'Voting in the Council of the European Union', SIEPS 2012: 2, p. 35.

operation with qualified majority voting currently governing most of its decisions. Moreover, while it is becoming more and more like the high chamber of a
bicameral parliament, it still has significant executive powers regarding foreign
policy, criminal cooperation and through comitology. The name 'Council of
Ministers', which is currently used by the media and would have been formalized
by the failed Constitutional Treaty, adds to the confusion by evoking the idea of
a government as opposed to a chamber. Finally, the Council remains a place of
debate where ministers can take the opportunity to develop, outside any formal
procedure, new policies or activities not covered by the treaties.

As said previously, the Treaty of Lisbon allows us to describe the EU regime
as a quadripartite system, in which the Council would be – mainly – the high
chamber of a bicameral parliament. This is true if we consider institutions'
formal powers, but we must add that the Council does not function like a
traditional legislative assembly and, for the time being, its members have refused
to play along. Its deliberations are now public, when dealing with legislative
matters but the Council is not an institution for exchange and debate. First, it is
affected by a culture of secrecy: ministers are still behaving first and foremost
like diplomats, they do not like to flaunt their positions and their possible
discrepancies. And they prefer to discuss files outside of the meetings, during
mealtimes, breaks and informal consultations. Second, the rotating presidency is
playing a growing role in the activities of the Council, thanks notably to the
generalization of trialogues with the Commission and the European Parliament.
In this context, it gets a kind of negotiation mandate, and the Council is often
happy to approve the 'early agreements' reached with the other two institutions.
The importance of the role of the COREPER, which meets behind closed doors,
has similar effects. Finally, the existence of 10 configurations of the Council is
another major obstacle to the transformation of the Council into a legislative
chamber. Contrary to what could be expected, the 'General affairs' configuration does not play a role of coordination of the Council's activities, which is a
task for the rotating presidency and the European Council.

4.2 The European Parliament: from decorum to co-decision

The Parliamentary Assembly of the Communities was originally an essentially
consultative institution with symbolic functions. It was created for three reasons.
First, it should maintain a certain institutional equilibrium balance between the
institutions. The Assembly, though almost devoid of authority, should assure a
kind of symmetry with the Council, offering a dual representation of peoples
and states. It was also a symbol of European reunification which is the reason
why the first sessions were held in Strasbourg, a recurring bone of contention

between France and Germany. Second, the creation of the Assembly responded to an institutional mimicry of other international organizations established at the time (UN, Union of Western Europe, Council of Europe, NATO, etc.) each of which had a parliamentary assembly. Finally, the later EP should ensure legitimacy of the Communities through control: even if the capacity of the assembly was limited in this respect, it was important that the High Authority (later the Commission) was subject to democratic control, at least formally.[40]

The Parliamentary Assembly has seen its composition, its powers and role evolving considerably since the 1950s. Its rise in power is the chief development of the European institutional system.

4.2.1 The composition of the European Parliament

Members of European Parliament (MEPs)

Since 1979, as a result of a 1976 Council decision, members of the EP are elected by direct universal suffrage. This reform, which was foreseen by the treaties from the beginning, has given a new scope to the institution.[41] Previously, MEPs were only representatives of national parliaments which exercised a dual mandate and were hardly devoted to the activities of the European Assembly.[42] The treaties related to the Communities' own resources (1970 and 1975), and the then following reforms of the treaties (Single European Act, Maastricht, Amsterdam, Nice and Lisbon) have substantially increased the Parliament's powers of decision-making and control with the aim to create an assembly which, through its influence, is similar to those of parliamentary monarchies of the nineteenth century or of the US Congress.[43]

There are currently 751 deputies, after peaking at 785 at the end of the 2004–2009 legislature (see Table 4.2). The Lisbon Treaty was supposed to set the number of elected members to 751 after the June 2009 elections, but due to the vicissitudes of its ratification, it was not able to come into force in time. Thus, the 2009 elections were organized in accordance with the provisions of the Nice Treaty which allowed for 736 seats. To remedy this inconvenience, the European Council decided in December 2008 that the number of MPs would be re-evaluated during the legislature, after the entry into force of the Lisbon Treaty with each state being responsible to appoint any future additional members. The German case, however, posed a problem since the number of elected officials was actually reduced from 99 to 96 by the Treaty of Lisbon. Faced with the inability to end the current term of three duly elected members of the legislature, the European Council temporarily increased the number of members to 754 (18 more than in June 2009), not to 751. This decision represented a major practical and judicial headache which the European Parliament could have done without.

With the accession of Croatia on 1 July 2013, the number of MEPs has temporarily increased to 766: Croatia had 12 deputies until the elections of May 2014, when their number was reduced to 11. Moreover, at the end of June 2013, an agreement between the European Council and the Parliament has been reached concerning the allocation of seats. After the 2014 elections, Germany's seats were reduced to 96 and 12 Member States have each lost one seat in order to comply with the 751-seat limit of the Lisbon Treaty and at the same time to make room for the Croatian MEPs. But the agreement also states that this allocation of seats should be revised before the 2019 elections on the basis of a proposal by the Parliament to ensure that seats are distributed in an 'objective, fair, durable and transparent way'. Moreover, because of Brexit, the EP will have to decide the fate of the United Kingdom's 73 seats.

Nowadays, the national allocation of seats is indeed not the result of the application of a given formula but of negotiations between Member States during the revision of treaties and negotiation of the accession treaties. Discussions are still built around a principle of 'degressive proportionality', which aims to guarantee a balance between the representation of citizens according to the demographics of their Member State, and a minimum representation of the less populous states. This method results in an overrepresentation of the latter, which decreases with the reforms but remains very noticeable. Each elected Maltese MEP represents 80,500 citizens, while a Bulgarian MEP representing 427,000 and a German one 839,000 (2015 figures). The persistent distortions in the ratio of national population to the number of members have negative repercussions on the representativeness of the Assembly.

Like any assembly, the current functioning of the European Parliament does not rely solely on the MEPs but on entities that have significant powers: political groups, European parties, parliamentary committees and hierarchical bodies. They enjoy a particularly important role in the European Parliament due to the high number of its members and the specific constraints that weigh on this unparalleled, supranational assembly.

The political groups

Without the treaties encouraging or compelling them to do so, the MEPs decided from June 1953 to give precedence to their political beliefs over their nationality by choosing to sit according to their ideological views.[44] They distinguished themselves from parliamentary assemblies of other international organizations, whereby members sit in alphabetical order or by national delegations. This de facto organization of Parliament seating resulted from the creation of transnational political groups and the codification of their existence in the internal regulation of the Assembly. From the outset, the multinational groups have been encouraged: the higher the number of implicated national delegations, the lower the number of MEPs to meet to create a group. Current regulations even prohibit mono-national groups. Today a group requires 25 members from at least one-quarter of the Member States (seven in the EU-28).[45]

The history of political groups is a reflection of the history of the Parliament. Rapid growth of the responsibilities and powers of the institution, evolution in the number of its members and also their election by direct universal suffrage, have contributed to the continuous transformation of the Parliament's political landscape. However, while the name and composition of the groups have been the subject of reconfigurations over time, particularly in response to the accession of members, the structure of the partisan game has maintained a certain stability. The number of political groups has remained relatively constant. The European Parliament had six political groups prior to the first European elections (1979) as compared to seven during the elections in September 2009 with a maximum of ten groups which was reached in 1989.[46] The Parliament's political landscape is therefore very stable, despite some name changes, including the permanent numerical domination of the two main groups, the Christian Democrats and the Social Democrats.[47]

Until 1965, the Parliament was composed merely of the three main political families of the time, each of which formed a group: Social Democrats, Christian Democrats and Liberals. The arrival of Gaullist deputies in 1965, and then communists in 1974 somewhat broadened the partisan spectrum, but the latter advanced mostly during the first direct election. Whereas previously many governments only sent elected representatives favourable to European integration to Strasbourg, the transition to universal suffrage led to the election of also Eurosceptic candidates. Their number increased significantly because of the second-order nature of European elections, which tend to favour protest and minority parties. Since then, the following six political families are routinely found in the Parliament: Christian Democrats, Social Democrats, Liberals, Environmentalists, the radical left and the Eurosceptics/sovereignists (see Tables 4.2, 4.3 and 4.4).[48]

The elections of May 2014 (see Table 4.5) were followed by the emergence of the 'block', i.e. an established alliance between the groups EPP, S&D and ALDE to support conjointly the election of J. C. Juncker as the President of the Commission and of Martin Schulz as the President of the EP (see below). The price for this alliance has been the integration in the Commission programme of elements likely to be suitable for the different parties; the large investment plan designed to boost growth within the EU was thus designed to meet the expectations of the S&D Group. If Juncker could count on the support of the 'block' for the important votes, it is not a stable coalition as it exists at national level in many parliamentary regimes, and the groups have not complied with any discipline of collective voting in the running of the assembly. In this respect, it remains traversed by a multitude of divisions.

In the absence of a stable cleavage between the majority and the opposition, coalitions permitting the adoption of legislation are variable. They are specific

Table 4.2 Number of seats per Member State (March 2017)

Country	1958	1973	1979	1984	1987	1994	1995	2004	2007	2009 Nice Revised	Lisbon	2014
Austria							21	18	18	17	19	18
Belgium		14	24	24	24	25	25	24	24	22	22	21
Bulgaria									18	17	18	17
Croatia											11	11
Cyprus								6	6	6	6	6
Czech Rep								24	24	22	22	21
Denmark		10	16	16	16	16	16	14	14	13	13	13
Estonia								6	6	6	6	6
Finland							16	14	14	13	13	13
France	36	36	81	81	81	87	87	78	78	72	74	74
Germany	36	36	81	81	81	99	99	99	99	99	96	96
Greece				24	24	25	25	24	24	22	22	21
Hungary								24	24	22	22	21
Ireland		10	15	15	15	15	15	13	13	12	12	11
Italy	36	36	81	81	81	87	87	78	78	72	73	73
Latvia								9	9	8	9	8
Lithuania								13	13	12	12	11
Luxembourg	6	6	6	6	6	6	6	6	6	6	6	6

(Continued)

Table 4.2 (continued)

Country	1958	1973	1979	1984	1987	1994	1995	2004	2007	2009 Nice	Lisbon (Revised)	2014
Malta								5	5	5	6	6
Netherlands	14	14	25	25	25	31	31	27	27	25	26	26
Poland								54	54	50	51	51
Portugal					24	25	25	24	24	22	22	21
Romania									35	33	33	32
Slovakia								14	14	13	13	13
Slovenia								7	7	7	8	8
Sweden							22	19	19	18	20	20
Spain					60	64	64	54	54	50	54	54
UK		36	81	81	81	87	87	78	78	72	73	73
TOTAL	142	198	410	434	518	567	626	732	785	736	751*	751

Source: European Parliament.

Notes: * Under the December 2008 European Council decision, Germany maintains its 99 MEPs for the entire 2009–2014 legislature, temporarily bringing the number of MEPs to 754. The number of seats was temporarily increased to 766 with the entry of Croatia on 1 July 2013.

The distribution of seats is set to change as a result of Brexit. A proposal, adopted by the EP on 7 February 2018, proposes to redistribute 27 of the UK's 73 seats to other countries, while keeping the remaining 46 seats for future enlargements. This would mean the number of MEPs to be elected in May 2019 would be 705.

Table 4.3 Political groups in the European Parliament (1979–2017)

ABBREVIATION	DATE OF CREATION	END DATE	DENOMINATION
ENF	15/06/2015		**Europe of Nations and Freedom Group**
EFDD	24/06/2014		**Europe of Freedom and Direct Democracy Group**
S&D	14/07/2009		**Progressive Alliance of Socialists and Democrats**
EPP	14/07/2009		**European People's Party (Christian Democrats)**
ECR	14/07/2009		**European Conservatives and Reformers**
EFD	14/07/2009	24/06/2014	Europe of Freedom and Democracy
ITS	15/01/2007	13/11/2007	Identity, Tradition and Sovereignty Group
ALDE	20/07/2004		**Alliance of Liberals and Democrats for Europe**
PES	20/07/2004	13/07/2009	Party of European Socialists
IND/DEM	20/07/2004	13/07/2009	Independence/Democracy Group
EDD	20/07/1999	19/07/2004	Group for a Europe of Democracies and Diversities
EPP-ED	20/07/1999	15/07/2009	European People's Party (Christian Democrats) and European Democrats
UEN	20/07/1999	15/07/2009	Union for Europe of the Nations
Greens-EFA	20/07/1999		**Group of the Greens/European Free Alliance**
TDI	20/07/1999	02/10/2001	Technical Group of Independent Members – mixed group
I-EN	20/12/1996	19/07/1999	Group of Independents for a Europe of Nations
UFE	06/07/1995	19/07/1999	Group Union for Europe
UEL/NGL	06/01/1995		**European United Left–Nordic Green Left**
ERA	19/07/1994	19/07/1999	Group of the Radical European Alliance
UEN	19/07/1994	10/11/1996	Union for Europe of the Nations (Coordination Group)
FE	19/07/1994	05/07/1995	Forza Europa
ELDR	19/07/1994	19/07/2004	Group of the European Liberal Democrat and Reform Party
EUL	19/07/1994	05/01/1995	Confederal Group of the European United Left

(Continued)

Table 4.3 (continued)

ABBREVIATION	DATE OF CREATION	END DATE	DENOMINATION
PES	21/04/1993	19/07/2004	Party of European Socialists
RBW	25/07/1989	18/07/1994	Rainbow Group in the European Parliament
DR	25/07/1989	18/07/1994	Technical Group of the European Right
CG	20/07/1989	18/07/1994	Left Unity
EUL	20/07/1989	11/01/1993	Group for the United European Left
G	19/07/1989	19/07/1999	Green Group in the European Parliament
CTDI	17/09/1987	17/11/1987	Group for the Technical Coordination and Defence of Independent Groups and Members
LDR	13/12/1985	18/07/1994	Liberal and Democratic Reformist Group
RBW	24/07/1984	24/07/1989	Rainbow Group: Federation of the Green Alternative European Left, Agalev-Ecolo, the Danish People's Movement against Membership of the European Community and the European Free Alliance in the European Parliament
DR	24/07/1984	24/07/1989	Technical Group of the European Right
EDA	23/07/1984	05/07/1995	Group of the European Democratic Alliance
ED	17/07/1979	01/05/1992	European Democrats
S	17/07/1979	20/04/1993	Socialist Group
EPP	17/07/1979	19/07/1999	European People's Party (Christian Democrat Group)
COM	17/07/1979	24/07/1989	Communist and Allies Group
LD	17/07/1979	12/12/1985	Liberal and Democratic Group
EPD	17/07/1979	30/09/1984	Group of European Progressive Democrats
CDI	17/07/1979	23/07/1984	Group the Technical Coordination and Defense of Independent Groups and Members

Source: European Parliament/authors.

Notes: Bold text: active groups (March 2017).

Table 4.4 Composition of the European Parliament since 1979 (after each election)

July 1979		July 1984		July 1989		July 1994		July 1999		July 2004		July 2009		June 2014	
S	112	S	130	PES	180	PES	198	EPP-ED	233	EPP-ED	268	EPP	265	EPP	221
EPP	108	EPP	110	EPP	121	EPP	156	PES	180	PES	200	S&D	184	S&D	191
ED	63	ED	50	LDR	49	ELDR	44	ELDR	50	ALDE	88	ALDE	84	ECR	70
COM	44	COM	41	ED	34	EUL	28	G/EFA	48	G/EFA	42	G/EFA	55	ALDE	67
LD	40	LD	31	G	30	FE	27	EUL-NGL	42	EUL-NGL	41	ECR	54	EUL/NGL	52
EPD	22	EDA	29	EUL	28	EDA	26	UEN	30	IND/DEM	37	EUL/NGL	35	G/EFA	50
CDI	11	RBW	20	EDA	20	G	23	TDI	18	UEN	27	EFD	32	EFDD	48
		DR	16	DR	17	ERA	19	EDD	16	UEN	18				
				CG	14	UEN	19								
				RBW	13										
NI	10	NI	7	NI	12	NI	27	NI	9	NI	9	NI	27	NI	52
TOT.	410	TOT.	434	TOT.	518	TOT.	567	TOT.	626	TOT.	626	TOT.	736	TOT.	751

Source: European Parliament/authors.

Table 4.5 Distribution of seats by political group and by Member State (November 2017)

	EPP	S&D	ALDE	G/EFA	ECR	UEL/NGL	EFDD	ENF	NI	Total
Belgium	4	4	6	2	4			1		21
Bulgaria	7	4	4		2					17
Czech Republic	7	4	4		2	3	1			21
Denmark	1	3	3	1	4	1				13
Germany	34	27	4	13	6	8	1	1	2	96
Estonia	1	1	3	1						6
Ireland	4	1	1		1	4				11
Greece	5	4			1	6			5	21
Spain	17	14	8	4		11			1	54
France	20	13	7	6		4	4	17	3	74
Croatia	5	2	2	1	1					11
Italy	15	31		1	2	3	15	6		73
Cyprus	1	2			1	2				6
Latvia	4	1		1	1				1	8
Lithuania	3	2	3	1	1		1			11
Luxemburg	3	1	1	1						6
Hungary	12	4		2					3	21
Malta	3	3								6
The Netherlands	5	3	7	2	2	3		4		26
Austria	5	5	1	3				4		18
Poland	22	5			19		1	2	2	51
Portugal	8	8	2			4				21

(Continued)

Table 4.5 (continued)

	EPP	S&D	ALDE	G/EFA	ECR	UEL/NGL	EFDD	ENF	NI	Total
Romania	13	14	3		1			1		32
Slovenia	5	1	1	1						8
Slovakia	6	4			3					13
Finland	3	2	4	1	2	1				13
Sweden	4	6	3	4		1	2			20
United Kingdom	20		1	6	21	1	20	1	3	73
	EPP	S&D	ALDE	G/EFA	ECR	UEL/NGL	EFDD	ENF	NI	Total
Total	217	189	68	51	74	52	45	37	18	751

Source: European Parliament.

to the issues considered and based on several levels of agreement.[49] The divide between the left and the right is evident on a growing number of topics: today, the European Union takes decisions that have a significant impact on many po.cies that generate contrasting approaches in different political families. Te.ions between Europhiles and Eurosceptics are nevertheless especially pervasive in particular following the many crises faced by the Union in recent years[50] and contribute to the ability of the Parliament to decide, by surmounting the divide between left and right. These tensions are even stronger when they are superimposed onto the divergent interests and views among major groups that are generally favourable to European integration and small groups which are more critical. The cleavage between pro- and anti-Europeans eases the decision because the former are far more numerous than the latter, and can thus easily reach the requested majorities. The Assembly's deliberations may further be governed by national divisions between big and small states, new and old, rich and poor, etc. or a return to specific geographical divisions. These national divisions are rarely explicit, especially in the plenary where MEPs avoid making re.rence to their nationality, but they are sometimes decisive in the conduct of negotiations within groups and committees or in MEPs votes.

All of these divisions are more or less perceptible depending on the inter-institutional context. Overall, the need to make Parliament's voice heard in the trialogue with the Council and the Commission is a powerful factor for reducing antagonisms within the Assembly. Parliament rarely remains divided when it comes to make a decision. The majority will lead most often to an agreement between the two large groups on the right (EPP) and the left (S&D). To understand the Parliament's ability to overcome a division between left and right, scholars emphasize the ideological proximity of the two main groups regarding European integration,[51] the constraints exerted by the treaty provisions related to the adoption of legislation (notably the need to bring together a majority of MEPs in many cases, and not the simple or absolute majority of voters),[52] the common interest of both groups to limit the influence of other formations[53] and/or their common desire to strengthen the weight of Parliament in the institutional triangle by speaking with one voice.[54] Since 2014, the existence of the 'bloc' is an additional explanation for the ability of the centre-left and the centre-right to vote jointly. Even if the politicization of issues is more and more sensitive in the debates, things haven't changed that much and the EPP and S&D continue to blend their voices in more than two-thirds of the cases.[55] For example, a recent study by VoteWatch shows that the frequency of the 'grand coalition' has increased in the last three legislatures, from 69 per cent of cases between 2004 and 2009, to 73 per cent of votes between 2009 and 2014 and 79.5 per cent of cases in the first six months of the 8th legislature.[56] The figure is even around 90 per cent in the more recent period of time (2016–2017).

The two main groups also illustrate a relatively high level of internal cohesion. About 70 per cent of MEPs respect the voting instructions adopted by their formation[57] (see Figures 4.4 and 4.5). However, it is necessary to keep the scope of this purely statistical fact in perspective.[58] While in the Member States such cohesion may be the product of group discipline, a shared vision of society, the collective defence of a political programme or an attitude of support or opposition to government policy, this is not the same at the level of the EU. For the

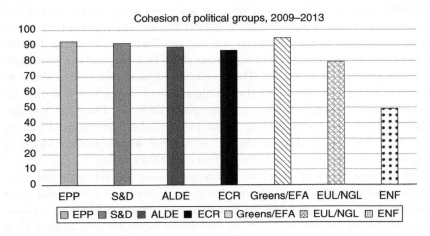

Figure 4.4 Cohesion of political groups, 7th legislature

Source: Votewatch.eu

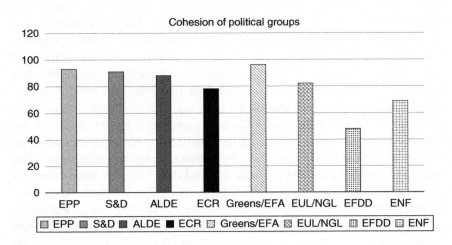

Figure 4.5 Cohesion of political groups, 8th legislature

Source: Votewatch.eu

European Parliament, it is primarily the result of an extensive division of labour, which encourages MEPs to rely on their group's positions for all issues which they have not followed closely and to seek support from their peers on issues for which they are responsible and of which they know the details and the issues. The European Parliament's political groups do not have the same functions or the same rapport with their members as those of national parliaments. The specific institutional context of the European political area and the Assembly itself induce specific functions for the groups which are not the product of highly structured parties, having campaigned on a specific programme and working to ensure a certain voting discipline to support the action of the executive.[59] The parliamentary activities of the MPs are mostly disconnected from electoral and campaign functions which remain largely associated with national parties,[60] due to the division of labour between national parties, European parties and political groups.[61] The political groups' primary mission is not to defend an elaborate political line but above all to provide the functional structure which allows elected officials to rationalize their work, to collectively increase their influence and to benefit from resources from which non-attached members are deprived. Therefore, one must carefully consider the argument that group cohesion in the European Parliament is indicative of a partisan structure comparable to national parliaments.

Political groups are equally central components to the EP's organization and deliberation. They play a crucial role in the socialization and training of the MEPs[62] as well as in the supervision and organization of the Assembly's work.[63] These groups control access to key resources such as the allocation of speaking time in plenary sessions, of appointments and mandates of responsibility and of reports. These resources are distributed amongst groups in proportion to their size (D'Hondt method). This tends to favour large groups but keeps small groups from being confined to futile opposition.

European Parliament political groups enjoy significant financial and logistical means available to them in order to carry out their tasks. The Assembly provides offices, meeting rooms, translation services and interpretation, a relatively large administrative staff and financial assistance for the European elections. Therefore, the groups are functional structures and vectors of influence essential for the MEPs. MEPs also derive substantial benefits from participating in a group, especially a large group.[64] In addition, the groups ensure MEPs' training. Since the European Parliament experiences high turnover after each election, the groups contribute to the continuity of its work, socialization of its members and assistance to them in their parliamentary activities (drafting of a report, chairing of a committee, preparation of questions, etc.).[65]

Finally, the groups play an essential role in the development of majority positions in the Assembly. As the principal place of resolution and occultation of conflicts between national delegations, they contribute to the aggregation of heterogeneous positions of their members through an internal deliberative process. The groups discuss each text as soon as it starts its consideration in parliamentary committee and before its discussion in plenary; the most integrated groups adopt a collective position by the majority and ensure that it is respected by their members. The two principle groups are veritable assemblies: during the 8th legislature, the EPP has around 220 members and the S&D 190. They have therefore been forced to implement precise procedures of internal organization: preparatory meetings, discussions in thematic working groups and validation of the position by the entire group. The group's president provides leadership and speaks in the name of his or her political group both inside and outside the parliamentary institution. Above all, he or she is a member of the Conference of Presidents (for political groups), a powerful management body of parliamentary work. We will come back to this.

European parties

The EP's parliamentary groups and European alliances of national parties with which they were aligned were the source of the creation of European parties (see Table 4.6).[66] The European People's Party (Christian Democrats) was established in 1978, followed in 1992 by the Party of European Socialists, in 1993 by the European Liberal Democrat and Reform Party (now the Alliance of Liberals and Democrats for Europe) and the European Federation of Green Parties (becoming the Green Party in 2004), in 1998 by the Democratic Party of the Peoples of Europe (now the European Free Alliance, autonomists and independents) and in 2004 by the Party of the European Left. Since 2005, many other parties were created: the Alliance for Europe of the Nations (Eurosceptic and nationalist parties, that stopped to meet the recognition threshold from 2010), the European Democratic Party (pro-European centrists), the EU Democrats (Europeans United for Democracy, Eurosceptics and Eurocritics), the Alliance of Independent Democrats in Europe (Eurosceptics and nationalists, dissolved at the end of 2008), the Alliance of European Conservatives and Reformists (Eurorealists), the European Christian Political Movement (Christian democrats), the European Alliance for Freedom (nationalist far right Eurosceptics, dissolved in 2014), the Alliance of European National Movements (nationalist far right Eurosceptics) and the Movement for a Europe of Liberties and Democracy (nationalists and Eurosceptics). The two last received a grant of the EP for the first time in 2012. In 2014, two new parties were recognized and then financed starting in 2015: the Movement for a Europe of Nations and Freedoms (a radical right-wing and Eurosceptic party, and the successor to the European Alliance for Freedom) and the Alliance for Direct Democracy in Europe (Eurosceptic and right-wing).

Table 4.6 European political parties (under regulation 2004/2003, as of March 2017)

Name	Abbr.	Date of creation	Number of members		of associate members		of observers		total members
			EU	Non EU	EU	Non EU	EU	Non EU	
1 European People's Party	EPP	1976	52	0	0	6	3	16	77
2 Party of European Socialists	PES	1992	33	0	1	10	2	9	55
3 Alliance of Liberals and Democrats for Europe Party*	ALDE	2004	45	16	0	0	0	0	61
4 European Green Party	EGP	2004	31	7	0	0	0	3	41
5 European Free Alliance	EFA	1981	36	0	0	0	6	0	42
6 Party of the European Left	EL	2004	24	5	0	0	0	0	29
7 European Christian Political Movement	ECPM	2002	10	6	0	0	0	0	16
8 European Democratic Party*	EDP	2004	13	1	0	0	0	0	14
9 Alliance of European National Movements	AENM	2009	8	0	8	0	0	1	17
10 Alliance of European Conservatives and Reformists	ECR	2009	16	8	0	5	0	0	29
11 Movement for a Europe of Liberties and Democracy	MELD	2011	9	0	0	0	0	0	9
12 Movement for a Europe of Nations and Freedoms*	MENF	2014	5	0	0	0	0	0	5
13 European Alliance for Freedom[67]	EAF	2010	19	0	0	0	0	0	19
14 EU Democrats*	EUD	2005	8	0	1	0	0	0	9
TOTAL			283	39	34	20	23	35	434

*The party does not specify the status of party members (full, associated or observers).

Source: European Parliament.

This inflation in the number of European parties is the result of a deliberate policy. The role of these bodies has indeed been recognized by the Maastricht Treaty, which states that:

> Political parties at European level are important as a factor for integration within the Union. They contribute to forming a European awareness and to expressing the political will of the citizens of the Union.
>
> (Art. 191, TEC)

With the same concern of 'politicizing' the functioning of the EU, the Nice Treaty evokes a statute of European parties, adopted in 2003 and amended for the first time in 2007. It accords the parties a legal status, provides funding and equips them with foundations. However, discussions are underway about reducing or eliminating the funding of European parties in order to combat the multiplication of extreme right-wing Eurosceptic groups whose only 'raison d'être' is the acquisition of public funds.

Despite their institutionalization, European parties play only a limited role in the EU's political life. During the campaign for European elections, they have developed common manifestos, even slogans and logos, but their party members have not always emphasized this within the national campaigns and no dynamic became apparent at the European level in this context. Taking into consideration the 2014 European elections, the Council and Parliament amended the regulation on the financing and legal status of European political parties and their foundations.[68] The aim was to increase their visibility and strengthen their role in European political life.

This allowed the European parties to acquire a new role at the occasion of the 2014 elections, since five of them (EPP, PES, Greens, ALDE and UEL/NGL) have agreed to organize the campaign around their respective candidates for the Presidency of the European Commission. This new procedure, inspired by the German system of *Spitzenkandidaten* (frontrunners of the lists, who are competing to become Chancellor), has attracted some attention from the media and the electors (see below).[69] Given that the EP was finally able to impose the 'winner' of the European election, EPP leader J. C. Juncker, as the new President of the Commission, it is quite likely that European parties will be very mobilized in 2019, in order to implement this practice over time, and will become key actors of the campaign.

Parliamentary committees

In addition to the political groups, the parliamentary committees are another principal setting for MEP socialization. Like all parliaments in contemporary democracies, the EP organizes much of its work in committees, based on a division of labour logic.[70] Much of the discussion, technical work and negotiations take place in the committees and political groups and not in the plenary session. Thus, some analysts refer to the EU as a system of 'governance by commit-tees',[71] in reference to the key role played by working groups and Council com-mittees, the Commission's advisory committees and the European Parliament committees. Improperly, some denounce 'comitology' which prevails in the institutions of the EU, including the Parliament, and clashes with the fundamen-tals of parliamentary government, especially relating to the principles of author-ization, responsibility and representation.

From an organizational perspective, the European Parliament has total freedom in this concern. MEPs can create as many committees as they deem necessary as well as temporary committees and committees of inquiry (under certain conditions). This ability enables them to adapt to the EU's fluctuating responsibilities and policies. The organizational autonomy of the Parliament has played a decisive role in the MEPs' exercise of their legislative, budgetary and control powers, and their demand for the extension of the latter. The European Parliament currently has 20 parliamentary committees (see Table 4.7).

Inter-parliamentary delegations

In addition to being a member of one or more committees, each MEP belongs to an inter-parliamentary delegation. These bodies are responsible for main-taining and developing international contacts for the European Parliament by building relationships with national parliaments and parliamentary bodies of certain international organizations (PAP, MERCOSUR, etc.). There are 25 traditional inter-parliamentary delegations (with a country, a group of coun-tries or an inter-parliamentary organization), 5 parliamentary cooperation committees (which refer to association agreements), 10 joint parliamentary committees and 5 delegations to the parliamentary assemblies in which the EU is represented (ACP-EU, Union for the Mediterranean, NATO, etc.). De. gations develop cooperation with the parliaments of the EU's traditional partners and promote the EU's values in other states. There are 13 parliamen-tary delegations in Europe (broadly defined and including NATO, Euronest, etc.) and 32 outside of Europe. These bodies have played a key role in the development of the EP's 'para-diplomacy' and currently allow it to offset the relative weakness of its powers regarding external relations.

The Assembly's hierarchical bodies

The European Parliament has four hierarchical bodies: the Bureau, the Confer-ence of Presidents (of the political groups), the Conference of Committee Chairs and the Conference of Delegation Chairs. These bodies make important decisions concerning the Assembly's organization of work (resource allocation,

Table 4.7   Parliamentary committees (March 2017)

Permanent Committees

AFET	Foreign Affairs
DROI Human Rights (subcommittee)	
SEDE Security and Defense (subcommittee)	
DEVE	Development
INTA	International Trade
BUDG	Budgets
CONT	Budgetary Control
ECON	Economic and Monetary Affairs
EMPL	Employment and Social Affairs
ENVI	Environment, Public Health and Food Safety
ITRE	Industry, Research and Energy
IMCO	Internal Market and Consumer Protection
TRAN	Transport and Tourism
REGI	Regional Development
AGRI	Agriculture and Rural Development
PECH	Fisheries
CULT	Culture and Education
JURI	Legal Affairs
LIBE	Civil Liberties, Justice and Home Affairs
AFCO	Constitutional Affairs
FEMM	Women's Rights and Gender Equality
PETI	Petitions

Special Committees

TERR	Terrorism
TAXE	Tax Rulings and Other Measures Similar in Nature or Effect (activity ended on the 30th of November 2015)
TAX2	Tax Rulings and Other Measures Similar in Nature or Effect (TAXE 2) (The work of the committee was completed on 2 August 2016)
EMIS	Emission Measurements in the Automotive Sector (the work of the committee was completed on 4 April 2017)

Committee of inquiry

PANA	Money laundering, tax avoidance and tax evasion

Source: European Parliament.

agenda, distribution of reports between committees, relations with other institutions, etc.) and provide most of the 'rationalization' of its operations.

The **Bureau** is the governing body in charge of financial and administrative matters. It is responsible for establishing the Parliament's projected budget and to settle all administrative, personnel and organizational questions. It is composed of the EP President, 14 Vice-Presidents and as many as six Quaestors elected by the Assembly. In accordance with Article 28 of the Rules of procedure (July 2014 edition):

> The Quaestors shall be responsible for administrative and financial matters directly concerning Members, pursuant to guidelines established by the Bureau.

This applies especially in relation to services and facilities available to the Members. They have only a consultative voice in the Bureau's deliberations. In the event of a tie, the president has the deciding vote. The president and the vice-presidents are the chairs of the plenary sessions of the Assembly. The president also plays an important role in representing the Parliament vis-à-vis other institutions, Member States, outside countries and other international organizations.[72]

The **Conference of Presidents** is composed of the president of the Parliament and the presidents of the political groups. The Chair invites one non-attached MEP to the meetings, where he or she participates without the right to vote. This is a key body for the Parliament's operation since it is responsible for the organization of work and legislative planning, the allocation of responsibilities and the composition of committees and delegations, as well as for the relations with other EU institutions, national parliaments and outside countries. The very sensitive responsibility to establish the institution's work schedule as well as the adoption of the agenda for the plenary sessions also falls under the accountability of the Conference of Presidents. The Conference usually meets twice a month behind closed doors. From now on, the presidents of the different groups shall have a weighted vote according to their respective headcount; in fact, the chairpersons of the bloc (EPP, S & D, ALDE), or even only the EPP and S&D groups, can impose their views. In practice, however, the President of the Parliament always tries to find broad compromises. Depending on current events, some extraordinary Conferences of Presidents provide an opportunity for all members to exchange views with a guest speaker on the sidlines of the plenary sessions or also to learn of the European Commission's proposals first-hand.[73]

The **Conference of Committee Chairs** was an informal body before being recognized by the Rules of procedure in 1993. Composed of the presidents of each permanent or temporary committee, it meets approximately once a month and may make recommendations to the Conference of Presidents regarding the work of the committees and the establishment of the agenda. Its president attends the Conference of Presidents. According to the Rules of procedure, the Bureau and the Conference of Presidents delegate certain tasks to the

Conference of Committee Chairs. The **Conference of Presidents of Delegations** is a replica of this body at the level of the inter-parliamentary delegations. These two bodies battle the effects of 'sectorization' which affect the activities of the EU's major institutions. Just as the various Council configurations and Commission DGs which tend to develop visions for specific actions and even advance some competing projects, the EP committees, and to a lesser extent its delegations, are also affected by these phenomena of specialization and competition that undermine the effectiveness, or even the consistency, of the Parliament's work. The Conference of Committee Chairs and the Conference of the Presidents of the Delegations are places of interface which permit the correction of centrifugal effects and ensure a better planning of Assembly's activities.

4.2.2 Functions and powers of the European Parliament

From the perspective of its functions and powers, the EP is no exception to the rule among the EU institutions: it is distinguished, like the Commission and the Council, by some originality. It has six main powers which correspond only partially to those of a national parliament, but which by far exceed those of the parliamentary assemblies of international organizations.[74]

1   The Parliament has always had a power of deliberation, which we can call a '**tribunitian power**', based on the right to adopt non-legislative resolutions (also called 'initiative resolutions'). Originally, due to the lack of other powers, the adoption of these resolutions was central to Parliament's deliberations. The EP still uses it today to express an opinion on internal EU issues, such as racism, the institutional future of the EU or the crisis of the eurozone; to take a position on international issues (conflicts, human rights violations, natural disasters); to make legislative proposals to the Commission; to speaking out about issues beyond its abilities (CFSP, Eurozone governance, Brexit, etc.) as well as to make constitutional proposals.[75] However, this role as a forum for expression tends to diminish as EP's legislative powers increase and weigh on its agenda.

2   The EP has significant **powers of control**. Since 1957, the Parliament can collectively censure the Commission during its term with a two-thirds majority of those voting, representing at least half of the members. The procedure has never succeeded and is in fact a poor instrument of control, since the EP has little interest to dismiss the Commission given that it has little control over the choice of a new college. Censorship is therefore the most conspicuous manifestation of the EP's significant power to control the Commission, but not the most important one. The Parliament's powers also include the right to question the Commission (and the Council); the

creation of temporary committees of inquiry; extensive budgetary control in collaboration with the European Court of Auditors (ECA) and the use of information from various sources (European Ombudsman, citizen petitions to Parliament, documents provided by interest groups, reports submitted by other institutions, public hearings, etc.). The Parliament also monitors executive tasks delegated to the Commission through the delegated act procedure and the examination procedure of the comitology.

3   With the Council, the EP is now the EU's **co-legislator** for the adoption of the vast majority of European laws. While its legislative power has long been anecdotal, it has grown considerably as a result of treaty reform and the evolution of inter-institutional relations. Today the Parliament has significant influence in the EU's decision-making system (see Box 4.6).[76] It co-legislates in all domains relevant to co-decision, which, after the Lisbon Treaty, became the ordinary legislative procedure applicable to most areas of EU competence, including the Common Agricultural Policy. In other cases, the Parliament has decision-making powers through other procedures, including principally consultation and assent (also known as the consent procedure). In the consultation process, now restricted to a limited number of issues of an intergovernmental nature, the Parliament can only issue a non-binding opinion. In the assent procedure, which applies mainly to international agreements and accession treaties, the Parliament must render, by a simple majority, a binding opinion but cannot propose amendments.

4   Regarding **budgetary matters**, since the Community is financed by its own resources and not only by Member State contributions (treaties of 1970 and 1975), the EP shares with the Council the power to amend, adopt and reject the draft budget prepared by the Commission. The Lisbon Treaty removed restrictions that applied to the Parliament's budgetary powers through the specious distinction of 'mandatory' and 'not mandatory' expenditures. Parliament now enjoys a power equal to that of the Council for all expenses; it anyway remains restricted by the ceiling that applies to the overall budget for expenses, by annual budget programming established by the European Council and its complete absence of power related to resources. However, its budgetary power allows the Parliament to influence EU policies by acting on their funding. Parliament is also responsible for ensuring the proper implementation of the EU budget through the process of 'budget discharge', which provides the Parliament with substantial information on EU policies and the activities of the Commission.

5   The Parliament has **powers of appointment**. Since the entry into force of the Treaty on the European Union (1 November 1993), it has already enjoyed a formal role in the Commission's appointment procedure by national governments. Today, the treaty provides that the Commission's president shall be chosen by the European Council based on the outcome of European

Box 4.6 Decision-making in the Parliament

In the EP, the adoption of a legislative text follows a very formal process with eight steps:

I   The proposal from the Commission is transmitted by the President of Parliament to the relevant parliamentary committee, which becomes the 'committee responsible', and eventually to other committees, 'for their opinion'. If there is a conflict over competence, for example the matter falls almost equally within the competences of two or more committees, several committees will be associated or joint meetings and votes will be organized.

II The committee responsible or the one asked for an opinion designates a rapporteur. Based on the model of 'continental' parliamentarism, the rapporteurs play a critical role in parliamentary work. In committee, they must prepare for the discussions, compose a draft report and modify it to reflect various positions. Groups that have not received the report follow it through their coordinator (the person responsible for the members of a group within a parliamentary committee) or a 'shadow rapporteur' (the member appointed by a group, who did not get the written version of the report, in order to follow its development).

III Open discussions with the MEPs are held during committee meetings following the oral presentation by the rapporteur's overview of the issue, which is informed by contact with the coordinators and shadow rapporteurs, Parliament officials, Commission officials responsible for the dossier, representatives of civil society, the research units of the EP, and possibly independent experts.

IV Once the report is written, it is translated and distributed to committee members.

V   The committee evokes the report a second time, which allows the rapporteur to change the text if necessary. A deadline for depositing amendments is fixed.

VI At the next meeting, the committee will vote on the amendments, then the points of the rapporteur's proposed resolution and finally, on the entire text.

VII After its adoption in committee, the report is translated, printed and distributed to all MEPs. It is then included on the plenary session agenda.

VIII The rapporteur presents the report to the Assembly. His or her presentation is followed by a relatively brief discussion of the text, involving speakers from each group and a limited number of MEPs. In general, the speaking time is limited and strictly controlled. Then the presentation of amendments takes place. The rapporteur gives an opinion on each on behalf of the parliamentary committee. The vote does not take place directly after the discussions but during a voting period when parliamentary participation is at its highest.

In case of the co-decision procedure, Parliament's vote only concludes the first reading. It allows the Council to define its common position. If it does not coincide with EP's vote, it is passed by the president of the assembly to the appropriate committee so that it can adopt a recommendation for the second reading.

elections and then has to be elected by a majority of the Parliament's members, i.e. currently 376 out of 751. Since the treaties do not, a priori, allow the MEPs to decide on the candidate, this was to remain a simple investiture. For the 2014 EP elections, the main European parties have however organized the campaign around a competition between their respective leaders, and then requested – and obtained – from the European Council the appointment of the leader of the winning party (J. C. Juncker, from the EPP) as President of the Commission. Despite its limitations, this new procedure reinforces the authority of the President of the Commission vis-à-vis the other Commissioners, national governments and public opinion. It also contributes to the politicization and dramatization of European elections, opening up the possibility of political alternation at the head of the Commission. After the election of the President, the Parliament then approves the College of Commissioners by a second vote (by a majority of voters), next to the individual audition of candidates by the relevant parliamentary committees. The Parliament also elects the European Ombudsman and participates in the appointment of other actors, such as the President of the European Central Bank or the members of the European Court of Auditors.

6 Regarding the **Common Foreign and Security Policy,** aspects of the policy of 'Justice and Home Affairs' and the **matters covered by the European Fiscal Compact**, the Parliament plays a more marginal role. The High Representative for Foreign Affairs and Security Policy informs and consults the Parliament on the main aspects and choices in foreign and security policy. It can only pose questions and make recommendations on the matter to both the High Representative and the Council.[77] Similarly, the European Parliament has no effective influence on most intergovernmental aspects of cooperation in criminal matters or on the governance of the eurozone and is granted no formal power by the Fiscal Compact.

Parliament's powers are distinguished from those of parliaments in advanced democracies in that it is not recognized as a sovereign institution, i.e. the only institution capable (with the people) of creating the law. In the EU, it is possible to adopt laws without the Parliament when it fails to take a position in the co-decision procedure or when the Council adopts decisions on intergovernmental matters. The Lisbon Treaty has nevertheless made a qualitative leap. It recognizes, for the first time, the cross-cutting and general powers of the Parliament: Article 11 of the Treaty on European Union states that it 'shall, jointly with the Council, exercise the legislative and budgetary functions'. The treaty also devotes a title to 'democratic principles': Article 10 states that 'the functioning of the Union is founded on representative democracy' and acknowledges the principle of a dual representation of citizens, directly, in Parliament, and indirectly, in the European Council and the Council.

4.2.3 The EP and the new 'Spitzenkandidaten' procedure for selecting the President of the Commission

As noted above, in 2014, the three main European political parties and the EP have succeeded in imposing the leader of the EPP as the new President of the Commission, through an audacious interpretation of the Lisbon treaty.[78] This event has affected relations between the EP and the Commission, but its medium-term impact, beyond configurations that rely heavily on interpersonal relations, will depend on a complex set of factors. The *entente cordiale* between Jean-Claude Juncker and his unfortunate S&D competitor Martin Schulz – who was re-elected President of the European Parliament after the 2014 elections – has indeed contributed greatly to the pacification of relations between the two institutions. The election of Antonio Tajani to head the Parliament in January 2017 may change the situation. In the longer term, it is not certain that the European Council will once again choose to accept the Parliament candidate in 2019 or allow him or her to be formalized in the context of treaty reform.

From a scientific point of view, the analysis is no less complex. The election of J. C. Juncker in 2014 can be analysed as a 'critical juncture', capable to provoke a major shift of the EU institutional balance and a strengthening of political contestation of the EU at the national level.[79] By reference to Article 10 TEU, a conflict of legitimacies exists between the EP, representing the citizens, and the European Council, representing the Member States, which led in 2014 to the victory of the first over the second. However, the *Spitzenkandidaten* procedure and the election of J. C. Juncker can also be regarded as the result of old practices and dynamics dominated by path dependency, which tend to irresistibly increase the involvement of the EP in the appointment of the Commission.

In any case it is, at least from a symbolic point of view, a new step in the process of parliamentarization of the EU political system. Even if the *Spitzenkandidaten* procedure does not fundamentally change the structure of the regime, it will have three medium-term consequences. First, it will necessarily impact groups and parties, and the relations between them. As we have seen, they adapt to the new procedure of *Spitzenkandidaten* by increasing their centralization and, if it is renewed in 2019, will certainly focus their campaigns on their candidate to the Presidency of the Commission. The procedure also modifies the relations between the political groups as we have seen with the 'block': the agreement between the groups EPP, S&D and ALDE on the programme proposed by J. C. Juncker goes indeed beyond what existed before, within the frame of the 'technical agreement' between the EPP and the S&D initiated at the end of the 1980s. During the first half of J. C. Juncker's term, those three groups have been quite supportive to the Commission, even if this has created tensions within the S&D and ALDE groups. The arrival of Antonio Tajani at the head of the European Parliament at the beginning of 2017, however, calls this arrangement into question.

Second, the reinforcement of the cleavage between Eurosceptical and pro-European parties within the EP is part of a wider movement of polarization of opinions and parties around European issues at the national level. The clarification in Strasbourg and Brussels is likely to fuel the electoral success of Eurosceptical parties in national elections or referendums. Finally, the *Spitzenkandidaten* experience will potentially increase the connexions between the Commission and the EP, at the expense of the Council and European Council.

From a political point of view, the 2014 European elections have already led to a new situation. The election of J. C. Juncker was admittedly the result of the European elections, but it nevertheless is part of a wider negotiation on the appointment of EU leaders, including the President of the EP. As soon as 20 June 2014, i.e. before the inaugural session of the newly elected Parliament, the German Chancellor Angela Merkel publicly called for the re-election of Martin Schulz as President of the assembly, by reference to an agreement between the CDU/CSU and the SPD. This claim resulted in the idea that the choice of the EP president should no longer be subject to a deal between the EPP and the S&D groups related to the internal organization of the assembly, but from a broader arrangement concerning all the leaders of the EU: President of the Commission, President of the European Council, High Representative of the EU and President of the EP. The price to pay for a greater involvement of the MEPs in the appointment of the President of the Commission was thus an intrusion of Member States' representatives in the choice of their own President.

At first, MEPs have strongly criticized that 'global' approach of EU leadership. However, the negotiations between the three main groups (EPP, S&D and ALDE) have quickly led to linking the two elections: socialist MEPs have thus accepted to support J. C. Juncker in exchange for the vote of EPP and ALDE members in favour of M. Schulz. On 1 July 2014, he was indeed re-elected at the first round, with a large majority (409 voices out of 612 valid votes). Two weeks after, J. C. Juncker was 'elected' with a majority of the same order (422 voices out of 729 valid votes).

It is on this occasion that the concept of 'block' appeared in the European jargon to qualify the new tripartite alliance between the groups EPP, S&D and ALDE, supporting both Juncker and Schulz. As said, we witnessed the emergence of a new logic: the election of the EP President does not result anymore from a deal between the two main groups, but of a wider negotiation, including the Liberals and even the Greens, that aims at finding a partisan balance at the level of the EU political system. Hence, the historical 'technical agreement' linking the EPP and the S&D since 1989 provides for a rule of alternation under which the EPP should have got the Presidency of the EP after the May 2014 elections. Also, for the very first time in the history of the EP, an outgoing President has been re-elected. Martin Schulz tried to avail himself of this arrangement for a third term as president in December 2016, but eventually turned it down in order to return to German political life. This decision opened a new sequence, already experimented with from 1999 to 2004: contrary to a practice established previously, the EPP and S&D groups both presented a candidate. Under the rule of alternation – which had experienced a glitch in 2014 when responding to a new logic of partisan balance of presidencies – the S&D group refused to rally behind the EPP candidate. It was therefore necessary to wait until the third ballot for the conservative Antonio Tajani to prevail over the socialist Gianni Pittella (291 against 199 votes).

The evolution of the European Parliament since May 2014 shows that the MEPs have now two options regarding their relations with the Commission that refer to two different institutional logics. The first one is a logic of independence, as part of the constitutional tradition of the EU and of the 'Community method'. The EP does not support the Commission, but screens all its legislative proposals in detail and exert a tight scrutiny on its activities. The second option is a logic of majority, in which the groups of the 'block' support the action of the Commission and develops strategies with it vis-à-vis the Council and European Council. This implies maintaining peaceful relations between the main political groups, which is not easy if we consider the ideological cleavages and the rivalries between individuals within the 'block'. The crises encountered by the EU since the end of the 2000s have, moreover, provoked profound divisions between the S&D and the EPP groups. For instance, in 2011, the EP legislative resolution on macroeconomic supervision was adopted by a right-wing coalition, the S&D voted against it. The same was true at the end of 2013 regarding the resolution calling for a strengthening of the internal services market. As for the motion for a resolution calling for better investor protection under the Transatlantic Treaty (TAFTA), it could not be adopted because of the opposition of the EPP Group.

4.2.4 The nature of the European Parliament: true Parliament or International Assembly?

Due to the nature of relations between the three vertices of the EU's institutional triangle, the Parliament has a margin of flexibility and influence that is much greater than its formal powers might make to believe. Above all, it enjoys a freedom of action that has nothing in common with the assemblies in parliamentary regimes and is more akin to that of the US Congress. The European Parliament does not, however, have the broad constitutional powers or the budgetary and human resources of the latter. As we will see, it faces also many constraints. Its autonomy follows in large part the skills and perseverance which the MEPs have demonstrated for 65 years in the organization of their work.[80]

The Parliament's powers have always depended on the MEPs' ability to organize their deliberations. Initially, before the Assembly had significant legislative powers, its influence stemmed in large part from its deliberative activity, that is to say, the adoption of declarative, non-binding resolutions. As a result of its tribunician power, its influence on Community action was certainly indirect, but more than what was formally provided for by the treaties.[81]

Even today, the question of the organization of Parliament's deliberations is crucial. Despite the dramatic evolution of its powers, it is still not designed to be sovereign: literally, the EP exercises the powers conferred upon it by the treaties. Beyond a fairly general definition of its functions (Article 14 TEU), no particular right is tied to its 'democratic' representativeness; thus, certain policies and jurisdictions escape it in part or almost completely. One must also note that some of its powers remain 'negative'. This means that they fall within its original function of control and limitation: the Parliament does not intervene so much to 'create' the law itself than to review the action of the Commission, amend its proposals and counterbalance the Council. In most cases, moreover, the EP only has influence if it acts, which means to manage the overcoming of its divisions and to meet the demands of majorities and deadlines set by the treaties. The absence of internal compromise decreases its influence on the elaboration of the budget and laws and in the following it cannot effectively exercise its oversight role or make its voice heard. It is therefore important that the MEPs find a balance in the organization of their deliberation between the freedom necessary to preserve the representativeness of their Assembly, and the indispensable rationalization for its active participation in the institutional functioning of the EU.

This difficulty is a result of the many constraints faced by the Parliament's deliberations which require constant redefinition of this aspired equilibrium. One can list five principles in this matter. The first set of constraints is related to the Assembly's supranational character which implies that it has 3 seats, 24 actual working languages (in contrast to what prevails in the Commission or the

COREPER) and a problematically high number of MEPs (over 750). Second, the Parliament suffers from the heterogeneity of European representation, be it a partisan (approximately 200 national parties are represented) and cultural point of view or in terms of the objectives, expectations, visions and logics of the MEPs actions. Third, the persistent 'second order' nature of European elections should be mentioned because it entails a significant abstention rate (especially as compared to national legislative elections), a rapid turnover of MEPs and a weak capacity of the elected to invoke their representative mandate in order to be heard by the Commission and Council. The hybrid nature of the entire EU regime also implies its share of difficulties. It induces complex and permanently changing relations between institutions that lack the partisan dimension and, further, does not allow the Parliament to benefit from significant support from the citizens. Finally, the EP must deal with structural constraints such as its lack of sovereignty (which implies that decisions can be made without it), the large number and sophistication of the texts submitted to it or the strict deadlines and overabundant majorities requested by the treaties for most of its legislative, budgetary and control activities.[82]

However, one need not stop at this bleak portrayal of the EP's situation. MEPs also have uncommon resources. First, they benefit from the 'youth' of the institution. The Assembly is a flexible and pragmatic organization not subject to historical and ceremonial stiffness which evolves always depending on the constraints, objectives and policy context. In this regard, the high turnover of MEPs has also its positive aspects: it induces creativity, flexibility and closer contact with the 'civil society', EU territories and citizens. Second, the EP has substantial organizational autonomy: its members are completely free to define the terms of their deliberation, their Rules of procedure, their work schedule and their agenda. They have incidentally mastered the art of using some powers to their own ends, to interpret new treaty provisions to their advantage and to leverage their formal powers to increase their overall influence. This has been once again illustrated at the occasion of the 2014, when MEPs imposed to the European Council the procedure of '*Spitzenkandidaten*' by relying on a very creative interpretation of the treaties. The Parliament also has a certain independence vis-à-vis national and European parties. MEPs use their powers with great freedom – as compared to their national counterparts – after open deliberations instead of the confrontation of fixed partisan positions or execution of external instructions. The EP does not, in fact, have to aid other institutions to implement a government programme (this was the case for a while with the Juncker Commission), but to control and influence their actions on a case-by-case basis, by making heard a different perspective: that of the 'people' or, according to the Lisbon Treaty, 'citizens'. To return to Bernard Manin's typology of the 'three ages' of representative government (parliamentarism of notables; party democracy; public democracy),[83] the EU seems to be in the first age whereby the

Parliament still has a central role and is not subject to the parties or deprived of its power to benefit the public and the media. Finally, the Assembly benefits from the sustainably dominant character of the divide between pro-and anti-Europeans which facilitates the 'centre coalition' between the pro-European groups (EPP, S&D, ALDE, Greens) to achieve the overabundant majorities required by the treaties.

Since the mid 1980s, MEPs have faced a steady increase in constraints as a result of several EU enlargements, the EU's augmented powers and the allocation of new competences to the Parliament. Anyway, they used their independence to regulate and rationalize their deliberations in an increasingly rigorous manner. This resulted indeed in a rise of the prerogatives of the political groups, the development of committee work and strengthening of the authority of its hierarchical bodies (President, Bureau and Conference of Presidents).[84] But the MEPs have nevertheless managed to preserve the central character of the deliberative logic in its overall functioning, even if the Plenary Assembly is far from conforming to the ideal of deliberative democracy.[85]

Notes

1 Mikko Mattila and Jan-Erik Lane, 'Why unanimity in the council? A roll call analysis of Council Voting,' *European Union Politics* 2(1) (2001): 31–52; Bjørn Høyland and Vibeke Wøien Hansen, 'Issue-specific policy-positions and voting in the council,' *European Union Politics* 15(1) (2014): 59–81.

2 Fiona Hayes-Renshaw and Helen S. Wallace, *The Council of Ministers* (London: Palgrave MacMillan, coll. 'The European Union series,' 2006).

3 On the Council Presidency, see Jelmer Schalk, René Torenvlied, Jeroen Weesie and Frans Stokman, 'The power of the presidency in EU council decision-making,' *European Union Politics* 8(2) (2007): 229–249; Jonas Tallberg, 'The agenda-shaping power of the EU council presidency,' *Journal of European Public Policy* 10(1) (2003): 1–19; Robert Thomson, 'The council presidency in the European Union. Responsibility with power,' *Journal of Common Market Studies* 46(3) (2008): 593–617; Peter Bursens and Steven Van Hecke, *Readjusting the Council Presidency: Belgian Leadership in the EU* (Brussels: ASP, 2011).

4 Andreas Warntjen, 'The rotating Council presidency hinders legislative continuity in the Council of the European Union,', http://blogs.lse.ac.uk/europpblog/2013/12/11/the-rotating-council-presidency-hinders-legislative-continuity-in-the-council-of-the-european-union/.

5 See Luciano Bardia and Eugenio Pizzimenti, 'Old logics for new games: the appointment of the EU's high representative for foreign affairs and security policy,' *Contemporary Italian Politics* 5(1) (2013): 55–70.

6 For an evaluation of the mandate held by Catherine Ashton, see: Niklas Helwig and Carolin Rüger, 'In search of a role for the high representative: The legacy of Catherine Ashton,' *The International Spectator* 49 (4) (2014) 1–17.

7 Article 236, Treaty on the Functioning of the European Union.

8 Edward Best, Thomas Christiansen and Pierpaolo Settembri, eds, *The Institutions of the Enlarged European Union: Continuity and Change* (Cheltenham: Edward Elgar Publishing, coll. 'Studies in EU reform and enlargement,' 2008); Martin Westlake and David Galloway, *The Council of the European Union* (London: John Harper Publishing, 2004).

9 Michel Mangenot, 'The invention and transformation of a governmental body: the Council Secretariat,' in *A Political Sociology of the European Union. Reassessing Constructivism*, eds Jay Rowell and Michel Mangenot (Manchester-New York: Manchester University Press, coll. 'Europe in Change,' 2010), 46–67.

10 Neill Nugent, *The Government and Politics of the European Union* (Basingstoke: Palgrave MacMillan, 7th ed., 2010), 147.

11 Jean-Paul Jacqué, 'The principle of institutional balance,' *Common Market Law Review,' 41 (2004) 383–391.

12 For a complete overview of all committee and working groups, see the frequently updated note of the Secretary General on 'The inventory of groups and committees involved in the preparatory work of the Council.'

13 The PCS is a permanent structure composed of the ambassadors of the 28 Member States and is formally under the control of the COREPER. As a result of Article 38 of the TEU, the PCS monitors the international situation in the domain of the CFSP, contributes to the definition of policies by issuing opinions to the Council and exercises political control and strategic direction of crisis management operations conducted by the EU.

14 Hayes-Renshaw and Wallace, *The Council of Ministers;* Jeffrey Lewis, 'Is the "Hard Bargaining" Image of the Council Misleading? The Committee of Permanent Representatives and the Local Elections Directive,' *Journal of Common Market Studies* 36(4) (1998): 479–504.

15 Birgit Hanny and Wolfgang Wessels, The Monetary Committee of the European Communities: A significant though not typical case. EU committees as influential policymakers (Aldershot, 1998, 109–126); Jolyon Howorth, The Political and Security Committee: A Case Study in 'Supranational Intergovernmentalism.' *The 'Community Method': Obstinate or Obsolete?*, 91–117; Uwe Puetter, 'Providing venues for contestation: the role of expert committees and informal dialogue among ministers in European Economic Policy Coordination,' *Comparative European Politics* 5(1) (2007): 18–35.

16 Jan Beyers and Guido Dierickx, 'The working groups of the council of the European union: supranational or intergovernmental negotiations?,' *Journal of Common Market Studies* 36(3) (1998): 289–317; Eve Fouilleux, Jacques de Maillard and Andy Smith, 'Council Working Groups: Their role in the production of European problems and policies,' in *Governance by Committee, the Role of Committees in European Policy-Making and Policy Implementation*, ed. Günther F. Schaefer (Maastricht: European Institute of Public Administration, 2002).

17 Article 155 of the EEC Treaty (1957). Alexander Ballmann, David Epstein and Sharyn O'Halloran, 'Delegation, comitology, and the separation of powers in the EU,' *International Organization* 56(3) (2002): 551–574.

18 Carl Fredrik Bergström, *Comitology: Delegation of Powers in the European Union and the Committee System* (Oxford: Oxford University Press, 2005); Thomas Christiansen and

Torbjorn Larsson,eds, *The Role of Committees in Policy-Process of the European Union: Legislation, Implementation and Deliberation* (Cheltenham/Northampton, Edward Elgar, 2007); Rhys Dogan, 'Comitology: Little procedures with big implications,' *West European Politics* 20(3) (1997): 31–60; Georg Haibach,'Council decision 1999/468—a new comitology decision for the 21st century!?,' *Eipascope* 3, 1999: 10–18; Wolfgang Wessels, 'Comitology: fusion in action. Politico-administrative trends in the EU system,' *Journal of European Public Policy* 5(2), (1998): 209–234.

19 Report from the Commission on the Working of Committees during 2011 (COM (2012) 685 final).

20 (EU) Rule no 182/2011 of the European Parliament and of the Council of 16 February 2011, establishing the rules and general principles concerning the mechanisms of control by the Member States for the exercise of implementing powers by the Commission, or Comitology Regulation.

21 There is also an 'urgency procedure' for immediately applicable implementing acts which allows a basic act to give the Commission the option to adopt immediately applicable implementing acts on imperative grounds of urgency. This 'urgency procedure' is not a separate comitology procedure, but rather a 'variant' of the examination or advisory procedure.

22 The regulatory procedure with scrutiny will still be used in the committees until July 2014.

23 CJ, 18 March 2014, Commission c. Parliament and Council, C-427/12 (ECLI:EU: C:2014:170).

24 Kathrin Böhling, 'Sidelined member states: commission-learning from experts in the face of comitology,' *Journal of European Integration* 36(2) (2014): 117–134; Katrijn Siderius and Gijs Jan Brandsma, 'The effect of removing voting rules: consultation practices in the commission's delegated act expert groups and comitology committees,' *Journal of Common Market Studies* 54(6) (2016): 1265–1279.

25 Rapport du Parlement européen, sur la procédure législative ordinaire, 4 juillet 2014—31 décembre 2016, PE 595.931

26 G. J. BRANDSMA, 'Responsabiliser la Commission européenne: la promesse des actes délégués,' *Revue Internationale des Sciences Administratives* 82(4) (2016): 695–712.

27 Thomas Christiansen, 'The Council of Ministers: Facilitating interaction and developing actorness in the EU,' in *European Union: Power and Policy-Making*, ed. Jeremy J. Richardson (London/New York: Routledge, coll. 'European public policy,' 2006), 147–170; Hayes-Renshaw and Wallace, *The Council of Ministers*.

28 Dennis Leech, 'Designing the voting system for the council of the European Union,' *Public Choice* 113(3–4) (2002): 437–464; Mikka Mattila and Jan-Erik Lane, 'Why Unanimity in the Council? A roll call analysis of council voting,' *European Union Politics* 2(1) (2001): 31–52.

29 There are a few special cases: if all the Member States do not take part in the vote, for example because some have an opt-out option, the decision is adopted if 55% of the participants, representing at least 65% of the population of participating Member States, vote in favour. Moreover, if the Council votes on a proposal which does not emanate from the Commission or the High Representative, this proposal is only adopted if 72% of the Member States, representing 65% of the EU population, are in favour.

30 Moreover, until 31 March 2017, a Member State may insist that in a particular vote, the Nice voting rules should still apply.

31 Renaud Dehousse, Florence Deloche-Gaudez, and Olivier Duhamel, eds, *Elargissement: Comment l'Europe s'adapte* (Paris: Presses de Sciences Po, coll. 'Evaluer l'Europe,' 2006).

32 Thomas Christiansen, 'The Council of Ministers: Facilitating interaction and developing actorness in the EU,' 147–170; Hayes-Renshaw and Wallace, *The Council of Ministers*.

33 Council of the EU, Règlement intérieur du Conseil—commentaire, Luxembourg: Office des publications de l'Union européenne, 2016, 119 p.

34 F. Deloche-Gaudez and L. Beaudonnet, 'Decision-Making in the Enlarged EU Council of Ministers: A Softer Consensus Norm as an Explanation for its Apparent Adaptability?,' Fifth Pan-European Conference on EU Politics Porto, Portugal, 23–26 June 2010.

35 Madeleine O. Hosli, Mikko Mattila and Marc Uriot, 'Voting in the Council of the European Union after the 2004 enlargement: a comparison of old and new member states,' *Journal of Common Market Studies* 49(6) (2011): 1249–1270.

36 VoteWatch, 'Agreeing to Disagree,' Votewatch Europe Annual Report 2012.

37 Javier Arregui and Robert Thomson, 'Domestic adjustment costs, interdependence and dissent in the Council of the European Union,' *European Journal of Political Research* 53(4) (2014): 692–708; Mikko Mattila, 'Contested decisions: empirical analysis of voting in the European Union Council of Ministers,' *European Journal of Political Research* 43(1) (2004): 29–50; Mikko Mattila, 'Roll call analysis of voting in the European Union Council of Ministers after the 2004 enlargement,' *European Journal of Political Research* 48(6) (2009): 840–857; Běla Plechanovová, 'The EU Council enlarged: North-south-east or core-periphery?,' *European Union Politics* 12(1) (2011): 87–106.

38 Stéphanie Novak, 'The silence of ministers: consensus and blame avoidance in the council of the European Union,' *Journal of Common Market Studies* 51(6) (2013): 1091–1107; Robert Thomson, *Resolving controversy in the European Union* (Cambridge: Cambridge University Press, 2011).

39 Bjørn Høyland and Vibeke Wøien Hansen, 'Issue-specific policy-positions and voting in the Council,' *European Union Politics* 15(1) (2014): 59–81.

40 Berthold Rittberger, *Building Europe's Parliament: Democratic Representation beyond the Nation-State* (Oxford/New York: Oxford University Press, 2005).

41 Yves Mény, ed., *La construction d'un parlement: 50 ans d'histoire du Parlement européen: 1958–2008* (Luxembourg: Publications Office of the European Union, coll. '50ᵉ anniversaire du Parlement européen' 2009), 90; Marc Abélès, *La vie quotidienne au Parlement européen* (Paris: Hachette, 1992), 70.

42 Abélès, *La vie quotidienne au Parlement européen*, 71.

43 Olivier Costa, *Le Parlement européen, assemblée délibérante* (Brussels: Éd. de l'Université de Bruxelles, coll. 'Études européennes,' 2001); David Judge and David Earnshaw, *The European Parliament* (Basingstoke/New York: Palgrave MacMillan, 2nd ed., 2008).

44 Abélès, *La vie quotidienne au Parlement européen*, 151.

45 Richard Corbett, Francis Jacobs and Michael Shackleton, *The European Parliament* (London: J. Harper, 7th ed., 2007), 71–75; Simon Hix, Amie Kreppel and Abdul Noury, 'The party system in the European Parliament: collusive or competitive?,' *Journal of Common Market Studies* 41(2) (2003): 309–331.

46 Costa and Saint Martin, *Le Parlement européen*, 34.

47 Whereas in 1979, the two largest groups (EPP and PES) together represented 53.4% of the MEPs, they accounted for 61% of the MEPs after the 2009 elections. See Steven Van Hecke, 'Democracy, Power and Europarties: plus ça change, plus ça reste la même chose,' (paper to the 'Conférence Élections 2009: Challenges pour un système politique européen,' Luxemburg University, December 11–12, 2009.

48 Corbett, Jacobs and Shackleton, *The European Parliament*, 2007, 71–75; Pascal Delwit and Jean-Michel De Waele, 'Les élections européennes et l'évolution des groupes politiques au Parlement européen,' in *Démocratie et construction européenne*, ed. Mario Telò (Brussels: Éd. de l'Université de Bruxelles, coll. 'Études européennes,' 1995), 277–291.

49 Olivier Rozenberg, 'L'influence du Parlement européen et l'indifférence de ses électeurs: une corrélation fallacieuse?,' *Politique européenne* 28 (2009): 23.

50 Nathalie Brack, 'The roles of Eurosceptic Members of the European Parliament and their implications for the EU,' *International Political Science Review*, 36(3) (2015): 337–350; Simon Otjes, Harmen and van der Veer, 'The Eurozone crisis and the European Parliament's changing lines of conflict,' *European Union Politics*, 17(2) (2016): 242–261 DOI 1465116515622567.

51 Simon Hix, Abdul G. Noury and Gérard Roland, *Democratic Politics in the European Parliament* (Cambridge: Cambridge University Press, 2007).

52 Richard Corbett, Francis Jacobs and Michael Shackleton, *The European Parliament* (London: J. Harper, 7th ed., 2007).

53 Martin Westlake, *A Modern Guide to the European Parliament* (London: Pinter, 1994).

54 Richard Corbett, *The European Parliament's Role in Closer EU Integration* (Houndmills/ Basingstoke/Hampshire/New York: Macmillan Press/St. Martin's Press, 1998); Simon Hix and Chris Lord, *Political Parties in the European Union* (Basingstoke: Macmillan, coll. 'The European Union series,' 1997); Hix, Noury and Roland, *Democratic Politics in the European Parliament*; Amie Kreppel and George Tsebelis, 'Coalition Formation in the European Parliament,' *Comparative Political Studies* 32(8) (1999): 933–966.

55 [www.votewatch.eu/]. See also: Pierpaolo Settembri, 'Is the European Parliament competitive or consensual. . . and why bother?' (Paper presented at the Conference 'The European Parliament and the European Political Space,' Federal Trust, Berlin, 2006); Pierpaolo Settembri and Christine Neuhold, 'Achieving consensus through committees: does the European parliament manage?,' *Journal of Common Market Studies* 4(1) (2009): 127–151.

56 VoteWatch, 'The make up and break-up of the EU governing coalition'?, 27 February 2015.

57 Amie Kreppel, *The European Parliament and the Supranational Party System: A Study in Institutional Development* (Cambridge: Cambridge University Press, coll. 'Cambridge studies in comparative politics,' 2002); Hix, Noury and Roland, *Democratic Politics in the European Parliament*.

58 Almost all studies on the behaviour of MEPs and the cohesion of the EP's political groups have been based on the analysis of roll-call votes, the methodological limits and faults of which are well known. See among others: Bernard Steunenberg and Jacques Thomassen, eds, *The European Parliament: Moving Toward Democracy in the EU* (Lanham/Oxford: Rowman & Littlefield, coll. 'Governance in Europe,' 2002).

59 Olivier Costa, 'Équilibres partisans et comportement parlementaire dans l'Union à vingt-cinq: le Parlement européen entre continuité et bipolarisation,' in *Dynamiques et résistances politiques dans le nouvel espace européen*, eds Elisabeth du Réau, Christine Manigand and Traian Sandu (Paris: l'Harmattan, 2005), 154.

60 Robert Ladrech, 'Political parties in the European Parliament,' in *Political Parties in the European Union*, ed. John Gaffney (London/New York: Routledge, 1996), 293–294.

61 The absence of a strong connection between the MEPs and their electoral accountability has resulted from this division of labour, their activities not serving as the first criteria for reselection or re-election of MEPs. Judge and Earnshaw, *The European Parliament*, 117; Hix, Noury and Roland, *Democratic Politics in the European* Parliament, 28.

62 Abélès, *La vie quotidienne au Parlement européen*, 148.

63 Olivier Costa and Olivier Rozenberg, 'Parlementarisme,' in *Science politique de l'Union européenne*, eds Céline Belot, Paul Magnette and Sabine Saurugger (Paris: Economica, coll. 'Études politiques,' 2008), 254.

64 Corbett, Jacobs and Shackleton, *The European Parliament*, 2005; Judge and Earnshaw, *The European Parliament*.

65 Abélès, *La vie quotidienne au Parlement européen*, 148; Tim Bale and Paul Taggart, 'Finding Their Way: The Socialisation of Freshmen MEPs in the European Parliament,' (Paper presented at the 'European Union Studies Association (EUSA)' conference, Austin, Texas, 31 March to 2 April 2005), 1–22.

66 Luciano Bardi, 'Transnational Party Federation, European Parliamentary Party Groups and the Building of Europarties,' in *How Parties Organize: Change and Adaptation in Party Organization in Western Democracies*, eds Richard S. Katz and Peter Mair (London: Sage Publications, 1994), 361–364; Knut Heidar and Ruud Koole, eds, *Parliamentary Party Groups in European Democracies: Political Parties Behind Closed Doors* (London/New York: Routledge, 2000); Simon Hix, *The Political System of the European Union* (Basingstoke/New York: Palgrave Macmillan, 2nd ed., 2005), 186–190; Virginie Mamadouh and Tapio Raunio, 'The Committee System: powers, appointments and report allocation,' *Journal of Common Market Studies* 41(2) (2003): 333–351; Shaun Bowler and David M. Farrell, 'The organizing of the European Parliament: committees, specialization and coordination,' *British Journal of Political Science* 25(2) (1995): 219–243.

67 Unlike the other Europarties, members of the EAF are only individuals and not national parties.

68 The latest reform: Regulation No 1141/2014 of the European Parliament and of the Council, 22 October 2014, on the regulations governing the financing of European political parties and political foundations, Official Journal L317/1.

69 Hermann Schmitt, Sara Hobolt and Sebastian Adrian Popa, 'Does personalization increase turnout? Spitzenkandidaten in the 2014 European Parliament elections,' *European Union Politics* 16(3) (2015): 347–368.

70 Richard Whitaker, *The European Parliament's Committees. National Party Influence and Legislative Empowerment* (London: Routledge, 2011); Cristina Fasone, *Sistemi di commissioni parlamentari e forme di governo* (Padova: Cedam, 2012).

71 Thomas Christiansen and Emil J. Kirchner, *Committee Governance in the European Union* (Manchester: Manchester University Press, 2000); Morton Egeberg, *An organisational approach to European Integration—What organisations tells us about system transformation*,

committee governance and Commission decision making (University of Oslo: ARENA Working papers, 19, 2002).

72 Olivier Costa, 'The President of the European Parliament,' *Il Filangieri*, vol. 2012–2013, 'Le trasformazioni del ruolo dei Presidenti delle Camere,' ed. Jovene, Naples (2013), 143–160.

73 Corbett, Jacobs and Shackleton, *The European Parliament*, 2007, 101.

74 Y. Mény, *La construction d'un parlement: 50 ans d'histoire du Parlement européen: 1958–2008.*

75 Since 1984, the EP has adopted six significant reports proposing draft constitutions or calling for the adoption of a constitution, which had an indirect impact on treaty reform and the work of the Convention.

76 Olivier Costa, 'The European Parliament and the Community Method,' in *The 'Community Method'. Obstinate or Obsolete?*, ed. Renaud Dehousse (Basingstoke: Palgrave, coll. 'Studies in European Union Politics,' 2011), 60–75.

77 Article 36 TEU.

78 Sara B Hobolt, 'A vote for the president? The role of Spitzenkandidaten in the 2014 European parliament elections,' *Journal of European Public Policy* 21(10) (2014): 1528–1540; Peñalver García, Nereo and Priestley, Julian, *The Making of a European President* (London: Palgrave, 2015); Fabbrini, Sergio, *Which European Union? Europe After the Euro Crisis* (Cambridge: Cambridge University Press, 2015).

79 Ruth Collier and David Collier, 'Critical Junctures and Historical Legacies,' *Shaping the Political Arena; Critical Junctures, The Labor Movement, and Regime Dynamics in Latin America* (Princeton: Princeton University Press, 1991).

80 Judge and Earnshaw, *The European Parliament*; Corbett, Jacobs and Shackleton, *The European Parliament*, 2007.

81 Costa, *Le Parlement européen, assemblée délibérante.*

82 Corbett, Jacobs and Shackleton, *The European Parliament*, 2011; Judge and Earnshaw, *The European Parliament*, 2008.

83 Bernard Manin, *The Principles of Representative Government* (Cambridge: Cambridge University Press, 1997).

84 Nathalie Brack, Olivier Costa and Clarissa Dri, 'Le Parlement européen à la recherche de l'efficacité législative : Une analyse des évolutions de son organisation,' Bruges Political Research Papers, College of Europe, Bruges, no 39, 2015, 47 p.

85 Costa, *Le Parlement européen, assemblée délibérante.*

Organs of control 5

To be effective and legitimate, decision-making processes need to be supervised by bodies of control, i.e. independent authorities who monitor the responsibilities and activities of EU institutions but also of Member States and ensure that all actors in the EU respect the treaties, secondary legislation and internal rules of the institutions. In this chapter, we will briefly present the four organs of control in the EU: the Court of Justice ensures that European treaties and laws are applied uniformly in all Member States and gives independent rulings; the Court of Auditors monitors the EU budget; the European Ombudsman investigates complaints about maladministration in the institutions and bodies of the Union; and the European Anti-fraud Office, or OLAF, investigates fraud against the EU budget as well as corruption and misconduct within the European institutions.

5.1 The Court of Justice of the European Union

The Court of Justice of the European Union includes the Court of Justice itself, the General Court (previously known as the Court of First Instance) and the specialized courts.[1] In general, it ensures compliance with primary legislation (treaties) as well as secondary legislation (standards adopted by EU institutions) and monitors the legality of the acts of the Council, Commission and the European Central Bank (other than recommendations and opinions) as well as the acts of the Parliament and the European Council (and of the EU's bodies and agencies) that produce legal effects against third parties.[2]

5.1.1 Composition and powers

The Court of Justice is based in Luxembourg. It is composed of one judge per Member State. Since the Lisbon Treaty, the suitability of the candidates has to be evaluated by a panel of seven members, consisting of former EU and national Supreme Court judges and legal experts, one of whom is proposed by the EP. In practice however, Member States remain free to choose their judges. The Court designates a president from amongst these judges for a three year, renewable term. Judges are assisted by legal secretaries (three each) and by Advocates-General appointed by the Member States, from whom they are also independent. Both the judges and the Advocates-General are appointed for a term of six years that may be renewed.

Since the Lisbon Treaty's entry into force, the Court has jurisdiction over all EU policies. Before that, most of the activities that the EU institutions developed outside the Community pillar were beyond the Court's jurisdiction. Several types of appeal (infringement, annulment, failure to fulfil an obligation, preliminary ruling procedure, etc.) are available, as appropriate, to Member States, EU institutions and 'any natural or legal person' (with significant restrictions). Through these various procedures the Court helps guarantee that all relevant actors (institutions, states, governments, economic and social actors, etc.) comply with European law.

Since the Single Act, the Court of Justice is assisted by a General Court responsible for minor cases, which can be appealed on points of law before the Court of Justice. The General Court is composed of 47 judges; in 2019, this number will be increased to 56 (2 judges from each EU country).

There is no Advocate-General in the General Court but, if necessary, a judge can assume the role and does not take part in the judgment of the case under consideration. This court is responsible for matters that are generally more routine in nature. The division of labour between the Court of Justice and the General Court is as follows: the Court of Justice generally considers the failures of Member States to fulfil obligations, most preliminary rulings, and appeals against General Court decisions on direct actions. The General Court deals with annulments, failures to act, disputes relating to compensation for non-contractual liability and appeals from the European Union Civil Service Tribunal.

5.1.2 The role of the Court in EU integration

Since the 1960s, the Court has played a fundamental role in the integration process and is now a key player in the functioning of the EU.[3] Originally created to protect Member States and their citizens from the actions and any excesses of the High Authority (as an Administrative Court)[4] and to mediate disputes between Member State governments (as an International Court), it used its power of Community law interpretation (in the manner of a Constitutional Court) to render judgments that were quite audacious in their interpretation of treaties, especially from 1957 to 1990.[5] In doing so, it helped forge a comprehensive and quasi-federal legal order which is the basis of European integration.[6]

Indeed, the Court has gone far beyond the technical and grammatical interpretation of written rules. It has mobilized its power to give Community law
constitutional force, establish the key principles of European order, advance
integration and stimulate the development of new policies when the Council
and the Commission were relatively inactive. Although at first the judges were
fairly cautious, they later showed strong activism,[7] especially through the means
of preliminary rulings which allow a national jurisdiction to refer a case to the
Court of Justice so that it can interpret Community law without judging on the
merits of the case.[8]

An overview of legal integration

Over time, the Court progressively strengthened the status of EU law through
the establishment of two principles: the direct effect (or direct applicability)
of EU law and its primacy over national laws. The Van Gend en Loos (ECJ
26/62) decision allowed the Court to constitutionalize European law by
establishing that treaties confer rights and obligations not only to Member
States but also to their citizens, a fact that national courts have to recognize
and enforce. It extended the 'direct effect' principle of European law through
other decisions in the following years, so that it applies today to most provisions of the treaties but also to most secondary legislation. The Costa v. ENEL
(ECJ 6/64) case allowed the Court to establish the principle of 'primacy' of
European law over national law; in so doing, it created a hierarchy of norms
in the Community and established itself as a Constitutional Court.[9] Since
then, when a conflict arises between national and European laws, national
courts have to apply EU law, even if it contradicts provisions of the national
constitution. This principle is vital for the functioning of the EU as without
it, Member States could disregard all EU laws that are inconvenient to them
or even adopt contrary national standards, and a uniform EU legal order
would be impossible. Since the Lisbon Treaty, this principle is explicitly mentioned in the treaties (declaration n°17).

In the 1980s, the increased complexity of the European system led to many
disputes between European institutions that the Court had to arbitrate. By doing
so, it clarified the powers and functioning of the EU institutions. It ruled that
institutions should provide a legal justification for drafting European legislation
(ECJ 45/86 Commission v. Council). This reduced the scale of action of institutions that had, in the past, opted for the legal basis most conducive to achieving
their own political objectives. The Court also and especially upheld the rights
of the EP by establishing that it was obligatory to consult it when provided for
by the treaty (Isoglucose case, ECJ 138/79), even if its opinions were not binding, and by recognizing the EP's right to submit a case to the Court, despite the
silence of the treaties in this regard (ECJ 294/83 Greens).[10] Similarly, the Court

reinforced the power of EU institutions vis-à-vis non-EU companies as it ruled that they could take legal actions against them if certain conditions were met (Wood Pulp case, Joined Cases 89, 104, 114–117, 125–129/85).

The Court also strengthened EU policy competences in key areas such as social policy and stimulated development of new policies, for example, on gender equality. Through numerous rulings, it pushed Member States to coordinate their policies and even harmonize some of their practices (see for instance ECJ 80/70 Defrenne I; ECJ 43/75 Defrenne II ECJ 262/88 Barber v. Royal Exchange Assurance). More recently, the Court's rulings have greatly influenced national healthcare systems. Through several cases, it has defined the maximum allowable working hours for doctors in Europe and has defined patients' rights, such as the right to seek non-emergency health care across borders (Kholl v. Union des Caisses de Maladie, Case C- 158/96; Decker v. Caisse de Maladie des Employés Privés, Case C 120/95; Yvonne Watts v. Bedford Primary Care Trust, Case C 372/04).

Finally, it played a major role in the promotion of the 'four freedoms' that are the cornerstone of the single market (free movement of people, goods, services and capital) and in the liberalization of the trade of goods at a time when the Council was not very active (ECJ 8/74 Dassonville).[11] The Cassis de Dijon Case (ECJ 120/78) for instance established the famous principle of 'mutual recognition', i.e. a product lawfully produced and marketed in one Member State has to be accepted in another Member State, and greatly facilitated intra-EU trade while reducing the need to legislate in order to harmonize standards. The Court also extended EU policy competences in the internal market with the Nouvelles Frontières case (Joined cases 209–213/84) in 1986 for example, which allowed for the deregulation of air transport, and the case Spain, Belgium and Italy v. Commission (Joined cases 271, 281 and 289/90), which extended the Commission's powers in matters of competition policy to the ability to break monopolies. In more recent rulings, the Court once again took highly controversial positions when national systems of industrial relations were in conflict with the right of free movement of services within the internal market (see Case C 341/05, known as the Laval case; Case C 346/06, known as the Rüffert case and Case C 438/05 known as the Viking case).

The Court has therefore promoted negative integration, by limiting the capacity of Member States' regulation in the internal market as well as positive integration by promoting the adoption of common standards in a range of policy areas.[12]

A government by the judges?

The ambitious and controversial legal doctrines of the European Court of Justice have led some scholars to examine the 'judicialization of politics'[13] in the EU and its consequences.

Overall, the judicialization of politics has had differentiated results. In some areas, it has prompted institutions to legislate; the judgments regarding gender equality for example have contributed to the adoption of directives on working hours and equal treatment. In other cases, the Court's activism has sharpened the vigilance of national governments. They have attempted to reverse the effects of certain decisions through treaty reforms and have taken care to limit the Court's freedom of interpretation by surrounding certain provisions with multiple precautions.[14]

In any case, the often-criticized European 'government of judges', or juristocracy, does not have absolute power. It is true that Member States have little ability to retaliate against the Court (other than an unlikely treaty reform), because of the considerable independence of its members, and that they have found it difficult to constrain the powers of the Court.[15] But we must also remember that the Court's actions are not one-sided and often protect Member State interests. As noted by Carruba and his colleagues, the case-law of the Court has certainly favoured greater integration, but this development tended to match the preferences of the governments rather than oppose them.[16] Additionally, the Court does not control the cases brought before it: it cannot self-refer a case and must wait for the actors to take action. Moreover, it needs a treaty or legislative base upon which to act. As Wincott explained, the Court cannot, in itself, create a fully-fledged policy and its rulings should be seen rather as a provocation for further legislation.[17] It also lacks the means to implement its own judgments and therefore must rely on national courts. If lower national courts have emerged as crucial partners of the European Court over time, some national courts, especially higher ones, have proved reluctant to accept the rulings of the European Court of Justice and resisted unwelcome doctrine, in particular the principles of direct effect and of the rule of European law.[18] Moreover, national courts have considerable discretion in the concrete applications of the European Court's rulings, which may circumvent the practical effect of its case law.[19] Finally, as Kelemen noted, the judicialization of politics may have a positive impact in the European context. He argues that the growing role of courts in the policy-making process does not render this process less democratic as it rather pushes Member States to increase the transparency, legal certainty and access to justice at the national level: 'By emphasizing transparency, accountability and individual rights, European law is enhancing opportunities for public participation in governance and thus promises to improve the quality of democracy across Europe'.[20]

However, in recent years, the Court's judges, aware of the negative reactions within national governments or even among the general public (i.e. the Bosman verdict ECJ 415/93),[21] have become more vigilant in their decisions. In the years to come, they are likely to remain cautious as a result of the overall reluctance towards European integration, of the expected increase of vertical conflicts (with, in particular, recognition of the right of national parliaments to submit cases to the Court to enforce the principle of subsidiarity by the Lisbon Treaty) as well as of the traditional reluctance of the Court to resolve political disputes.[22]

5.2 The Court of Auditors

The EU's Court of Auditors was created by the Treaty of 1975 but it is only with the Maastricht Treaty that it became a fully-fledged Community institution. It is based in Luxembourg and is composed of one member per country. Members of the Court of Auditors must belong or have belonged to an external audit body at the national level or have the appropriate expertise. They are appointed by the Council, under the qualified-majority voting system after consultation of the European Parliament. The latter very quickly established the habit of holding hearings of the candidates before the budgetary control committee. However, its power is relatively limited and cannot be compared with the nomination of the College of Commissioners. Indeed, on several occasions, the Parliament expressed reservations or rejected candidates but the Council did not usually take this into account. There are two exceptions though: the first in 1989, when the EP rejected the Greek and the French candidate, leading to France proposing a new name. The second was in 2004 when after a negative vote in the budgetary control committee, the Cypriot candidate withdrew his name from consideration.

The Court of Auditors is responsible for the external audit of the EU general budget as well as of some financial transactions such as aid to developing countries. It monitors the EU's financial operations and oversees the management of its finances. It assists the Council and the Parliament in their powers of control over the Commission's budget implementation by preparing an annual report and providing them with the information necessary for their supervision. It also delivers special reports and opinions and EU institutions may ask the Court to submit an opinion on a topic. The information provided by the Court of Auditors plays an essential role in the budgetary 'discharge' procedure, that is to say, the validation by the Parliament of the implementation of the previous year's budget (see Box 5.1). It should be remembered that it is partly because of its lax financial management (pointed out by the Court of Auditors) that the College of Commissioners was forced to resign in 1999, after threats from the EP to vote a censure of the college.

The Court provides the EP with all the material it needs to exercise the discharge procedure in a way that has reinforced its control over the Commission. Therefore, Member States that are net contributors to the EU budget, argue for increased control over the Court of Auditors on the use of EU funds in both the EU and in outside countries.[23] In recent years, the Court has adopted a more

Box 5.1 The budgetary discharge procedure

The financial controllers of the Commission perform an internal audit, draw up an analysis of the financial year, a financial statement of the assets and liabilities of the EU and explain how the budget has been implemented. The Commission must deliver this documentation to the Council, the Parliament and the Court of Auditors by 1 June of each year.

The Court performs its external audit on the basis of these documents and of its own investigations (including on-the-spot investigations). It remains in close contact with the national audit bodies and agencies as well as with the EU institutions. The Court transmits to all relevant institutions any comments that it intends to include in its report and to which the institution may want to reply. After receiving the replies, the Court issues the final version of its annual report and sends it to the other EU institutions by 30 November.

The Council then sends its recommendation to the Parliament which is supposed to give discharge to the Commission for its implementation of the budget by 30 April.

political approach to its work by demonstrating its claims to define broad principles of good budgetary governance and by demanding an increasing number of documents and more information from the European institutions. This approach has created considerable reluctance within the Commission, where the Court is considered to be trying to overstretch its powers. But so far, the ability of the Court to perform its various oversight functions remains limited by its small staff of 900 people, with only 400 directly involved in audit duties who can thus only examine a small proportion of EU expenditure.[24]

5.3 The European Ombudsman

The European Ombudsman was established by the Maastricht Treaty in an effort to increase the democratic guarantees offered by the EU. He or she is elected by the Parliament for a five-year term, renewable. Acting at 'the intersection of a parliamentary review committee and a quasi-judicial institution',[25] the Ombudsman is responsible for monitoring and investigating complaints about maladministration in the institutions and bodies of the European Union, such as administrative irregularities, unfairness, discrimination, abuse of power, failure to reply, refusal of information, unnecessary delay, etc. He or she can act on his or her own initiative or at the request of a citizen, a company or association based in the EU. Since 1996, he or she can rely on the European Network of Ombudsmen, consisting of over 90 offices in 32 European countries. The network includes the European Ombudsman him or herself, national and regional ombudsmen and similar bodies of the Member States as well as of the candidate countries for EU membership and other European Economic Area countries, and finally the Committee on Petitions of the European Parliament.

Each year the Ombudsman receives on average more than 2,000 complaints generally concerning alleged maladministration of the Commission. He or she is able to assist petitioners in approximately 70 per cent of cases.[26] In 2014, the Ombudsman Emilie O'Reilly, registered 2,079 complaints. The office of the Ombudsman opened 325 inquiries and closed 387 inquiries over the course of the year. It also handled 1,823 information requests. Most (87 per cent) of the complaints came from EU citizens and 59.6 per cent concerned the Commission, compared to 13.4 per cent for EU agencies and 9.4 per cent for the European Personnel Selection Office (EPSO).[27]

While he or she is able to make the process of EU policy more open, his or her impact is often considered to be relatively marginal.[28] His or her sphere of competence is limited: he/she cannot investigate complaints against national, regional or local administrations of Member States which have their own national ombudsmen. However, a recent study has shown that the impact of the Ombudsman is far from negligible, and that he/she has contributed to significantly improving the accountability and transparency of EU institutions.[29] Thus, in most cases his/her investigations lead to an improvement of the practices of the European administration. In more than half the cases, EU institutions tend to respond positively to the Ombudsman's recommendations and adopt new practices in order to better meet the requirements of transparency and accountability in their activities.[30]

5.4 The European Anti-Fraud Office (OLAF)

The European Anti-Fraud Office, or OLAF (from the French: Office de Lutte Anti-Fraude), was created in 1999 as a result of a new concern for the prevention and repression of fraud and other illegal activities detrimental to the EU's financial interests. The actors of the EU started to consider that fraud and corruption were of direct concern when the Community institutions were granted their 'own resources' in the 1970s. A first initiative was taken by the Commission in 1987, with the creation of a Task Force for the Co-ordination of Fraud Prevention (UCLAF) that was divided into 'anti-fraud units' within four DGs of the Commission.[31] In 1995, it was placed under the responsibility of the Commissioner in charge of Financial Control. Its efficiency was nevertheless criticized; in 1996, the investigation committee on the Common Transit Regime created by the Parliament underlined the failures in UCLAF's activities of control and concluded that it was unable to fight against irregularities within the European institutions. On 15 March 1999, the day after the resignation of the College of Commissioners because of severe accusations of mismanagement and misconduct of some commissioners and services, the Anti-Fraud Office was set up.

Today, OLAF is a General Service of the Commission, under the responsibility of the Commissioner in charge of the budget and human resources. It is an administrative investigative body: it has no judicial or disciplinary powers and it cannot oblige national prosecutors to act. It however enjoys full independence for its investigations. OLAF's power and functional independence have been much extended, compared to UCLAF, but its statute and institutional environment are still ambiguous.

Some authors, as well as European and national MPs, have denounced its limitations and called for a stronger organ. However, its hybrid statute also allows OLAF to get administrative and logistical support from the Commission and to influence it in the development of anti-fraud legislation that applies to EU institutions as well as to all actors involved in EU policies and funding. Also, even if OLAF is administratively part of the Commission, it is fully independent and works under the sole authority of its Director-General – currently Giovanni Kessler, former Italian anti-fraud chief. It is even entitled to bring an action against the Commission before the Court of Justice. OLAF has 160 investigators and a total of around 422 staff members (in March 2017), among which two-thirds are lawyers and accountants working on fraud investigations.

OLAF is called to protect the financial interests of the EU. Concretely, it fights fraud affecting the EU budget, as well as corruption and any other irregular activity within the EU institutions. To do so, it conducts internal and external investigations, plays a role in the coordination of the competent authorities of the Member States and provides them with technical support. More generally, OLAF contributes to the anti-fraud strategy of the EU and can even take initiatives to strengthen EU legislation in this field.

OLAF's investigations mainly concern cases of fraud and professional misconduct. Regarding the former, it has been very active in fighting irregular use of EU funds for projects in areas such as external aid (illegal uses), agriculture (non-existent agricultural products) and environment, against evasion of customs duties and taxes by importers, and against smuggling (cigarettes, alcohol, etc.) by organized crime groups. Regarding cases of professional misconduct, OLAF has focused on irregularities in tender procedures, conflicts of interest, and leaking of information for EU recruitment exams.

From its creation to the end of 2011, OLAF has completed 3,500 investigations. As a result, 335 individuals have received prison sentences totalling 900 years.[32] In 2015, irregularities represented around 3.8 per cent of total EU expenditure, i.e. 5.5 billion euros. Recovery rate of unduly used sums was more than 50 per cent.

OLAF went through a reorganization in 2012. Its structure and powers did not change, but internal reform made it more effective: OLAF has increased the number of open investigations by 86 per cent, the number of investigations closed by 93 per cent, and makes 83 per cent more recommendations.[33] In 2015 OLAF opened 219 new investigations, closed 304, issued 364 recommendations and recommended the recovery of 888 million euros. It also appears that the surveys contribute to a greater efficiency of European funds. OLAF also provides advice to national authorities, for example in the fight against smuggling of products such as cigarettes. It has also supported the Union's institutions in setting up a legal framework to better protect the EU's budget. Recently, OLAF has made several media headlines. In 2016, it dismantled a large, illegal criminal network of clothing and footwear from China to the United Kingdom, and demanded that the UK government repay €2 billion of non-country duties. OLAF also contributed, at the same time, to the investigation into the misappropriations of Members of the National Front in the employment of parliamentary assistants.

Despite this, experts and politicians have always been quite critical of OLAF, underlining its limited capacity to pursue fraud and misadministration. According to them, the organ suffers from several shortcomings. First, it faces problems of international judicial cooperation, which is far beyond its scope. Second, it has to deal with very different national legislations on the definitions of the most current types of corruption offences. Finally, OLAF has no judicial capacity and national authorities tend to regard it as an ordinary service within the Commission.

During discussions on the annual report of the Supervisory Committee of OLAF (a body of four independent experts which monitors it) by the Budget Control Committee of the European Parliament, MEPs are often quite critical of its methods and lack of independence from the Commission. OLAF has also been criticized for its excesses in the way it uses its competences. After its creation, MEPs protested the idea that OLAF could investigate the EP, because of the principle of parliamentary immunity. In March 2011, MEPs objected to the action of OLAF in the 'cash-for-amendments' scandal that followed the announcement by the *Sunday Times* that three MEPs agreed to table amendments in exchange for money. The President of the EP, after a period of hesitations, invited OLAF to investigate the allegations in the Parliament.

In April 2013, OLAF was accused by its Supervisory Committee of having violated its mandate and broken EU laws in its 'Dalligate' probe – a four-month investigation conducted in 2012 which led to the removal of EU Health Commissioner John Dalli over allegations that he solicited a €60 million bribe from a tobacco firm. OLAF was accused of having conducted unlawful interrogations in Malta, of having intercepted a private telephone conversation, of having involved the help of Maltese authorities without a proper legal basis and of having overlooked the legality of its actions in order to speed up the process. OLAF was also blamed for using the Commission as the main source of information to launch the proceedings, in violation of its duty to remain independent from it.

More generally, OLAF is accused of failing to carry out its investigations adequately and therefore of seeing its findings ignored by many Member States. Indeed, these do not always see sufficient foundations in the decisions, and are often not in a hurry to recover funds which in all cases return 'to Brussels'. Thus, out of the 317 files submitted to national authorities from 2007 to 2015, 169 were closed. In response to these criticisms, in 2016 the Commission reactivated a proposal for a European Public Ministry, which had already been put forward in a Green Paper in late 2001. According to the Commission's proposal, the European Public Prosecutor's Office would resume and expand OLAF's role and would be responsible in all Member States for investigating cases of fraud in the European budget for amounts over €10 million, but also of VAT fraud – whose losses are estimated at €50 billion per year. OLAF would be made accountable to the Council, the EP as well as to national parliaments. It would consist of a European Public Prosecutor and delegated prosecutors in the Member States, who would investigate cases with the help of national civil servants.

The proposal, examined by the Council in December 2016, provoked considerable resistance from the authorities of a dozen Member States, anxious to preserve their sovereignty (in particular Denmark, Ireland, Sweden and the Netherlands). To overcome this opposition, enhanced cooperation was launched on the basis of the Commission proposal on 4 April 2017. It involves 16 Member States: Belgium, Bulgaria, Croatia, Cyprus, Czech Republic, Germany, Greece, Spain, Finland, France, Lithuania, Luxembourg, Portugal, Romania, Slovenia and Slovakia. At the time of writing, this regulation must still be approved by the EP.[34]

*

One of the most important developments within Western democracies in recent years is the demand for more democratic control and accountability.[35] This trend has particularly affected the EU, since its institutions are at the centre of various criticisms and growing distrust of citizens since the 1990s. The enlargement of the EU to Sweden and Finland in 1995 reinforced this concern by introducing in the EU debate references to new norms and new forms of good governance as well as new criteria of democracy, such as accountability and transparency. As a result, an increasing number of bodies have been established with the aim of controlling the actions of the European institutions, and were formalized in the Lisbon Treaty. The EU political system has therefore experienced a diversification of control mechanisms and the institution of new forms of control that do not involve the Parliament.[36]

Whereas the Court of Justice was created and developed since the beginning of the Communities to solve potential conflicts between Member States or between EU institutions and Member States and also to make sure all states comply with and implement EU laws uniformly, the other controlling bodies were set up much later and reflect another philosophy. Contrary to the Court, they have not received a complete delegation in a given area. The current reluctance of States to see OLAF transformed into a European Public Prosecutor's Office shows that it is difficult to question the sovereignty of States in matters of control. As noted by P. Magnette and his colleagues, 'their task is limited to controlling the agents and the trustees, on the basis of open principles such as legality, regularity, openness, good administration.'[37] They were created as a way to increase the accountability and legitimacy of the EU in a time of growing popular discontent and distrust towards the supranational institutions, but without affecting the independence of these institutions. They are not specific to the EU though: 'the multiplication of control mechanisms in the EU is part and parcel of a general trend towards more accountability from decision-making authorities in the Western world over the past twenty years.'[38]

They may alleviate the accountability deficits in EU governance by providing formal and informal checks and balances. However, they are not perfect and cannot replace traditional forms of popular control and political accountability.[39] Numerous activities in the EU multi-level system remain formally shielded from any parliamentary or judicial control. Moreover, the concrete impact of such control bodies remains limited due to their cost, their lack of visibility to the public and the resistance of the EU institutions that reluctantly accept external control.

Notes

1 Article 257 of the Treaty on the Functioning of the Union stipulates that specialized courts can be created to rule on certain categories of recourse in specific matters. This is done by a resolution of the Parliament and the Council, acting according to the ordinary legislative procedure. A Civil Service Tribunal was created in 2004 for internal EU staffing disputes.

2 Article 19 TEU.

3 Karen J. Alter, 'The European Court's political power,' *West European Politics* 19 (1996): 458–487; Anne-Marie Burley and Walter Mattli, 'Europe before the Court: a political theory of legal integration,' *International Organization* 47(1) (1993): 41–76; Lisa Conant, 'Review article: the politics of legal integration,' *Journal of Common Market Studies* 45 (1) (2007): 45–66; Renaud Dehousse, *The European Court of Justice: The Politics of Judicial Integration* (New York: St Martin's Press, coll. 'The European Union series,' 1998); Margaret McCown, 'Judicial law-making and European integration: The European court of justice,' in *European Union: Power and Policy-Making*, ed. Jeremy J. Richardson (Abingdon/New York: Routledge, coll. 'Routledge research in

European public policy,' 3rd ed., 2006), 171–185; Alec Stone Sweet, *The Judicial Construction of Europe* (Oxford/New York: Oxford University Press, 2004).

4 In fact, it appears that the Member States have further encouraged non-judicial ways to resolve their differences.

5 Koen Lenaerts, 'Some reflections on the separation of powers in the EU,' *Common Market Law Review* 28 (1991): 11–35.

6 Alec Stone Sweet and James A. Caporaso, 'La Cour de Justice et l'intégration européenne,' *Revue Française de Science Politique* 48(2) (1998): 195–244; Daniel Wincott, 'The role of law or the rule of the court of justice? An "institutional" account of judicial politics in the European Community,' *Journal of European Public Policy* 2(4) (1995): 583–602.

7 On the importance of the political context and the cautiousness of the Court, see Karen Alter, 'Who are the masters of the treaty? European governments and the European court of justice,' *International Organization* 52 (1998): 125–152.

8 Joseph Weiler, 'A quiet revolution: the European court of justice and its interlocutors,' *Comparative Political Studies* 24 (1994): 510–534; Susanne Schmidt and Daniel Kelemen, *The Power of the European Court of Justice* (London: Routledge, 2013).

9 Karen J. Alter, 'The European Court's political power: the emergence of an authoritative international court in the European Union,' *West European Politics* 19 (1996): 458–487; Karen J. Alter, *Establishing the Supremacy of European Law: The Making of an International Law in Europe* (Oxford: Oxford University Press, coll. 'Oxford studies in European law,' 2001); Stone Sweet, *The Judicial Construction of Europe.*

10 Jean-Paul Jacqué, *Droit constitutionnel de l'Union européenne* (Paris: Dalloz, 2004); Margaret McCown, 'Judicial law-making and European Integration: The European Court of Justice'; Margaret McCown, 'The European Parliament before the bench: ECJ precedent and European parliament litigation strategies,' *Journal of European Public Policy* 10(6) (2003): 974–995.

11 Miguel P. Maduro, *We, the Court: the European Court of Justice and the European Economic Constitution* (Oxford: Hart Publishing, 1998).

12 Karen J. Alter and Sophie Meunier-Aitsahalia, 'Judicial politics in the European Community: European integration and the pathbreaking Cassis de Dijon decision,' *Comparative Political Studies* 26(4) (1994): 535–561; Rachel A. Cichowski, 'Women's rights, the European court and supranational constitutionalism,' *Law and Society Review* 38(3) (2004): 489–512; Dehousse, *The European Court of Justice: The Politics of Judicial Integration*; Jonas Tallberg, 'Delegation to supranational institutions: why, how, and with what consequences?' *West European Politics* 25(1) (2002): 23–46.

13 Alec Stone Sweet defines the judicialization of politics as 'how judicial law-making – defined as the law produced by a judge through normative interpretation, reason-giving and the application of legal norms to facts in the course of resolving disputes – influences the strategic behaviour of non-judicial agents' (Alec Stone Sweet, 'The European Court of Justice and the Judicialization of EU governance,' *Living Reviews in European Governance* 5(2) (2010): 7). See also Jacques Commaille, Laurence Dumoulin and Cécile Robert, *La juridicisation du politique: leçons scientifiques* (Paris: LGDJ/Maison des sciences de l'homme, coll. 'Droit et société, Recherches et travaux,' tome 7, 1st ed., 2000); Ran Hirschl, 'The judicialization of politics,' in *The Oxford Handbook of Law and Politics*, eds Keith E. Whittington and Gregory A. Caldeira (Oxford: Oxford

University Press, 2008), 119–141; Alec Stone Sweet, *Governing with Judges: Constitutional Politics in Europe* (Oxford/New York: Oxford University Press, 2000).

14 Dorte Sindbjerg Martinsen, *An Ever More Powerful Court? The Political Constraints of Legal Integration in the European Union* (Oxford, Oxford University Press, 2015).

15 Alter, 'The European Court's Political Power'; Alec Stone Sweet and Thomas Brunell, 'The European court of justice, state non-compliance and the politics of override,' *American Political Science Review* 106 (2012): 204–213.

16 Clifford Carruba, Matthew Gabel and Charles Hankla, 'Understanding the role of the European court of justice in European integration,' *American Political Science Review* 106(1) (2012): 214–223; Olof Larsson and Daniel Naurin, 'Judicial independence and political uncertainty: how the risk of override impacts on the Court of Justice of the EU,' *Comparative Political Studies* 49 (2016): 1–29.

17 Daniel Wincott, 'The court of justice and the legal system,' in *Developments in the European Union*, eds Laura Cram, Desmond Dinan and Neill Nugent (Basingstoke: Macmillan, 1999), 84–104.

18 Matthias Herdegen, 'Maastricht and the German constitutional court: constitutional restraints for an ever closer Europe,' *Common Market Law Review* 31 (1994): 235–244; Jonathan Golub, 'The politics of judicial discretion: rethinking the interaction between national courts and the European court of justice,' *West European Politics* 19(2) (1996): 360–385; Anne-Marie Slaughter, Alec Stone Sweet and Joseph H. H. Weiler, eds, *The European Court and the National Courts – Doctrine and Jurisprudence* (Oxford: Hart Publishing, 1998).

19 Lisa Conant, *Justice Contained* (Ithaca: Cornell University Press, 2002); Mark A. Pollack, 'The new EU legal history: what's new, what's missing?,' *American University International Law Review* (2013).

20 R. Daniel Kelemen, 'Eurolegalism and democracy,' *Journal of Common Market Studies* 50(1) (2012): 65.

21 Luca Barani, 'The role of the European Court of Justice as a political actor in the integration process: the case of sport regulation after the Bosman Ruling,' *Journal of Contemporary European Research* 1(1) (2005): 42–58.

22 R. Daniel Kelemen, 'Suing for Europe: adversarial legalism and European governance,' *Comparative Political Studies* 39(1) (2006): 101–127; Paul Magnette, *Le régime politique de l'Union européenne* (Paris: Les Presses de Sciences Po, coll. 'Références,' 3rd ed., 2009). A case has recently caused a commotion. On the basis of a reference to a preliminary ruling by the Council of Litigation of Foreigners (Belgium), the Court had to rule on the interpretation of the visa code, while the EU is going through a migratory crisis. In particular, the Grand Court ruled in a case concerning visa applications with the Belgian embassy in Beirut by a Syrian couple from Aleppo and their three children, after repeated refusals by the Belgian state. Considering the tense political climate (since a crisis meeting was planned for the Commission as soon as the judgment was made public), it is not surprising that the Court did not follow the Advocate General's reasoning or the Belgian State. Otherwise, its ruling would have been a strong precedent, which would have had the potential to force states to legislate urgently on European migration policies and the definition of borders.

23 Brigid Laffan, 'Auditing and accountability in the European Union,' *Journal of European Public Policy* 10(5) (2003): 762–777; Brigid Laffan, 'The court of auditors and

OLAF,' in *The Institutions of the European Union*, eds John Peterson and Michael Schakelton (Oxford/New York: Oxford University Press, coll. 'The New European Union Series,' 2002), 233–254; Paul Magnette, *Contrôler l'Europe: pouvoirs et responsabilité dans l'Union européenne* (Brussels: Éd. de l'Université de Bruxelles, coll. 'Études européennes,' 2003).

24 Neill Nugent, *The Government and Politics of the European Union* (Basingstoke: Palgrave Macmillan, 7th ed., 2010), 241.

25 Petia Kostadinova, 'Improving the transparency and accountability of EU institutions: the impact of the Office of the European Ombudsman,' *Journal of Common Market Studies*, Early view 2015, DOI: 10.1111/jcms.12245.

26 Yves Doutriaux and Christian Lequesne, *Les institutions de l'Union européenne* (Paris: La Documentation française, 2007), 94.

27 European Ombudsman Annual Report 2014.

28 Paul Magnette, 'Between parliamentary control and the rule of law: the political role of the Ombudsman in the European Union,' *Journal of European Public Policy* 10(5) (2003): 677–694.

29 Petia Kostadinova, 'Improving the transparency and accountability of EU institutions: the impact of the Office of the European Ombudsman,' *Journal of Common Market Studies*, Early view 2015, DOI: 10.1111/jcms.12245.

30 P. Kostadinova, op. cit.

31 Véronique Pujas, 'The European anti-fraud office (OLAF): a European policy to fight against economic and financial fraud?' *Journal of European Public Policy* 10(5) (2003): 778–797.

32 'Office européen de lutte antifraude,' European Commission, accessed 28 July 2015, http://ec.europa.eu/anti_fraud/index_fr.htm.

33 Sixteenth report of the European Anti-Fraud Office, 1 January–31 December 2015, 2016, 48 p.

34 European Council, 'Parquet européen: 16 États membres vont s'associer pour lutter contre la fraude au détriment du budget de l'UE,' press release, 3 April 2017

35 See in particular Anchrit Wille, 'L'évolution du paysage de l'imputabilité dans l'Union européenne : une Union de plus en plus dense,' *Revue Internationale des Sciences Administratives* 82(4) (2016): 733–754.

36 See the special issue of the *Journal of European Public Policy* 10(5) (2003): 'The diffusion of democracy.'

37 Paul Magnette, Christian Lequesne, Nicolas Jabko and Olivier Costa, 'Conclusion: diffuse democracy in the European Union: the pathologies of delegation,' *Journal of European Public Policy* 10(5) (2003): 834–840.

38 Olivier Costa, Nicolas Jabko, Christian Lequesne and Paul Magnette, 'Introduction: diffuse control mechanisms in the European Union: towards a new democracy?' *Journal of European Public Policy* 10(5) (2003): 666–676.

39 Mark Bovens, 'New forms of accountability and EU-Governance,' *Comparative European Politics* 5(1) (2004): 104–120.

Other organs involved in EU policy making

6

Usually, the EU is described as a system based on three (Commission, Council and European Parliament), four (add the Court of Justice) or five (add the European Council) institutions. Analysts underline the role of the institutional triangle, which has become a square since the institutionalization of the European Council, and insist on the elitism and the closeness of the European microcosm. However, even if the EU is clearly perceived as an elitist political system,[1] it nevertheless involves many actors who do not belong to the five main institutions.

This chapter will present the EU political system in a broader sense, by taking into account all the organs established by the treaties or by EU legislative norms. We must also address the growing role played by national parliaments in EU policy making. Despite treaty reforms their involvement was quite limited for a very long time, but they are now much more mobilized. Finally, we will deal with the numerous non-institutional actors (experts, national civil servants, lobbyists, civil society representatives, etc.) that surround the EU institutions in Brussels and Strasbourg.

We will, however, not expand our thinking too much. The chapter will not deal with citizen's perceptions of the EU. Neither will it address in a broader sense the relationship of Member States with the EU. The objective is to remain focused on the very places and procedures of EU decision-making.

6.1 The consultative bodies

There are many consultative bodies in the EU whose roles and importance are quite weak. We will present here the two main ones who are also the most institutionalized: the Economic and Social Committee and the Committee of the Regions.[2]

6.1.1 The European Economic and Social Committee

The European Economic and Social Committee (EESC) was established by the treaty of Rome in 1957 and represents the various socio-professional groups (unions, businesses, farmers, artisans, families, consumers, etc.) across the EU. It defines itself, in its motto, as 'a bridge between Europe and organised civil society'.[3]

It must be consulted on certain texts as provided for in the treaties, but with little consequence as its opinions are not binding and not much considered by the Commission, the EP and the Council. The treaty on the functioning of the EU states that the EESC is composed by no more than 350 members. There is a principle of national allocation of seats based on a vague criterion of the 'size' of the Member States: Malta has 5 representatives while the largest Member States are granted 24. EESC members are appointed in a personal capacity for a renewable term of five years by the Council on proposals from Member States and after consultation with the Commission. The current mandate runs from October 2015 to September 2020. Members are expected to act independently. The membership is divided into three main groups: employers (stemming mostly from industry but also from banks, insurance companies, public enterprises, etc.); employees (most are members of national trade unions); and 'various interests' (about half are associated with agriculture, small and medium-sized businesses as well as trades but there are also representatives from consumer groups, public agencies, etc.). The EESC has its seat in Brussels, in buildings formerly occupied by the EP and can rely on the administrative support of a Secretariat General.

6.1.2 The Committee of the Regions

The Committee of the Regions (CoR), established by the Maastricht Treaty, represents regional and local authorities to the Council and Commission, in the same way as the EESC. It must be consulted in some areas (culture, economic and social cohesion, employment, public health, education, vocational training, social issues, trans-European networks, transport, regional planning) and may issue opinions on its own initiative. It is composed of 350 members, and as many deputy members, according to the same national allocation key as the EESC. They must be elected members of regional or local authorities or be politically accountable to an elected assembly. Within the CoR, there are five political groups paralleling the main groups of the EP: the European People's Party, the Party of European Socialists, the Group of the Alliance of Liberals and Democrats for Europe and the European Alliance Group and the European Conservative and Reformist Group.

6.2 Financial agencies

6.2.1 European Investment Bank

The European Investment Bank (EIB) finances long-term, large-scale projects such as trans-European transport and telecommunications networks. It is owned by the EU Member States and works with EU institutions to implement EU policy. It provides financial support for investment projects linked to EU policy objectives: more than 90 per cent of its activity is focused on Europe. The EIB also has an advisory role – through a team of 300 engineers and economists. It is called upon to give priority to projects that contribute to growth, employment, economic and social cohesion and environmental sustainability. The EIB's main decision-making bodies are the Board of Governors (composed of one Minister per Member State), the Board of Directors (one director nominated by each Member State and one nominated by the European Commission) and the Management Committee (the Bank's President and eight Vice-Presidents). The EIB has a staff of 2,900, mainly located in Luxembourg; it also has a network of local and regional offices in Europe and beyond. The European Investment Fund (EIF), created by the EIB, the EU (represented by the Commission) and other European private and public bodies, focuses on 'innovative' financing for SMEs.

The EIB cooperates with the Commission to use EU funds to support special programmes to help countries that experience economic difficulties. It played a central role in Member States' attempts to fight the economic crisis. Indeed, since 2009, the Corporate Operational Plans, which frame the EIB policy, prioritize actions related to the mitigation of the effects of the credit and economic crisis. In 2012, the Member States decided to increase the EIB capital by €10 billion, which allowed the bank to plan for €60 billion additional lending between 2013 and 2015. In 2015, the annual loan volume represented €77.5 billion.

6.2.2 European Central Bank

The European Central Bank (ECB), created by the Maastricht Treaty and established in June 1998, defines and implements monetary policy in the eurozone (19 Member States in 2017).[4] It replaced the European Monetary Institute (EMI) established by the Treaty of Maastricht. With the Treaty of Lisbon, the ECB has gained the official status of an EU institution (Article 13 of TEU). The Amsterdam Treaty defined the seat of the major EU institutions: according to it, the ECB is based in Frankfurt, Germany. This was a request of the German government in the global bargaining over seats. It also made sense since Frankfurt is the largest financial centre in the eurozone.

The ECB is governed by EU norms, but its organization resembles that of a private corporation, since it has shareholders and stock capital. Its capital is €5 billion, held by the central banks of the Member States. The ECB is the central bank for the euro and is responsible for the monetary policy of the Member States within the eurozone. The European System of Central Banks (ESCB) includes the ECB and the National Central Banks (NCBs) of all EU Member States. According to the treaties, the ESCB's main objective is to maintain price stability within the eurozone. The Governing Council of the ECB has interpreted this objective as the need to keep inflation below 2 per cent. The Lisbon Treaty also states that 'the ESCB shall support the general economic policies of the Union with a view to contributing to the achievement of the objectives of the Union' (Article 105.1 TFEU), but without prejudice to the objective of low inflation.

The ECB has the exclusive right to issue euro banknotes; Member States can only issue euro coins, with a specific national side, within a given amount. The ECB also conducts foreign-exchange operations, manages the foreign reserves of the European System of Central Banks and organizes the financial market infrastructure. The ECB finally contributes to maintaining a stable financial system and to monitoring the banking sector. Contrary to the US Federal reserve, the ECB normally does not buy bonds outright but uses 'refinancing facilities'. This approach was challenged by the sovereign-debt crisis that started in late 2009. In 2011, the ECB purchased bonds issued by the weaker states – mainly Spain and Italy – to fight against international speculation. It also set up, in December 2011 and February 2012, a system of low-interest loans to European banks (mainly in Greece, Ireland, Italy and Spain), for a total of nearly €1,000 billion.

The ECB is governed by three main bodies.

1   The Executive Board is composed of the President of the Bank (currently Mario Draghi, former governor of the Bank of Italy), the Vice-President (currently Vitor Constâncio) and four other members. It is responsible for the implementation of monetary policy and for the current operations of the ECB. The members are appointed for a non-renewable term of eight years by the European Council, on a recommendation from the Council, after consultation of the EP and the Governing Council of the ECB.

2   The Governing Council defines the monetary policy. This organ comprises the members of the Executive Board and the governors of the National Central Banks of the eurozone countries. The governors are appointed by their respective government and tend to vote along national lines – even if votes are secret.[5]

3   The General Council is made up of the President and Vice-President of the ECB and of the governors of all of the EU's National Central Banks. It takes decisions relating to the adoption of the euro by EU Member States.

The ECB has played a key role in the increased regulation of the eurozone following the financial crisis. Already in October 2007, its President, J. C. Trichet, had underlined the need for the EU to pursue further economic and financial integration, for a coordination of national fiscal policies, and even for a fiscal union. In the context of the sovereign debt crisis, the President of the ECB has participated, with his pairs from the Commission, Council and Eurogroup, in the brainstorming on the ways to save the euro. This resulted notably in the 'blueprint for a deep and genuine EMU'[6] released in November 2012, outlining the elements of a fiscal union that could be achieved in the short, medium and long term.

In the meanwhile, a group of several Member States, led by Germany, made proposals to enforce a better coordination of economic policies between eurozone members, so that all states take an active part in their policymaking. These proposals gave birth to new European agreements or regulations (Two pack and Six pack[7]) and to the negotiation of what would become the Fiscal Compact. In the frame of this new treaty, the ECB contributes to the governance of the eurozone particularly through the participation of its President in the Euro summits.

The ECB has been designed as an agency, according to the liberal theory of international politics. As a Non-Majoritarian Institution (NMI) it is supposed to take its decisions independently, only taking into account economic data and the long-term objectives mentioned in the treaty. Neither public opinion's expectations, elections' results or other EU institutions' points of view should come into play. Members of the Executive Board have a non-renewable term, to guarantee their independence from their governments. They cannot be removed from office, except in case of incapacity or grave misconduct. The political independence of the ECB is designed as a key element of its capacity to maintain price stability: EU institutions and national governments are bound by the treaties to respect this independence.

However, this does not mean that the ECB is not accountable at all: it must publish regular reports on its activities and address its annual report to the EP, the Commission, the Council and the European Council. Since its creation, the ECB has gone beyond these statutory obligations in matters of accountability. It, for instance, issues a Monthly Bulletin, rather than a quarterly report. Members of the Governing Council also deliver many speeches to explain their action to the public. The President and Vice-President also often explain the bank's monetary-policy decisions during the press conferences that follow each monthly Governing Council meeting. The EP can question candidates for the Executive Board during hearings and gives its opinion about them. Finally, since the ECB was elevated to the status of an institution by the Lisbon Treaty, it must respect the principle of faithful cooperation between the institutions.

The ECB's action has always attracted criticism from politicians who think that it should pay more attention to growth, employment and parity with other currencies, or at least have a less strict conception of is 'low inflation', understood as less than 2 per cent by the ECB.[8]

Some left-wing politicians also criticize the very idea of giving an NMI the right to define the monetary policy of the eurozone, and even to interfere in the fiscal and budgetary policies of the Member States; these politicians consider that elected bodies and actors (EP, National parliaments, Member States' governments, etc.) should be able to define the priorities between competing objectives, such as inflation, growth, employment or exportation capabilities. Since the beginning of the financial crisis, at the end of 2009, there have also been tough discussions on the role of the ECB and the ways to develop mechanisms of macro-economic stabilization for the eurozone countries along with stronger budgetary discipline. There is a kind of consensus over the fact that the ECB does not enjoy sufficient legitimacy to play a key role in the coordination and monitoring of Member States' budgetary policy, given their potential impact on national fiscal and social policies.

6.3 EU agencies

The treaties provide no definition of an 'agency'. EU agencies are independent legal entities created by European public law (i.e. EU regulation), that are distinct from the EU institutions (Council, EP, Commission, etc.). In common parlance, 'agency' is a generic term for a technical body, operating in a field of expertise and not of representation. In the EU, the term describes a wide range of organs that meet these criteria but have different names: centre, institute, foundation, office, authority, etc. They play an important role in the implementation of EU policies and deal mainly with technical, scientific, operational and regulatory questions. They also contribute to the cooperation of the EU and the pooling of Member States' expertise.

Today there are 54 agencies and assimilated bodies located in various Member States. The multiplication of agencies at the European level is one of the major recent institutional innovations.[9] There have been several periods of agencies creation: in the 1970s, in the 1990s and in the 2000s, with the emergence of 'executive agencies'. They can be considered as a new player in the EU's operations, even though each of them has a mandate, objectives and tasks that are specific. They do not form a network.

Another aspect defining their diversity is the extent of their independence. Some agencies assist the Commission in the management of European programmes and are subject to strict oversight. Others exercise executive functions by adopting measures intended to regulate specific sectors. Still others are responsible for the coordination of a specific domain such as the environment or professional training, they then collect data, exchange and analysis information and communicate the results to European decision-making bodies, the general public and professionals. In this case, they involve large networks of experts to advise EU officials in the conduct of specific policies, especially those that give rise to strong national or partisan divisions. The Commission now presents on its website European agencies that were set up under EU programs and public-private partnerships, although they have a different logic (see Box 6.1).

Box 6.1 EU Agencies (April 2017)

Decentralised Agencies:

1. Agency for the Cooperation of Energy Regulators (ACER)
2. Body of European Regulators for Electronic Communications (BEREC)
3. Community Plant Variety Office (CPVO)
4. European Agency for Safety and Health at Work (EU-OSHA)
5. European Agency for the Management of Operational Cooperation at the External Borders (FRONTEX)
6. European agency for the operational management of large-scale IT systems in the area of freedom, security and justice (eu-LISA)
7. European Asylum Support Office (EASO)
8. European Aviation Safety Agency (EASA)
9. European Banking Authority (EBA)
10. European Centre for Disease Prevention and Control (ECDC)
11. European Centre for the Development of Vocational Training (Cedefop)
12. European Chemicals Agency (ECHA)
13. European Environment Agency (EEA)
14. European Fisheries Control Agency (EFCA)
15. European Food Safety Authority (EFSA)
16. European Foundation for the Improvement of Living and Working Conditions (EUROFOUND)
17. European GNSS Agency (GSA)
18. European Institute for Gender Equality (EIGE)
19. European Insurance and Occupational Pensions Authority (EIOPA)
20. European Maritime Safety Agency (EMSA)
21. European Medicines Agency (EMA)
22. European Monitoring Centre for Drugs and Drug Addiction (EMCDDA)
23. European Network and Information Security Agency (ENISA)
24. European Police College (CEPOL)

25. European Police Office (EUROPOL)
26. European Public Prosecutor's Office (in preparation) (EPPO)
27. European Railway Agency (ERA)
28. European Securities and Markets Authority (ESMA)
29. European Training Foundation (ETF)
30. European Union Agency for Fundamental Rights (FRA)
31. Office for Harmonisation in the Internal Market (OHIM)
32. Single Resolution Board (in preparation) (SRB)
33. The European Union's Judicial Cooperation Unit (EUROJUST)
34. Translation Centre for the Bodies of the European Union (CdT)

Agencies under Common Security and Defence Policy:

1. European Defence Agency (EDA)
2. European Union Institute for Security Studies (EUISS)
3. European Union Satellite Centre (EUSC)

Executive agencies:

1. Education, Audiovisual and Culture Executive Agency (EACEA)
2. Executive Agency for Small and Medium-sized enterprises (EASME)
3. European Research Council Executive Agency (ERC Executive Agency)
4. Consumers, Health and Food Executive Agency (CHAFEA)
5. Research Executive Agency (REA)
6. Innovation & Networks Executive Agency (INEA)

EURATOM agencies and bodies:

1. EURATOM Supply Agency (ESA)
2. European Joint Undertaking for ITER and the Development of Fusion Energy (Fusion for Energy)

Other:

1. European Institute of Innovation and Technology (EIT)
2. Bio-based Industries Joint Undertaking (BBI)
3. Joint Undertaking ECSEL
4. Fuel Cells and Hydrogen 2 Joint Undertaking
5. IMI 2 Joint Undertaking (IMI 2 JU)
6. Joint Undertaking SESAR
7. Shift2Rail Joint Undertaking
8. Clean Sky 2 Joint Undertaking

The first agencies, created in the 1970s, had only a limited mandate and few discretional powers; in that sense, they were not 'agencies' as theorized by liberal economists, i.e. independent organs endowed with executive powers.[10] Even if they are often called 'regulatory agencies', most EU agencies do not enjoy regulatory powers. Until the late 1980s, the creation of this type of agency was guided by the jurisprudence of the Court, and particularly the Meroni decision (ECJ 9/56 Meroni v. High Authority), which set strict and clear criteria for the delegation of powers to agencies.

There are several ways to classify agencies. If we look at their functions and powers, there are five categories[11] – from the least to the most powerful:

- agencies providing services to other agencies and institutions, with only one agency of that type: the Translation Centre for the Bodies of the EU (CDT);
- agencies in charge of gathering and analysing information, like the European Environment Agency (EEA) or the European Monitoring Centre for Drugs and Drug Addiction (EMCDDA);
- agencies providing scientific or technical advice to EU institutions or Member States, such as the European Food Safety Authority (EFSA) or the European Medicines Agency (EMA);
- agencies that take individual legally binding decisions like the Office for Harmonisation in the Internal Market (Trade Marks and Designs) (OHIM) or the European Chemicals Agency (ECHA);
- agencies that oversee operational activities, such as the European Fisheries Control Agency (EFCA) or the European Agency for the Management of Operational Cooperation at the External Borders (FRONTEX).

Another way to present agencies is to refer to the former three pillars of the EU: Community policies, foreign affairs and political and judicial cooperation. The implementation of these last two policy fields following the entry into force of the Maastricht Treaty has led to the creation of many ad hoc agencies, intended to offset the Commission's weak involvement. This typology, a priori, no longer makes legal sense, due to the merging of the pillars by the Treaty of Lisbon, but it remains enlightening nevertheless. Combining the typologies in terms of powers and policy fields, we can distinguish four categories of agencies:

1   **Community agencies** are bodies of public European law, distinct from EU institutions with their own legal personality. They are the most common. A Community agency is created by an act of secondary legislation to accomplish a task with a specific technical, scientific or managerial nature in the framework of what was the 'first pillar' of the EU before the entry into force of the Lisbon Treaty;

2   **Common foreign policy and security agencies** were created to fulfil specific tasks of a technical, scientific and managerial nature. There are three such agencies: the European Defence Agency (EDA), the European Union Satellite Centre (EUSC) and the Institute for Security Studies of the European Union (ISS);

3   **Agencies for police and judicial cooperation in criminal matters** have been created to facilitate cooperation between EU Member States in the fight against international organized crime. For instance, there is the European Police College (CEPOL) or the European Union Agency for Fundamental Rights (FRA);

4   **Executive agencies** are established to carry out the tasks relative to the management of one or more community programmes: in that sense, they are 'true' agencies, i.e. non-majoritarian institutions with executive powers.[12] They are created for a specific period. Unlike other agencies that are based in different EU countries, Executive agencies are hosted by the Commission in Brussels or Luxembourg. Among this category we can find for instance the Education, Audiovisual and Culture Executive Agency and the Research Executive Agency.

The creation of European agencies stems from a combination of factors and various incentives.

It is first supposed to free-up the EU institutions, mainly the Commission, to concentrate on policy-making and political issues. The establishment of the internal market in the late 1980s resulted in extra work for the Commission, which, due to budget constraints imposed by the Council and the EP, could not increase its staff.[13] Between 1989 and 1999, 10 agencies were established for this purpose. In the late 1990s, the repeated crises affecting the Commission (management of the mad cow disease, charges of nepotism, scandals in the technical assistance offices, etc.) attracted widespread criticism of its inability to conduct legitimate and effective policies. In response, President Romano Prodi (1999–2004) launched a reform including the establishment of six new agencies to restore the credibility of the Commission.

Many of these bodies were also created to end a specific political crisis. For example, the Food Safety Agency was set up in response to the mad cow disease and the Maritime Safety Agency in response to the Erika oil spill. In October 2004, José Manuel Barroso, then upcoming president of the Commission, promised the creation of a 'Fundamental Rights Agency'[14] when the EP demanded the replacement of Commissioner candidate Rocco Buttiglione after his comments on homosexuality before a parliamentary committee.

The creation of agencies also emanates from the political interests of institutions. Agencies, in a way, deprive the Commission from part of its executive powers and, to a large extent, escape the EP's control; however, both institutions have supported their creation. Agencies are indeed a way for the Commission and the EP to expand the scope of EU activities in general. By providing independent and technical expertise which the Commission does not have, they contribute to the development and implementation of European policies and can indirectly involve a wide range of recipients. Also, agencies are a way to leave some autonomy to Member States in the management of policies, since their representatives are always far more numerous than the representatives of supranational institutions (Commission, EP)[15] within said agencies. They can be a medium between the intergovernmental and supranational logics and thus contribute to the limitation of conflicts between the national and European levels of governance.[16] The Council also supports the creation of regulatory agencies, since many national leaders prefer to give new missions to agencies rather than to the Commission since they see these as less of a threat to their own independence. Finally, the governments and administrations of Member States approve of agencies, because they develop a new mode of governance that is less centralized and rigid as well as more responsive.[17]

Finally, agencies have also played a role in the discussions over the seats of EU institutions and organs. As all the main institutions are located in four cities in four different countries (Brussels, Luxembourg, Strasbourg and Frankfurt), the other Member States were given agency seats.

The multiplication of agencies has led to considerations about European governance and the nature of European politics.[18] They are seen as being adapted to the EU's missions, particularly to its function of European market regulation. This is especially the case when they are understood not as organs of information and advice, but as non-majoritarian institutions, i.e. independent bodies with a high degree of autonomy and broad decision-making power. Such agencies, composed of experts removed from the electoral process and from political and national pressures, can externalize the regulation of technical matters and take into account the speed of change in technology, knowledge and geographic diversity.[19] Some authors have advocated a systematic dismantling of the Commission into a multitude of independent agencies, thus escaping the politicization that increasingly affects the Commission.[20]

It should however be remembered that these agencies are not fully independent vis-à-vis national governments who establish and define their rules of operation. Moreover, they must deal with the contradictions between the dual imperatives of autonomy and accountability: the agencies' autonomy is, in fact, affected both by the Commission – which often believes that these bodies deviate from the priorities that it defines (*bureaucratic drift*) – and the presence of stakeholders within the agencies themselves – which influences their decisions.[21]

The issue of control of the agencies also remains problematic. If it is excessive, they lose their principle of efficiency but if it is too weak, it can lead them to follow their own interests and thus lose their credibility. The controversies surrounding the action and legitimacy of the European Central Bank (which, functionally, is an agency) illustrate the complexity of this problem.

There is still no common framework for agencies, regarding their missions, their governance or their accountability. At the end of the 1990s, the Commission launched an inter-institutional discussion on the functions of agencies in EU governance.[22] In 2012, the EU institutions rectified the historical case-by-case approach by adopting a comprehensive set of guiding principles to make the agencies more 'coherent, effective and accountable'.[23] This 'Common Approach', formalized on 12 July 2012 by the signature of an inter-institutional agreement between the Commission, the Council and the Parliament, was based on a working group that studied agencies' governance, functioning and oversight.

The Commission is responsible for the follow-up of agencies. It must search for a 'more balanced governance, improved efficiency and accountability and coherence of its action' and publishes annual reports.[24] A Roadmap from December 2012[25] includes details about how the Common Approach should be implemented and lists the initiatives to be taken by the Commission, by the agencies themselves, and by the Member States, the European Parliament and the Council. In parallel, the Commission is in charge of adapting the founding legal acts of existing agencies in a case-by-case approach. Recent progresses include provisions for headquarters of agencies, and for their communication, guidelines on conflicts of interest and on budgetary effectiveness along with the preparation of legislative proposals.

6.4 National parliaments and European integration

Originally, national parliaments were involved in European integration through the European Parliament which was composed of national MPs delegated by their institutions. These MPs had a double mandate and could participate in the debates at the EU level and inform their colleagues of European developments. The weak powers of the European Assembly did not permit them to significantly influence the decisions of the Community but because they were part of the EP, EU decisions did not seem to come from a disconnected level of government. The first direct elections of the EP in June 1979 put an end to this relationship without providing an alternative. National parliaments thus lost all contact with European integration, which greatly contributed to the rise of the theme of the 'democratic deficit'. This disconnection has indeed increased the feeling that European integration is a process that transfers growing responsibilities from the national to the European level, and is therefore an area where parliaments vote on legislation for a system dominated largely by the executive. By losing their representatives in the EP, national parliaments have, moreover, been deprived of any ability to control the European policy of their respective governments, especially when the Council decides by qualified majority and the positions of the various ministers are not publicly known.[26]

After some delay resulting as much from a lack of interest in European integration on the part of the national parliaments as from the EP's claim to exercise a monopoly of parliamentary representation at European level, the situation has changed.[27] Now, national parliaments can no longer be considered as elements outside the EU's institutional system[28] and one can see the emergence of a European parliamentary network which counterbalances those of the executives, the courts and the central banks.[29] From the beginning of European integration, the Council has in fact been a kind of network of national executives and administrations, while the Court of Justice has maintained an on-going dialogue with national courts through preliminary rulings. More recently, within the context of the economic and monetary union, one can observe the development of a network of national central banks closely linked to the European Central Bank. Now the national parliaments and the European Parliament are trying to weigh jointly on EU governance.

For years, the involvement of national parliaments in the EU's functioning was the result of initiatives by parliamentarians themselves. With declarations 13 and 14 of the Maastricht Treaty, the treaties only belatedly recognized the right for national parliaments to benefit from information on the activities of the EU. This role has been strengthened by Protocol 13 of the Amsterdam Treaty and the Protocol 'on the role of national parliaments in the European Union' annexed to the Treaty of Lisbon.[30] The financial crisis that hit the European Union in 2008 has also renewed the discussion on how to associate national parliaments in the governance of the eurozone to give more legitimacy to the important decisions taken in this area.[31]

6.4.1 The development of the means of unilateral information from national parliaments

We will not discuss here the various means of control gradually provided to parliaments to learn about the European policy of their respective governments, and in some cases, influence it. In fact, these mechanisms only have an indirect impact on the functioning of the EU when, for example, a national parliament warns its government about issues with a proposal or constrains the position of its minister during Council negotiations by an explicit negotiating mandate or a threat of sanctions. It is sufficient to observe that while all national parliaments now have such mechanisms, including a specialized body on European affairs (dedicated parliamentary committee or ad hoc structure), they vary greatly from one Member State to another, depending on the balance of power between the executive and legislative branches and the resources allocated to this task.

Because they are unable to achieve effective control over their government's European policy, some Parliaments favour collective mechanisms of information and influence over the EU, whether they are horizontal bilateral inter-parliamentary relations (between national parliaments), vertical relations (between national parliaments and the European Parliament), or multilateral inter-parliamentary relations (between all the national parliaments and the EP).

6.4.2 Bilateral parliamentary cooperation between national chambers and the European Parliament

Each national chamber maintains direct relations with the EU through the European Parliament. These relationships take the form of document and information exchange, joint meetings and parliamentary hearings. Due to physical as well as political constraints, these relationships have only developed since the 1990s. Today, all national parliaments have a liaison office to the EU, located in the EP buildings in Brussels, in order to develop contacts with its institutions and with other legislatures.[32] Today, 39 chambers are represented by at least one agent. They follow the work of the parliamentary committees of interest to their national parliamentarians and organize their trips to Brussels. They also play a key role in the Early Warning Mechanism created by the Lisbon Treaty (see below). Conversely, the specialized bodies on European affairs in national parliaments regularly invite MEPs to take part in their work. There are also bilateral 'encounters' between specialized bodies of various national parliaments, some of which are truly collaborative meetings.

Parallel to this bilateral cooperation (vertical and horizontal), whose scope is relatively limited, multilateral inter-parliamentary cooperation has been gradually institutionalized in various forms.

6.4.3 The Conference of Presidents of Parliaments

The Conference of Presidents is an old, informal forum for discussion which has intermittently played a leading role in inter-parliamentary cooperation. After two isolated meetings in Rome in 1963 and Strasbourg in 1973, the Presidents of Parliaments have met regularly since 1975 in the framework of two conferences. The 'restricted conference' brings together the Presidents of the Parliaments of the EU Member States and the President of the European Parliament. The 'full conference' brings together the Presidents of the Parliaments of the Member States of the Council of Europe (47 at present) and the Presidents of the Parliamentary Assembly of the Council of Europe, the Assembly of the Western European Union and the European Parliament. The 'full conference' typically meets every two years and discusses Europe in very general terms. The 'restricted conference' used to be held during the 'off' years. It was reactivated in 1999 and meets every year now with the goal to promote close cooperation between the EU parliaments. Its relative anonymity is explained by the inadequacies of its statute: despite the adoption of guiding principles for its operation and purpose in September 2000, this body only adopts declarative resolutions by unanimity. The wide variety of statutes and legal and political prerogatives of the Presidents of the assemblies does not facilitate the achievement of such a consensus.

6.4.4 The Conference of the Parliaments

The Conference of the Parliaments, or 'Assizes', held its inaugural session in Rome on 29 and 30 November 1990. This was the first manifestation of scale in matters of inter-parliamentary cooperation in the Community, bringing together a large number of delegates from the EP and national parliaments to discuss European integration and its future. The Assizes were held the day before the meeting of the two intergovernmental conferences that were to launch the comprehensive review of the founding treaties of the Communities and the creation of a European Union.

From the preparation of this event, however, it appeared that members of national parliaments and the EP did not share the same conception of this inter-institutional meeting. The former wanted to institutionalize these Assizes, while the latter were inclined towards a more limited strategy. The final resolution adopted by the Conference was a great political success for the EP[33]: the text covers its essential demands, while references to the national parliaments are limited to a strict minimum. The resolution states that European action by national parliaments should focus on the control of governments not on that of the supranational institutions. It establishes the principle of enhanced cooperation between national parliaments and the EP through the regular meetings of specialized bodies in the monitoring of European affairs. The idea of creating a second chamber representative of national parliaments in the Community was excluded in accordance with the EP's will. Despite its formal recognition by Declaration 14 annexed to the Maastricht Treaty, the Conference of the Parliaments no longer meets, because of a lack of political will. However, other forms of inter-parliamentary cooperation have been developed.

6.4.5 The COSAC

The Conference of Parliamentary Committees for Union Affairs of Parliaments of the European Union (COSAC) met for the first time in Paris in

November 1989. It quickly became the framework for inter-parliamentary cooperation and the involvement of national parliaments in European affairs. It is a forum for cooperation between national parliamentary committees specialized in European affairs and representatives of the EP, that meet every six months at the invitation of the Parliament of the Member State holding the EU presidency. COSAC is primarily a forum for exchange. In some cases, meetings are preceded by questionnaires sent to the specialized bodies according to the topics on the agenda so that discussions can be based on written submissions. Institutional questions, in particular concerning the role of national parliaments in the EU and the relations between national parliaments and the EP, are recurrent. COSAC also deals with the current functioning of the EU and treaty reforms, as well as topics related to inter-governmental cooperation, including the Common Foreign and Security Policy.

In the debates of the Convention on the Future of the European Union, the issue of COSAC's institutionalization in the form of a 'senate' of national parliaments was brought up once again. It had the favour of the President of the Convention, Valéry Giscard d'Estaing, but was quickly abandoned mainly because of the hostility of EP representatives to this idea. The progress proposed by the Constitution in terms of inter-parliamentary cooperation was therefore limited. It was included in the Protocol 'on the role of national Parliaments in the European Union' annexed to the Treaty of Lisbon. But this only carried minor changes to the treaties of Maastricht and Amsterdam and stated that COSAC's powers are strictly advisory. Article 10 of the Protocol states that *'a conference of Parliamentary Committees for Union Affairs may submit any contribution it deems appropriate'* for EU institutions and *'should promote the exchange of information and best practice between national Parliaments and the European Parliament, including their special committees'*. However, *'contributions from the conference shall not bind national Parliaments and shall not prejudge their positions.'*

Additionally, representatives of national parliaments have no delegation of authority, or mandate, that would allow them to bind national parliaments. While the COSAC cannot speak for national representatives, its work provides insight to the EP, the Council and the Commission as to how it comprehends certain issues.

Parallel to the COSAC, an electronic platform called 'IPEX' (InterParliamentary EXchange) was set up in 2004 between national parliaments and the EP to enhance information exchanges.[34]

More recently, the idea of setting up a chamber of national parliaments has returned to the debate, particularly in the context of reflections on ways to legitimize the economic and budgetary governance of the eurozone. Several authors and politicians have therefore proposed the constitution of a new body, composed of national parliamentarians and possibly European parliamentarians, who would oversee the important decisions in these matters.[35]

6.4.6 The Early Warning System

The Early Warning System (EWS) is an innovation of the Constitutional Treaty, and later the Lisbon Treaty, that aimed at improving the involvement of national parliaments in the EU political system. It was designed by two working groups of the Convention on the Future of Europe respectively in charge of the reflection on the subsidiarity principle and on the role of national parliaments in the EU system. The EWS was a kind of compromise that allowed the involvement of national parliaments through the control of the subsidiarity principle compliance, without creating a new institution. The objective was to improve the participation of national chambers – enjoying an unrivalled democratic legitimacy – at the EU level in order to reduce the alleged 'democratic deficit'.[36] The EWS was the result of long negotiations within the Convention and the two IGCs that led to the Constitutional treaty and to the Lisbon treaty. The mechanism is thus complex, has a restricted scope and was expected to have a limited operational record by both negotiators and academics.

Concretely, the EWS opens the possibility for national parliaments to review a European draft legislative act within an eight-week period after its transmission and to assess whether or not it complies with the subsidiarity principle. A chamber can issue and send a 'reasoned opinion' to the EU institutions asserting why this proposal breaches the principle. Each parliament has two votes, thus, in bicameral parliaments chambers have one vote each.

If the number of opinions denouncing a subsidiarity breach reaches one-third of the total votes of the national parliaments (58 by 1 August 2017), the so-called 'yellow card' is triggered. In such a case, the Commission must review its proposal and can decide to maintain, amend or withdraw it, and justify its choice. If the total of opinions represents half of the votes, the so-called 'orange card' is activated. The Commission must then review the proposal and can, again, maintain, amend or withdraw it; however, if it decides to maintain it, it must explain why, and the EP and the Council are called on to check the subsidiarity compliance of the proposal at the end of the first reading. They can then reject the proposal on subsidiarity grounds, by a simple majority in the EP or a qualified majority of 55 per cent in the Council.

The EWS procedure is quite constraining for national parliaments: it is, in theory, restricted to the control of the subsidiarity principle, and the eight-weeks period represents a tight timeframe. Moreover, national parliaments are requested to coordinate their action to trigger the mechanism collectively. For all these reasons, the EWS had quite a weak operation record during the first two years after its entry into force (1 December 2009). Until the first semester 2012, more than 200 draft legislative acts were transmitted to national parliaments in application of the EWS: only 145 reasoned opinions concerning 60 draft acts were adopted by 33 out of 38 parliamentary chambers.[37] By 2014, the Commission had received 506 opinions, while in 2015 this figure had decreased to 350, of which 8 were reasoned opinions in the terms of Protocol 2. In particular, three texts drew national parliaments' attention: the Commission's work programme (26 opinions), the proposal for a regulation establishing a relocation mechanism in the event of a migratory crisis (12 opinions including 5 reasoned opinions) and finally a proposal for a regulation on the possibility for Member States to restrict or prohibit the use of genetically modified food and animal feed in their territory (12 opinions, including 2 reasoned ones).[38]

The EWS has rebooted the interest of researchers in the involvement of national parliaments in EU affairs. Some were quite optimistic about the potential effect of the new procedure[39] but most were sceptical about the capacity of the chambers to use the mechanism and about its effective contribution to the legitimation of the EU.[40] They considered that the EWS was suffering from incentive, political and practical problems, and that even if a yellow or orange card was used, this would have little influence on EU law-making. Finally, many authors considered the EWS as a symbolic and virtual procedure that would, in the end, lead to a reinforcement of the Commission.[41]

Despite those analyses and predictions, and to general surprise, the EWS was triggered against the 'Monti II' legislative proposal in late May 2009. This use of the procedure is the result of a conjunction of factors. First, chambers have adapted to the EWS: they have made efforts to reduce transaction-costs and asymmetrical information by using the existing inter-parliamentary cooperation instruments, i.e. the COSAC, the IPEX and the permanent representative network. Also, the Monti II proposal was a very controversial one: it was an answer to a debated ruling of the European Court of Justice relating to the rights to take collective action.[42] To clarify the legal situation on this topic, the Commission proposed two texts in March 2012 (called the 'Monti II' package): a 'regulation on the exercise of the right to take collective action within the context of the freedom of establishment and the freedom to provide services' and a 'directive for the enforcement of Directive 96/71 on the Posting of workers'. They immediately induced a strong opposition from social partners, which contributed to the mobilization of national MPs. The trigger of the EWS was also made possible by the mobilization of 'policy entrepreneurs' (mainly the Danish parliament) who initiated a ripple effect and progressively mobilized other chambers in order to reach the threshold.[43]

Commissioners were surprised by the first trigger of the EWS, since most of them considered it to be a cosmetic procedure or communication operation, unlikely ever to be activated. They were also considering the yellow card as a harmless procedure, since it imposed no legal obligation for the Commission apart from reviewing the proposal. Thus, they were not really prepared to deal with the event and failed at lessening the impact of the objections made by national chambers on this proposal.

The relations of the Commission with the national parliaments fall under the responsibility of the General Secretariat. Some guidelines were set up to manage the EWS and anticipate a yellow or orange card, but they remained quite vague. Thus, when the yellow card was used against the Monti II proposals, there was some confusion about what to do and internal divergences arose. The Commission's leaders were surprised that the proposals were contested not only regarding the respect of the subsidiarity principle, but more generally, regarding their content and opportuneness. Also, they did not expect the Council and the EP to support the position of the national parliaments.

The College of Commissioners adopted a solution of compromise to overcome its internal disagreements. At the end of the summer of 2012, they decided to use the withdrawal procedure (Article 293 TFEU), and not one of the three possible options provided by the treaty within the framework of the EWS. National MPs criticized this choice for being a tactical answer, an attempt to deny the impact of the yellow card and a refusal to undertake political discussions with national parliaments on the topic and on the true notion of subsidiarity.

It is arguable that the Monti II case provoked a change in both the attitude of national MPs and of agents of the Commission. The former have started to be more offensive towards the European Commission, while the latter have adopted a more careful approach on Commission's relations with national chambers.

However, national parliaments have not made regular use of the EWS and the mechanism has only been triggered twice again (by 1 April 2017). In October 2013, the chambers of fourteen Member States expressed their reluctance regarding the creation of a European Public Prosecutor's Office and thus brandished a new 'yellow card'. A few days later, the Commission decided, however, to go ahead, considering that the proposal for a regulation was not an infringement of the principle of subsidiarity and that it would certainly be the subject of enhanced cooperation – which was eventually the case. A third 'yellow card' was voted by 14 chambers of 11 Member States in May 2016 on the proposal to revise the Directive on the Posting of Workers. Once again, the Commission chose to maintain its proposal.

It is difficult to determine whether parliaments will make more regular use of the early warning mechanism in the future. Today, MPs are clearly more mobilized by the issue, since they are now all aware of their capacity to truly influence EU law-making.[44] Also, some actors within EU institutions are favourable to a political approach of subsidiarity, and consider that national parliaments should have a key role in defining this principle and in legitimizing European legislative proposals. The Commission has adopted a more constructive approach to its relations with national parliaments, which may limit the cases of conflicts. Some pro-European MPs who contested the Monti II package were not satisfied by the withdrawal of the proposal and considered that national parliaments should not be an obstacle to EU policy-making. The decision of the Commission to maintain its proposal, after the last two yellow cards, is also likely to discourage the national parliamentarians.

Recently, MPs have discussed ways to improve the 'yellow card' procedure, via the introduction of voluntary guidelines and a political dialogue with the Commission. They especially ask the Commission for more detailed and swift answers to reasoned opinions. Some chambers have also launched a reflexion on the possibility for them to get involved more actively in the EU legislative process. The House of Lords, in a report of March 2014,[45] has thus proposed a system of 'green card' enabling national parliaments to make legislative suggestions to the Commission, as the EP and the Council can already do.[46] During the 53rd meeting of the COSAC Chairpersons (Riga, 31 May to 2 June 2015), a working group was set up to examine the possibility of the creation of a 'green card' and of an improvement of the 'yellow card'. A few days later (12 June 2015), the chairman of the European Affairs Committee of the House of Lords had sent a letter to his peers in the other Member States to invite them to support a 'green card' on the issue of food waste.[47] Finally, by the end of June 2015, the House of Lords sent a letter signed by 14 other parliaments to the Commission to request a legislative proposal on that topic.

During the meeting of the 54th COSAC (Luxembourg, 29 November to 1 December 2017), Frans Timmermans, Vice-Chair of the Commission, expressed his sympathy for the initiative, but stressed that the Commission would not abdicate its exclusive right to introduce legal acts, and recalled the need to respect the EU treaties and the national constitutions. He also underlined the growing importance attached by the new Commission to a dialogue with national parliaments, insisting on the 160 visits made by its members to National Chambers since their appointment.

To this day, the 'green card' has remained a unilateral and informal initiative. Its formalization would request a reform of the EU treaties and of many national constitutions, and it is quite likely that several national leaders would be reluctant to allow such changes. This initiative shows, however, that national MPs, or at least some of them, are now very much concerned about what happens at the EU level and about the legitimation of EU policies and norms to the point where they have decided to get involved. It should also be noted that for the first time, national chambers have decided to take initiatives without the participation of the EP. The most intriguing feature of parliamentary cooperation in the EU is, indeed that it always involved the EP, thanks to the efforts deployed by MEPs to avoid the constitution of an independent parliamentary network capable of competing with their institution. Hence, the COSAC can paradoxically send 'contributions' to EU institutions, including the EP, even if the EP itself is represented within the COSAC . . . The 'green card' procedure proposes another approach of interparliamentary cooperation that formally excludes the EP and even attempts to compete with it, because the national chambers are claiming a right of 'indirect initiative' that is comparable to that of the EP (Art. 225 TFEU).

6.4.7 National parliaments and treaty reform

In principle, national parliaments do not directly intervene in treaty reform. Their role is limited to the ratification of treaties negotiated and signed by representatives of the executive branch – Head of Government or State and Minister of Foreign Affairs. Their role is even more limited in case of ratification by referendum. However, the recourse to the conventional method to prepare the Charter of Fundamental Rights in 1999 and reflect on the institutional future of the Union in 2001, marked a dramatic reversal on this matter. In 1999, national MPs were asked to participate in the development of the Charter to increase its legitimacy and its political and symbolic scope, and to overcome national divisions which would have resulted from the use of a classical intergovernmental conference. Originally, the French government expressed its preference for a body composed only of European and national MPs. This solution was rejected, but delegates from national parliaments still constituted almost half of the members of the Working Group, which proclaimed itself a 'Convention'. Each Parliament delegated two of its members to make the representation of bicameral parliaments and opposition parties possible. The Convention adopted an ambitious text and, as was hoped, overcame the divisions which often paralyze intergovernmental conferences.

After the relative failure of the Treaty of Nice (2000), which revealed the impossibility of any significant reform of the institutional architecture of the Union by means of classic intergovernmental negotiations, state representatives decided to fuel the debate by organizing a new Convention, tasked with making suggestions as to the place of the European Council. However, members of the Convention decided to exceed their original mandate and proceed with drafting a European constitution.

For the first time, the Convention on the Future of the Union led national and European MPs to mix with representatives of the national executive bodies and the European Commission in an exercise of reflection on treaty reform. Again, the Convention included two representatives (and alternates) of the Parliament of each Member State and each candidate state, i.e. 56 members out of a total of 105 members of the Convention. The European Parliament, with 16 representatives, enjoyed an impressive domination over the Commission, which only had 2 representatives.

This Convention marked a paradigm shift for the MEPs, who had previously opposed any form of direct involvement in European construction by their national counterparts. Acknowledging the illusory nature of their claim to the monopoly of parliamentary representation at the EU level, the MEPs called for a participation of national parliaments in treaty reform, hoping to bring together the representatives of parliaments against those of governments. During the

Convention on the Future of the EU, the MEPs implemented this strategy with some success.[48] The concerted efforts of European and national parliamentarians, who together enjoyed significant influence in the Convention (72 representatives out of a total of 105), explain most of the advances proposed by the draft European constitution regarding the EP's powers and the participation of national parliaments in EU governance.

After the failure of the European Constitution, the reform of the EU was revived according to classic intergovernmental modalities and resulted in the signing of the Treaty of Lisbon on 13 December 2007. Despite the abandonment of the conventional method, the European Parliament has been associated more closely than in the past with the process of treaty negotiation through three representatives. It sought to maintain contact with national MPs on the issue of reform by convening the three joint parliamentary meetings on the theme 'The future of Europe: together, but how?' (Brussels, 8–9 May 2006, 4–5 December 2006 and 11–12 June 2007). During the third meeting, representatives of national and European Parliaments adopted a joint appeal to the Heads of State and government to preserve the substance of the Constitutional Treaty and called for strengthening the supervisory role of national parliaments in the European legislative process. The Intergovernmental Conference and the European Council heard these calls: the Lisbon Treaty not only increased the direct involvement of national parliaments in the EU's political system by tasking them with ensuring the observance of the principle of subsidiarity but also gave them the opportunity to complain to the Court of Justice and formalized their role in treaty reform.

Article 48 TEU states that the treaties may be amended in accordance with two procedures. The 'ordinary' procedure includes the convening of a Convention 'composed of representatives of the national Parliaments, of the Heads of state or government of the Member States, of the European Parliament and of the Commission' in charge of adopting a recommendation to an IGC. The European Council can decide by a simple majority, with the consent of the EP, not to convene a Convention if the proposed amendments are minor. The 'simplified' procedure does not involve the national parliaments, but it is restricted to the revision of part three of the TFEU relating to the internal policies and action of the Union.

The Article 48.7 TEU also allows the European Council to authorize the Council to act by a qualified majority rather than unanimity in some areas and to substitute the ordinary legislative procedure to a special legislative procedure in some cases. However, any initiative of that kind must be notified to the national parliaments. If a Parliament expresses its opposition within a delay of six months, the decision cannot be adopted.

On 15 June 2010, the European Parliament amended its internal rules to reflect the entry into force of the Lisbon Treaty, especially the provisions concerning the role of national parliaments. The revised rules provide that the Bureau of the EP appoints two Vice-Presidents among its own members who are responsible for the implementation of relations with national parliaments; one leads the European Parliament delegation to the COSAC together with the President of the Committee on Constitutional Affairs. The rules also detail the conditions under which European Parliament representatives can negotiate the terms of inter-parliamentary cooperation with national counterparts. Finally, it is provided that a parliamentary committee may engage in direct dialogue with committees of national Parliaments for pre-legislative and post-legislative cooperation within the limits of budgetary appropriations provided for this purpose.

The role of national parliaments remains, despite everything, still relatively limited in the functioning of the EU, despite a real awareness among national parliamentarians of the importance of this issue. Their involvement is fraught with both practical and political problems. Practically speaking, one can mention the complexity of EU decision-making, the aridity of most legislative proposals or even the lack of motivation of national parliamentarians to engage in this thankless task. From the political point of view, the reluctance of European institutions and most governments over the effective participation of national parliaments in the functioning of the EU is to be underlined, as well as the different views among national parliaments on the modalities and objectives of inter-parliamentary cooperation and the shortcomings of its bodies (Conference of Presidents, COSAC), which can be more dedicated to examining their own operating procedures than to controlling the EU's activities. Finally, we note that many national parliamentarians refuse to recognize the importance of the control of the Union's activities, believing that this amounts to acknowledging the loss of sovereignty from which parliaments have suffered since the early 1950s.

6.5 Non-institutional actors in the EU

The presentation of actors in the EU decision-making system would be biased if we did not refer to the increasingly crucial role of 'non-institutional' actors. Because of the many peculiarities of the EU political system (polycentrism and absence of hierarchy, complexity of norms, importance of technical regulations, weakness of political parties, absence of a European public sphere, limitations of the logic of representation, governance by committees, limitation of national and political conflicts through expertise and so on), non-institutional actors are able to play an important role. They are even called to do so by institutional actors who are always in search of expertise and legitimation.

First, one should mention the various experts (independent consultants, Member States' officials, researchers, academics, think tanks, etc.) directly and indirectly involved in the development and implementation of many policies.

Second, there is a multitude of interest groups (representatives) gravitating around EU institutions and developing more or less regular and close contacts with EU actors.[49] In Brussels, there are over 5,000 lobbies, which employ around 30,000 people. These actors, often presented as a homogeneous group, have profiles and motivations which vary widely. Thus, a typology is useful.

European federations, numbering about 500, represent companies, associations and unions, which have advanced structures (representation bureau in Brussels, permanent staff) and significant financial resources. These 'Eurogroups' (in EU jargon) are the preferred interlocutors of the Commission and EP who appreciate their ability to limit interference between players originating from the same sector, to create synergies between them and to contribute to the emergence of common positions. Organizations such as the COPA (Committee of Agricultural Organizations) and BusinessEurope (the Confederation of European Business, representing 40 member federations and 20 million companies from 34 countries) limit the counter-productive effects of the dispersed interferences of their constituents with European institutions. However, their united front often hides conflicts of interest. Many Eurogroups have indeed the sole effective function of reporting to their members on the actions of EU institutions and the state of current legislative procedures. Based on this information, members are then free to entrust the defence of their interests to the federation or to opt for an independent approach by sending representatives, relying on the services of professional lobbying groups in Brussels or by soliciting a national government or party.[50]

Approximately 250 **large companies**, both European and foreign, also have their own representational structure in Brussels, with means comparable to the Eurogroups.[51] Given that their representatives clearly defend very specific private interests, they are considered with caution within the institutions.

There are several thousand **professional lobbyists** in Brussels, with various statuses. They work in audit firms, consulting and public policy firms, and business law firms. They perform two types of functions. First, they may act promptly on behalf of a client who has a specific need: a big business or Eurogroup which does not have enough resources to handle an issue, an informal grouping of economic or social actors involved in the same issue, a state government outside of the EU, etc. Their objective in this case is to influence the development or implementation of a European norm or a decision of the Commission.[52] Second, lobbyists may provide a monitoring function. In this case, they systematically collect information to inform their customers about current EU activities. MEPs and EU officials are particularly suspicious of them, insofar as they are making business out of public or confidential data and provide no expertise.[53]

Over the past 30 years, **regions and local communities** have demonstrated a lot of dynamism in order to be represented in Brussels. They do so in three distinct modes:

- on an individual basis: the regions or local communities are running representative offices in Brussels. Currently, there are almost 200. Some are primarily symbolic while others have means comparable to those of a permanent national representation;
- in a mode comparable to the 'Eurogroups', regions create thematic (i.e. AREV: Assembly of European Wine Regions) or geographical (i.e. the Atlantic Arc Commission) associations that have offices and representatives in Brussels[54];
- in a general mode: the Assembly of European Regions and the Council of Municipalities and Regions of Europe, general(ist) associations of subnational authorities, have offices in Brussels.

Representatives of regions and communities benefit from a favourable reception within European institutions as a result of the legitimacy attached to territorial representation. In return, they can take advantage of this legitimacy to make privileged contacts with some commissioners, officials and MEPs. In the EP, they find attentive interlocutors within the intergroup of local and regional elected officials and specialized intergroups, and enjoy fewer constraints than other lobbyists.

Diplomats or representatives from countries outside the EU can also act as lobbyists and many countries are represented towards the EU not only through an embassy, but through structures similar to groups of interest – such as the American Chamber of Commerce. Foreign countries are, indeed, impacted by many of the EU's activities (conventional politics, actions in favour of development and protection of human rights, legislative activities that affect their economic activities, accession prospects, etc.) and thus seek to get information or influence over them.

One might add – if not afraid to stretch the notion of lobbying – that **Member States** are called upon to defend their own interests towards EU institutions in addition to their action within the Council and the European Council. National ministries and administrations are developing unilateral means of information and influence in Brussels. In the Commission, this practice takes forms similar to lobbying, with occasionally more 'political' interventions in the direction of the national commissioner. In the EP, this appears mostly in the context of links that national delegations maintain with their national parties and governments.[55] Ministries or administrations in charge of EU affairs regularly send detailed memos to their MEPs to provide explanations on the texts, to underline the national interests at stake and, punctually, to give them more precise instructions. Officials from the Permanent Representations in Brussels spend nowadays a lot of time in the EP to meet MEPs of their nationality. They are more or less inclined to listen to them and follow their recommendations, depending on their view of their mandate and their degree of dependence on their government or party.

Finally, if the notion of **civil society** has appeared belatedly at the European level, contact with it has been around a long time, especially in the EP. The first explicit reflections on dialogue with the non-profit sector took place in 1995 within DG V (Social Affairs and Employment) of the Commission and from 1996 within the Economic and Social Committee. The EP, on the other hand, opened a broad dialogue with civil society organizations during the Intergovernmental Conference that led, in 1997, to the Treaty of Amsterdam. Meanwhile, some organizations have tried to structure their work on behalf of 'European civil society'. In 1995, we witnessed the creation of the Permanent Forum of European Civil Society which sought to defend the project of a Europe closer to its citizens in the framework of treaty reform.

Progressively, all EU institutions have included civil-society organizations among their interlocutors and have often treated them in a privileged way, since they represent public interests.[56] Many representatives of economic and private interests also claim to belong to 'civil society', fully aware of the favourable reception that await them in the institutions. To do so, they emphasize the public dimension of the issues that motivate their actions or hide behind various kinds of think tanks or associations.[57]

At the end of the 1990s, the notion of 'European civil society' has been defined in detail by an opinion of the Economic and Social Committee[58] and has been widely disseminated in public debate through the White Paper on European Governance of the Commission.[59] The latter defines European civil society as all of the trade and employer unions ('social partners'), non-governmental organizations, professional associations, charitable organizations, grassroots organizations, organizations that involve citizens in local and municipal life, and recognizes the specific contribution of churches and religious communities. The European Convention has provided a significant portion of its debates to the participation of civil society in the functioning of the EU. The Treaty of Lisbon echoes this concern and mentions several times civil society and the principle of openness of the institutions – including the Council. It provides in particular that institutions 'maintain an open, transparent and regular dialogue with representative associations and civil society' (Article 10 TEU).

All of these lobbyists and interest representatives form a European elite which follows closely the EU's activities, understands them and undertakes a whole range of lobbying practices: formal and informal contacts with institutional and non-institutional actors, observation of institutions' activities, preparation and diffusion of statements, organization of press campaigns, public events or demonstrations, participation in the Commission's advisory committees, etc.

In addition, lobbyists also make a proficient use of the possibilities for action offered to citizens by the treaties such as:

- participation in various consultation activities (public and expert hearings, conferences, forums, seminars, transmission of reports in response to Green papers, participation in consultation exercises over the Internet, etc.);
- complaints to the Commission;
- direct appeals before the Court of Justice;
- petitions to the EP;
- referral to the European Ombudsman;
- requests for access to documents;
- use of the mechanism of the European Citizens' Initiative, provided by the Lisbon Treaty, which allows one million citizens to demand the Commission to adopt a legislative proposal.

Paradoxically, the more EU institutions try to be opened to civil society and try to ensure some pluralism in interest representation, the more they offer channels of influence for lobbyists representing private interests.

In the European area of Brussels, representatives of interest groups occupy a vast majority of the buildings that do not pertain to EU institutions. Lobbying is today a major economic activity in the EU capital; representing a billion-euro a year and employing 30,000 people – to be compared to the 31,000 staff of the Commission. This makes Brussels the second city in the world, after Washington, regarding the number of lobbyists.

Interest representatives are supposed to provide actors of EU institutions with information and arguments, and not put pressure on them. Concretely, they try to meet all the key persons dealing with a file, to explain to them their concerns, to transmit arguments and reports to them, and potentially to send drafts of amendments to MEPs, and to be present in all the arenas and forums of discussions.

EU institutions have developed over years a set of rules to frame the activities of interest groups and freelance lobbyists, and to ensure some clearness in that respect. These rules are particularly trying to provide more transparency about the interests represented. Lobbyists are called to sign a transparency register common to the EP and the Commission and to declare their employers' identity. They must also respect a code of conduct allowing EU actors to complain efficiently against those who misbehave. However, the register is not mandatory and not all lobbyists are explicit about their allegiances (thus the graph in Figure 6.1 shows the extent to which the number of interest representatives is underestimated on the basis of the transparency register). Some of them thus appear as neutral experts or enact on several statuses, and EU actors sometimes judge lobbyists' pressure excessive.

The EU institutions are confronted with another phenomenon that is widespread in Brussels: revolving doors. It refers to the tendency of private

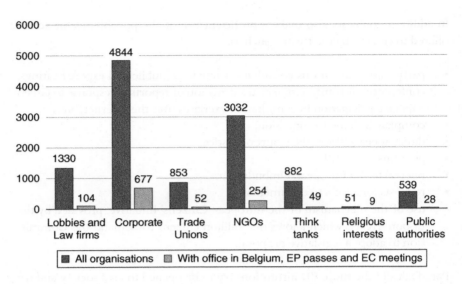

Figure 6.1 Lobbies and associations according to the Transparency register
Source: Lobbyfacts, https://lobbyfacts.eu/charts-graphs, 8 December 2017.

companies to hire senior EU civil servants, cabinet members, friends of politicians or MEPs, or even Commissioners or MEPs when they retire or quit their functions in order to benefit from their networks and their knowledge of specific files. In these circumstances, key players in the EU may also be rewarded afterwards by a highly compensated position for their complacency towards private interests. There are rules forbidding certain actors to work in the sector for which they were responsible for a given period of time, but there are always possible wrongdoings, as in the polemic following the hiring of José Manuel Barroso by the Goldman Sachs Bank in 2016.[60]

It is very difficult to estimate the overall influence of lobbying on the EU policy making, beyond a case-by-case approach. It is nevertheless considered to be high by researchers and observers, especially by way of comparison with national situations.[61] Corporate Europe Observatory (http://corporateeurope.org), an association campaigning for greater transparency in the EU sphere, considers that the lobbies influence, to a varying extent, 75 per cent of EU norms.

Sectors such as energy, the sector of chemical products, the insurance industry, tobacco, medicine and high technologies are massively represented in Brussels, and have huge human and financial means to try to influence EU actors. Many civil-society organizations try to limit lobbies' impact using similar methods. For instance, health-promotion associations fight efficiently the powerful lobbies of the alcohol and tobacco industries. But the fight is often unbalanced. Thus, the financial resources available to the chemical or Eurochamber sectors are in no way comparable to those of trade unions or non-governmental organizations.

For instance, the only organization representing consumers, the European Consumer Organisation (BEUC), has only 35 employees. Even if it benefits from the support of the EU – which finances half of its budget – and if it enjoys privileged access to institutions, it is incapable to counterbalance efficiently the numerous pressure groups that work for the private sector.

Conclusion

The EU is a complex political system that should not be reduced to its four main institutions – EP, Commission, Council and European Council. It involves many other institutions, organs and actors that exert several functions. They contribute to its legitimation by creating a complex system of checks and balances, ensuring a very high level of political and legal control, or enriching the reflexion on policies. At the same time, this institutional profusion is confusing for citizens and does not ease the enunciation of a coherent narrative to describe the nature and principles of the EU regime.

Also, despite the efforts made to involve national parliaments and civil society organizations, the EU is not really able to overcome its image of a centralized and elitist system, driven by intergovernmental deals and sensitive to lobbying. It shows the greatest difficulties in developing a real dialogue with citizens, civil society organizations, trade unions, local authorities, etc., capable of increasing its legitimation.

In order to fully understand those challenges and difficulties, we must first analyse how all those institutions, organs and actors interact in the decision-making system.

Notes

1 Olivier Costa and Paul Magnette, eds, *Une Europe des élites? Réflexions sur la fracture démocratique de l'Union européenne* (Brussels: Editions de l'Université de Bruxelles, 2007), 284.

2 Charlie Jeffery, 'Social and regional interests: ESC and the committee of the regions,' in *The Institutions of the European Union*, eds John Peterson and Michael Shackleton (Oxford/New York: Oxford University Press, coll. 'The New European Union Series,' 1st ed., 2002), 326–345; Juliet Lodge and Valentine Herman, 'The economic and social committee in EEC decision making,' *International Organization* 34(2) (1980): 265–284.

3 www.eesc.europa.eu.

4 Kathleen McNamara, 'Managing the Euro: The European Central Bank,' in *The Institutions of the European Union*, eds John Peterson and Michael Shackleton (Oxford/New York: Oxford University Press, coll. 'The New European Union Series,' 1st ed., 2002), 164–184; Simon Hix, *The Political System of the European Union* (London: Macmillan Press, coll. 'The European Union series,' 1999).

5 Friedrich Heinemann and Felix Huefner, 'Is the view from the Eurotower purely European? National divergence and ECB interest rate policy,' *Scottish Journal of Political Economy* 51(4) (2004): 544–558.

6 http://europa.eu/rapid/press-release_MEMO-12-909_en.htm.

7 The six-pack consists of five regulations and a directive which entered into force at the end of 2011 throughout the EU. It reforms the Stability and Growth Pact and deepens the Member States' budgetary surveillance thanks to the 'European Semester', a system for coordinating the economic and budgetary policies of the Member States, which authorizes the Commission to request amendments and even impose sanctions on national budget projects. The 'two-pack' consists of two regulations entered into force at the end of May 2013 to strengthen the six-pack. It improves the transparency and coordination of the States' budgetary decisions and takes better account of their needs. It aims more broadly to deepen EMU and improve its resistance to crises.

8 Karl Kaltenhaler, *Policy-Making in the European Central Bank: The Masters of Europe's Money* (Lanham: Rowman & Littlefield, 2006).

9 Edoardo Chiti, 'The emergence of a community administration: the case of the European agencies,' *Common Market Law Review* 37 (2000): 309–343; Giandomenico Majone, ed., *Regulating Europe* (London/New York: Routledge, coll. 'European public policy,' 1996); Madalina Busuioc, Martijn Groenleer and Jarle Trondal, *The Agency Phenomenon in the European Union: Emergence, Institutionalisation and Everyday Decision-Making* (Manchester: Manchester University Press, 2012).

10 Mark Thatcher and Alec Stone Sweet, 'Theory and practice of delegation to non-majoritarian institutions,' *West European Politics* 25(1) (2002): 1–22.

11 Neil Nugent, *The Government and Politics of the European Union* (Basingstoke, Palgrave MacMillan, 7th ed., 2010), 234–235.

12 Deirdre Curtin, 'Delegation to EU non-majoritarian agencies and emerging practices of public accountability,' in *Regulation Through Agencies in The EU, A New Paradigm Of European Govenance?*, eds Damien Géradin, Rodolphe Múñoz and Nicolas Petit (Cheltenham, UK; Northhampton, MA: Edward Elgar, 2005), 88–119.

13 R. Daniel Kelemen, *The European 'independent' Agencies and Regulation in the EU* (Brussels: CEPS Working Documents no 112, 1997), 3; Daniel R. Kelemen, 'The politics of "Eurocratic" structure and the New European agencies,' *West European Politics* 25(4) (2002): 93–118.

14 Martijn Groenleer, 'The European Commission and Agencies,' in *European Union: Power and Policy-Making*, ed. Jeremy J. Richardson (Abingdon/New York: Routledge, 3rd ed., coll. 'Routledge research in European public policy,' 2006), 156–172; Knud Erik Jørgensen, Mark A. Pollack and Ben Rosamond, eds, *Handbook of European Union Politics* (London/Thousand Oaks: Sage, 2006); Mark Thatcher, 'Delegation to Independent Regulatory Agencies: Pressures, functions and Contextual Mediation,' *West European Politics* 25(1) (2002): 125–147.

15 Daniel R. Kelemen, *The European 'independent' agencies and regulation in the EU*, 4.

16 Mark Bovens, Deirdre Curtin and Paul 't Hart, eds, *The Real World of EU Accountability. What Deficit?* (Oxford: Oxford University Press, 2010), 87.

17 Govin Permanand and Ellen Vos, 'EU regulatory agencies and health protection,' in *The Role of European Union Law and Policy*, eds Elias Mossialos, Govin Permanand, Rita Baeten and Tamara Hervey (Cambridge: Cambridge University Press, 2010), 140.

18 Renaud Dehousse, 'Regulation by networks in the European Community: The Role of the European Agencies,' *Journal of European Public Policy* 4(2) (1997): 246–261; Majone, ed., *Regulating Europe;* Paul Magnette, *Le régime politique de l'Union européenne* (Paris: Presses de Sciences, 2009).

19 Burkard Eberlein and Dieter Kerwer, 'New governance in the European Union: A theoretical perspective,' *Journal of Common Market Studies* 42(1) (2002): 121–142; Giandomenico Majone, 'Delegation of regulatory powers in a mixed polity,' *European Law Journal* 8(3) (2002): 319–339; Giandomenico Majone, 'The new European agencies: Regulation by information,' *Journal of European Public Policy* 4(2) (1997): 262–275; Majone, ed., *Regulating Europe.*

20 Giandomenico Majone, *The European Community as a Regulatory State* (Leiden: Nijhoff, coll. 'Series of Lectures of the Academy of European Law,' 1995); Michelle Everson, 'Independent agencies,' in *Sources and Categories of European Union Law*, ed. Gerd Winter (Baden-Baden: Nomos, coll. 'Schriftenreihe des Zentrums für europäische Rechtspolitik' 22, 1996).

21 Martijn Groenleer, *'The European Commission and Agencies,'* 156–172.

22 European Commission, *Participation of candidate countries in Community programmes, agencies and committees* (Communication to the Council of 20 December 1999), COM(1999) 710 final.; European Commission, *Draft Interinstitutional Agreement of 25 February 2005 on the operating framework for the European regulatory agencies,* COM(2005) 59 final; European Commission: *European Agencies—The way forward SEC* (Communication to the European Parliament and the Council of 11 March 2008) COM(2008) 135 final, 323.

23 'Decentralised agencies,' European Union, accessed 7 June 2013, http://europa.eu/agencies/regulatory_agencies_bodies/.

24 European Commission, Progress report on the implementation of the Common Approach on EU decentralised agencies, Brussels, 24.4.2015 COM(2015) 179 final-http://eur-lex.europa.eu/legal-content/EN/TXT/PDF/?uri=COM:2015:179:FIN& from=EN.

25 European Commission, Roadmap on the follow-up to the Common Approach on EU decentralised agencies, 19 December 2012. http://europa.eu/agencies/documents/2012-12-18_roadmap_on_the_follow_up_to_the_common_approach_on_eu_decentralised_agencies_en.pdf.

26 Katrin Auel, 'Democratic accountability and National Parliaments: redefining the impact of parliamentary scrutiny in EU Affairs,' *European Law Journal* 13 (2006): 487–504.

27 Karl-Heinz Neunreither, 'The European parliament and national parliaments: conflict or cooperation?,' *Journal of Legislative Studies* 11(3–4) (2005): 466–489.

28 Katrin Auel and Arthur Benz, eds, *The Europeanisation of Parliamentary Democracy* (Abingdon/New York: Routledge, coll. 'The library of legislative studies,' 2006).

29 Nicola Lupo and Cristina Fasone, eds., *Interparliamentary Cooperation in the Composite European Constitution* (Oxford: Hart, 2016, 366).

30 Christine Neuhold, Olivier Rozenberg, Julie Smith. Smith, Claudia Hefftler, *The Palgrave Handbook of National Parliaments and the European Union* (London: Palgrave, 2016, 760 p).

31 Katrin Auel and Oliver Höing, National parliaments and the Eurozone crisis: taking ownership in difficult times?, *West European Politics* 38(2) (2015): 375–395 ; Katrin Auel

and Oliver Höing, Parliaments in the Euro crisis: Can the losers of integration still fight back? *JCMS: Journal of Common Market Studies* 52(6) (2014): 1184–1193.

32 Maria Teresa Paulo, 'National parliaments in the EU: after Lisbon and beyond subsidiarity—the (positive) side-effects and (unintended) achievements of the treaty provisions,' *OPAL Online Paper* 5 (2012): 15.

33 Prepared and developed by a drafting committee composed of the chairmen of 20 specialized parliamentary bodies and 8 Members of the European Parliament.

34 see: www.ipex.eu.

35 Stéphanie Hennette, Thomas Piketty, Guillaume Sacriste and Antoine Vauchez, *Pour un traité de démocratisation de l'Europe*, Paris, Le Seuil, 2017.

36 Pieter De Wilde, *Why the Early Warning Mechanism does not Alleviate the Democratic Deficit* (Observatory of Parliament after the Lisbon Treaty (OPAL), Online Paper no. 6 (2012): 3.

37 Assemblée nationale, *Analyse de l'exercice du mécanisme d'alerte précoce sur la période 2010–2012* (Brussels: Juillet, 2012), 3.

38 Annual report 2015 on relations between the European Commission and the national parliaments, 15 July 2016.

39 Ian Cooper, 'The watchdogs of subsidiarity: national parliaments and the logic of arguing in the European Union,' *Journal of the Common Market* 44(2) (2006): 281–304; Ian Cooper, 'The subsidiarity early mechanism: making it work,' *Intereconomics* (2006): 254–257; Philipp Kiiver, 'The treaty of Lisbon, the national parliaments and the principle of subsidiarity,' *Maastricht Journal of European and Comparative Law* 15 (2008): 77–83.

40 Tapio Raunio, *National Parliaments and European Integration: What we know and what we should know* (ARENA—Centre of European Studies, University of Oslo, Working Paper no 2, 2009).

41 Philipp Kiiver, 'The early-warning system for the principle of subsidiarity: the national parliament as a Conseil d'Etat for Europe,' *European Law Review* 1 (2011): 98–108.

42 European Court of Justice, Case C-341/05: *Laval and Partners v. Svendska Byggnadsar-betareförbundet and others* (2007), ECR I-11767; European Court of Justice, Case C-438-05: *International Transport Workers' Federation and Finnish Seamen's Union v. Viking Line ABP and another* (2007), ECR I-10779; European Court of Justice, Case C-346/06: *Rüffert v. Land Niedersachsen* (2008), ECR I-1989; European Court of Justice, Case C-319/06: *Commission v. Luxembourg* (2008), ECR I-4323.

43 Clément Vernet, 'Yellow card to the European Commission for the "Monti II proposal". Assessing the future of the early warning system for the principle of subsidiarity' (Master thesis, College of Europe, Bruges, 2013).

44 *West European Politics*, Special Issue: After Lisbon: National Parliaments in the European Union, eds Kathrin Auel and Thomas Christiansen 38(2), 2015; Thomas Christiansen, Anna-lena Högenauer and Christine Neuhold, 'National Parliaments in the post-Lisbon European Union: Bureaucratization rather than Democratization,' *Comparative European Politics* 12(2) (2014): 121–140; Katjana Gattermann and Claudia Hefftler, 'Beyond institutional capacity: political motivation and parliamentary behaviour in the early warning system,' *West European Politics* 38(2) (2015): 305–334.

45 House of Lords, European Union Committee 9th Report of Session 2013–14, 24 March 2014 www.publications.parliament.uk/pa/ld201314/ldselect/ldeucom/151/151.pdf.

46 Chambre des lords, Comité de l'Union européenne 9e rapport de la session 2013–14, 24 mars 2014.

47 www.parliament.uk/documents/lords-committees/eu-select/green-card/green-card-letter-to-np-chairs.pdf.

48 Olivier Costa, 'La contribution de la composante « Parlement européen » à la Convention européenne,' *Politique européenne* 13 (2004): 21–41.

49 Sonia Mazey and Jeremy J. Richardson, 'Interest groups and EU policy-making: Organisational logic and venue shopping,' in *European Union: Power and Policy-Making*, ed. Jeremy J. Richardson (Abingdon/New York: Routledge, 3rd ed., coll. 'Routledge research in European public policy,' 2006), 247–265.

50 Justin Greenwood, *Interest Representation in the European Union* (Basingstoke/New York: Palgrave, coll. 'The European union series,' 3rd ed., 2011); Justin Greenwood, Linda Strangward and Lara Stancich, 'The capacities of Euro groups in the Integration Process,' *Political Studies* 47(1) (1999):127–138; Emiliano Grossman, 'Bringing politics back: rethinking the role of economic interest groups in European integration,' *Journal of European Public Policy* 11(4) (2004): 637–656.; Beate Kohler-Koch, 'Organized interests in European integration: the evolution of a new type of governance?,' in *Participation and Policy-Making in the European Union*, eds Helen S. Wallace and Alasdair R. Young (Oxford/New York: Clarendon Press/Oxford University Press, 1997).

51 Robert J. Bennett, 'Business routes of influence in Brussels: exploring the choice of direct representation,' *Political Studies* 47(2) (1999): 240–257.

52 Justin Greenwood and Karsten Ronit, 'Interest groups in the European community: newly emerging dynamics and forms,' *West European Politics* 17(1) (1994): 31–52; Bernhard Wessels, 'European parliament and the interest groups,' in *The European Parliament, the National Parliaments and European Integration*, eds Richard S. Katz and Bernhard Wessels (Oxford: Oxford University Press, 1999).

53 Sonia Mazey and Jeremy J. Richardson, 'Promiscuous policymaking: the European policy style?,' in *The State of the Union, vol. 3: Building A European Polity?*, eds Carolyn Rhodes and Sonia Mazey (Harlow/Boulder: Longman/Lynne Rienner, 1995); Hélène Michel, ed., *Lobbyistes et lobbying de l'Union européenne: trajectoires, formations et pratiques des représentants d'intérêts* (Strasbourg: Presses universitaires de Strasbourg, coll. 'Sociologie politique européenne,' 2005).

54 Liesbet Hooghe and Gary Marks, '"Europe with the Regions": channels of regional representation in the European Union,' *Publius, the Journal of Federalism* 26(1) (1996): 73–92.

55 Stefano Braghiroli, *Home Sweet Home: Assessing the Weight and Effectiveness of National Parties' Interference on MEPs' everyday Activity* (SEI Working Paper, no. 108, 2008); Sonia Mazey and Jeremy J. Richardson, eds, *Lobbying in the European Community* (Oxford: Oxford University Press, coll. 'Nuffield European studies,' 1993).

56 Stijn Smismans, ed., *European Governance and Civil Society* (Cheltenham: Edward Elgar, 2006).

57 For an overview of the literature on Interest Representation and the representativeness of representatives of the 'civil society,' see Andreas Dür, 'Interest groups in the European Union: how powerful are they?,' *West European Politics* 31(6) (2008) 1212–1230;

Sabine Saurugger, 'Interest groups and democracy in the European Union,' *West European Politics* 31(6) (2008): 1274–1291.

58 Economic and Social Committee, *Opinion on the role and contribution of civil society organizations in the building of Europe* (17 November 1999), JO C 329: 30f.

59 European Commission, *European governance: a white paper* (25 July 2001), COM document (2001) 428 final.

60 Alberto Alemanno and Benjamin Bodson, How to nudge Barroso out of the revolving door. LSE European Politics and Policy (EUROPP) Blog, 2016.

61 Justin Greenwood, 2011.

Decision-making in the European Union

7

After explaining the complex history of the EU decision-making system and describing its numerous actors, we now turn to its operations. First, one must mention its legislative work, which has always been its central activity and now includes the three main institutions (Commission, Council, EP) in a highly integrated process. Similar mechanisms and logics, though specific, apply to the budget process and key international agreements that must be ratified by the Council and the Parliament. Other decisions are beyond this general framework, such as when the Commission independently implements European legislation or acts in domains where it has specific powers (competition policy, state aids, the CAP, etc.). There are other exceptions for the decisions that the Council adopts regarding the CFSP or criminal cooperation, or for the implementation of certain standards. We should also mention – even though they have no legal impact – the resolutions of initiative that the EP continues to adopt. Further, the procedures for appointments also call for specific institutional patterns.

In this wide range of activities, we will focus on the legislative work which is now as ever at the centre of the functions of EU institutions. Its elaboration is particularly important for at least three reasons.

First, the resounding failure of the 'constitutionalization' process of the 2000s and the rejection of a political Union by public opinion essentially confirm the EU's mainly functional vocation: in other words, European integration mainly exists through its capacity to develop policies. Their implementation remains essentially a matter for the governments, administrations and courts of the Member States and for sub-state entities. Also, EU institutions are struggling to emerge as political actors in their own right and exist in national public spheres. Despite the increasing politicization of European issues, the notion of a 'European public space' does not make sense to the ordinary citizen. Not content with words alone as are national politicians, EU actors are forced to focus on making public policy, which takes on particular importance. Faced with the rise of Euroscepticism all over Europe, they are obliged daily to prove the usefulness and relevance of their action.

'Policy-making' is also crucial because it is the main place of interaction between EU institutions. The relationships between the Commission, Council and Parliament, which are inherently tense and cause frequent conflicts, take place essentially during the decision-making process. Given the weakness of European political parties and limited media interest in the EU, 'political' inter-actions between the institutions can only take place in the EP and are restricted to a few key moments: oral questions, question time, Commissioner's hearings, timely interventions by Commission members or by the Council's presidency in front of the MEPs. Relations between the Commission and the Council only have a few opportunities for public appearances. In sum, the balance of power between the institutions is manifested above all during the decision-making process which allows them to express their views and to criticize, implicitly or explicitly, their partners' positions.

Third, one must recognize that the EU's legislative process is far from being a purely technical matter and that it is, on the contrary, underpinned by a triple dynamic. Discussions and negotiations deal primarily with the content of the texts, which most often generate contrasting views. The Commission tends to favour a technical perspective and is sensitive to the discourse of the most estab-lished special interests in Brussels. The Parliament is committed to its respon-siveness to citizens and has a different approach to lobbyists so it is more attentive (in appearance at least) to civil-society organizations and infra-state authorities than to private-interest groups. The Council generally gives precedence to national interests (be they private or public), favouring the lowest common denominator, which leads it to prefer less ambitious texts. The Committee of the Regions and the Economic and Social Committee are also trying to make their respective points of view heard, even if it is purely advisory.

Generally speaking, the dynamic of law-making in the EU is very different from what it is at the national level. Historically, there is no systematic political support for the Commission from the Parliament, and each proposal is the subject of intense negotiations between the three institutions – even if they happen more and more behind closed doors, within the framework of 'trialogues', and thus with little publicity. The situation changed somewhat in 2014, with the creation of the 'block' – i.e. the alliance of Christian-Democrats, Socialists and Liberals – supporting the nomination of J. C. Juncker. However, the EP has a critical view of the legislative proposals transmitted by the Commission, and does not have to systematically support its action like lower chambers do in governments of most Member States. Second, given the relative flexibility that characterizes the EU's institutional system and its evolving nature, the institutions' perspectives often include strategies that have little to do with policy content. The Commission may well want to pass a text at all costs to extend its jurisdiction; the Council may wish to challenge the Commission's proposal to give priority to another legal basis, such as giving less influence to the EP; and the Parliament can in turn reject a text to protest its partners' attitude in the inter-institutional dialogue. Even within institutions, some bodies and actors (Commission DGs, parliamentary committees, expert groups, or Council formations, etc.) engage in power struggles that are sometimes unrelated to the policies themselves. A third factor complicating EU decision-making is the attitude towards European integration. Actors within the institutions may support or oppose a reform based on its potential impact on the degree of integration and not on its actual purpose. Such a proposal for codification or legislative revision will be opposed in the Parliament not because of its content (since it only has to synthesize existing law) but because the MEPs most favourable to integration will see a lack of political ambition from the Commission and those more Eurosceptic will see the systematization of a bureaucratic approach to integration of which they disapprove. Conversely, some Member States can block a proposal for fear that it helps to widen the scope of EU intervention at the expense of national authorities. To grasp the logic and complexity of EU decision-making, it is thus important to always consider three levels of issues: the public-policy itself, the inter-institutional balance of power and the degree of resulting European integration.

In order to provide a comprehensive overview of EU decision-making, we will first examine the division of power between the different levels of government which strictly determines the capacity for action by each European institution. Second, we will present the decision-making procedures themselves with particular emphasis on co-decision, which is now the common legal procedure. The next chapter will adopt a more analytical approach by distinguishing several EU decision-making 'models'. This typology will be complemented and enriched by the explanation of three distinctive features of the functioning of the EU.

7.1 The EU's competences

In order to analyse the EU's operations, we must begin by reviewing its powers and highlighting the issues associated with their definitions.

7.1.1 A historically confused division of competences

The division of powers between Member States and Community/EU institutions has always been complex. Originally, one could distinguish three broad categories: the powers of the Member States, over which the Community had no direct influence; powers of the Community, which Member States renounced in totality, apart from their representation in European institutions and their role in implementation; and the so-called 'shared' competences, the most numerous, for which the two levels of government are likely to intervene. This third category follows a principle of reality: with the entry into force of the treaties, Community institutions could not directly develop all the standards and norms necessary to achieve the objectives of the treaties or to set up effective policies. Therefore, they had a right to intervene in the sectors concerned, which they could use as they deemed necessary. Concretely, if the institutions decided to intervene, states were required not to and to accept if necessary to override national norms. Thus, no right of 'shared' action per se exists and the priority of intervention always goes to the EU. As recognized by the Court of Justice, full use of its joint competences can lead the EU to have exclusive power in a sector.

The EU has gradually developed two new types of competence. 'Parallel' competences correspond to actions led by the EU in areas where states remain fully sovereign, such as development aid policy or the CFSP. 'Limited' competences (today: 'supporting' competences) correspond to EU actions aimed at strengthening the effectiveness of Member State policies without constraining or replacing them. This is the case of framework programmes for research and development that do not challenge the state's powers and are intended to foster collaboration on a European scale.

The Court of Justice has produced a wealth of case law as a result of the treaties' grey areas and jurisdictional disputes arising between Member States and EU institutions, particularly due to the Commission's tendency to exceed its formal powers. Two 'theories' have strongly influenced the interpretation of the treaties and the evolution of European powers.

The first is the *theory of implied powers*. The Court acknowledges that Community institutions are entitled to exercise the powers which, though not expressly mentioned in the treaties, are necessary to effectively exercise their formal powers.[1] The argument is that treaty negotiators could not have granted some powers to the Community, without having implicitly accepted to endow it with the powers that are intimately linked to them but for which they could not establish an *a priori* list (ERTA Decision, ECJ, March 31, 1971). The Court also extricated a principle of parallelism of powers: any internal competence corresponds implicitly with an external competence which may be exercised if the internal competence has already been exercised. We find a trace of this principle in Article 3.2 TFEU:

> The Union shall also have exclusive competence for the conclusion of an international agreement when its conclusion is provided for in the legislative act of the Union or is necessary to enable the Union to exercise its internal competence, or insofar as its conclusion may affect common rules or alter their scope.

The second is the theory of subsidiary powers, which stems from an article in the Rome Treaty, now Article 352 TFEU. It provides that if an action of the Union should prove necessary within the framework of its policies to achieve one of the objectives set by the treaty, although the treaties do not mention the necessary powers of action, the Council, acting unanimously on a proposal from the Commission and after approval by Parliament, shall adopt the appropriate measures. This article allows the EU to adjust its power to the objectives of the treaties without having to revise them whenever it is found that it lacks jurisdiction. This possibility has played a major role in extending the powers of the EU, permitting, for example, the creation of the European Monetary Cooperation Fund (EMCF), the European Development Fund (EDF) and the launch of actions in social, energy, environmental, research, and consumer-protection matters. The powers acquired through this article are often included a posteriori in the treaties: revisions are indeed used both to develop new policies and to provide a stable legal basis for existing actions (*aggiornamento*). The theory of subsidiary powers allows the Union to intervene in almost any domain, provided that there is unanimity within the Council and it is possible to prove that this action is related to the implementation of one of the objectives set by the treaties. However, the Court of Justice has prompted Member States to be cautious by sanctioning repeated misuse of this stratagem.

The division of competences between EU institutions and the Member States has proven to be increasingly complex over time. Establishing the state of national and European law in any given sector is a major headache, particularly as a result of the lack of systematic codification of Community law, which is spread through multiple treaties and norms adopted by the institutions since the 1950s. For the record, the Community acquis currently represents 100,000 pages of the Official Journal of the EU and 17,000 acts (Celex database). Approximately 80 per cent of this acquis consists of binding standards. The situation is further complicated by frequent jurisdictional disputes between European and national actors, representing different public or private interests.

Past efforts to categorize competences by level of government have clashed with an extremely complex legal and political reality which has given rise to theories of the EU as a system of multilevel governance. The Commission has quickly taken over this concept. One can interpret its White Paper on European Governance (July 2001) as an attempt to legitimize and objectify this situation, by presenting it as a new form of government, where multiple actors of different levels and natures (public institutions but also private actors) interact in a network of negotiations.[2]

7.1.2 EU competences after the Lisbon Treaty

In the face of the practical and legitimation difficulties that this mix-up of roles and competences arouses, one of the missions of the Convention on the Future of the Union was to clarify the situation by proposing a simpler and more systematic typology. The draft Constitutional Treaty, which largely inspired the Lisbon Treaty, proposed a new presentation of the situation. It does not change the distribution of competences but it does define them a bit more clearly.

Today, Article 2 TFEU provides that where the treaties attribute an *exclusive competence* to the Union, it may legislate and adopt legally binding acts. The Member States may do so only if so empowered by the EU or if they implement EU acts.

When the treaties confer a *shared competence* on the EU with Member States, Member States only exercise this power inasmuch as the EU has not exercised this competence. However, the Treaty provides that they can exercise it if the EU ceases to do so.

The same article also provides that Member States shall *coordinate their economic and employment policies* according to specific modalities. It further mentions the competences of the EU to define and implement a *Common Foreign and Security Policy* (CFSP), including the progressive definition of a Common Defence Policy. Finally, the EU shall have the competence to carry out actions *to support, coordinate or supplement* the Member States' actions, in areas like industry, culture or education, without thereby superseding their competence, which notably excludes any harmonization of their laws and regulations (Article 6, TFEU). Those competences can be called supporting competences.

The TFEU provides a list of exclusive (Art. 3) and shared (Art. 4) competences, the latter being recognized as the default category (Box 7.1 on the EU's competences). The list of shared competences includes the EU's activities in the fields of research, technological development and space, on the one hand, and development and humanitarian aid, on the other, but the treaty specifies that the EU's action cannot be construed to prevent Member States from exercising their competences in these areas. This creates a specific category of competences which can be called, as aforesaid, the 'parallel' competences. Finally, Article 5 TFEU specifies the conditions for coordination of Member States' economic policies, particularly for states in the eurozone, and employment policies. Article 5 TFEU also establishes, rather vaguely, that the EU may take initiatives to ensure coordination of Member States' social policies.

In addition, to clarify somewhat the nature and distribution of competences, the Treaty on the EU states in Article 5 the three principles governing the exercise of the EU's competences. These principles have been gradually included in the treaties to address the concerns of some national leaders who did not appreciate the tendency of the Commission and the EP to use the vagueness of the treaty to increase their competences. These three key principles thus govern their use: conferral, subsidiarity and proportionality.

- Under the principle of **conferral** (attribution), which may seem somewhat tautological, the Union must act only within the limits of the competences conferred upon it by the treaties. By default, competences remain with the Member States.

Box 7.1 The competences of the EU (Lisbon Treaty)

Exclusive competences (Art. 3 TFEU):

- customs union;
- establishment of the competition rules necessary for the functioning of the internal market;
- monetary policy for the Member States whose currency is the euro;
- the conservation of marine biological resources under the common fisheries policy;
- common commercial policy;
- conclusion of an international agreement when it is provided for in a legislative act of the Union, necessary to enable the Union to exercise its internal competence, or likely to affect common rules or to alter their scope.

Shared competences (Art. 4 TFEU):

- internal market;
- social policy, for the aspects defined in this Treaty;
- economic, social and territorial cohesion;
- agriculture and fisheries, excluding the conservation of marine biological resources;
- environment;
- consumer protection;
- transport;
- trans-European networks (transport, telecommunications and energy);
- energy;
- area of freedom, security and justice;
- common safety concerns in public health matters, for the aspects defined in this treaty;
- research, technological development and space (European programmes, respecting the autonomy of the states);
- development cooperation and humanitarian aid (with respect for the autonomy of the states).

Supporting competences:

- protection and improvement of human health;
- industry;
- culture;
- tourism;
- education, vocational training, youth and sport;
- civil protection;
- administrative cooperation.

- Under the principle of **subsidiarity**, in areas which do not fall within its exclusive competence, the Union can act only if and in so far as the objectives of the proposed action cannot be sufficiently achieved by the Member States (at the central government level or at regional and/or local levels), but can rather, by reason of the scale or effects of the proposed action, be better achieved at EU level.
- Under the principle of **proportionality**, the content and form of EU action may not exceed that which is necessary to achieve the objectives of the treaties.

A protocol annexed to the Lisbon Treaty defines the conditions of application of these principles. Control of subsidiarity is made a priori and a posteriori. A priori, the institutions involved in the legislative process (Commission, Parliament and Council) must ensure compliance with the principle; the protocol also gives national parliaments a supervisory role in this area (see Chapter 6). A posteriori, control is exercised by the Court of Justice which can annul an act for that reason – something that it has never done.

With regard to shared and support competences, one recalls that the degree of normative activity of the EU institutions has been quite variable across the sectors. Some sectors are saturated with EU directives and regulations (internal market, environment) while others have only been the object of limited initiatives (transport, social, energy) and could still experience significant developments.

The distribution of powers between the Member States and the EU is not less complex than that of the European institutional system itself, for similar reasons. Several factors explain this situation as well as the differentiated use EU institutions have made of the various shared competences.

First, one must take into account the choices made by the negotiators during the drafting of treaties. The transfer of certain policies to the Community seemed inevitable to further the goals of European integration and has therefore been implemented without restrictions (customs union, competition, trade policy). For other policies, just as crucial, some Member States were more reluctant to abandon their jurisdiction. They were thus only partially attributed to the Community in the form of shared competences (internal market, consumer protection, economic and social cohesion). Other policies, whose exercise could usefully contribute to European integration but for which the states preferred to maintain control, were subjected to very restrictive joint-decision procedures (taxation, social policy, education, sovereign policies). These choices have evolved through time and been revised on the occasion of each treaty reform. However, developments were limited in that they require unanimity of all national representatives. At every stage, the negotiators had to find a balance between the principle of 'exact adequation' (which means that certain kinds of powers should be exerted at certain levels of government by reference to criteria of efficiency and political relevance[3]) and the preferences of the Member States (which manifest reluctance to the transfer of a particular policy to the EU, according to their interests, cultural factors or domestic policy constraints).

In the current functioning of the EU, other power relationships contributed to shape the division of competences between the levels of government. First, it is an issue, once again, of the positions of Member State representatives within the Council and the European Council. Even if the treaties provide a legal basis for EU action, opposition by one or more Member States, especially when unanimity is required in the Council or when an impetus from the European Council is necessary, may reduce the Commission's efforts to nothing. A particular state is also able to promote or hinder an action in a certain domain when it is exercising the Council's six-month presidency.

The strategies of the EU institutions are a third factor. The various institutions do not have the same priorities and therefore intend to favour – for ideological or organizational reasons – some policies that are not necessarily the same. The inter-institutional balance of power thus affects the division of competences. The political composition of institutions has a similar effect, since they have become more and more partisan. As has been demonstrated at a national level by research dealing with the competition between parties and their way of appropriating topics,[4] not all parties have the same priorities and focus regarding policies. The fact that right-wing parties dominate today the four central institutions of the EU (Commission, Council, EP, and European Council) obviously has an impact on its priorities and on the kind of public policies that are developed at a European level.

Finally, this division of competences may well be affected by a range of external pressures, such as current events, changes in the economic and social context, political situations in the Member States, changes in public opinion, relations between the EU and other international organizations or outside countries, etc.

7.1.3 A growing differentiated integration

Over the past 30 years, in order to cope with the growing number of Member States and their increasingly divergent interests, the EU has had to be flexible. EU treaties thus include many clauses of 'opting out' that allow some Member States to be exempted from a given policy. For instance, EMU only involves 19 Member States: 2 have obtained an opt-out (The United Kingdom and Denmark) and 7 have not yet met the criteria to participate (Bulgaria, Croatia, Czech Republic, Hungary, Poland, Romania and Sweden[5]) but are legally required to enter the eurozone once they meet the relative criteria. Similarly, as previously explained, the Fiscal Compact has not been signed by three Member States (Croatia, the

United Kingdom and the Czech Republic). The treaties also include a 'Mechanism for cooperation and verification' that is a safeguard measure invoked by the Commission when a new Member State has failed to implement part of the acquis in the fields of the area of freedom, security and justice, or internal market policy. It can then impose a permanent 'acquis suspension' that is conditional on benchmarks to be met by the Member State. Finally, the treaties allow a minimum of nine Member States of the EU to launch reinforced integration or cooperation in an area within EU competencies, but for which it is impossible to act on a European scale. Although so far the number of enhanced cooperation is limited, they might become more popular as a solution to some of the EU's current challenges.

So, while treaty negotiators have always tried to preserve the singularity of European integration, especially of its institutional system, EU policies are in fact organized as a set of non-concentric 'circles' that include various configurations of Member States (see Table 7.1). This situation obviously increases the complexity of the share of competences between the EU and Member States, which differs from one state to another.[6]

Even if we set aside differential integration, the EU's overall activities have a very different structure from those of a modern state. Regarding its legislative output, the EU's principle activities relate to agriculture and fisheries, macroeconomic policies and economic regulation (see Figure 7.1). Its activities are next to nothing regarding the fields of rights and freedoms, health, education, defence and cultural policies. In contrast, the focal points for Member States in terms of legislative activity are foreign policy, cultural and sports policy and management of the state and its personnel.[7]

Since the beginning of the eighth parliamentary term (2014–2019), there has been a noticeable change: due to the salience of the migratory crisis and security issues, the number of legislative proposals related to immigration and internal affairs has increased significantly. Thus, with almost 20 per cent of the files under the co-decision procedure, DG Home was the most active in terms of proposals between 2014 and 2016 (see Figure 7.2).

The gap between the activities of the EU and the Member States is also considerable if we look at it from the point of view of their respective state budgets. There is an historical tropism of EU expenditure towards agricultural and regional policies while most other European policies are essentially regulatory. Although, due to European integration, Member States had to put an end to certain expenditures (state aid to companies, some agricultural and regional aid), they retained full power over most policies with a significant budgetary component (education, defence, health, safety, social affairs, etc.). Thus, while Member State budgets (all levels of government combined including welfare) range between 30 and 45 per cent of their gross national product, the EU represents under 1 per cent and is unlikely to increase in the years ahead.

Table 7.1 Differentiated integration in the EU

Opt-outs mentioned by the treaties:

	Denmark	Ireland	Poland	United Kingdom
Schengen Area	Inter-governmental participation	Opt-out (opt-in)		Opt-out (opt-in)
EMU	Opt-out			Opt-out
CSDP	Opt-out			
Area of freedom, security and justice		Opt-out (opt-in)		Opt-out (opt-in)
Charter of Fundamental Rights	Opt-out (referendum scheduled)		Opt-out	Opt-out

Permanent acquis suspension, conditional on benchmarks to be met by the Member State:

	Bulgaria	Croatia	Cyprus	Czech Republic	Hungary	Poland	Romania	Sweden
Schengen Area	+	+	+				+	
EMU	+	+		+	+	+	+	+
Criminal law mutual recognition	*						*	
Civil matters mutual recognition	*						*	

Suspension: + Potential suspension: *

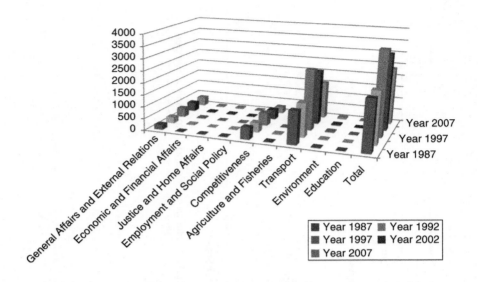

Figure 7.1 Number of norms and decisions adopted by EU institutions, by sector of activity

Source: Based on data taken from the 'Delors' myth project' directed by S. Brouard, O. Costa and T. König. See: Sylvain Brouard, Olivier Costa and Thomas König, (eds), *The Europeanization of domestic legislatures. The empirical implications of the Delors' Myth in nine countries* (New York: Springer, 2012).

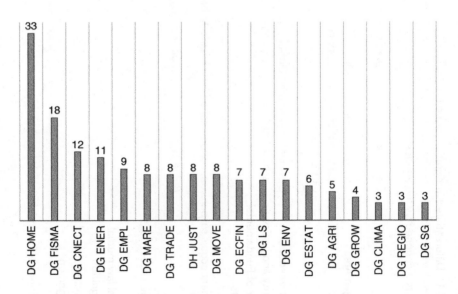

Figure 7.2 Number of proposals under the co-decision procedure (2014–2016)

Source: European Parliament, Report on co-decision activity (4 July 2014 to 31 December 2016).

7.2 Decision-making procedures in the EU

EU decision-making procedures, like its institutional design, mirror the turbulent history of European integration. Through time, new procedures have been created, while the old ones have remained. Some have seen their scope extended while others have progressively disappeared. Since the late 1980s, several approaches to decision-making have co-existed, corresponding to different conceptions of European integration. The Treaty of Maastricht has systematized this diversity by introducing the 'three pillars' legal structure, in order to find a consensus between Member States' negotiators. It thus provided 22 different decision-making procedures and 60 legal instruments. After a difficult process of simplification of the decision-making procedures by the Treaties of Amsterdam, Nice and Lisbon, we can distinguish four main procedures, plus the special case of enhanced cooperation.

7.2.1 The ordinary legislative procedure

The 'co-decision' (the treaties have never used this term) procedure was introduced by the Maastricht Treaty in order to increase the Parliament's legislative power. It was amended by the Treaty of Amsterdam which simplified it and established a perfect equality between the Council and the European Parliament. The scope of this procedure has been progressively extended by the treaties that have entered into force since the mid 1990s. The Treaty of Lisbon made it the method for common-law decisions by calling it the 'ordinary legislative procedure' (OLP). Article 289 TFEU states that it is 'the adoption of a regulation, directive or decision jointly by the European Parliament and the Council on a proposal from the Commission' (see Box 7.2). It now applies to three-quarters of European legislation (see Figure 7.3).

Upon entry into force of the Maastricht Treaty (1 November 1993), the Commission, Council and Parliament clarified the modalities of application of the co-decision procedure in a very detailed inter-institutional agreement. Agreements of this type do not constitute a homogeneous category of acts and may take on many forms: inter-institutional agreements strictly speaking, but also joint statements, declarations of Presidents, exchanges of letters, notes, communications, codes of conduct, *modus vivendi*, framework agreements, decisions of the Secretary General, etc.[8] Since 1957, over 100 agreements of various natures have come to organize the relations between the three institutions, especially in legislative and budgetary domains. They specify the procedures under the treaties and, without being contrary to them, may propose alternative arrangements that facilitate decision-making, and limit inter-institutional conflicts. To put an end to the negotiation of secret agreements between the Commission and the EP, the Nice Treaty states that inter-institutional agreements are allowed only if

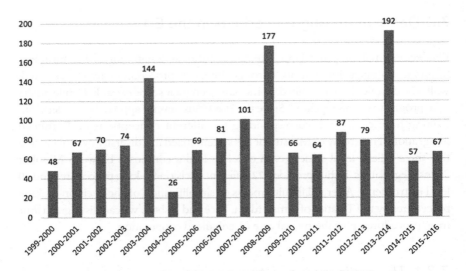

Figure 7.3   Number of files covered by the co-decision procedure (1999–2016)

Source: European Parliament, Progress report on the ordinary legislative procedure, 4 July 2014 to 31 December 2016, EN PE 595.931.

Box 7.2 The ordinary legislative procedure

The procedure can take up to three readings. The following are the main steps:

Proposal:

- The Commission presents a proposal to the European Parliament and the Council.

First Reading:

- the EP adopts (by simple majority) a position that approves the proposal as it is or suggests amendments, and sends it to the Council;
- the Commission can alter its original legislative proposal – incorporating eventual EP amendments – in order to facilitate an agreement (this is only possible during first reading);
- if the Council approves the Parliament's position or a revised proposal including EP's amendments, the act is adopted;
- if the Council does not approve the Parliament's position, it adopts its own position (called 'common position') and sends it to Parliament. The treaty provides that the Council and the Commission 'fully' inform the Parliament of their respective positions.

The treaty mentions no time limit for the first reading.

Second Reading:

- the EP has three months (with possible extension of one month) to review the Council's position. It can:
    - approve or refrain from comment: the act is thus deemed adopted as the position of the Council;
    - reject it by a majority of its members: the proposed act is not adopted and the procedure ends;
    - propose amendments by a majority of its members. The amended text is forwarded to the Council and the Commission and the latter submits an opinion on Parliament's amendments;

- the Council has three months (with possible extension of one month) to review the Parliament's amendments. It acts by qualified majority for amendments that were approved by the Commission and unanimously for amendments that have received a negative opinion.
  It can:
    - approve all of Parliament's amendments: the act is then adopted;
    - reject some amendments. In this case, the Council President, in consultation with the President of the Parliament, convenes the Conciliation Committee within six weeks.

Conciliation:

- the Conciliation Committee brings together members of the Council (or their representatives) and as many deputies representing the Parliament (concretely: 28 + 28). Its mission is to reach an agreement on a common draft by a qualified majority of Council members and a majority of Members of Parliament within six weeks. The Commission participates in the work and can take initiatives to help achieve an agreement;
- if the Conciliation Committee does not reach an agreement within the prescribed period the act is not adopted.

Third Reading:

- if the Conciliation Committee agrees on a common draft, the Parliament and the Council each have six weeks to adopt it: the Parliament by a majority of the votes cast and the Council by qualified majority. Otherwise, the proposed act is not adopted;
- the periods of three months and six weeks respectively may be extended one month and two weeks respectively at the initiative of the Parliament or the Council.

the three main institutions are involved. The Treaty of Lisbon now recognizes the existence of these agreements and provides that they may be legally binding (see below).

Regarding co-decision, Parliament instantly called for the establishment of a structured dialogue with the Commission and the Council. The latter did not respond to this claim and even expressed reservations about the conciliation process. To begin with, the ministers only sent officials to sit on the committee. This attitude led the MEPs to reject a number of texts until obtaining a modification of the procedure in the Treaty of Amsterdam and a change of attitude from the Council.[9] Council officials, however, accepted the principle of a 'trialogue' with the Parliament and the Commission on legislative matters only by the end of the 1990s. In fact, Council actors really started to get involved in such an exchange when they began to fear a widespread blockage of European institutions, and sought consequently to appease inter-institutional relations.[10] The aim was to limit the conflictual nature of the decision-making process and to preserve the EU's capacity to fulfil its tasks.

Since then, the three institutions have become accustomed to charging a limited number of representatives with negotiating the relevant texts on the sidelines of the formal procedure at an increasingly early stage in order to shorten the adoption procedure and to appease it. This process of 'pre-cooking' the texts, inspired by the conciliation committee of the co-decision, allowed an increasing number of them to vote straight after the first reading; a decrease in the number of rejected proposals as well as a decrease in the number of amendments proposed by the EP and the Council. Ministers and deputies have not given up on amending the legislative proposals, but their views are now most often incorporated into informal negotiations, carried out by a limited number of representatives of the three institutions.[11] Whereas during the 1994–1999 legislative term, no text had been adopted at an early stage[12] (at the end of the Council's first reading or at the end of Parliament's second reading) and nearly 40 per cent required the meeting of the Conciliation Committee, a vast majority of texts are now adopted at the first reading and use of the conciliation procedure is the exception (see Figure 7.4).

The use of trialogues has also made it possible to speed up the decision-making process, at least for the texts adopted at first reading (Table 7.2).

This practice was formalized on 30 June 2007 by the adoption of a joint declaration by the three institutions on practical arrangements for co-decision (including trialogues). It was also guided by codes of good conduct, internal use guidelines, and by the amendment of the Rules of Procedure of the three institutions (see Box 7.3).[13] In recent years, between 80 and 90 per cent of the texts adopted under the co-decision procedure have been agreed upon during the first reading, and the conciliation committee meeting (third reading) has become very rare. During the first half of the eighth legislature (July 2014–December 2016), approximately 300 trialogue meetings were held on 86 texts.

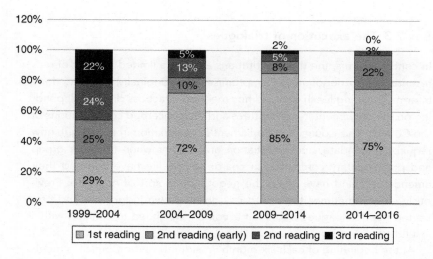

Figure 7.4 Percentages of co-decision files adopted in 1st, 2nd or 3rd reading (1999–2016)

Total number of files: 1999–2004 = 403; 2004–2009 = 454; 2009–2014 = 488; 2014–2016 = 152

Source: European Parliament, Progress report on the ordinary legislative procedure, 4 July 2014 to 31 December 2016, EN PE 595.931.

Table 7.2 Average duration of cases under the co-decision procedure

	1999–2004	*2004–2009*	*2009–2014*	*2014–2016*
1st reading	11 months	16 months	17 months	16 months
2nd early reading	24 months	29 months	32 months	37 months
3rd reading	31 months	43 months	29 months	/
Average total duration	22 months	21 months	19 months	22 months

Source: European Parliament, Progress report on the ordinary legislative procedure, 4 July 2014 to 31 December 2016, EN PE 595.931.

The generalization of trialogues is explained by the widely shared desire to avoid conflicts and accelerate the decision-making process, but also by the advantages that the various actors appreciate:

- The trialogues allow the state that holds the Presidency of the Council to publish a flattering report at the end of its six-month mandate. The length of the legislative procedure does not allow the Presidency to hope for the text to be adopted before the end of its six-month period, unless it is subject to an early agreement. The trialogues also give the Presidency a leading role in the negotiations.

Box 7.3 The execution of trialogues

In concrete terms, the three institutions appoint a limited number of representatives to negotiate a compromise text. Originally, this was done informally, during lunch or an ad hoc meeting. Practices differed depending on the parliamentary committees and the concerned configurations of the Council. The Council's or Parliament's participation in a trialogue now requires a mandate, and negotiation only begins when the work group and parliamentary committee in charge of the file have adopted their amendments and have given the negotiators a sort of mandate. Previously, they sometimes tended to rely on their own judgement and presented their colleagues with a fait accompli, which led to conflicts within institutions.

At the beginning of each six-month Presidency of the Council, a meeting with the chairs of the parliamentary committees and the rapporteurs is organized by the President of COREPER. Collectively, they decide on an agenda to promote the adoption of texts during the first reading. Once started, a trialogue, based on an average of 4 meetings, lasts about 6 months. In some cases, for very long or technical texts, there may be up to 30 meetings. The delegations were originally restricted, so that the trialogue involved only about 10 people. Now it's roughly around 40. Parliament has the largest delegation (about 20 members) composed of the rapporteur, the chair of the parliamentary committee, the shadow rapporteurs or co-ordinators, the administrators of the groups and the administrators of the general secretariat. The Council is represented by about 10 people: the President of COREPER or the working group, one or two representatives of the Presidency, 3 or 4 administrators of the unit in charge of the case, and a representative of the Legal Service. The Commission is represented by a dozen or so people: the Director-General, the Director or Head of the unit concerned, the administrators of the unit dealing with the case, the administrators of the units responsible for relations with the Council and the Parliament, and an agent from the Legal Service.

In reality, there are different kinds of trialogues, the compositions of which vary[14]: an informal dialogue made up of bilateral meetings between the Parliament and the Council without the Commission; technical preparatory trialogues intended to deal with 'technical' details; and the 'political' trialogue where the final agreement is negotiated. The more important the matter, the more the negotiation stage is advanced, and the more important the representatives are. The negotiation takes place with a document in four columns, including the initial positions of the Commission, that of Parliament, that of the Council and, finally, the compromise text that is likely to be agreed upon. The trialogue may take place during the first or second reading; in the case of conciliation, negotiations are always held in a trialogue, and the Conciliation Committee only validates the final result.

- Since the co-decision procedure provides that the Commission can only amend its proposal at first reading, resorting to the strategy of an early agreement allows it to remain actively involved in the discussion. During the second reading or third reading, an agreement between the Council and the EP is likely to be reached on the grounds of amendments which could seriously distort the original proposal.
- In the European Parliament, trialogues have been part of the 'rationalization' process that has been in effect since the mid 1980s under the leadership of the two main political groups. This also strengthens the power of hierarchs of the assembly and of the most influential MEPs who regularly participate in the negotiations.

The Joint Declaration of 2007 also refers to the quality of the legislation. On 30 June 2007, the EP, the Council and the Commission adopted a joint declaration on practical modalities for co-decision, which specified the role of each institution at different stages. It complements the Inter-institutional 'Better Regulation' Agreement signed on 16 December 2003, which defines 'best practices' and sets targets and the commitments of each institution in the matter of commitments (see Box 7.4 on 'Better Regulation'). Those agreements are responding to Declaration No. 34 annexed to the Amsterdam Treaty, which calls on institutions to make every effort to ensure that proceedings are conducted as quickly as possible. Article 295 TFEU also encourages the development of inter-institutional procedures on the sidelines of the treaties:

the European Parliament, the Council and the Commission shall consult each other and by common agreement make arrangements for their cooperation. To that end, they may, in compliance with the treaties, conclude inter-institutional agreements which may be of a binding nature.

The reactivation of the BRS in May 2014, through a new communication, has led to the adoption of a new inter-institutional agreement on 9 March 2016, replacing the one of 2003.

The Program for Better Regulation adopted by the Juncker Commission immediately after taking office (see Box 7.4) includes two main elements: a new

Box 7.4 'Better Regulation' (Better Regulation Strategy – BRS)[15]

The complexity and opacity of the Community acquis and of the decision-making procedures have been among the concerns of European institutions since the 1990s. At the European Summit in Edinburgh (1992), the Heads of State and Government had already instructed the Commission to simplify and improve the regulatory environment. It was not until 2002, following the White Paper on European Governance and the Mandelkern Report that the Prodi Commission adopted an action-plan identifying steps to improve the various stages of the legislative cycle.

Having taken the form of an agenda, an action plan, and a programme, the 'Better Regulation Strategy' was formally adopted by the Commission in March 2005. The document 'Better regulation for growth and employment in the EU' defines the problem schematically: less bureaucracy equals more growth. In order to simplify the Community acquis and improve the quality of legislation, the strategy includes some ideas from the Lisbon Strategy (action and development plan devised by the European Council in March 2000, for the economy of the EU) and promotes the reduction of administrative burdens and the improvement of business competitiveness. It has three main objectives: limiting the overall level of European regulation, improving the quality of regulation, and improving the effective implementation of European laws by the Member States.

The strategy is based on **three lines of action:**

- production of better European regulation through simplification and reduction of administrative burdens and through systematic impact assessments;
- close cooperation with Member States to ensure the consistent application of the principles of better regulation; and
- strengthening the dialogue between regulators and stakeholders.

institutional agreement and a notification entitled 'Improving regulation for better results. A priority issue for the EU'. The latter applies only to the Commission and explains how the Commission will apply the Better Regulation strategy. It also urges the institution to be more open and transparent in its work methods.

To achieve these objectives, various tools and techniques have been developed by the Commission. Thus, any new proposal must be based on an impact assessment, must define the appropriate level of action in accordance with the principles of proportionality and subsidiarity, and must assess the potential repercussions of the measure on economic, social and environmental plans. These impact assessments have varying durations and degrees of precision and are conducted according to guidelines set by the Commission. The BRS also provides for consultation with stakeholders to improve both the transparency and legitimacy of EU measures. The dialogue between these actors and the Commission takes place throughout the process of law-making and can take many forms (green and white papers,[16] advisory committees, panels, workshops, forums, and conferences, online consultation, etc.). Finally, to reduce the volume of legislation, to improve its readability and to reinforce legal certainty in the EU, the Commission has embarked on a process of elimination, reformulation and simplification of existing legislation with tools such as codification, repeal, revision and co-regulation.

As part of this strategy, several inter-institutional agreements were signed: the 'Better Regulation' Agreement (2003), the 'Common Approach to Impact Assessment' Agreement (2005) as well as agreements regarding editorial quality or codification and revision of legislation.

Concretely, any major initiative of the Commission now includes: an overview of the consultation with stakeholders; an analysis of the expected impact of the measure; a justification of the level of legal constraints in accordance with the principles of subsidiarity and proportionality.

Jean-Claude Juncker, the new President of the Commission (2014–2019), has made the BRS one of its priorities and put **Franz Timmermans**, the First vice-President, in charge of this dossier.[17] Upon taking office, he launched a very ambitious plan to revitalize the strategy of improving the legislation,[18] which led to the adoption of a new inter-institutional agreement in 2016.

In his State of the Union address in 2016, J. C. Juncker emphasized the importance of the 'better regulation' approach and welcomed the success of 'withdrawing 100 proposals in the first two years of its mandate, to reduce by 80% the number of initiatives presented compared with the previous five years and to launch an in-depth review of all the legislation in effect.'

The Commission aims at fixing some of the major failures and challenges of European integration through BRS. It is founded on the idea of public policies that are based on the main concept of 'evidence-based' policies, supposed to 'deliver tangible and sustainable benefits for citizens, business, and society as a whole'.

The three main elements of this renewed strategy are:

1   **Openness and transparency**: the Commission wants to consult more and to listen better to stakeholders, social partners, and the whole society, and to explain and justify its action better.

2   **Better tools for better policies**: in a quite tautological way, the Commission claims its will is to use new 'integrated Guidelines on Better Regulation' to result in better regulations. In particular, it intends to use impact assessments more systematically. It also aims to be more open to scrutiny, especially through the systematic use of impact assessments and of a board dedicated to that.

3   **Renewing the legislation**: the objective is to systematically assess the effect of policies that have been adopted and implemented, and then, if needed, to reform them. This is notably the objective of the Regulatory Fitness and Performance Programme (REFIT), launched in 2012 in order to: 'keeping EU Law fit for purpose'. The Commission wants to strengthen this system of monitoring and to use it, as well, to identify the legislation that deserves to be repealed, that no longer serves its purpose, and to repeal it. In this process, the Commission seeks stakeholder input in particular. Since the beginning of the 8th Parliament, 41 legislative proposals have been withdrawn under the REFIT programme.

While the goals of the BRS are relatively clear and generally approved, the processes and procedures, however, are subject to discussions in the EU sphere. Many EU experts and practitioners indeed consider that their complexity may override their achievement. We have witnessed a constant inflation of the number of reports, reviews and public consultations on the tools and procedures, the BRS itself, and the creation of new committees, such as on the impact-assessment committee. The strategy of introducing new procedures and creating new bodies and tools tends to increase the intricacy of the EU's governance. It threatens to become even more cumbersome, time and energy consuming, contradicting its original objectives. Also, it tends to depoliticize the functioning of the EU, by increasing the role of experts and technocrats, and to reduce the level of legislative activity. There is thus strong resistance against the BRS within the EP and the Council; in its communication of 19 May 2015, the Commission thus insists on the necessity for the two institutions to participate actively in the BRS; it especially deplores the fact that, between 2007 and 2014, the EP only asked for 20 impact assessments and the Council produced none, while the Commission produced over 700.

Although the Better Regulation strategy does not seem to be a panacea for responding to criticism of EU action, the Juncker Commission is determined drastically to reduce the number of new legislative proposals. Thus, the first two years of the 8th legislature are distinguished by the low number of new co-decision proposals. The Commission proposed only 192 texts in the ordinary legislative procedure, which represents a significant decrease compared with the first two years of the 6th legislature (321 new proposals) and those of the 7th legislature (244 new co-decision texts) (see Figure 7.5).

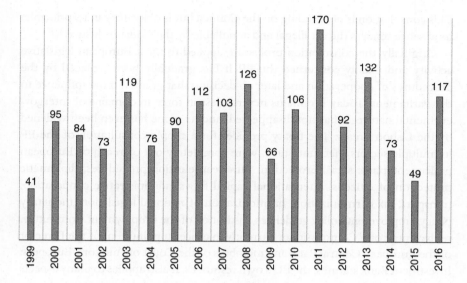

Figure 7.5 Number of co-decision proposals
Source: European Parliament.

7.2.2 The special legislative procedures

Article 294 TFEU provides that:

> in the specific cases provided for in the Treaties, the adoption of a regulation, directive or decision by the European Parliament with the participation of the Council or by the latter with participation of the European Parliament is a special legislative procedure.

The notion of a 'special legislative procedure' in fact covers a heterogeneous set of specific procedures whose primary purpose is to limit the influence of the Parliament. Among them, the two main ones are the consultation procedure and the assent procedure: we will focus on these.

The consultation procedure

The consultation procedure is a legacy of the EEC Treaty. It provides for a Council decision (by unanimity or qualified majority) on a proposal from the Commission or another institution with a simple consultation of certain bodies: mainly the European Parliament, but also the Economic and Social Committee or the Committee of the Regions or, more rarely, the European Central Bank.

This consultation is not binding on the Council but is obligatory in its principle: its absence renders the act illegal and annullable by the Court of Justice.[19]

Originally, the consultation procedure applied to most European legislative activity and mainly concerned the EP. It has gradually been replaced by the procedures of cooperation and later co-decision that granted more influence to the Parliament. Today it remains nevertheless in force in domains of intergovernmental nature. It has not disappeared, and its scope has even been widened by the Lisbon Treaty. The treaty provides for a simple consultation of the EP in multiple sectors that, until now, were completely out of reach of European parliamentarians: social protection, European election procedures, diplomatic protection of citizens, international capital flows, administrative cooperation, transport, tax harmonization, harmonization of national legislation, monetary policy, employment policy guidelines, institution of the Employment Committee, replacement of a Commissioner currently in office, appointment of the Director of the European Central Bank and members of the Court of Auditors, European Investment Bank statutes, the EU's own resources. It also applies to many aspects of various policies: free movement of persons, asylum and immigration, family law, cooperation in criminal and police matters, company agreements, state aid, internal market, intellectual property, research and development, environment, monetary policy, and strengthened cooperation. In particular it concerns all decisions with fiscal implications and certain international agreements.

The consultation procedure symbolizes the enduring intergovernmental character of several EU policies: in these areas, the Member States' representatives have refused to give the right of co-decision to the EP. However, it also represents an improvement in the areas in which consultation is not a heritage of 1957, but an innovation of the Lisbon Treaty. Indeed, the EP is now consulted on most of the decisions relating to intergovernmental topics (foreign affairs, defence, cooperation in criminal and police matters, etc.) on which MEPs only enjoyed, at most, a right of information before.

Here again, the concern with simplification invigorates the drafters of the treaties and tends to reinforce the supranational character of European integration. This concern for simplification materializes in the application of the consultation procedure to all matters which do not fall under the co-decision or assent procedure.

The assent procedure

The assent procedure (commonly referred to as 'assent' or, formerly, 'consent') was established by the Single European Act for certain international agreements and other matters. It provides that the Parliament considers a draft act forwarded by the Council and decides on its approval, with no possibility for amendments, by the absolute majority of votes cast. A possible rejection by the Parliament is binding on the Council. The procedure allows a legitimation of the decision by the EP without, however, permitting it to modify the text. This is necessary for international agreements that cannot be amended and was also considered useful for some other decisions (for instance, to regional policy) that resulted from very subtle intergovernmental agreements. The Treaty of Lisbon has limited the use of the assent procedure for legislative matters but has extended it to some budgetary questions.

The current treaties provide for the Parliament to approve various types of international agreements: agreements of association, of the EU's accession to the European Convention of Human Rights, institutionalization of cooperation procedures, agreements having budgetary implications or covering areas in which the Parliament is involved in the legislative process. Parliament is also content to approve various Council decisions with no recourse to amendments: the establishment of a uniform procedure for the election of the Parliament, some aspects of the EU's own resources, the definition of a long-term financial framework, establishment of enhanced cooperation, use of implied powers, combatting discrimination, some aspects of European citizenship, and criminal cooperation.

7.2.3 A special case: the budgetary procedure

Since the budget treaties of 1970 and 1975, the EU has its own resources, which are of three main types: customs duties on imports from outside the EU and sugar levies, for which the Member States retain 20 per cent of the amounts for collection costs; a standard percentage of the harmonized VAT base for each Member State, levied at the rate of 0.3 per cent (1 per cent before 2004) ; and a contribution from each Member State based on a standard percentage of its Gross National Income (GNI), in 2015 it accounted for 68.9 per cent of the EU's revenue). Over time the latter has become the largest source of revenue for the EU. There are also other minor sources of revenue, accounting for 1 per cent of the budget such as taxes on EU staff salaries, fines on companies breaking competition laws, and contributions from non-EU countries to certain programmes. National compensation mechanisms have been put in place when some countries have considered that their contribution to the European budget is excessive compared to that of other states. Thus, the United Kingdom benefits from a 'correction': it is reimbursed 66 per cent of the difference between its contribution and what it receives in return from the budget. Denmark, Sweden, the Netherlands and Austria receive flat-rate reimbursements, and Sweden, Germany and the Netherlands benefit from lower VAT rates. In total, these resources are not allowed to exceed 1.23 per cent of the EU's GNI, which is little if we compare it with national budgets that represent 30 to 40 per cent of the national GNI.[20] In practice, the Multi-annual Financial Framework (MFF) 2014–2020 sets the budget ceiling at around 1 per cent of the EU's GNI. For 2013, the EU budget thus represents 1.13 per cent of the EU's GNI, i.e. €150.9 billion, whereas in 2017 commitment appropriations totalled €157.86 billion (approximately 1.05 per cent of the Member States' GNI), and payment appropriations made up €134.49 billion (about 0.93 per cent of GNI) in commitment appropriations and is mainly made up of GNI-based resources from the Member States (see Figure 7.6).

As far as the expenses are concerned, the annual budget is divided into five main categories (or headings): 1) competitiveness for growth and employment; 2) economic, social and territorial cohesion; 3) sustainable growth; 4) security and citizenship; and 5) Europe in the world. As we can see in Figure 7.7, today

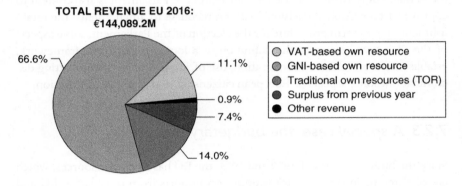

Figure 7.6   The EU budgetary resources in 2016

Source: European Commission.

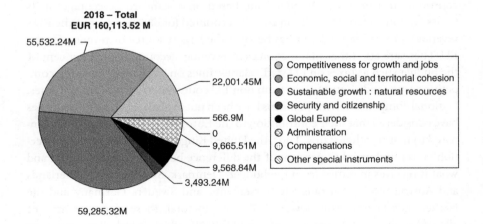

Figure 7.7   The EU expenditures in 2018 (commitments)

Source: European Commission.

most of the EU's budget is spent on two main categories: 'economic, social and territorial cohesion' (including the regional policy) and 'sustainable growth: natural resources' (including the CAP agriculture and rural development) (see Figure 7.7).

The labels of the budget headings have undergone many changes in recent years, notably for communication purposes. For example, under the heading 'agriculture' in the 2005 budget, 'natural resources' were reclassified from 2006 onwards, while the heading 'regional aid' was renamed 'competitiveness', as a result of its association with other expenditures, in particular with the Research policy. This evolution has led to the selection of titles that are more in line with the supposed expectations of citizens. And it allowed the highly criticized agricultural expenditures to be shifted from the first EU expenditure chapter to the second, and disguise them under a title with an ecological connotation ('natural resources').

The EU's budget had been at the heart of heated discussions at the end of the 1970s and during the 1980s, leading to numerous budgetary crises and conflicts between the Parliament, the Council and the Commission. A first compromise was made at the Fontainebleau Summit in 1984 with the adoption of new rules on budgetary discipline. In 1986, a new inter-institutional agreement was signed, known as the 'Brussels reform', stating that the three institutions were committed to a framework for a financial perspective for the period 1988–1992, tighter budgetary discipline and an increase in the EU's resources through the creation of a new category based on the GNI of each Member State.

Since 1988, all annual budgets have been framed within multi-annual financial perspectives, i.e. seven year-frameworks containing annual ceilings on EU's expenditure in general and for each main category of expenditure. The establishment of this multi-annual programming has pacified the negotiations of the annual budget. It does not mean that there is no longer any conflict: indeed, the tensions have been transferred to the negotiations of the multi-annual financial frameworks (MFF) every seven years. The MFF are package deals whose negotiations constitute a long, highly contentious, and politicized process with conflicts between supranational institutions and the Member States but also among Member States themselves, and more particularly, between net contributors that want their contribution to be cut and net beneficiaries that want to maintain their benefits.[21]

The Lisbon Treaty brought some changes to the budgetary procedure, for both the multi-annual financial framework and the annual budget.[22] It aimed at simplifying the budgetary procedures and giving equal powers to the Council and the Parliament. However, the result is quite peculiar: on the one hand, the Parliament now has equal power with the Council on the annual budget and even has the last say in that respect, and on the other hand, it can only approve or reject the constraining multi-annual framework, without any formal possibility of amending it. Together with the Commission and the Council, the Parliament is closely involved in the expenses, but the Commission, the Council and the European Council are the only institutions to have a formal say in the EU's resources. As the current negotiations attest, the situation is likely to produce gridlocks and an institutional crisis as the Parliament may, from now on, use its current power to block the adoption of the multi-annual financial framework in order to see its position taken into account.

We will examine first the multi-annual framework and then the annual budgetary procedure but it is important to keep in mind that the two are closely related.

The multi-annual financial framework

The Lisbon Treaty gives a new status to the multi-annual financial framework (Art. 312 TFEU). Previously, financial perspectives took the form of inter-institutional agreements between the European Parliament, the Commission, and the Council, binding only these three institutions. Now, the treaty requires that the multi-annual financial framework be set out in a regulation, directly applicable, and binding for all Member States.

The Commission is responsible for proposing the multi-annual financial framework, composed of the MFF regulation as such but also of several legislative acts and sector-specific proposals. This package defines how much money the EU can spend, how the money should be spent, and how the expenses should be financed. It constitutes the basis for negotiations, which then follow a twin-track process: a political track and a legislative track (which run in parallel). Given the very sensitive nature of the issue, there is a political track involving the European Council. The 28 Heads of State and Governments have to reach an agreement on the key political issues. The content of this agreement provides guidance to the Council and feeds into the legislative track. At the same time, there are negotiations between the Commission, the Council, and the Parliament under the legislative track. Different rules apply for the different parts of the multi-annual financial framework package. The multi-annual financial framework regulation as such is adopted by the Council by unanimity after having obtained the consent of the Parliament. The legislative acts and implementing acts are also adopted by the Council under different rules depending on the type of act. In 2011, the Commission proposed, as part of the package, five acts on the EU's own resources. Among these five acts, one decision has to be adopted by the Council by unanimity while the Parliament is simply consulted. Then the decision needs to be ratified by the national parliaments of all Member States. One implementing act has to be adopted by the Council by qualified majority after having received the consent of the Parliament. And three Council regulations have to be adopted by qualified majority with the consultation of the Parliament. Finally, there are numerous sector-specific legal acts (70 proposed by the Commission in 2011) which follow the ordinary legislative procedure.

The negotiations for the 2014–2020 financial framework proved to be very difficult. They started in June 2011 with the proposal of the Commission – along with a communication entitled 'a budget for Europe 2020 strategy'. In March 2012, Member States started negotiating and the European Council reached an agreement in February 2013 but it was rejected by the Parliament on 13 March 2013. More particularly, three issues are contentious. The first is related to how much money the EU can spend. On the one hand, in a time of economic crisis and rising Euroscepticism, Member States face strong incentives to oppose an increased EU budget although most acknowledge the need for a European solution to the crisis and for a coordinated approach to stimulate growth and employment. In their agreement, they decreased the amount of the EU budget for the next seven years. On the other hand, the Parliament requires a larger budget to launch pan-European policies to counter the crisis. Second, the priorities are diverging between the Parliament and the Member States. The Parliament generally asks for a reduced budget for the Common Agricultural Policy to focus on innovation and growth. In the European Council, in contrast, each Member State has its own priorities and interests, according to its domestic situation, and each tries to put its own agenda forward. Third, the question of the EU's resources is quite controversial. The Commission proposed to reform the current system either by suppressing the VAT-based resources and the corrections or by establishing a new system based on a new own resource. The Parliament considers the current system unfair, opaque and anti-democratic. It proposes to increase the transparency of the budget by relying solely on the GNI-based resource, with potentially other own resources. Some have suggested considering air tax, a financial transaction tax, or a CO^2 emissions tax to support the EU budget. Also, there have always been some debates about a European tax as a potential way to increase the EU's independence vis-à-vis the Member States through fiscal autonomy and to increase the EU's visibility among citizens but, in the current context, it seems rather impossible to implement this politically.

On 19 June 2013, the Irish Presidency of the Council claimed to have reached a political agreement with the negotiators of the Parliament and the Commission but soon after, the EP's President announced that his institution would not approve this compromise. The Parliament demanded an increase of the 2013 budget, a greater flexibility in the way the money was spent, the possibility to evaluate the multi-annual financial framework at mid-term, and to amend it according to the economic context. The situation turned out to be further complicated by the configuration inside the European Council as six Member States (United Kingdom, the Netherlands, Finland, Sweden, Denmark and Austria) already opposed or expressed strong reservations over any increase in the budget as proposed by the compromise put forward by the Irish Presidency (and which the EP found insufficient). On 27 June, the Presidents of the European Council, the Commission, and the Parliament reached an agreement which was then approved by the European Council later that day. On 4 July 2013, the Parliament approved this compromise as it includes more flexibility as requested by the

MEPs: it will be possible to transfer the unspent money to priority areas or to the following year rather than returning it to national budgets and the compromise also includes a revision clause for 2016.

In addition, a 'high-level group', comprised of representatives of the Commission, the Council and the European Parliament and chaired by former Commissioner Mario Monti, was instructed to examine the question of own resources and was responsible for formulating proposals for the adoption in 2020 of the next MFF. The outcome of the work of this high-level group was published in January 2017 in a final report containing a series of recommendations.[23] It is now up to the Commission to judge the desirability of reforming own resources on the basis of this report.

The final vote of the MFF 2014–2020 was to take place in autumn 2013, along with the adoption of budgetary regulations, implementing acts, and an interinstitutional agreement on the conditions for the implementation of the budget. The last legally binding vote took place in Parliament in September 2014 along with the votes on other budgetary regulations, implementing acts and an interinstitutional agreement on how to spend the budget. The Council adopted the regulation laying down the EU's multi-annual financial framework for 2014–2020 on 2 December 2014, after more than two years of negotiations. The final legally binding vote took place in Parliament in September 2014 along with the votes on other budgetary regulations, implementing acts and an inter-institutional agreement on how to spend the budget. The Council adopted the regulation laying down the EU's multi-annual financial framework for 2014–2020 on 2 December 2014, after more than two years of negotiation. In June 2017, the first steps of the discussions on the next MFF (2021–2027) have shown that the negotiations will be once again very arduous.

The annual budgetary procedure

The Lisbon Treaty also changed the procedure for the annual budget. The purpose was to simplify and shorten the procedure but also to give equal power to the Council and the Parliament. Since then, there is only one reading in the budgetary procedure and the Parliament has not only a decision on all components of the budget but also a final say in the budgetary procedure (Art. 314 TFEU).

In practice, the draft budget must be proposed by the Commission by 1 September of each year. In order to prepare the draft, the Commissioner for the budget and his/her DG meet informally with national representatives, EP representatives, and lobbyists but also organize formal trialogues to discuss priorities. In practice, the Commission tries to present its draft budget much earlier, at the end of April or in early May.

Once the draft is issued by the Commission, the Council has until 1 October to adopt its position by qualified majority and transmit it to the Parliament.

Within 42 days, if the Parliament either approves the position of the Council or does not take a decision, the budget is adopted. If the Parliament adopts amendments by the majority of its component members, these amendments are sent to the Council and the conciliation committee is convened.

If within 10 days of receiving the EP's amendments the Council approves all of them, the budget is adopted without conciliation. If not, the conciliation committee has 21 days to be convened, to reach an agreement by qualified majority for the Council representatives and by the majority of EP representatives (if no agreement is reached, the Commission has to submit a revised draft of the budget).

The joint text agreed by the conciliation committee is referred to the Parliament and the Council and it must be approved by both within 14 days. There are then three options:

- If both approve, or one approves and the other takes no decision, or both take no decision, the budget is approved.
- If the Council and the Parliament both reject the joint draft, or one rejects the text while the other fails to decide, or the Parliament rejects the joint text while the Council approves, the budget is rejected and the Commission submits a new draft budget and the whole procedure must start afresh.
- If the EP approves the joint text while the Council rejects it, the Parliament has 14 days from the date of the rejection by the Council to confirm some or all of its amendments by a majority of its component members and 3/5 of the votes cast and the EP President may then declare the EU budget adopted.

The budget should be adopted by the end of December. If this is not the case (as happened several times in the 1980s), a fall-back position consists in allowing funding to continue on the basis of provisional twelfths, i.e. the spending is limited to the monthly average of the expenditure of the previous year until a new budget is adopted (Art. 315 TFEU). In the event of an exceptional or unforeseen situation, the Commission may propose draft amending budgets during the year, which are subject to the same adoption rules as the general budget.

Although the establishment of the multi-annual financial perspective tends to pacify the negotiations of the annual budget, there are still recurring tensions. For instance, the Council, Commission and the EP long-failed to find an agreement on the 2015 budget and some feared the EU would be obliged to resort to the system of the provisional twelfths. After long boisterous discussions, in November 2014 the Council rejected the proposal of the Commission to bridge the gap of €4.7 billion in the 2014 budget using additional resources available in the EU budget, coming from fines. The EP supported the Commission's approach but Member States, especially net contributors, asked for this money to be sent back to national budgets. A deal was finally made in mid-December 2014. The compromise provided for an increase in payments of €3.5 billion to tackle unpaid bills as well as an increase in the funds for research and education, as requested by the EP. The Commission also had to present a plan to reduce the amount of the unpaid bills to a sustainable level by 2016. With this compromise, a major budgetary crisis was avoided but in times of economic crisis and tight finances, the adoption of the annual budget remains a fundamentally conflictual procedure. We can expect the annual budget to remain controversial in the years to come.

7.2.4 The open method of coordination and enhanced cooperation

To conclude this overview of the decision process in the European Union, we must also briefly discuss the open method of coordination and of enhanced cooperation. We shall return to these two modes of decision in the next chapter in more detail.

The open method of coordination

As of the late 1990s, the Open Method of Coordination (OMC) is another form of EU decision-making. The origin of the OMC is controversial inasmuch as it has only recently been analysed. In a broad sense, we consider that its principle already underpins the Economic and Monetary Union established by the Treaty of Maastricht. The Member States adopting the euro agreed to coordinate their economic and fiscal policies without using constraining European norms. This logic, based on the goodwill of the states, has also been applied to certain elements of social and employment policy (European Employment Strategy) by the Amsterdam Treaty: there was indeed a consensus to develop action at the European level in this field, given the expectations of public opinion, but with respect for the sovereignty of states. However, it was impossible to transfer competences to the EU, given the absence of unanimity among the negotiators. The Amsterdam Treaty thus provided flexible and non-constraining mechanisms for coordination of national policies in this domain. Though only a germ of an idea in the Treaties of Maastricht and Amsterdam, this approach was codified as part of the 'Lisbon Strategy'. Launched in March 2000 by the Heads of State and Government meeting in Lisbon under the Portuguese Presidency, it was with the ambition of making Europe 'the most competitive and dynamic economy in the world by 2010 capable of sustainable economic growth with more and better jobs and greater social cohesion'.[24] Again, the members of the European Council agreed to take coordinated initiatives and converge their policies, but not to transfer new formal powers to the EU. Formally, the document presenting the strategy consisted of three parts (excluding the introduction): 1. 'Preparing the transition to a society and economy based on knowledge'; 2. 'modernizing the European social model by investing in people and fighting against social exclusion'; and 3. 'the implementation of decisions: a more coherent and systematic approach'.

The third part is a formalization of the OMC based on previous experience. It provides a new framework for cooperation between Member States through the exchange of best practices in an attempt to make national policies converge and to achieve certain common objectives. In this intergovernmental method, Member States' performances are evaluated by representatives of other Member States (peer review) and the Commission must be satisfied with a role of supervision and assistance. The Parliament and the Court of Justice are almost completely excluded from this process, which raises the issue of its democratic character. The Treaty of Nice extended the OMC to a host of new areas related to social security and vocational training. The Lisbon Treaty still has not institutionalized the OMC and makes no reference to it as such but refers to it implicitly in various domains of Member States' competences where a convergence of policies is desired: employment, social protection, social inclusion, education, youth, and training, as well as the coordination of economic and monetary policies.

Specifically, the OMC is based on three operations: 1. joint identification and definition of objectives to be fulfilled in a specific domain by the Council; 2. joint definition of instruments to measure progress made by states (statistics, indicators, guidelines); 3. benchmarking or comparison of individual Member State performance by Member States themselves or by the Commission, and the identification and diffusion of best practices.

According to the relevant domains, the OMC can involve 'soft law' mechanisms. They are more or less binding on Member States but never take the form of directives, evaluation procedures, regulations or decisions ('hard law'). As part of the Lisbon Strategy, the OMC requires Member States to develop national reform plans and to transmit them to the Commission for their information and evaluation, it is thus a minor constraint. The coordination of budgetary policies within the framework of the Stability and Growth Pact and macroeconomic policies (Broad Economic Policy Guidelines – BEPG) is much more supervised than that of research and innovation policies. Recently, the OMC has taken on even more restrictive forms.[25] Another example of such a plan is the Euro Plus Pact, which is quite constraining. It is an arrangement adopted in March 2011 to improve the cooperation in economic matters that involves all the EU Member States except the Czech Republic, Hungary, Sweden and the United Kingdom. The Pact includes a list of political reforms intended to improve the fiscal strength and competitiveness of the participating countries. It was designed to be more coercive than the Stability and Growth Pact, which has not been implemented consistently. For other policies, such as youth policy, there is no question of targets or coordinated national action plans; Member States remain more independent.

The European Council has gradually extended this method to new areas as part of the Lisbon Strategy, as for example social inclusion (Nice, 2000), pensions (Stockholm, 2001), health care (Gothenburg, 2001) or research and innovation (European Council, spring 2003). While the corresponding processes share the same name (OMC), they vary according to format, status or the presence or absence of specific targets and sanction mechanisms. Coordination of fiscal policies within the framework of the Growth and Stability Pact, and macroeconomic policies (Broad Economic Policy Guidelines – BEPG), for example, are much more restricted than research and innovation policy.[26]

7.2.5 Enhanced cooperation

To be exhaustive, this overview of EU decision-making must include discussion of the 'enhanced cooperation' system introduced by the Amsterdam Treaty in 1997. It was created in response, mostly symbolic, to discussions held since the early 1990s on the conditions for a differentiated European integration.[27] As we saw earlier, under the Maastricht Treaty, certain Member States were already exempted on a case-by-case basis from specific policies – European citizenship or Economic and Monetary Union. Enhanced cooperation is of a different nature and constitutes a new modality of integration, enabling a limited number of Member States to develop a policy that does not receive the consent of all. These have been largely fuelled by federalists' fears of continuous EU enlargement. The accession of countries little motivated by a political Europe as well as the foreseeable difficulties of the functioning of an EU of 25 or 30 Member States has given rise to all kinds of proposals to reconcile EU enlargement with further integration. With enhanced cooperation, for the first time, the Treaty of Amsterdam formalized a system of differentiation for Member State involvement. Under the Maastricht Treaty, some Member States were already exempt from specific policies – European citizenship and Economic and Monetary Union – but these were exceptions negotiated on a case-by-case basis. On the contrary, enhanced cooperation can be seen as a new form of integration.

The Treaty of Amsterdam has placed very restrictive conditions on the introduction of enhanced cooperation, thus confirming the primarily symbolic character of the procedure which was not intended to compete with conventional forms of integration. It gives hope to supporters of further European integration who can initiate enhanced cooperation or invoke the possibility of its use in order to convince their less Europhile peers to make concessions. Conversely, with this option, the latter need not be alarmed at the prospect of a federal Europe and are able to oppose a decision without being accused of blocking the integration process. The Treaty of Nice has relaxed the system and extended its potential use to the CFSP. It abolished the right of veto to the introduction of enhanced cooperation which all Member States previously had (except in the CFSP which is still governed by unanimity) and reduced the number of states required to initiate the process (eight, regardless of the total number of Member States and no longer the majority). The Lisbon Treaty has continued to expand the scope of enhanced cooperation, which now covers all of the EU's non-exclusive powers. However, it has clarified the conditions under which the procedure can be enabled and reaffirmed its exceptional and limited character.

This possibility remains very restrictive. States that wish to establish enhanced cooperation must ensure scrupulous compliance with EU treaties and the EU's institutional framework, including preservation of rights for Member States who do not take part in it as well as respect for the Community acquis. Enhanced cooperation should contribute to the EU integration process, should not undermine the internal market and the EU's economic and social cohesion, and should create no interference, discrimination in trade between Member States or distortion of competition. The use of this device cannot be considered as a last resort when it appears that the objective can be achieved within a reasonable time through normal procedures. Enhanced cooperation should be open to participation for all Member States who may request to join at any time.

Since the entry into force of the Lisbon Treaty, enhanced cooperation requires the participation of at least nine Member States – regardless of their total number. It is adopted, on a proposal from the Commission and after consulting the Parliament, by a Council decision of qualified majority – all members participating in the vote. Regarding CFSP, unanimity in the Council is required. Overall, enhanced cooperation replicates decision-making rules (type of majority required in the Council, role and influence of the Parliament) under the treaties according to the EU's areas of competence. The main difference is that only representatives of Member States involved in the cooperation shall vote in the Council. Conversely, all MEPs, irrespective of their nationality, participate in the EP decision, under a principle of 'generality' of the European parliamentary mandate. This had already been the case after the entry into force of the Maastricht Treaty in domains which do not concern all Member States or when the EP is dealing with the euro and the eurozone. Once the cooperation is in place, all national representatives may participate in Council deliberation but only those states involved in enhanced cooperation can vote. The measures adopted are only binding on participating Member States and are not considered a part of the acquis that must be accepted by candidate states for EU accession. Despite the easing of the device, implementation of enhanced cooperation requires highly motivated supporters and goodwill from other national representatives (see Section III, TFEU).

For a long time, enhanced cooperation remained a purely theoretical issue of European integration. It was not until 2010 that the device became a concrete initiative. Thirteen Member States have adopted a directive aimed at facilitating the separation of spouses from two Member States. This directive falls under the premise of the former pillar 'justice and home affairs'. In this area, implementing procedures or any changes require a unanimous decision of the participating states in the Council; the Parliament is only consulted on these decisions.

The second case of enhanced cooperation was the EU patent. In December 2010, 12 states proposed to use this procedure in order to overcome a dispute with Italy and Spain over the languages to be used for a common EU Patent. As a consequence, 25 Member States (all except Italy and Spain) have joined a proposal of enhanced cooperation in that field. It will apply to a state once it has ratified the Agreement on a Unified Patent Court.

At the beginning of April 2017, 16 Member States (Belgium, Bulgaria, Croatia, Cyprus, Czech Republic, Germany, Greece, Spain, Finland, France, Lithuania, Luxembourg, Portugal, Romania, Slovenia and Slovakia) notified the three institutions of their intention to launch an enhanced cooperation for the creation of a European Public Prosecutor's Office, in the absence of a consensus of 28 on this dossier.

Finally, on 13 November 2017 ministers from 23 Member States signed a joint notification on the Permanent Structured Cooperation (PESCO) and handed it over to the High Representative and the Council. The possibility of such a cooperation in the area of defence security and policy was introduced by the Lisbon Treaty; it allows for the Member States involved to jointly develop defence capabilities, invest in shared projects, or enhance the operational readiness and contribution of their armed forces.

The future of the procedure will likely depend on the success of these first experiments in enhanced cooperation. Under the present circumstances and given the technical difficulties of its implementation and the willingness of national and European politicians to maintain the homogeneity of European integration, the use of enhanced cooperation has not propagated However, given the growing divergences in an enlarged Union, the desire to preserve the homogeneity of integration appears to be diminishing, as evidenced by the inclusion among the five proposed scenarios of an option called 'those who want more do more' introduced by the Commissions White Paper on the Future of Europe (in March 2017). This change in sensitivity could increase the attractiveness of differentiated integration through the enhanced cooperation procedure or via a new, more ambitious treaty limited to certain Member States only.

Conclusion

Since the beginning of the sovereign-debt crises, there have been several changes in the EU decision-making. Negotiations took place in an intergovernmental mode, given the uncertain context, and included only some of EU members (sometimes the eurozone members, sometimes other configurations). They are not formally 'enhanced cooperations', but they follow the same logic. As such, this trend is not new.

This was already the case of the Schengen Treaty, signed in 1985 by only 5 of the then 10 Member States of the Communities, and later included in the Amsterdam Treaty. But it still does not include the UK (to leave the EU in 2019) and Ireland but includes non-EU countries such as Norway or Switzerland. The Social Charter was adopted in 1989 by only 11 of the then 12 Member States, since the United Kingdom refused to sign it and subsequently vetoed it being included as the 'Social Chapter' in the 1992 Maastricht Treaty. Instead, an 'Agreement on Social Policy' was added as a protocol applying to only 11 Member States. The 'Prüm Convention' was also negotiated in a way similar to an enhanced cooperation: it is a treaty for cooperation in criminal matters adopted in 2005 by Germany, Spain, France, Luxembourg, Netherlands, Austria and Belgium. It is external to the EU, but it asserts that EU law takes precedence over its provisions and it is open to any Member State of the EU willing to join it.

The eurozone crisis has led to an inflation of initiatives located outside of the treaties, because of the conjunction of an urgent need of further integration in the field of macro-economic coordination and national budgetary and fiscal policies monitoring, and not at least because of clear divergences between the Member States regarding these matters. More recently, the European Stability Mechanism, established to replace the European Financial Stability Facility (EFSF) and the European Financial Stabilisation Mechanism (EFSM) in 2012, was negotiated outside of the EU framework by the Eurozone members. This treaty has created a new international organization located in Luxembourg that aims at providing financial assistance programmes for Member States of the eurozone that experience difficulties. The European Fiscal Compact (2012) is, as well, an intergovernmental treaty signed by all of the Member States, except the Czech Republic and the United Kingdom. Formally, it is not part of EU law but nevertheless contains a provision to attempt to incorporate it in the EU Treaties – as recalled by J. C. Juncker in December 2017.

We must thus account for the existence of a multi-speed European integration. The leaders of the Member States and of the European institutions have always been reluctant acknowledge this, and the EU's theoretical approaches don't really take it into account so far.[28] This situation is a major obstacle to understanding for EU citizens, whether it concerns its structure, its purposes or its working methods, and therefore its legitimacy. But things are changing. The taboo has fallen because of Brexit and recognition of the institutional and political difficulties caused by the massive enlargement of the EU to the countries of Central and Eastern Europe. The 60th anniversary celebration of the Treaty of Rome thus saw the emergence of the idea of a formalization of a multispeed integration,[29] because of those various intergovernmental initiatives and treaties, but also of the multiplication of *de facto* or *de jure* opt-outs for policies such as the

EMU, European Citizenship, the Common Security and Defence Policy (CSDP), the Area of Freedom, Security and Justice (AFSJ) and the Charter of Fundamental Rights.[30]

Notes

1 See Fédéchar Decision, case 8/55 and the Italian Republic v. the High Authority Decision, case 20/59, and the establishment of the implied powers in the ERTA Decision, Case 22/70, the Commission v. the Council.

2 Liesbet Hooghe, *The European Commission and the Integration of Governance* (Cambridge: Cambridge University Press, 2001); Andreas Foellesdal, 'The political theory of the white paper on governance: hidden and fascinating,' *European Public Law* 9(1) (2003): 73–86; Beate Kohler-Koch and Rainer Eising, *The Transformation of Governance* (London: Routledge, 1999); Gary Marks and Liesbet Hooghe, *Multi-level Governance and European Integration* (Boulder: Rowman and Littlefield, 2001).

3 Guy Héraud, *Les Principes du Fédéralisme et la Fédération Européenne* (Presses d'Europe, 1968).

4 Robertson, *A Theory of Party Competition* (London: Wiley, 1976); John R. Petrocik, 'Issue ownership in presidential elections, with a 1980 case study,' *American Journal of Political Science* 40 (1996): 825–850. Rune Stubager and Rune Slothuus, 'What are the sources of political parties' issue ownership? Testing four explanations at the individual level,' *Political Behavior* 35(3): 567–588; Christoffer Green-Pedersen and Peter B. Mortensen, 'Avoidance and engagement: issue competition in multiparty systems,' *Political Studies* 63(4) (2015): 747–764.

5 Sweden has intentionally avoided the fulfilment of the adoption requirements. Swedish leaders consider that joining the ERM II (European Exchange Rate Mechanism, a requirement for euro adoption) is not compulsory and have chosen to remain outside the EMU pending public approval by a referendum.

6 On differentiated integration, see in particular: Katharina Holzinger and Frank Schimmelfennig, 'Differentiated integration in the European Union: Many concepts, sparse theory, few data,' *Journal of European Public Policy* 19(2) (2012): 292–305; Dirk Leuffen, Berthold Rittberger and Frank Schimmelfennig, *Differentiated Integration: Explaining Variation in the European Union* (Palgrave Macmillan, 2012); Benjamin Leruth, 'Operationalizing national preferences on Europe and differentiated integration,' *Journal of European Public Policy*, 22(6) (2015): 816–835; Daniela A. Kroll and Dirk Leuffen, 'Enhanced cooperation in practice. An analysis of differentiated integration in EU secondary law,' *Journal of European Public Policy* 22(3) 2015: 353–373.

7 Emiliano Grossman and Sylvain Brouard, 'La production législative de l'UE par secteurs: premières analyses et comparaisons,' in *Que fait l'Europe?* eds Renaud Dehousse, Florence Deloche-Gaudez and Sophie Jacquot (Paris: Presses de Sciences Po, 2009), 15–27.

8 Jörg Monar, 'Inter-institutional agreements: the phenomenon and its new dynamics after Maastricht,' *Common Market Law Review* 31 (1994): 693–719; Sonja Puntscher

Riekmann, 'The cocoon of power: democratic implications of inter-institutional agreements,' *European Law Journal* 13(1) (2007): 4–19.

9 Simon Hix, 'Constitutional agenda-setting through discretion in rule interpretation: why the European Parliament won at Amsterdam,' *British Journal of Political Science* 32(2) (2002): 259–280.

10 Olivier Costa, Renaud Dehousse, Aneta Trakalova, 'La Codécision et les 'accords précoces'. Progrès ou détournement de la procédure législative?' *Notes de la Fondation Notre Europe* 84 (2011): 47.

11 Olivier Costa, 'Parlement Européen et élargissement: entre fantasme et réalité,' in *Elargissement: Comment l'Europe s'Adapte*, eds Renaud Dehousse, Florence Deloche-Gaudez and Olivier Duhamel (Paris: Presses de Sciences Po, 2007); Henry Farrell and Adrienne Héritier, 'Interorganizational negotiation and intraorganizational power in shared decision making. Early agreements under codecision and their impact on the European Parliament and Council,' *Comparative Political Studies* 27 (2004): 1184–1212; Anne Rasmussen and Christine Reh, 'The consequences of concluding codecision early: trilogues and intra-institutional bargaining success,' *Journal of European Public Policy* 20(7) (2013): 1006–1024.

12 This was impossible under the Treaty of Maastricht; it became possible thanks to the Treaty of Amsterdam on 1 May 1999.

13 Brandsma, Gijs Jan (2015): 'Co-decision after Lisbon: the politics of informal trilogues in European Union lawmaking', *European Union Politics* 16(2): 300–319.

14 Greenwood, Justin; Roederer-Rynning, Christilla 'The culture of trilogies,' *Journal of European Public Policy* 22(8) (2015), 1148–1165.

15 See the Commission website dedicated to 'Better Regulation': http://ec.europa.eu/governance/better_regulation/index_en.htm; as well as Eric Van den Abeele, 'L'agenda Mieux légiférer de l'Union européenne,' *Courrier Hebdomadaire du Crisp*, 2028–2029 (2009); Claudio Radaelli, 'Whither better regulation for the Lisbon agenda,' *Journal of European Public Policy* 14(2) (2007): 190–207.

16 A green paper is a consultation document of policy proposals on a precise topic that is drawn by the Commission and diffused on a large scale in order to favour debate and discussion with all kinds of stakeholders and between EU institutions and organs. There is no commitment to action: it is only a first step in a process that may lead (or not) to a policy change. At the end of the consultation process, a green paper can result in the production of a white paper. It is a document of the Commission containing more precise proposals regarding a reform or an action plan in a specific area. If the Council and the EP agree on the main objectives and on the necessity to adopt new norms, the Commission then draws up detailed proposals for legislation.

17 See his official webpage: https://ec.europa.eu/commission/2014-2019/timmermans_en

18 Communication from the Commission to the European Parliament, the Council, the European Economic and Social Committee and the Committee of the Regions, 'Improving regulation for better results – a priority issue for the EU', 19 May 2015, COM (2015) 215 final, 14 p.

19 European Commission – Press release Juncker Commission presents third annual Work Programme: Delivering a Europe that protects, empowers and defends Strasbourg, 25 October 2016.

20 Brigid Laffan and Johannes Lindner, 'The budget. Who gets what, when and how?,' in *Policy-Making in the European Union,* eds Helen Wallace, Mark A. Pollack and Alasdair R. Young (Oxford: Oxford University Press, 2010), 207–228.

21 Neill Nugent, *The Government and Politics of the European Union* (Basingstoke: Palgrave MacMillan, 7th ed., 2010), 401–415.

22 See: Giacomo Benedetto and Simona Milio, *European Union Budget Reform. Institutions, Policy and Economic Crisis* (Basingstoke: Palgrave MacMillan, 2012).

23 Future Financing of the EU, Final Report and Recommendations of the High Level Group on Own Resources December 2016, http://ec.europa.eu/budget/mff/hlgor/library/reports-communication/hlgor-report_20170104.pdf.

24 *Conclusions of the European Council of Lisbon,* 23 and 24 March 2000, p. 2.

25 See: Manuele Citi and Martin Rhodes, 'New modes of governance in the European Union: a critical survey and analysis,' in *Handbook of European Union Politics,* eds Knud Erik Jørgensen, Mark A. Pollack and Ben Rosamond (London: Sage, 2007), 463–482.

26 Citi and Rhodes, op. cit.

27 For this subject see: Kerstin Junge, 'Differentiated European integration,' in *European Union Politics,* ed. Michelle Cini (Oxford: Oxford University Press, 2007), 391–404; Alex Warleigh, *Flexible Integration: Which Model for the European Union?* (Sheffield: Sheffield Academic Press, 2005).

28 Katharina Holzinger and Frank Schimmelfennig, 'Differentiated integration in the European Union: many concepts, sparse theory, few data,' *Journal of European Public Policy* 19(2) (2012): 292–305; Christian B. Jensen and Jonathan B. Slapin, 'Institutional hokey-pokey: the politics of multispeed integration in the European Union,' *Journal of European Public Policy* 19(6) (2012): 779–795.

29 'L'Europe à plusieurs vitesses ressurgit au 60ème anniversaire du traité de Rome,' Les Echos, 5 February 2017.

30 Katharina Holzinger and Frank Schimmelfennig, 'Differentiated integration in the European Union: many concepts, sparse theory, few data,' *Journal of European Public Policy* 19(2) (2012): 292–305; Christian B. Jensen and Jonathan B. Slapin, 'Institutional hokey-pokey: the politics of multispeed integration in the European Union,' *Journal of European Public Policy* 19(6) (2012): 779–795.

EU decision-making models

8

It is impossible to understand EU policies, their elaboration, nature and evolution without considering the specificities of the EU's institutional framework. Because of them, some policies are possible, others are not, and further, they determine the EU's mode of governance. To analyse them, one must not insist on the *sui generis* nature of the institutions but on their experimental characteristics and on the considerable changes they have undergone since 1951. After the strengthening of EU powers and after each enlargement, the decision-making system has experienced both a formal and a practical evolution. This is still the case today with the Lisbon Treaty, which has had a significant impact on the relationship between institutions and on the decision-making dynamics. Similarly, the economic and financial crisis that shook the EU from late 2008 has profoundly changed both the relations between institutions and the decision-making methods. The experience of *Spitzenkandidaten* – unilaterally promoted by the five major European political parties in 2014 – also had a significant impact on the overall logic of the EU regime and on the way European policies are produced.

As mentioned earlier in this volume, actors in European institutions have always tried to influence the institutional framework to serve their political and organizational objectives. They alter procedures and affect the equilibrium through the practice and strategy of *fait accompli*, take advantage of the treaties' grey areas, negotiate various types of inter-institutional agreements, demand improvements in the treaties, etc. The treaties encourage these practices, calling on the institutions to cooperate and recognizing the existence of – potentially binding – inter-institutional agreements to clarify their wording.

The visions of these actors towards European integration must also be considered. Their individual approaches to decision-making are not the same depending on whether they perceive it as a benefit to support, a necessary evil to control or a danger to combat. In recent years, the institutions (European

Parliament, Council, European Council) have welcomed a growing number of overtly Eurosceptic actors, openly obstructing any progress in integration. Finally, we must pay attention to the impact of the complexity of EU decision-making on the actors themselves. Acute awareness of the unusual nature of the EU's institutional structure and functioning and of the suspicion surrounding its activities explains their sensitivity to norms such as transparency, subsidiarity and openness as well as their propensity to want to publicly justify their choices. We must add that it is essential to acknowledge the historical depth of the phenomena studied which, by itself, helps us to understand the Byzantine character of the distribution of powers between the EU and its Member States, the subtlety and dynamics of power relations between institutions and the multiplicity of decision-making mechanisms.

8.1 The plurality of decision-making styles

The initial treaties already held a dual logic of decision-making in the legislative domain. Based on a Commission proposal, decisions could be taken by the Council either unanimously or (after a 10-year transition period and only in certain domains) by a qualified majority. In both cases, the EP was only consulted originally and had virtually no influence. The rationale was that the second method, called the 'Community method', would gradually become more widespread. The French President Charles De Gaulle protested this method in 1965 when he triggered the 'empty chair' crisis. Even if this was not its original purpose, the Luxembourg compromise, which was adopted to put an end to French obstruction, gradually led to a systematic questioning of the Community method. Without legally affecting the treaties, it provoked a profound change in the expanding institutional equilibrium by suspending the use of the majority rule in the Council. The Council gradually became the central EU decision-making actor. Its rise came with the involvement of a growing number of national officials in its work. In turn, the Commission saw its room for manoeuvre shrink as it has been forced to anticipate potential blockages within the Council; it has gradually lost its power of impetus and has favoured bland legislative proposals. Meanwhile, the institutional development of the EP has come to a stop. Only the Court of Justice has escaped the inter-governmental evolution of the Communities' institutional framework. The Court has been able, by virtue of its independence and daring interpretations, to preserve the European integration process by asserting the binding force of the treaties and of secondary legislation.

The creation of the European Council in 1974 and its inclusion in the Single European Act reinforced this dual logic of decision-making. The Community method was applied to routine decisions or those of minor importance and to the management of core policies (low politics); while inter-governmental decision-making was relied upon for key decisions and less integrated policies (high politics). This duality was long implicit, hidden behind the veil of institutional community; it was finally formalized with the Maastricht Treaty, which entered into force in late 1993.

This treaty was the fruit of a great political ambition: to make the European Communities a European Union, to transform a group of functional organizations created to conduct a limited number of market policies, in partnership with the economic, political and administrative elites, into a single policy organization, expected to develop activities in all areas and establish direct relations with its 'citizens'. As a result of complex negotiations and the targeted reluctance of the negotiators, who each had a veto, the end-result was mixed. The original goal was to replicate the success of the Single European Act in other domains (foreign affairs, defence, currency, justice). However, unlike the prospect of opening economic borders on 31 December 1992, which had mobilized the general public and had led to the emergence of broad coalitions of support for the efforts of European institutions, the idea of integration in these new domains only stimulated the enthusiasm of a limited number of groups. This integration concerned mainly sovereignty-related policies that were historically linked to the national framework and for which a (simple) transfer to Community institutions was not self-evident. It thus provoked strong reactions among certain citizens, opinion leaders and national policy makers.[1]

Negotiations have long centred on the structure of the EU: should one maintain a single institutional and legal framework? During the two Intergovernmental Conferences tasked with considering respectively the conditions necessary for the creation of a Political Union and of an Economic and Monetary Union, it soon became apparent that defence, currency and homeland security could only enter the scope of responsibilities exercised at the European level if an institutional arrangement different from the one of the Community was established. In the face of the prospect of a failure of treaty reform, negotiators proposed the creation, alongside the Community 'pillar', of a second and a third pillar with a more intergovernmental form of cooperation, largely based on Council and European Council actions. The Court would be more or less excluded, the Commission would only have a technical role and Parliament would benefit from a simple right of scrutiny. However, the decision was made to include the Economic and Monetary Union in the Community pillar though it is (still) subject to a specific decision-making process and does not concern all Member States.

At the end of this difficult negotiation process, in February 1992, the European Council adopted a new Treaty 'on the European Union' in Maastricht. This text created the expected European Union but designed a complex institutional landscape consisting of three 'pillars' (the European Community, including an Economic and Monetary Union; a cooperation in the domains of Justice and Home Affairs; and a Common Foreign and Security Policy), backed by 22 distinct decision-making procedures and more than 30 legal instruments by which the jurisdictions, influence and mode of operations of the institutions varied greatly according to the policy. In this plan, the Community 'lends', so to speak, its institutions to the non-Community pillars of the EU, who then operate according to other rationales. Creating a single structure was the object of a consensus among the negotiators. In addition to avoiding the multiplication of European organizations, it raised the hopes of EU federalists that the EU could eventually be governed entirely by the Community method on the one hand, and of their opponents that the intergovernmental mechanisms would contaminate the Community pillar and thus impede the prospect of a supranational Europe on the other.

The Treaty of Amsterdam, signed on 2 October 1997, simplified the Maastricht scheme by streamlining the decision-making process and by beginning to integrate the cooperation on matters of Justice and Home Affairs into the Community pillar. In doing so, it also introduced intergovernmental procedures in the Community pillar, further increasing the confusion. The Amsterdam Treaty also provided the possibility of enhanced cooperation among limited groups of Member States wishing to go further in certain areas. The Treaty of Nice signed in December 2000 relaxed the conditions for the implementation of this procedure, seeking to simplify EU decision-making and, again, extended the scope of the application of co-decision and qualified majority voting within the Council.

The Treaty of Lisbon – which resumed the major points of the constitutional treaty that had not been ratified – continued this work of clarification and simplification. It merged the three pillars into one and conferred the legal capacity on the EU; it also made co-decision the 'ordinary legislative procedure', applying to most texts, and extended once more the use of qualified majority voting in the Council. But it did not question the fundamental duality of European integration, which still blends the community method and the intergovernmental method. Formally, the latter appears to be residual, limited to exceptions, but the management of the sovereign debt and the refugee crises has shown that intergovernmental logic could quickly become preponderant again.

The Maastricht, Amsterdam and Nice Treaties are the results of attempts to find a balance between two, difficult to reconcile, imperatives: the expansion of EU activities in a single institutional framework and the preservation of the efficiency and originality of the Community method. This process therefore has mixed assessments. On the one hand, these treaties have formalized the latent competition that exists within the EU between different modes of decision-making, primarily the Community and intergovernmental methods. On the other hand, they created a single institutional framework to pre-existing forms of cooperation in Foreign Affairs and Justice and Home Affairs and avoided a proliferation of regional organizations in Europe. The formalization of the existence of an 'intergovernmental method' alongside the 'Community method' which was intended to govern all the activities of the communities is not fortuitous or insignificant. This decision clearly reflects the reluctance of a growing number of national officials regarding the initial approach which they perceived to be too federal.

The Treaty of Lisbon's entry into force (1 December 2009) did not fundamentally change the situation. Even if co-decision became the norm, other, more intergovernmental decision-making procedures stayed in place. The turbulent history of European integration has led to a stratification of the diverse kinds of decision-making processes, evidencing very stable political arrangements and making sense in this regard. When Member States agree on clear, broad priorities (for the single market long ago and the policies that are currently directly and indirectly related to it), they establish decision procedures governed by qualified majority voting and which involved heavily the most integrated institutions (Commission, Parliament, Court). In areas where consensus on the objectives and the urgency of the action remains less broad (foreign policy, cooperation in criminal matters), States have focused on intergovernmental mechanisms, leaving little influence to supranational institutions.

The Lisbon Treaty does not challenge this duality despite the difficulties it creates. The Convention on the Future of the Union reached an agreement to radically simplify EU policy instruments. It proposed to replace existing instruments with two simple categories: 'European laws' and 'European framework laws', both adopted according to a single legislative procedure. State representatives, however, did not reach an agreement on this perspective. Therefore, even today, we can distinguish five decision-making methods in the EU.[2]

8.1.1 The Community method

The 'Community method', also known as the Monnet method, is based on a partnership between state representatives, the main policy recipients ('stakeholders') and the actors from supranational institutions. It was originally based on the relationship between the Commission and the Council; the Parliament only gradually came into the frame in the late 1980s. Originally, the Commission was charged with proposing and implementing legislation; the Council adapted it to the States' expectations and legitimized it. The Court ensured that the decision-making process worked efficiently, avoided conflicts between institutions, ensured the correct application of the texts by the Member States and defended the rights of the recipients of the standards. This scheme resulted in the neo-functionalist interpretations of the Community experience[3] that emphasized the autonomy of the Commission and described European integration as a process beyond the reach of Member States, gradually depriving them of their sovereignty.

The Community method, which never disappeared despite the emergence of other policy-making processes, is symbolic of the original Community. Decisions were based on a partnership between the political, administrative and economic elites and on a permissive consensus among citizens. The legitimacy of the Community method was primarily rational–legal. It resulted from duly negotiated treaties ratified by the Member States, compliance and respect for which was assured by the Court of Justice. The Council could also rely on the legitimacy of its members, who represented and defended state interests. The Commission became, in turn, worthy of the confidence placed in it by its dynamism and innovative solutions. It designed and implemented effective policies, responding to real problems in order to meet the interests of the political, administrative and economic elites involved in the European integration process, thereby strengthening their allegiance to it. The institutional framework and the Community method have been developed to meet these requirements and they have done so successfully. The 'empty chair' crisis (June 1965 to January 1966) may have hampered the development of this method and restricted its scope, but it was never called into question.

In breaking down the barriers of the Luxembourg Compromise, and therefore of the systematic search for unanimity, the Single European Act (entered into force on 1 July 1987) largely restored the use of the Community method. It also amended it by upgrading the role of the European Parliament. This has contributed to further politicizing the process of developing standards but it has not affected the ability of the method to develop broad consensus and to aggregate different interests (national, partisan, sectorial, institutional). Though they institutionalized the intergovernmental method, the following treaties (Maastricht, Amsterdam, Nice and Lisbon) continued to expand the scope of the Community method. They also continued the 'parliamentarization' of this approach, acknowledging the ability of the Parliament to contribute constructively.[4]

With the generalization of co-decision and the evolution of the budgetary procedure, the 'Community method' is now the EU's principle method of decision-making. It is also the most binding for three distinct reasons. First, it gives broad influence to the supranational institutions that control the agenda (Commission), actively contribute to the development of standards (Commission, Parliament) and ensure their compliance (Court of Justice). Second, it provides that the Council decides by qualified majority, with some exceptions that are fading off. Finally, it leads to binding standards (directives, regulations). This implies that a state is legally bound by a European standard even if it is adopted against the opinion of its representatives in the Council and in Parliament.

Today, this method of decision-making primarily governs the regulation of the single market, the market 'support' policies (protection of public health, consumer rights and environment), some sectorial policies (research, transport, development cooperation) and some specific social measures (anti-discrimination).

Despite its centrality in the decision-making process, the Community method has been called into question since the beginning of the economic and financial crisis (2008). Due to the political sensitivity of the issues on the agenda, Member States preferred turning to other decision-making methods. Indeed, there has been a form of integration without supranationalization, where the integration process is essentially pursued via the intergovernmental method at the expense of the Community method. This is particularly the case in the EU's new areas of intervention, which hybridize legislative and non-legislative mechanisms, such as foreign policy, action in the energy sector, economic regulation or Internal Affairs.[5] This has led some researchers to think that the crisis in the EU is not so much a crisis of integration as a crisis of the Community method.[6] More generally, the increasing power of Euroscepticism within the institutions and in most Member States has aroused the reluctance of many actors to develop new initiatives at the Community level, which is clearly visible in the decrease in the number or even the scope of legislative proposals.

8.1.2 Intergovernmental cooperation

As we have seen, the 'empty chair' crisis (1965–1966) seriously undermined the 'Community method' and challenged neo-functionalist analysis. Neo-realist authors reminded the neo-functionalists that European integration (only) happened with the consent of the States and was not a process beyond their control.[7] It sufficed for General de Gaulle to ask his ministers not to serve on the Council to force a gridlock and compel his partners to change the rules of the game. De Gaulle, who returned to power shortly after the signing of the Treaty of Rome, initially accommodated European integration because of the benefits that France drew from the Common Agricultural Policy and commitments made by his predecessors. However, the Community process gradually became too 'costly' in his eyes in terms of loss of sovereignty, with the increased autonomy of the Commission, the prospects for strengthened EP powers as well as the introduction of qualified majority voting to the Council. The refusal of other Member States to engage in forms of intergovernmental cooperation proposed by the Fouchet plans in 1961 and 1962 was perceived as another affront to his vision of European cooperation.

More generally, Member State representatives have always been very reluctant to apply the Community method to the areas they consider to be at the heart of their sovereignty, including foreign policy, security and defence, judicial and police cooperation, monetary, fiscal and social policy. Therefore, they decided to submit some domains to the rule of unanimity, and, in the context of the negotiation of the Maastricht Treaty, include certain policies within specific mechanisms, governed by less supranational decision-making rules.[8] This logic is also partly implemented in the Treaty on Stability, Coordination and Governance (TSCG), signed in 2012 to provide lasting solutions to the financial crisis.

Today, intergovernmental cooperation (or 'joint decision') includes the following three characteristics:

1   supranational institutions enjoy limited powers: the Commission has only a partial right of initiative which it shares with governments; the Parliament is, at best, consulted or informed; the Court of Justice plays a minor role – even if the Lisbon Treaty strengthens its powers;

2   as for the Council, unanimity prevails: a negative consensus is sufficient to take a decision, however. This means that a decision does not require the explicit support of all members, through a formal vote, but only the absence of a veto;

3   decisions are often ad hoc or atypical legal instruments, but they are just as binding on Member States as directives and regulations.[9]

The intergovernmental method makes national governments mediators. They are the main interlocutors of the Commission (and now of the Parliament), on the one hand, and of national parliaments, as well as socio-economic, administrative and public-opinion elites, on the other. After 1965, governments have gradually applied it to all 'high politics', that is to say, to the major decisions and most sensitive policies, leaving the Monnet method to operate only within limited fields and for routine decisions. Strictly speaking, the intergovernmental method is not opposed to the Community method. Instead, it is a restrictive approach which limits the extension of European policies and puts the defence of national interests at the forefront.

The intergovernmental method has led to a proliferation of committees and working groups around the Council and COREPER ('Comité des représentants permanents'[10]). Armies of national officials were mobilized by the Permanent Representations to continuously negotiate every conceivable topic, leading to a gradual shift of the centre of power from the Commission to the Council. This has greatly affected the dynamics of the integration process as committee participants openly defend the interests of their respective states. Paradoxically, it has improved the functioning of the Council: individual positions and strategies are more exposed and better understood, making it often easier to reach a compromise than in the past. Similarly, the relationship between the Commission and the Council has become simpler. Finally, one must recall that 'intergovernmental' does not mean 'diplomatic': to capture the dynamics of the Council's discussions, even when deciding unanimously, it is necessary to consider the routines and habits of negotiation, the stabilized arrangements that exist on certain subjects, the effects of socialization and institutionalization and the role of established coalitions like the 'Franco-German' couple. Above all, one must remember that the 'cost' of the use of its veto for a Member State is much higher in the EU than in a traditional diplomatic framework because of the unwritten rules of behaviour that irrigate European institutions, the considerable impact of European integration on the States and, therefore, the existence of multiple means of retaliation available to other Member States and supranational institutions.

The Lisbon Treaty reduced the scope of the intergovernmental method and increased the powers of EU institutions. Nevertheless, unanimity will continue to be required in certain areas. In addition, one should not focus excessively on decision-making procedures but also take into account the specificities of policies. Regarding defence policy, for example, the mere use of qualified majority voting would not put an end to the divergent views of states and would be unlikely to overcome the opposition of some of them to an EU action under dramatic circumstances. In such a case, it is safe to wager that the procedures provided for in the treaties remain a dead letter. Even the most ardent advocates of the Community method acknowledge that, for issues that exacerbate national sensibilities, it is more effective to encourage dialogue between Member States with a unanimity rule and to wait for the evolution of the political context and for opinion to be suitable for recourse to qualified majority. Thus, the Treaty of Lisbon simplifies the intergovernmental method, formalizes it (through the institutionalization of the European Council) and also restricts its scope but does not question it.

The intergovernmental method has thus surged back vigorously since the financial crisis occurred at the end of 2008. The European Council has been strongly mobilized to save the euro and develop the necessary mechanisms of regulation. It has then played a prominent role in addressing the crisis of refugees, the situation in Ukraine and Brexit. Progressively, it has exceeded this role and gained an important influence in the setting of the legislative agenda. It is now the main initiator for the EU.[11] Today, the European Council not only gives precise instructions to the Commission regarding the normative and political priorities, but also the content of some legislative proposals, which is unprecedented.

8.1.3 Open coordination

Since the late 1990s, one must consider a new form of EU decision-making: the Open Method of Coordination (OMC). This is the third decision-making method in addition to the Community method and intergovernmental cooperation. It allows states to lessen the incompatibilities between their national policies without giving supranational institutions (Parliament, Commission, Court of Justice, European Central Bank, etc.) too much influence. There were objective needs for European action in areas such as the coordination of economic, employment, health and retirement policies and high expectations in public opinion, but some Member States were reluctant to attribute formal powers to the EU institutions in these fields. Failing this, a consensus emerged in order to develop flexible and non-binding coordination mechanisms for certain policies, which remain fundamentally within the states' competences. Governments do not engage in the creation of common policies but simply establish criteria that channel national policies and promote their convergence. To do so, governments adopt general guidelines and criteria which they take on to respect the design of national policies. Fundamentally, the OMC provides a new framework for cooperation between Member States, which promotes the exchange of best practices in a given sector in order to converge national policies and achieve certain common objectives.

The OMC is the result of a variety of initiatives that initially were carried out without a clear framework. The coordination of macroeconomic policies foreseen in the Stability and Growth Pact (Amsterdam European Council, June 1997) or the employment measures encouraged by the Treaty of Amsterdam fall under this rationale. This was formalized in the Lisbon Strategy adopted by the European Council in March 2000 to promote a 'knowledge society' at the EU level.[12]

Formally, the strategy's presentation leaflet was divided into three parts (excluding the introduction):

1   'prepare for the transition to a knowledge-based society and economy';
2   'modernize the European social model by investing in human resources and fighting against social exclusion';
3   'the implementation of decisions: a more coherent and systematic approach'.

This third part is a formalization of the OMC, based on previous experiences.

Over the years, the European Council has extended the OMC to new areas within the Lisbon Strategy's framework: social inclusion and vocational training (Nice, 2000), pensions (Stockholm, 2001), health care (Gothenburg, 2001), research and innovation (Spring European Council, 2003), etc.

The OMC has to be distinguished from both the Community method and the intergovernmental method. First, the degree of involvement of Community institutions is low. The Commission's power of initiative is limited; it can make suggestions or recommendations, but only on the basis of reports and findings established by governments in the Council. Its power of control is equally diluted. The Commission may, at best, analyse national situations on the basis of reports by governments and propose the adoption of recommendations by the Council. The system is based on mechanisms of multilateral surveillance in which it is the governments themselves who decide to issue reprimands or recommendations to States that do not meet the criteria. Decisions are made by unanimity in the Council. The European Parliament and the Court are removed from the entire process.[13]

Member State representatives engage the OMC because they know that in the absence of cooperation, they will be forced to compromise and because they seek to avoid fierce competition due to social or fiscal dumping. However, they are not sufficiently committed to the principle of collective action to accept the risks inherent in the Community method or even intergovernmental cooperation which involves the use of legally binding instruments. The OMC distinguishes itself by the weak level of constraint of the decisions reached. The OMC is meant to encourage a gradual convergence of national policies without imposing anything and is based on emulation rather than coercion. National leaders seek to promote mutual learning through the establishment of indicators based on benchmarks by which the States' respective results can be compared, and possibly named or shamed, an acceptance that the advantages will be evaluated by their peers (peer review) and by the Commission (monitoring) and through the sharing of best practices among partners.[14]

Initially, EU actors and experts were quite optimistic about the OMC, which was supposed to overcome the limits of the Community method and of intergovernmental cooperation. Given the lack of formal pressure, Member State representatives and senior officials were supposed to be more likely to agree. In the end, more rapid agreement was expected from the OMC than that permitted by other methods of integration which led States to surround themselves with precautions or raise objections on principle.

Fifteen years later, the results of the OMC and especially of the Lisbon Strategy, illustrate that informal coordination based on very flexible intergovernmental exchange and on recommendations adopted by consensus and addressed to Member States, does not have the desired effect.[15] The use of 'soft law' instead of the traditional integration instruments (directives, regulations, Commission decisions, the EU budget, etc.) has permitted the imposition of certain themes and objectives (i.e. employment rates, 'flexicurity') and stimulation of 'the exchange of best practices' between Member State governments. But it has also resulted in blurring the respective EU and Member State jurisdictions and contaminating the Community process itself through an 'à la carte' rationale. These failings of open coordination, as well as weak performance in areas where it applies, explain the lack of codification of the OMC by the Constitutional Treaty and the Lisbon Treaty. Nevertheless, the treaty implicitly refers to it regarding different areas that fall within the Member States' competences but where a certain convergence of policies is desired: employment, social protection, social inclusion, education, youth and training as well as the coordination of economic and monetary policies.

8.1.4 Centralized regulation

Centralized regulation applies only in certain defined and limited domains where governments agree that proper decisions can only be taken by a supranational and independent institution on behalf of the general interest. In this case, the rationale is similar to that of 'non-majoritarian institutions' or 'agencies', intended, according to the liberal theory, to address the clientelist policies engaged in by elected institutions for the benefit of their electorate. The intellectual relationship to the 'non-majoritarian' logic is even stronger, as the EU, as we have seen, is led above all by regulatory and redistribution policies: their goal is not to improve the situation of a part of the population at the expense of another but to achieve a better situation of society overall through regulations that apply to all. In a Pareto view, only an independent agency is able to make decisions likely to lead to overall progress in the medium and long term, majoritarian institutions having a tendency to try to privilege the immediate satisfaction of their customers via redistribution mechanisms that cannot lead to these collective benefits.[16]

Since the Treaty of Paris, it was in this regard that Member States established the High Authority of the ECSC, an institution with strong guarantees of independence and important means of expertise. Its goal was to ensure the compliance of Member States with European law and defend the general objectives of European integration. National leaders knew that it was in their interest that policies be defined by expertise, according to the general European interest, and that they be applied by all partners. They also opted for the creation of a supranational institution able to play the role of arbiter and guardian. A similar rationale was behind the attribution of specific powers to the Commission to supervise the proper implementation of free-market principles. It was also in this spirit that, during the euro's introduction, the ECB was responsible for monetary-policy decisions and limiting inflation. Finally, as we have seen, the recent creation of European executive agencies also falls under this rationale.

Centralized control implies supranational institutions in a mode distinct from that of the Community method. The European Parliament, as an elected institution and therefore sensitive to voter demands, is left out. At best, it has a right to information. The same applies to the Council, which is too prone to reflect the demands of the states. Decisions are taken according to the domains, by supranational and independent institutions appointed by Member State representatives, as are the Commission, the ECB and certain executive agencies. The decisions are as binding, legally speaking, as legislative acts, but they often do not have a general application and are specific to a stakeholder (CAP, competition policy, research policy, etc.).

8.1.5 Enhanced cooperation

As we saw in the previous chapter, enhanced cooperation enables a group of states that so wish to go further with European integration, when it is not possible to achieve progress in this area collectively. They are subject to strict conditions in order to avoid too much heterogeneity when it comes to European law. Enhanced cooperation was largely fuelled by the fears that the federalists insist on a continued enlargement of the EU. The membership of countries who are not motivated by a political Europe or who wish to retain competitive advantages linked to national regulatory or social-economic contrasts, as well as the foreseeable difficulties of the functioning of the EU with 25 or 30 Member States have generated all kinds of proposals (multi-speed Europe, concentric circles, etc.) that were designed to reconcile the enlargement of the EU with the pursuit of integration. Since the Nice Treaty, the right of veto on the establishment of enhanced cooperation without a provision for all Member States has been abolished (except in the area of CFSP, which is still governed by the rule of unanimity) and the number of states required to initiate the process has been reduced (to eight, whatever the number of Member States, and no longer the majority of them). The Treaty of Lisbon slightly increased the number of participants to nine, and created a special category of 'permanent enhanced cooperation' concerning defence, the details of which are dealt with in Protocol No. 10.

The principle of enhanced cooperation was subject to contrasting assessments. Some felt that this system would halt community integration, based on the principle of uniformity in the integration pace and the degree of participation of Member States. By opening up the possibility of a formal heterogeneity of European integration, they feared that the EU would become an 'à la carte' Europe based solely on the needs of Member States, where each one would only participate in the policies that serve its own interests.

The supporters of enhanced cooperation have demolished these arguments by insisting on the multiple guarantees offered by the system, on the exceptional nature of its use and by invoking a reality principle. Given that Member States had increasingly mixed expectations and integration capacities, and that it was becoming very difficult to reach an agreement on an increasing number of subjects in the Council, forms of differentiated integration became an obligatory alternative, at least on a temporary basis, to pursue European integration. The system of enhanced cooperation should not be an alternative to the existing modalities of integration, but a last resort. In addition, its promoters were counting on a ripple effect, with non-participating states destined to join the initiators of the process. Moreover, this perspective was supposed to strongly motivate the states involved, which had to succeed in their mission to encourage others to join them. In the spirit of the designers of enhanced cooperation, therefore, it was not a matter of proposing an 'à la carte' Europe but a multispeed Europe, as a transitionary tool in order to allow further integration. This differentiation was intended to be functional: it sought to take into account the variable capacity of states to engage in new sectors of integration (in particular new members, who already had to digest the whole of the EC acquis), and not to satisfy the contrasting expectations of the Member States regarding the European integration process.

8.2 Two distinctive features of EU decision-making

To better understand this typology of decision-making styles, it is useful to highlight two of the specificities of the EU political system: the segmentation of public policy making; and the 'co-optation' of interlocutors by European institutions.

8.2.1 The segmentation of European policy making

Following the Luxembourg Compromise, the considerable increase in Member State investment in decision-making led to an inflation of the number and activities of the committees and working groups assisting COREPER and the Council and to a tightening of intergovernmental negotiations. In order to avoid a general deadlock, states have chosen to increase the number of Council configurations and to grant them broad autonomy. The various configurations began working at different rates and with a contrasting ability to compromise. They have developed various approaches to European negotiations: some are attached to the Monnet model while others are more intergovernmental in nature. Quickly, competitive situations arose between different Council configurations over particular proposals and, more broadly, for control of certain European policy areas. The General Affairs configuration tried to challenge this phenomenon of 'segmentation' (or 'sectorization') of the Council's operations, but with limited results. The six-month rotating presidency has not helped matters: while some have mobilized around the issue of coordination, the lack of consistency of these efforts has deprived them of any effect. In addition, segmentation has long been tolerated because of certain virtues. The most dynamic and harmonious Council configurations have indeed profited from their independence to develop ambitious policies without suffering from the conflicts that crippled others.

In the medium term, however, this situation affected the Council's overall coherence, created more or less open conflicts between the different configurations and caused long-term blockage of certain important dossiers. In the 1970s and 1980s, the phenomenon of segmentation, added to the debate on the British contribution to the EU budget and the oil crises, made the Council an extremely adversarial institution. In some domains, it lost its character as a European institution and its action amounted to informal consultations of a diplomatic nature. The search for unanimity became systematic and the unwritten rules of the construction of compromise limited the field of possibilities. The easiest solution soon became the systematic rejection of the Commission's proposals.

This segmentation has gradually contaminated the Commission. The difficulties of negotiating within the Council have in effect forced the Commission to anticipate the reactions to legislative proposals and thus to adapt to the differentiated functioning of the Council. The increasing divergences between the

Council configurations have encouraged the segmentation of the Directorates-General (DG). The enlargements have increased the problem by creating a steady growth in the number of Commissioners and, indirectly, the DGs. Accordingly, the Commission has suffered from rising tensions between the Commissioners and the DGs which have been overcome through negotiations and permanent arbitrations. The various DGs have gradually gained autonomy and developed specific working methods and diverse conceptions of the type of policy to be pursued, particularly to accommodate the operations and dynamics of their Council configuration. DG IV (competition) favoured a regulatory approach, DG VI (Agriculture) clientelism, DGIII (Industry) interventionism, etc. Moreover, they developed diversified contacts with the outside world (interest groups, NGOs, etc.) and with other institutions.

The internal coordination of the Commission's actions became difficult in the 1970s as the president gradually lost his authority over a college whose members claimed increasing autonomy, thereby strengthening the DGs placed under their responsibility. Commissioners' cabinets expanded and became key sites of negotiation by performing a function similar to that of COREPER in the Council. In addition, committees proliferated within the Commission and played an increasing role in the drafting stage of standards (advisory committees) and their application (committees of the 'comitology').[17]

As in the Council, this situation had different effects. In becoming autonomous, Commissioners and DG agents were able to build their own 'network' of contacts within other institutions and among the recipients of the policy for which they were responsible. This enabled them to develop bold policies in certain sectors despite a political environment not conducive to further European integration. This was the case for environmental protection in the 1980s and 1990s or the establishment of major research programmes. This evolution has however led to a loss of leadership for the President of the Commission, a weakening of the cohesion and overall coherence of the institution's actions and an opacification of its operation.

This segmentation of European policy making was one of the reasons for the creation of the European Council in 1974. As we have seen, the new body had among its tasks to overcome the conflicts that affected the Council, to return coherence to EC action and, ultimately, to provide leadership which the Commission and its president were no longer capable of. A new method of governance appeared, characterized by the role of the Franco-German partnership (initiated by Valery Giscard d'Estaing and Helmut Schmidt), which was at the basis of the most important initiatives.[18] From the mid 1970s, the Council's work was based more systematically on a proposal of a Franco-German compromise, with the result that other national representatives discussed less the merits of the case than the Franco-German proposal itself which simplified the conduct of debates and negotiations.

The creation of the European Council has not, however, decreased the difficulties in elaborating EU policy. In some respects, it has even amplified them by disempowering Council members: with the knowledge that the European Council's mission was to arbitrate intergovernmental or inter-institutional conflicts, the ministers felt freer to obstruct negotiations within the Council or oppose Commission's proposals. Therefore, the decision-making ability of the Community's institutional system declined: the Commission and the Council have adopted a more defensive attitude and have become less open to negotiation. Within the Commission, procedures and attitudes were subjected to a certain codification and the development of new legislative proposals was more difficult and complex. Routine settled in and most of the legislative initiatives were soon justified by the authority of precedent in order to facilitate their development and reach an agreement within the Council. Commission officials were encouraged to re-use previous solutions and increase the number of proposals and similar initiatives, sometimes losing sight of their purpose.

In the 1990s, the segmentation process began to affect the European Parliament as it gained new powers. MEPs, with complete autonomy over internal organization, have been able to replicate the organization of the Council and the Commission at the level of parliamentary committees with the aim of strengthening inter-institutional dialogue, improving their influence in decision-making and their capacity to control. Like in the Council and the Commission, the segmentation of the Parliament's activity into multiple committees has created conflicts amongst them in the examination of certain proposals or the definition of the assembly's position on a given topic. As the parliamentary committees have asserted their autonomy, the institutionalization and the development of specific visions for policies as well as the allocation of legislative proposals to parliamentary committees has become increasingly strategic.

The leaders of the three main institutions progressively realized the perverse effects of this segmentation on the decision-making process. Reforms were undertaken in the 1970s and 1980s in the Council, the Commission and then in the European Parliament to increase the coherence of Community action and to resist sectorial conflicts. In the Council, as we have seen, the number of configurations (which exceeded 20 in the 1980s) has been reduced, and is limited to 10 today. In the Commission, inter-service consultations have grown, as have exchanges and coordination meetings between the Directors-General and the Chiefs of Staff and Assistant Chiefs of Staff of the Commissioners. The Secretaries-General of the Council, the Commission and the European Parliament were enrolled to ensure better internal and inter-institutional coordination of normative activities. More recently, the reorganization of the Commission, through the system of 'groups of projects' instituted by Jean-Claude Juncker, sought to politicize its running but also to enhance the coherence of its action. However, these reforms have only partially achieved their goal inasmuch as many European governance actors (interest groups, lobbyists, civil society, experts, national authorities, etc.) take advantage of this segmented mode of operation and are not favourable to decisions being taken in a more transversal way. This would indeed most likely lead to political or intergovernmental arbitration, which would in turn challenge current pluralist and neo-corporatist arrangements and thus limit their influence.

8.2.2 From 'co-option' to civil European dialogue: the omnipresence of interest groups

The segmentation of Community policy-making has encouraged the emergence of a pluralistic system – within the meaning of north American political theory[19] – which gives potentially significant influence to interest groups. This was already in the Communities' genetic code since the Community method makes these actors indispensable partners of the Commission during its dialogue with the Member States. The heavy presence of these actors in the Brussels microcosm is also the result of the Commission's deliberate strategy in the early 1980s to fight intergovernmentalism and restore the Community method. Faced with the rigidities of the Council's operations and with the European Council's prevarications, the Commission has tried to modify Community policies by relying on non-institutional actors. For example, it gained industry's support to improve research and development programmes, the support of business and consumer groups to complete the internal market and the support of regional and local authorities to develop structural policies. Today, the same applies to energy, transport and digital technology. To bypass obstructions, the Commission has also trivialized the use of 'soft law', or non-legally binding forms of integration which may strongly involve policy recipients and interest-group representatives.

The Commission was able to fully develop these practices in the late 1980s and 'co-opt' large-scale interest group representatives within reflection and consultation bodies acting in the institution. Several factors contributed to this process. The first is the Single European Act, which entered into force on 1 July 1987 and gave back to the Commission a political agenda and the means to act. This new treaty significantly expanded the scope of Community powers and prepared it for the establishment of a single market which required the adoption of over 200 directives and regulations before 31 December 1992.[20] There was thus a need to reactivate the contacts between the Commission and the numerous stakeholders that were concerned by these norms. The Single Act also increased the powers of the European Parliament, which, at that time, was inclined to support the Commission given the Council's failure to act. Finally, this new treaty restored voting by qualified majority within the Council and thus ended the recurring obstacles to the legislative process.

Second, the Commission benefited from the emergence of neo-liberalism in the European political and economic debate in the early 1980s. Its proponents stressed the need to find a new balance of powers between the national and European levels believing the nation-state to be unable to ensure the optimal functioning of a market economy. Many national politicians, who were seduced by the neo-liberal doctrine but did not intend to assume its political cost, were in favour of the Commission undertaking structural reforms across Europe (challenging national monopolies and the central role of the state, opening the market for services, increasing global economic competition, etc.).

Third, we must mention the new interest major industrial and financial groups have focused on European integration. While they deserted the European capital in the 1970s, mostly as a result of the essentially intergovernmental nature of major Community arbitrations, they increased their efforts towards European and national politicians in the 1980s to demand new Community policies and the completion of the common market. The Commission's action has benefited greatly from the investigation of traditional political connections at the national level by neo-liberals and the emergence of transnational networks which demanded strengthened European policies. Jacques Delors, President of the Commission (1985–95), relied heavily on these players who had much to gain from the internal market.

The enlargement of the Community to Spain and Portugal also strengthened the Commission by including new states with strong political demands and major budgetary needs.

This change in the political context led to the development of regulatory and redistributive policies that required the cooperation of public and private organizations throughout Europe. A growing number of interests of increasing size have been mobilized during the formulation, implementation and evaluation stages of European policies. The Commission established a system of stakeholder (lobbyists, territory representatives, experts, etc.) 'cooption' for all the policies for which it was responsible. Transnational groups have been particularly mobilized in the context of advisory committees to assist the Commission in identifying policy issues, providing expertise, outlining potential solutions and areas of stakeholder consensus as well as legitimizing legislative proposals to national governments, Council and Parliament. These representatives did not need to be persuaded. Indeed, even an informal position within the Commission gave them privileged access to information and allowed them to expect some influence over law-making. In the 1990s, the European Parliament also developed an open policy towards interest groups. Like the Commission, the MEPs' objective was to benefit from a better understanding of policy issues, to identify proposals and the points of view of the policy recipients, to improve the expertise available to them and to legitimate their action. This generalized process of co-option helped solidify the segments that appeared in the three main institutions by surrounding them with a host of actors reproducing and perpetuating these numerous thematic divisions.[21]

Since the late 1990s, concern for institutional dialogue has extended to 'European civil society'.[22] If, at first sight, this trend is favourable to a de-segmentation of the debate, one should not exaggerate its significance for at least two reasons. First, civil dialogue is largely a trompe-l'œil which responds to the desire to legitimize past pluralist and neo-corporatist practices through readjustments in favour of civil society. Second, through the faulty and discriminatory definition of civil society, representatives of private interests can claim membership on behalf of any particular population, or, if this is not possible, hide behind an association or a think tank to do so.[23]

The generalization of the 'trialogues' in legislative matters only accentuates the phenomenon of sectorization, which has been a reality in the EU since the 1970s. Today, the debate is essentially limited to officials and elected representatives who are directly in touch with a given dossier within the three institutions and who are also the privileged interlocutors of the lobbies. More than ever, policies are developed in a specialized network, composed of a limited number of public and private actors who share knowledge and often maintain sociable relations.

Notes

1 Ian Down and Carole J. Wilson, 'From "permissive consensus" to "constraining dissensus": a polarizing union?,' *Acta Politica* 43(1) (2008): 26–49; Richard C. Eichenberg and Russell J. Dalton, 'Post-Maastricht blues: the transformation of citizen support for European integration,' *Acta Politica* 42(2/3) (2007): 128–152; Robert Harmsen and Menno Ewout Spiering, *Euroscepticism. Party Politics, National Identity and European Integration* (Amsterdam: Rodopi, 2004).

2 To establish this typology of decision-making methods, we rely on the treaties and practices of the institutions and not on the theories and approaches of integration. For an alternative classification of decision-making methods, refer, for example, to the work of H. Wallace, who distinguishes the community method, the regulatory mode, the distributive mode, the coordination of policies, and finally, intensive trans-governmentalism. Helen Wallace, 'An institutional Anatomy and Five Policy Modes,' in *Policy-Making in the European Union*, eds Helen Wallace, Mark A. Pollack and Alasdair R. Young (Oxford: Oxford University Press, 6th edition, 2010), 70–104.

3 Ernst B. Haas, *The Uniting of Europe, Political, Social and Economic Forces, 1950–1957* (London: Stevens & Sons, 1958); Leon N. Lindberg, *The Political Dynamics of European Economic Integration* (Stanford: Stanford University Press, 1963).

4 Renaud Dehousse, ed., *The Community Method: Obstinate or Obsolete?* (Basingstoke: Palgrave MacMillan, 2011); Renaud Dehousse, 'The community method: chronicle of a death too early foretold,' in *The Transformation of European Governance*, ed. Renaud Dehousse (Mannheim: Connex Report Series, 2008); Helen Wallace, William Wallace

and Mark A. Pollack, eds, *Policy-Making in the European Union* (Oxford: Oxford University Press, 2005).

5 Sergio Fabbrini and Uwe Puetter, 'Integration without supranationalisation: studying the lead roles of the European Council and the Council in post-Lisbon EU politics,' *Journal of European Integration*, 38(5) (2016): 481–495.

6 Giandomenico Majone, 'The general crisis of the European Union: a genetic approach,' in *The European Union in Crises or the European Union as Crises, Arena Report n° 2*, eds John Erik Fossum and Agustín José Menéndez, 2014, 211–244.

7 Stanley Hoffman, 'Obstinate or Obsolete? The case of the Nation-state and the case of Western Europe,' *Daedalus* 95 (1966): 862–915; Stanley Hoffman, *The European Sisyphus. Essays on Europe 1964–1994* (Boulder: Westview Press, 1995).

8 Laura Cram, *Policy-Making in the EU: Conceptual Lenses and the Integration Process* (London: Routledge, 1999).

9 Wallace, Wallace and Pollack, *Policy-Making in the European Union.*

10 See Chapter 4.

11 Christopher J. Bickerton, Dermot Hodson and Uwe Puetter, 'The new intergovernmentalism: European integration in the post–Maastricht era,' *JCMS: Journal of Common Market Studies* 53(4) (2015): 703–722.

12 Charles F. Sabel and Jonathan Zeitlin, 'Learning from difference: the new architecture of experimentalist governance in the EU,' *European Law Journal* 14(3) (2008): 271–327; Renaud Dehousse, 'Has the European Union moved towards soft governance?,' *Comparative European Politics* (2015).

13 Wallace, Wallace and Pollack, *Policy-Making in the European Union.*

14 James Arrowsmith, Keith Sisson and Paul Marginson, 'What can "benchmarking" offer the open method of co-ordination?,' *Journal of European Public Policy* 11(2) (2004): 311–328; Robert Kaiser and Heiko Prange, 'Managing diversity in a system of multi-level governance: the open method of co-ordination in innovation policy,' *Journal of European Public Policy* 11(2) (2004): 249–266.

15 See especially the Kok group report, 'Relever le défi. La Stratégie de Lisbonne pour la croissance et l'emploi,' November 2004. See also Susana Borrás and Bent Greve, 'New method or just cheap talk?,' *Journal of European Public Policy* 11(2) (2004): 329–336; Jonathan Zeitlin, 'The open method of co-ordination and the governance of the Lisbon Strategy,' *Journal of Common Market Studies* 46(2) (2008): 436–450.

16 Giandomenico Majone, *Regulating Europe* (London/New York: Routledge, 1996); Gary Miller, 'Above politics: credible commitment and efficiency in the design of public agencies,' *Journal of Public Administration Research and Theory* 10(2) (2000): 289–328.

17 Michelle Cini, '*Administrative Culture in the European Commission: the case of competition and environment*' (paper presented at the European Community Studies Association, Fourth Biennial International Conference, Charleston, South Carolina, USA, 1995); Liesbet Hooghe, *The European Commission and the Integration of Europe. Images of Governance* (Cambridge: Cambridge University Press, 2001); David Spence, 'The directorates general and the services: structures, functions and procedures,' in *The European Commission*, eds David Spence and Geoffrey Edwards (London: John Harper Publishing, 2006), 128–155; Arndt Wonka, 'Decision making dynamics in the European Commission: partisan, national or sectoral?' *Journal of European Public Policy* 15(8) (2008): 1145–1163.

18 Alistair Cole, *Franco-German Relations* (Pearson Education, 2001).
19 Elmer Eric Schattschneider, *The Semi-Sovereign People: A Realist's View of Democracy in America* (1975).
20 Commission of the European Communities, *The Finalisation of the Internal Market, Commission White Paper for the European Council* (Brussels, 1985), 54.
21 Andreas Dür, 'Interest groups in the European Union: how powerful are they?,' *West European Politics* 31(6) (2008): 1212–1230; Justin Greenwood, *Interest Representation in the European Union* (Basingstoke: Palgrave MacMillan, 3rd ed., 2011); Andrew M. McLaughlin, Grant Jordan and William A. Maloney, 'Corporate lobbying in the European Community,' *Journal of Common Market Studies* 31(2) (1993): 191–212.
22 Stijn Smismans, 'European civil society: shaped by discourses and institutional interests,' *European Law Journal*, 9(4) (2003): 473–495.
23 Sabine Saurugger, 'Interest groups and democracy in the European Union,' *West European Politics* 31(6) (2008): 1274–1291.

The EU decision-making process from a public policy network perspective

9

The significant role played by non-institutional actors, especially lobbyists and experts, in the EU's daily functioning exceeds the typology of decision-making methods presented in the previous chapter. Although it captures the various logics of decision-making, it should be accompanied by an approach that is more sensitive to the practical and informal aspects. In other words, this chapter will answer the following questions: who actually participates in the decision-making and implementation of EU policies? With what information does the Commission prepare its proposals? Which data feeds the legislative work of the Council and Parliament? How are compromises negotiated? How can the inertia of European public policies be explained? Why are some non-institutional actors more able to influence EU policies than others? To answer these questions, one should analyse EU decision-making with the tools and schemes developed by public policy analysis.

9.1 A sequential analysis of public policies

The study of the EU in the light of public policy analysis has grown significantly since the mid 1980s.[1] This approach is particularly attractive since it can be applied without precondition to any organization with powers. It is thus possible to study the EU without the burden of interminable theoretical controversies about its nature, its purpose and its relation to sovereignty, and compare it with other political systems.[2]

Public policy analysis is largely based on the systemic approach inspired in particular by David Easton. Systemists consider political systems in a very abstract manner, like black boxes sustained by *inputs* (internal and external events, elections, lobbying, information, various pressures, etc.) and producing *outputs* (policies, decisions, speeches). Instead of seeing a complex set of institutions with uneven, conflicting and incomprehensible operations, they describe an on-going, harmonious and logical political process made up of inputs and outputs. Systemists try to link the one to the other to establish general rules of political activity: as a result of an event (*input*), the system will produce a policy (*output*).

Charles O. Jones[3] elaborated on this systematic model and developed the idea of a 'public policy cycle' in the national context to describe in more detail the operations of political organizations. It refrains from considering them as black boxes where one might know what feeds them and what they produce but not how this occurs. Jones describes the production of policies ('programmes') as a logical sequence of recurring events, i.e. a cycle. He outlines five major steps: programme identification; programme development; programme implementation; programme evaluation; and programme termination.

This somewhat esoteric language has been simplified and adapted by many other authors and various approaches to the public policy cycle coexist.[4] In this chapter, we put forward a typology overview, and distinguish five stages in the production of public policy:

1 Agenda-setting: issues are raised by various actors and organizations and problems are identified by the members of the executive and the legislative power. Concretely, not all actors try to add issues to the agenda: some simply aim at impeding this process, which is particularly true in the EU where many actors hold veto power or are trying to hinder legislative initiatives that would be detrimental to their interests.

2 Formulation: an agenda item is translated into a decision by political institutions (law, regulation, administrative decision, etc.). Initially, alternative policy proposals are defended by experts to policy makers; the latter make their choice or choose to do nothing. Formulation usually involves a majority and decision-making by elected or appointed actors (politicians, officials, members of agencies), presumably accountable to the public.

3 Budgeting: the policy or decision must be funded as part of developing the annual budget. Even a purely regulatory policy often remains a dead letter if the minimum resources are not made available to ensure implementation and compliance. Budget decisions are difficult because they are usually made in a context of partial information. Due to the structural deficits that affect virtually all political systems today, they have become increasingly important and can lead to a reconsideration of previous decisions.

4   Implementation: the policy or decision must be implemented by the government, local authorities (Member States for the EU), an administration or an agency. This body must often fill out the missing elements and make decisions concerning the objectives, timelines, procedures, reporting methods, etc. The most ambitious policies may face insurmountable resistance at this stage, especially in the EU.

5   Evaluation: after a given period of time, the impact of the policy or decision is assessed. Its effectiveness is evaluated in terms of its initial objectives and its unintended or perverse consequences. The assessment may lead to adjustments or provoke the abrogation of a policy which proved to be ineffective or had no purpose. The information collected in the evaluation stage is thus injected back into the agenda-setting stage, closing the loop of the cycle.

The large number of institutional actors in EU decision-making and the significant place held by non-institutional actors explain why this political system is particularly suited to public policy analysis. Various authors have drawn on such public policy concepts as 'network' and 'community'[5] as their use can bypass some of the issues raised by the theorization of the EU. By employing these terms, one envisages the EU not only as a political system exercising sovereign powers (which implies broaching issues of sovereignty and democracy, as well as the allocation of power), but as an organization implementing public policy based on a quasi-federal legal system. This choice can be justified to the extent that the EU is not only a political project at the level of the continent; it is also and above all a machine managing ever-increasing, detailed and technical public policies. This point of view joins the one developed by the neo-functionalists in the 1960s.[6] More than ever, European institutions mobilize transnational elites and interest groups and rely on the participation of such actors to develop and legitimize policies, even when relations between the Member States are deteriorating. Contrary to the intergovernmental approach to the EU, these policies are not seen as the product of a simple adjustment of the preferences of state representatives but as the result of a broader negotiation that includes many supranational or transnational players (supranational European institutions, Euro-groups, European parties, lobbyists, civil society organizations, etc.).

More generally, the phenomenon of the Europeanization of national political spaces has led to the mobilization of all types of actors (political, administrative, economic, social, associative, etc.) in the EU and at all levels of government (local, regional, national). According to the so-called 'uploading' Europeanization phenomenon, these players are now very attentive to the actions of European institutions. They are involved through their participation in transnational organizations or on an individual basis and may consider

Box 9.1 Biofuels and the impact of interest groups

Environmental issues are an area of European public policy in which the influence of interest groups is particularly visible. For instance, this was the case with biofuels, and more specifically with the issue of the impact of indirect land-use change on greenhouse gas emissions, i.e., the awareness of the negative effects of the production of biofuel through farming.[7]

Since 2006, while the Commission was preparing guidelines related to the 'climate and energy package 2020', divisions have emerged between the DG Environment and the DG Energy. While the former was listening to the scientific community, which doubted the sustainability of the European biofuel policy, the second was reluctant to take these arguments into account. During the public consultations on the renewable energy directive, two 'coalitions of causes' (see below) emerged: the first focused on environmental issues and the second on those related to industry. Environmental organizations highlighted the negative impacts of biofuel production on the environment, but their arguments were not taken into account by the Commission, particularly because of the fact that so-called 'first generation' biofuel producers lobby DG Energy. Environmental interest groups then turned to the other institutions, in particular the EP, which seemed more open to their arguments than the Council. Their objective was to include in the EP's agenda the horizontal integration of environmental challenges into European transport and energy policies. It was notably a matter of drawing the attention of parliamentarians to these issues and countering the arguments of the coalition formed by the industry.

Environmental NGOs formed a coalition with associations that deal with development policy and which share the same core belief that the use of biofuels should be limited, whether for environmental reasons or to help developing countries. By sharing the resources of its components, this coalition was able to develop a diversified argument and reach out to different categories of MEPs. It has provided them with the results of complex scientific studies on the issue to not only attract their attention but also to convince them of the merits of their arguments and counter those of the industrial coalition (counter-expertise strategy).[8] The coalition of the 'environmental cause' has succeeded in convincing a majority of MEPs to adopt amendments supporting its position. However, as the Council and the Commission were more sensitive to the arguments of the 'industrial' coalition, the EP was ultimately unable to succeed on the issue of indirect changes in land-use during trialogues.

specific actions by using the services of companies specializing in European public action. Thus, EU institutions are in permanent contact with special-interest representatives of all types and scales, as part of a system of 'multi-level governance'.[9]

Moreover, European governance is distinguished above all by the significance of the informal and through the existence of multiple places for mediation with special-interest representatives. It is distinguished by its 'procedural logic' which establishes a partnership between multiple stakeholders so that they are able to find solutions acceptable to all. This participation by a wide range of players and officials in the process is an essential modality of EU operations which cannot resort to authoritarian or majoritarian decisions. An analysis in terms of policy cycle is thus particularly suitable.

Finally, this approach is equally pertinent because EU policies consist mostly in multi-annual programmes, subject to evaluation on an ad hoc or systematic basis, as with the REFIT programme,[10] and then renewed in a more or less amended form or terminated if they are deemed to be ineffective or if circumstances have changed.

9.2 Communities and networks of actors

Scholarly literature offers a wide range of concepts to account for the participation of various types of actors, public and private, in the different phases of public policy development. The central concept is that of the network.[11] The literature proposes a number of more specific concepts (communities, thematic networks, professional networks, intergovernmental networks, producer networks, iron triangles, sub-governments, etc.) and lets them interact with related concepts (clientelism, corporatism and neo-corporatism, pluralism, etc.) and various analytical models from the sociology of organizations.[12]

Many types of networks related to the EU have been theorized according to the number of their members, their sectorial or cross-sectorial nature, their degree of stability or the intensity of communication between them. Within the limited scope of this chapter, we will focus on three concepts which can account for the main configurations on which the EU's functioning depends: policy community; policy network; and thematic network.

9.2.1 Policy communities

The concept of 'community' was developed in the late 1970s in the UK in opposition to constitutional analyses which considered public policy creation only in terms of interactions between parliament and government and between majority and opposition.[13] This concept proposes to move the perspective from parliament – the historic and symbolic arena of politics – towards the informal relationships that exist between different types of actors, public and private, involved in decision-making. Literature related to public policy communities highlights the decline of boundaries between institutions and private groups and challenges the strictly formal analysis of the regime's operations. Policies are not only considered as the result of codified procedures in the Constitution and the law but as the product of the interconnection, interferences and dialogue of multiple public and private organizations. Proponents of public policy analysis thus pay particular attention to the practices of cooperation and the research of consensus beyond the divisions between majority and opposition and inter-institutional tensions that focus the attention of specialists of political life.[14]

The concept of public policy community was largely mobilized by the first EU policy analysts.[15] The notion of 'policy community' refers to a complex set of organizations connected to each other through phenomena of resource dependencies which maintain close and stable relationships, conduct exchanges and collectively participate in the creation of public policy in a given area.[16] Let's clarify this definition. These organizations are of all kinds: they may include 'segments' of EU institutions (Council configuration or group; DG or Commission unit; European Parliament committee, delegation or political group), private interest groups, national governments, civil society organizations, experts. They are dependent on each other in the sense that they have a common interest in belonging to this community: they draw resources from their ability to co-exist and thus ensure the community's survival. The boundaries between the different communities correspond to ruptures in this dependence on resources: actors and organizations do not follow the informal rules that govern the operations of any given community and determine membership – or cease to do so – if they judge it more useful to participate in another community or to act independently. All of these organizations maintain close and stable relations in the sense that their representatives contribute to community life. Even if they have very diverging views and objectives, they invite each other to meetings and conferences, organize public events together and circulate information amongst themselves. Finally, these organizations conduct exchanges to the extent they are able to effectively engage in negotiations and are not content to hold their ground.

The notion of community allows researchers to describe the relationships created between the Commission and the recipients of certain policies: coal and steel markets, common agricultural policy, internal market, industrial policy, regional policy, environmental protection, etc. This concept found a concrete translation in the institutionalization of many advisory committees within the Commission which include policy recipients, representatives of various transnational organizations, experts, members of national administrations, etc.[17]

The phenomenon of the 'segmentation' of the functioning of the institutions in the 1970s and 1980s led to the emergence of such communities. This was also strongly reinforced with the entry into force of the Single European Act (1 July 1987), since the Commission was willing to closely associate the stakeholders to the elaboration of the internal market and needed their support more generally. The bodies of the Commission, Council and Parliament dealing with the same issues have developed close contacts with each other and with key non-institutional actors in the relevant sector. A real negotiation takes place, bringing the different parties to change their respective positions or even to settle for very little progress. Today, the trialogues are formalizing the inter-institutional dimension of those contacts.

The community concept also accounts for the stability of European policies. Community members have relatively constant interests and preferences and the community is stable in its composition; thus, it is unlikely that the arrangements emerging from their interactions will radically change. In addition, each member of the community knows which change is possible for its partners and avoids needlessly putting them in a difficult situation. In fact, institutional actors fear an impasse in the decision-making process while non-institutional actors dread being excluded from a community or watching it disintegrate, since it offers them privileged access to the centre of the decision-making process. If they find a consensus, they can expect to contribute, with varying influence, to the management of the public policy sector. The cohesion of the community is also encouraged by the fact that its members share a language, expertise, ideas, set of behaviours and sometimes values as well as the criteria of what is acceptable in the negotiation. More broadly, they present the same sociological profile,[18] and come from the same academic backgrounds in European studies. It is common for an actor to go to work for another organization or company belonging to the public policy community, or for a European institution.

9.2.2 Policy networks

The concept of a policy network refers to arrangements of actors that are less cohesive, more specific and less stable than those of communities, implying less empathy and collusion between members.[19] These networks appear for policies that are not central, whose development is linked to a particular context or which experiences strong interference with other policies, with the result that a stable community is impossible. In the EU, the concept is very useful insofar as many policies are characterized by the large number and fluidity of actors they involve and their sensitivity to changing contexts.[20] Moreover, interactions between different policies are increasingly common in such a way that some players participate alternately in several networks.

The concepts of community and public policy networks can account for the complexity of EU decision-making processes and the distance that often exists between treaties and practice. Due to the phenomenon of segmentation, which has affected all European institutions since the 1970s, a multiplicity of micro-networks or communities associated with different EU policies or sub-policies has emerged, each functioning with its own logic and style.[21]

One must be careful not to caricature the functioning of the Union.[22] The reticular approach is analytically useful, but, since the early 1990s, the development of European policies has changed. The increasing number of bodies involved in policy making (European Parliament, European Council, Committee of the Regions, Economic and Social Committee, Executive Agencies, etc.) has disrupted the organization of communities and networks and limited their influence. Successive EU enlargements have also led to a significant increase in the number of players wishing to be involved in decision-making and a broadening of the spectrum of their interests and visions which has destabilized certain well-established networks. The growing mobilization of actors from political and national administrative systems in EU institutions has had a similar effect. Since the early 1990s, 'top-down' Europeanization, understood as the convergence of national systems under the impact of European policies was accompanied by a 'bottom-up' Europeanization, understood as the convergence of national actors to influence or obstruct decisions made in Brussels.[23] This mobilization has had a disruptive effect on the public policy communities and networks which have for a long time been composed mainly of transnational actors.

Four other factors, related to the very nature of policies developed by the EU, have undermined past arrangements. The first is the continuous extension of EU competences which has led to growing interferences between its various policies and to tensions between the communities and the networks which drive them. The need to arbitrate these conflicts and to organize priorities has led to a renewed influence of political and administrative actors as communities and networks were unable to do so as a result of their specialization. Moreover, we note that the EU is increasingly called upon to develop cross-cutting policies, with multiple implications and referring to general political issues (ethical questions, social problems and sovereign politics) or to global issues (climate change, innovation, competitiveness and economic, social and territorial cohesion, migrations). The inability to resolve these debates in the technical registry preferred by network members, the inflation in the number of actors claiming to be competent to comment on these issues (experts, lobbyists, think tanks, etc.) and the lack of consensus among them has favoured the return of political and administrative leadership.[24] Finally, since the beginning of the 1990s, we must underline the impact of the EU institutions' quest to establish a *European civil dialogue*.[25] In search of pluralism and a better legitimation of EU policy making, they have systematically favoured contacts with civil-society organizations (NGOs, associations, trade-unions, various kinds of forums, etc.) matching the stake-holders' seating in the consultative committees. The objectives of openness, transparency and consultation, mentioned by the treaties, have thus contributed to disrupt the prior situation. Lastly, the generalization of trialogues and the adoption of texts at an early stage (first reading or early second reading) since the mid 2000s encourage a more direct inter-institutional dialogue and thus limit the influence of non-institutional actors. However, they do remain influential within each institution separately, and contribute to the definition of their respective positions.

9.2.3 Thematic and issue networks

The above-mentioned changes in the functioning of the EU led to the emergence, in the 1990s, of a new concept: that of an issue or thematic network. These are networks of actors who form around a dossier or a specific policy for a limited time.[26] These actors share common knowledge and consider themselves competent enough to dialogue, respond to each other and decide to treat certain aspects of a policy. They agree to identify a 'problem' and demand its inclusion on the agenda. However, they do not inevitably share the same views and do not necessarily agree over the long term. 'Communities' and 'networks', better organized and more invested in duration and routine, are more likely to compromise. The concept of a thematic network is useful to understand the complex and conflicting policies that combine many areas in an uncertain manner. In these domains (for example, bioethics or climate change), the policy-making process leads to results whose genesis and logic are difficult to explain due to the appearance of sometimes unexpected and heterogeneous and often ephemeral and very inclusive coalitions of interest.

The concept of thematic network is particularly suited to the EU due to three characteristics. The first is the large number of interest groups around the European institutions: approximately 30,000 actors representing 5,000 organizations attempt to communicate with the EU institutions. Many of these fail: they were not 'co-opted' in stable communities, are unable to effectively assert their views and have no real influence on the decisions and policies that mobilize them. They stay on the sidelines and simply monitor the EU's activities for information until circumstances eventually allow them to enter the game. The second characteristic of the contemporary Brussels microcosm is that many groups are not in relationships of dependence vis-à-vis the others, so they may conduct individual strategies or participate in various thematic networks according to their interests at the time. Third, many groups do not share any values with their counterparts or are in positions of extreme conflict which makes the emergence of a policy community or network impossible.[27]

However, these groups engage in collaborative processes when their interests compel them to. Concretely, the establishment of a thematic network is divided into three stages. First, different actors mobilized by the same issue recognize each other as legitimate interlocutors, because of their reputation, their visibility, their representativeness, their expertise and their behaviour. Second, they share the idea that collaboration is the best way to maximize the satisfaction of their expectations and that it is preferable to a unilateral lobbying approach that may result in decisions that do not take stakeholders' positions into account. Third, they agree to formalize their network especially vis-à-vis EU institutions.

Analysis of the genesis of a thematic network allows us to understand how a new idea, new knowledge or a new 'problem' is added to the EU's agenda, in the absence of an obvious cause (treaty measures, European Council instructions or items of the Commission programme, deadlines, requests from the Council or the European Parliament, European citizens' initiatives, current affairs, etc.). It allows us to go beyond the disillusioned acknowledgement of the chaotic functioning of the Union and open the 'black box'.

How do we make sense of these approaches and concepts? One can imagine a continuum where one extreme is the public policy community (organized, visible, efficient, institutionalized, influent, stable over time and in its composition) and the other extreme is distinguished by the absence of any organized interest groups. The public policy network (relatively stable and clear with regular relationships with the EU institutions) and the thematic network (more nebulous and conflictual, ephemeral) can be found on this continuum. According to the policy and the political context, one of these configurations predominates.

Analysis in terms of networks, however, should not obscure the central role played by institutions and states. Even if in the EU, institutional leadership is limited, they are often the origin of political change, especially when confusion reigns among the interest groups and they are unable to effectively contribute to the management of a sector of public action. If the Commission and Parliament are open to contacts with interest representatives in certain domains, or even demand such contacts, these actors only influence decision-making through their contributions to the construction of a compromise. When interest groups are highly fragmented, institutions tend to revert to a more exegetical interpretation of the treaties and base their choices on their own conception (expert or political) of the dossiers.

Moreover, when relations between Member States deteriorate or one or more states express their opposition to a text, the intergovernmental logic tends to regain the upper hand and marginalize public policy networks. In this case, their non-institutional actors have no choice but to try to adapt to the situation including acting within their respective governments.

9.3 Emergence of consensus in a network: advocacy coalitions

With some exceptions, networks have only significant influence on the agenda, decision-making or public policy implementation when they manage to force a majority decision (see Box 9.1). Otherwise, political and administrative actors are called upon to decide according to their own rationales. In the most formal settings where institutional actors in charge of a sector can themselves be considered members of the network, the majority compromise will usually be reflected by them within the institutions to which they belong. In the case of more vague and limited networks, institutional players have no obligations; however, unless there is deep disagreement with the majority position which emerges from among interest representatives, they tend to favour this as a result of their preference for compromise and their need for legitimacy and support among policy recipients. As noted, faced with increasingly fragmented positions, institutional actors tend to rely on their own assessment of the situation.

But how does a network, inevitably heterogeneous, manage to identify majority solutions in the absence of institutional constraints and formal decision-making processes? Various sub-groups exist within the network which embrace the same belief system and are organized for joint mobilization. They represent 'sub-systems' of society, composed of activists, elected officials, journalists, citizens, etc. who carry out their work within the margins of decision-making spaces. In the scientific literature, various models try to account for the emergence of a majority position among the members of a network and, more broadly, for the reasons why a change in public policy is made. One of the most famous models is Paul Sabatier's 'advocacy coalition framework'.[28] Even though it was developed in a North American context, it is suitable for the analysis of public policy networks deployed throughout EU institutions.

According to Sabatier, each coalition implements its strategy by relying on its resources (money, competence, information, capacity to communicate, legal authority, etc.) in order to influence the course of public action.[29] When change occurs, it challenges the resources, strategies and belief systems of each coalition and creates a new global configuration. Advocacy coalitions are in fact deployed in an environment submitted to two categories of external variables. On the one hand, there are relatively constant factors: distribution of natural resources, fundamental cultural values and constitutional rules. On the other hand, there are flexible factors: socio-economic conditions, public opinion, the balance of power among political parties and the influence of other networks. The underlying beliefs of the coalition change very little. Sabatier considers that the actors perceive the world through a series of filters consisting of pre-existing beliefs which are resistant to change and which have a triptych structure:

1   'Deep core beliefs' are fundamental representations of what is good or bad, desirable or undesirable. They are elaborated from very general normative reasoning and are, for the most part, socially and culturally embedded and, de facto, almost impossible to change. Therefore, it is unlikely, for example, that a person opposed to euthanasia for religious or philosophical reasons will change his/her mind on the matter.
2   'Policy core beliefs' are applicable to a particular policy or set of policies. These include, for example, the vision of different values, perspectives on the relative authority of governments and markets, the conception of the importance of a public issue, etc. They are also unlikely to change.
3   'Secondary beliefs' focus on the details of a public policy, the tools to be used to reach a given objective on the means and not the ends. They do not require agreement between all parties of the coalition and are easily adjustable.

The theory of coalitions strongly emphasizes the path dependency that affects public policy, that is to say their resistance to change as a result of the weight of history, routines and established positions and stability of the basic values of the actors. It thereby seeks to explain reform situations that appear to be exceptional. According to Sabatier, change occurs primarily in two situations: when socio-economic conditions alter the balance of resources among coalitions or when a crisis makes reform or new policy development inevitable.[30] Proponents of financial market regulation, for example, saw their resources and audience grow significantly as a result of the 2008 financial crisis while, just a few months before, their perspective was considered backward-looking (see Box 9.2).

Box 9.2 The supervision of credit rating agencies and the financial crisis

Prior to the outbreak of the financial crisis in 2008, the Commission tended to be very reticent about any regulation of the financial sector: its priority was the creation of a set of voluntary rules, by the financial sector itself, rather than the adoption of a binding legislative framework by the EU institutions.[31]

Since then, it has made a 180-degree turn and has promoted a regulatory approach. In spite of the adverse opinions of the advisory committees, in May 2008 the Ministers of Finance adopted a roadmap for the stability of financial markets in order to assess the shortcomings of credit rating agencies, and the October 2008 European Council called for a strengthening of the supervisory rules for these agencies, through new legislation. A legally binding framework has been put in place and the responsibility for the supervision of rating agencies has been transferred to the newly created European Securities authority.

This shift can be explained by a combination of different factors. First of all, two coalitions trying to influence the Commission must be mentioned. The first, consisting of the United Kingdom, Ireland, the Benelux countries and the Nordic countries, supported by the banking federations, was in favour of slight market support, its vision grounded in market liberalization. The second, made up of France, Germany and the countries of Southern Europe and supported by the European Trade Union Confederation, was in favour of stricter regulation of the financial markets, through an elaborate legislative framework.[32]

The debt crisis, a major external shock, changed the balance of power between these coalitions. It indeed led to a change in the socio-economic conditions as well as the attitudes of public opinion towards the financial markets. The coalition in favour of stricter regulation could be federated around a narrative blaming the rating agencies for the crisis. The latter were American and presented by some governments as hostile towards the EU and perceived as responsible for the situation. The Commission was therefore able to take advantage of this window of opportunity. The commission acted as an intermediary between these coalitions and played the role of 'political entrepreneur', pushing for the adoption of new rules regulating rating agencies. The appointment of Commissioner Barnier in 2009 was crucial in this respect, due to his financial expertise but also to his motivation to reform the European approach to the regulation of financial markets which echoed the arguments of the 'regulatory' coalition.

Also, a crisis such as bovine spongiform encephalopathy (or 'mad cow disease') or a disaster like the sinking of the oil tanker Erika provides actors who had previously struggled to be heard with an audience within European institutions willing to support their demands for reform. In such a case, decision proposals, which are left lying in the drawers of interest groups or Commission services, due to lack of support, can suddenly be placed on the agenda and adopted, as a result of the mobilization of various actors in favour of reform and/or as a result of the difficulty for some to sustain their veto.[33]

Several of the following conditions must be met in order for a coalition to become a majority or for multiple coalitions to decide to coalesce around the outlines of a public policy agenda: an untenable deadlock situation, participation of a large number of stakeholders in the negotiations, the search for consensus among them, establishment of mutual trust, phenomena of exchange and apprenticeship between coalitions and the active presence of a trained mediator. In the EU, the last condition is fulfilled with great consistency by the European

Commission through the Community method. It is in fact up to the Commission to try to draw up proposals that take into account both its own vision of a dossier, those of the stakeholders, those of the Member States as well as that of the European Parliament. Competition between the Commission and now the Parliament in their contacts with interest groups is also an opportunity for networks. Segmentation is likewise conducive to the formation of advocacy coalitions: a more or less open competition exists between specialized bodies within each institution (Commission DGs, parliamentary committees and Council groups or configurations) for the imposition of their vision or control over a public policy sector. They are therefore very dependent on the support and ideas of non-institutional actors. It is often the encounter between an advocacy coalition seeking institutional support for a reform proposal and an institutional actor in search of reform and public support that creates change in public policy. Recently, the generalization of the 'trialogue' between the Commission, Parliament and Council in the late stages of legislative proposal development has at times facilitated the inclusion of solutions put forward by majority advocacy coalitions, although it may also have led to more political solutions.[34]

Advocacy coalition theory is particularly useful for understanding the evolution of public policy issues related to 'devious' problems which involve conflicts in terms of objectives and technical controversies, and involve multiple actors from different levels of government. Paul Sabatier's model stresses the dynamic relationship between these actors and emphasizes the formal and informal strategies and interactions which are forged between coalitions (see Figure 9.1). He also highlights the importance of ideas and standards in public policy implementation.

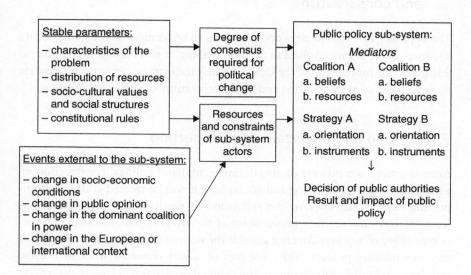

Figure 9.1 Schematic representation of advocacy coalitions

Source: Adapted by authors from P. Sabatier (1999).

It is often the emergence of a new concept or new idea that generates different coalitions which share a specific common interest and activates the mobilization of institutional actors. The Brussels microcosm is fond of these new concepts (sustainable development, 'flexicurity', carbon leakage, environmental technologies, corporate social responsibility, businesses 2.0, etc.) that can bring together actors with very different objectives. Opponents to European integration have understood this process well because they were able to coalesce around the very vague notion of a 'social Europe', which allowed the detractors of the Services Directive (Bolkestein) to obtain its substantial modification. If they had remained in the register of the neo-liberalism dispute, this would not have permitted them to massively mobilize the MEPs, and finally persuade the Council.[35]

Occasionally, advocacy coalitions can assemble actors who are total opposites *a priori*. In the early 1990s, environmentalists joined German car manufacturers to impose ambitious emissions standards. The environmentalists were worried about the preservation of nature and the German car manufacturers sought a competitive advantage over their French and Italian competitors who were less technologically advanced in this area. Today, the Brussels microcosm is teeming with industry players trying to take advantage of the interest of EU institutions in environmental issues and the power of environmental groups to promote reforms or decisions which serve their economic interests, whilst respecting 'green growth' principles.

9.4 EU decision-making: between openness and conservatism

The approach in terms of networks allows us to understand how change occurs and map all the actors involved in decision-making. It also highlights the general features of the functioning of the Union, namely the extreme asymmetry between the 'openness' of agenda-setting and the 'conservatism' of policy formulation.

9.4.1 Open and uncertain agenda-setting

Agenda-setting is a process of social, intellectual and political construction of a problem which has a strong impact on how it will be treated at the decision-making stage. Understanding the regulation of pesticide use in agriculture in terms of agricultural policy, preservation of the environment, consumer protection or safety of workers does not provide the same results. Given the complexity of contemporary politics, which are part of a very dense network of norms, standards and public interventions, the original proposal will largely determine the final text, amendments occurring most often in the details.[36]

As the EU is primarily a machine to manage and create policies, its agenda is the object of everyone's attention. A political system's agenda is defined by three types of elements. First, some points are automatically included: they depend on the annual budget or programmes which must be periodically reauthorized. Second, crises (health, social, ecological, international, political, etc.) are almost immediately included on the agenda, particularly when coalitions mobilizing around this issue exploit the vagaries of the media. Finally, policy makers can promote their own concerns, according to a political agenda, election results, analysis of the situation or solicitations for which they are the object of interest groups, civil society organizations or changes in public opinion.

The EU's agenda reflects the specificities of this atypical political system.[37] It is, first of all, highly structured by recurring or planned elements. Most EU policies (regional development, research, environment, agriculture, etc.) are adopted in the form of programmes whose duration are limited and must be periodically revised. The multi-annual financial framework (MFF) of the EU has led to a generalization of this approach and now strongly determines the European agenda in most sectors on the basis of five- and then seven-year periods (Delors 1 and 2 Packages for 1988–1992 and 1993–1999, Agenda 2000 for 2000–2006, Multiannual Financial Framework (MFF) for 2014–2020 and 2021–2027), with generally a mid-term policy review. Crises play a comparable role at the EU and national levels. They mostly contribute to disrupt the order of priorities and to enable advocacy coalitions to find the institutional support they lacked before. Regarding the agenda points that are set at the discretion of institutions, we recall that, while the Commission has a formal monopoly over legislative initiative in most EU domains, it no longer enjoys considerable autonomy in the matter. The Commission often implements the provisions of treaties and long-term agreements and responds to requests from other EU institutions, Member States, interest groups and civil-society organizations. The Citizen's initiative, created by the Treaty of Lisbon, even gives a capacity of indirect legislative initiative to one million Europeans. One also notes that European elections results had historically little weight on the European agenda and the Commission does not have a political programme comparable to that of an elected government. The conditions for the investiture of Jean-Claude Juncker have changed the situation, linking more closely the outcome of the European elections to the candidate for the presidency and to the Commission's programme. However, the latter is the result of clever compromises, designed to satisfy both the EPP, ALDE and S&D groups, so it is not marked by a very clear partisan approach. More generally, the work of the Juncker Commission since its inauguration is not distinguished by increased politicization.

The European agenda thus responds to other stimuli, specific to the EU.[38] Since the mid 1980s, it is regularly organized by the adoption of new treaties; their reform has gradually become an essential component of EU decision-making, a mode of governance designed to overcome the weakness of the Commission's leadership. During each revision, new chapters relating to new policies are introduced into the treaties. As they result from negotiations within the European Council, they help strongly structure the Commission's legislative agenda. The rotating presidency of the Council also has a significant impact on the EU's agenda. States that hold the presidency can define priorities or, alternatively, freeze some dossiers according to their interests or their conception of EU's best interests. The current troika system, according to which three presidencies define the EU agenda together for 18 months, helps to limit the inclusion of questions that only have interest for the one country holding the presidency. The establishment of a permanent President of the European Council by the Lisbon Treaty has reinforced this trend. Finally, we must emphasize the active role played by national and transnational interest groups in developing the agenda. The EU incites a strong interest from these actors, which, opportunistically, seek a setting or 'venue' to add an issue on the agenda ('venue shopping').[39] The multiplicity of EU institutional actors, the great 'openness' of some of them (Commission, European Parliament) to lobbyists, as well as the limited weight of European parties and partisan logic at the European level also contribute to the importance of this phenomenon.

9.4.2 Three characteristics of the European Agenda

The great 'openness' of EU agenda-setting stems in large part from three characteristics: systemic and broad institutional agendas (1) and a strong institutional (2) and territorial (3) fragmentation.

Broad systemic and institutional agendas

Public policy analysis distinguishes the real agenda (which includes all issues that are the object of a treatment through a given political system), the systemic agenda (i.e. all questions considered legitimate in this political system whether or not they are being discussed in the institution) and the institutional agenda (set of issues that an institution wishes to include in the systemic agenda). In the EU, the systemic agenda is particularly large since all the issues that can be legitimately raised in a Member State – and not necessarily in another – may also be raised at the European level. Even though the EU's powers are limited, they are broad enough for issues of a very diverse order to be discussed in the European microcosm. The EU's systemic agenda thus corresponds more or less to the sum of national systemic agendas. The institutional agenda is also broad and complex with several institutions developing contrasting, even conflicting, visions of the same problem. We will return to this.

This broad spectrum of possible visions creates strong conflicts and unpredictable results. There is a permanent competition between diverse advocacy coalitions, true political entrepreneurs who seek to make progress on issues or topics, or conversely, to ensure these issues are excluded from the agenda. This game is complex and perverse. It is frequent that an actor (government, interest group, institutional body, etc.) who does not want a policy, seeks to obtain its inclusion on the agenda under an unacceptable form or at an inauspicious moment to delegitimize competing initiatives. Many actors mobilize themselves to oppose, in principle, EU intervention in a given domain or to prevent the establishment of a policy that does not match their expectations or interests.

The situation is further complicated by the fact that 'European' interest groups (Eurogroups) often poorly fulfil their function of aggregation of interests, or do so in an overly superficial manner. Their general positions frequently boil down to the lowest common denominators without much consistency which badly conceals much more scattered specific interests. Many Eurogroup members do not feel bound by the positions taken in common and may seek to defend their interests by other means.[40]

Fragmented institutions

Institutional fragmentation vis-à-vis the agenda is much higher in the EU than in the Member States, due to the polycentrism of the regime, the weakness of its hierarchical logic within and between the institutions, and the limited nature of its partisan logic. By virtue of the Community method, strong tensions exist between the different institutions which each have their own interpretation of the European agenda. As noted, institutions are themselves criss-crossed by several division lines: each 'sector' (Commissioner and DG of the Commission, expert groups and Council formation, parliamentary committee or inter-parliamentary delegation to the EP, etc.) seeking to defend or increase its jurisdiction, and thus to set the agenda. Given the institutional arrangements specific to the EU, each institution is able to influence the agenda to some extent.

The European Council exercises strong influence on the matter. At a very early stage it sets the broad outlines of EU action, takes initiatives on intergovernmental matters and arbitrates the most conflictive dossiers. For the time being, the first two presidents of the European Council have not really been able to assert their own priorities and were first spokesmen for the 28 Heads of State and Government, but the institution itself has become a central part of the EU, which has a major influence on the legislative agenda.

The Commission maintains a key role in shaping the agenda. It may have lost to the European Council its impetus function exercised in the 1960s and late 1980s but it retains a monopoly over legislative initiative. The institution is, however, very segmented. Each Commissioner flaunts personal and sectorial goals and the actors of various DGs try to impose their vision. They attempt to capture the most important issues and adapt them to their own perspective and their operating constraints. The creation by J. C. Juncker of 'project teams', supervised by a Vice-President, is an attempt to limit this phenomenon. Within the DGs themselves, competition frequently divides management and units, despite 'inter-service' consultations. These conflicts over the division of powers between the different Commissioners and different components of the Commission instigate a subtle game over the definition of the problems and the concepts. Tensions between the College of Commissioners and DGs complicate matters further and increase the opportunities for action by interest groups who almost always find an interlocutor sensitive to their own perspective.

The influence of the Council on the agenda is indirect but real, in particular by virtue of the formal requests or informal instructions it sends to the Commission and the missions it is assigned by the European Council in intergovernmental matters. As noted, segmentation also affects the Council: its various formations and their respective working groups often have differing views on the agenda items and on how to approach cross-cutting issues.

The European Parliament has a formal right of indirect initiative and a very broad right of expression. These privileges allow it to ask for specific legislative initiatives from the Commission and, more broadly, to debate topics in the European microcosm. The absence of a stable majority and the segmentation of the Parliament according to its partisan and national divisions as well as to its parliamentary committees make its positions complex and variable, and provides uncertain but real opportunities for interest groups. The European Parliament also uses its power to amend legislation to ensure the inclusion of new issues and does so with great efficiency. It is a *conditional agenda-setter*[41] since it can introduce amendments that the Council and the Commission can more easily adopt than refuse.

A priori, a court does not intervene in the development of a political system's agenda. The European Court of Justice has nevertheless achieved policy changes or the inclusion of issues on the agenda in connection with the consideration of appeals against decisions of an institution or a Member State. In the 1970s and 1980s, the Court frequently exerted indirect pressure on the Commission and the Council to take the problems into account before they were raised by a plaintiff.[42]

Overall, the EU suffers from a lack of coordination of the positions of its various institutions. The absence of a single leader and the weakness of European political parties do not simplify the issues with imposing a precise programme or even limiting the range of possibilities. This offers many opportunities for all sorts of interest groups and gives a central role to expertise in determining the priorities of the moment.

A fragmented territory

Territorial fragmentation is another important aspect of EU agenda-setting. This in fact presents an emerging federal structure. Brussels can be regarded as a federal capital with close relations to national governments and, increasingly, with regional 'governments'. The development of interparliamentary cooperation and the rise in power of national chambers regarding the control of subsidiarity allow us to understand the emergence of a parallel parliamentary network.[43] National leaders often consider the EU as a way to add to the agenda issues that they dare not or cannot discuss at the national level. When reform seems impossible at home, Brussels can be an alternative for national governments allowing them to bypass conservatism while avoiding paying the political price for unpopular decisions. In addition, the complexity and opacity of the functioning of the Union allow national leaders to initiate a policy or a decision without taking responsibility for it.[44]

Regional and local authorities also play an increasing role in the process of preparing the EU's agenda. Since the late 1980s, European institutions are the privileged interlocutors of sub-state entities including those that cannot be heard at the national level (ethnic and linguistic minorities, regionalists and autonomists). After the entry into force of the Single European Act, the Commission has encouraged these entities to take action at the European level and to interact directly with it. It supported their claims to greater independence by allocating funds and advocating a general principle of subsidiarity. This dialogue has allowed the development of certain EU policies and a 'territorialization' of their implementation. It has provoked an overall movement towards decentralization in the Member States and the affirmation of the EU as a system of multilevel governance.[45]

All things considered, EU agenda-setting appears to be a chaotic process marked by great uncertainty. It is difficult to predict the evolution of the European agenda whereas, in the Member States, the platform or doctrine of the government parties, the positions of Head of State or Government and the demands of the most powerful interest groups allow anticipating the agenda's broad outlines. To account for this situation, we can mobilize the *garbage can* model.[46] In the EU, the extreme confusion that reigns during the setting of the agenda allows for the inclusion of items that do not collect broad support and do not seem particularly urgent. No one can determine the precise reasons for this choice. The EU is a chaos of institutional actors in search of solutions, interest groups that promote solutions and seek partners. It is, moreover, marked by a great instability of preferences and by the idea that the necessity to choose creates the choice and not vice versa. It is thus the antithesis of the rational model of decision-making described by the experts of Community law since the 1950s.

9.4.3 Very conservative policy 'formulation'

The openness of EU agenda-setting is largely offset by much more restrictive decision-making. The inclusion of an item on the EU's agenda is only the first step. It does not always lead to the adoption of a decision, or it may not be funded or implemented. Even in the absence of a result, having an issue added to the agenda is not without interest for the actors. It is essential to take into account the reality of democratic systems today: the role of the media and communication, focus on elections, predominance of words over action. Adding an issue to the agenda, in many cases, can be sufficient to satisfy governments or interest groups.

In a way, the cumbersome decision-making and implementation outweighs the excitement that characterizes agenda-setting. As explained in the previous chapters, decision-making requires multiple compromises within the three main institutions (Commission, Parliament, Council) first, and then, between them, particularly in the context of the co-decision procedure and today in the context of trialogues. This system, which emphasizes consensus, often tends toward the lowest common denominator. Fritz Scharpf discusses the pitfalls of joint decision ('joint-decision traps') which make reaching an agreement difficult (especially when unanimity is required in the Council) and favours some powerful interest groups (industry, agriculture exporters) over others (workers, consumers).[47] While the requirement for unanimity in the Council is now reduced, significant constraints weigh on EU decision-making: the search for consensus by the Commission for its legislative proposals, complex voting rules by qualified majority in the Council, the need in Parliament to cast the majority of its members to amend the legislation in the second reading, the necessity for the European Council to find the unanimity for the definition of the multi-annual financial framework, the main decisions of EU's external action and the governance of the Eurozone. Besides, we must add the informal veto power held by several actors who, while failing to impose their choice, can obstruct the adoption of a text.

All of this leads to 'conservative' decisions in the sense that they rarely question the order of things and are not conducive to major reforms. The proponents of historical neo-institutionalism apprehend this inertia with the notion of path dependency. Thus, an equilibrium exists: as a result of its openness, the agenda-setting makes it possible to start the debate on a great number of subjects and compensate for the loss of meaning and energy implied by a very demanding decision-making process. At the agenda-setting stage, the ability of Member States to block a dossier is limited: an institutional actor (Commissioner, Minister, Director General, parliamentary committee, etc.) or, indirectly, an advocacy coalition can, under certain conditions, obtain the inclusion of an item on the agenda. On the contrary, a broad consensus is required afterwards to reach a formal decision and, more importantly, an effective policy.

Agenda-setting is a kind of stockpile of ideas: it does not consist of the confrontation of clearly defined interests or of preferences but of more or less precise ideas. This game on the ideas, concepts and visions allows it to overcome blockages. Mechanisms of learning, teaching and argumentation are at work in the permanent back and forth between policy and expertise. At the decision stage, however, the actors are more pragmatic and the defence of individual and institutional interests takes over.

As a consequence, EU decision-making creates inequalities between policies: it favours those that would benefit the largest number of countries, regions or citizens and satisfy several categories of actors (political, administrative and private). These are policies of 'Pareto optimum', which essentially concern market regulation. The decision-making process harms redistributive policies that involve the designation of contributors and beneficiaries and are therefore less consensual.[48]

The difficulty arises because regulatory policies, intended to benefit all, have effects that are difficult to understand and evaluate and which are only noticeable in the medium term. Moreover, these policies also have indirect effects, especially when they change the rules of the functioning of the market. The 'adjustments' that are taking place are even more poorly perceived by the populations as they are presented as the inevitable consequences of European integration or of the modernity and globalization of which it is the vector. They are not the result of policy choices but of a rationality presented as indisputable, although increasingly challenged in its principle. Public opinions thus have the feeling that the EU imposes a certain economic and social model without making it a subject of public debate and that it provides no tangible benefit to the common individual.

Conclusion

Until now – and the Lisbon Treaty does not change this – the limited resources of the Commission, the institutional balance and the importance of interest groups have not allowed a more 'political' functioning of the Union. The Council has managed to overcome the systematic search for consensus but its composition cannot be politically homogeneous since it is dependent on disparate national electoral configurations. Moreover, it is inconceivable that a majority composed of certain Member States systematically imposes its views on a minority. The European Council could have the necessary legitimacy but it is sensitive to the situation and to national divisions, as it takes most of its decisions at unanimity. Its permanent president appears, in the current state of things, unlikely to assert its leadership, given the dispositions of national leaders towards him and the relatively unobtrusive personalities of the first two incumbents.

Parliament has contributed to a better legitimacy of EU policies but it arouses little interest among citizens and the media and did not increase the legibility of the decision-making process. Various constraints further prevent it from fully functioning according to the left–right divide that governs many national chambers. The rise of the Eurosceptics, election after election, forced the moderate groups to find forms of cooperation, which ended up with them forming a kind of coalition in 2014 to support the inauguration of Jean-Claude Juncker. Moreover, the EP is not in a position to impose a partisan logic on the system and, on the contrary, must cope with the other logics that animate it.

The European edifice rests on the ability of different institutions to extricate majority positions and to make them coincide, which does not favour the articulation of a clear political line. The importance accorded to the idea of 'evidence-based policies' by the Juncker Commission reflects the difficulty of handling the idea of politicization. The Constitution sought to simplify the functioning of the Union: division of powers between institutions and levels of government, assertion of the primacy of representative logic, improved mechanisms of political accountability, revaluation of the role of citizens and national parliaments, simplification of the decision-making process, 'politicization' of the institutional functioning, etc. The Lisbon Treaty only took up part of these provisions and did not profoundly modify the EU regime. The *Spitzenkandidaten* procedure generated some hope, but in a very difficult political context, Jean-Claude Juncker could not, or did not know how to impose a more political approach to the role of the Commission and restore its capacity for political initiatives. As for officials and interest groups structured in opaque networks, they appear to be at the origin of everything, leaving state representatives and peoples confined in a position of validation, veto or limitation of their initiatives.

Notes

1 Around one-third of contemporary political science research on the EU studies public policy. The *Journal of European Public Policy*, created in 1994 and published by Taylor & Francis, has significantly structured this field of the discipline. See also: Federiga Bindi and Kjell A. Eliassen, eds, *Analyzing European Union Politics* (Rome: Il Mulino, 2012).

2 Sabine Saurugger, *Theoretical Approaches to European Integration* (Palgrave Macmillan, 2013); Ben Rosamond, *Theories of European Integration* (Basingstoke/New York: MacMillan/St. Martin's Press, 2000).

3 See, among others: Charles O. Jones and Robert D. Thomas, *Public Policy Making in a Federal System* (Beverly Hills: Sage, 1976).

4 See, for instance: William N. Dunn, *Public Policy Analysis* (London: Routledge, 2015).

5 In a particularly abundant literature, see: Thomas Christiansen and Simona Piattoni, *Informal Governance in the European Union* (Cheltenham: Edward Elgar, 2003); John Peterson and Elizabeth Bomberg, *Decision-Making in the European Union* (London: Palgrave Macmillan, 1999); Rod A. W. Rhodes, *Understanding Governance. Policy*

Networks, Governance, Reflexivity and Accountability (Buckingham/Philadelphia: Open University Press, 1997); Jeremy J. Richardson, *European Union. Policy and Policy-Making* (London: Routledge, 1996); Carlo Ruzza and Vincent Della Sala, *Governance and Civil Society in the European Union* (Manchester: Manchester University Press, 2007); Helen Wallace, William Wallace and Mark A. Pollack, *Policy-Making in the European Union* (Oxford: Oxford University Press, 5th ed., 2005).

6 Ernst B. Haas, *The Uniting of Europe* (Stanford: Stanford University Press, 1958); Leon N. Lindberg, *The Political Dynamics of European Economic Integration* (Stanford: Stanford University Press, 1963); Leon N. Lindberg, 'Decision-making and integration in the European Community,' *International Organization* 19(1) (1965): 56–80.

7 This process has been studies in detail by Thijs Vandenbussche: 'For my next trick I'll need a volunteer. The role of ENGOs in integrating environmental concerns in the European biofuel policy through the European Parliament,' Bruges Political Research Papers, No 55, January 2017, 53 p.

8 Fischer, *Citizens, Experts, and the Environment*, op. cit., p. 22.

9 Ian Bache and Matthew V. Flinders, eds, *Multi-Level Governance. Interdisciplinary Perspectives* (Oxford: Oxford University Press, 2004); Liesbet Hooghe and Gary Marks, 'Types of multi-level governance,' *European Integration Online Papers (EIoP)* 5(11) (2001), accessed 27 June 2013, http://eiop.or.at/eiop/texte/2001-011a.htm; Justin Greenwood, *Interest Representation in the European Union* (Basingstoke: Palgrave Macmillan, 2007); David Coen and Jeremy J. Richardson, eds, *Lobbying the European Union* (Oxford: Oxford University Press, 2009).

10 The Commission's Regulatory Fitness and Performance program (REFIT) aims to ensure that EU legislation produces results for citizens and businesses in an efficient and effective way and at the lowest cost. The aim of the REFIT programme is to ensure that EU legislation remains simple, to remove unnecessary burdens and to adapt existing legislation without compromising policy objectives '(European Commission website, legislation / legislative process / presentation / evaluation and improvement of legislation existing, 10 May 2017).

11 Tanja A. Börzel and Karen Heard-Laureote, 'Networks in EU multi-level governance: concepts and contributions,' *Journal of Public Policy* 29(2) (2009): 135–152; John Peterson, 'Policy networks and European Union policy making: a reply to Kassim,' *West European Politics* 18(2) (1995): 389–407.

12 For a synthesis, see Mark Thatcher, 'Réseau (policy network),' in *Dictionnaire des politiques publiques*, eds Laurie Boussaguet, Sophie Jacquot and Pauline Ravinet (Paris: Les Presses de Sciences-Po, 2006), 384–390. See also: Tanja Börzel, 'Organizing Babylon—on the different conceptions of policy networks,' *Public Administration* 76 (1998): 253–273; Rod Rhodes, Ian Bache and Stephen George, 'Policy networks and policy making in the European Union,' in *Cohesion Policy and European Integration: Building Multilevel Governance*, ed. Liesbet Hooghe (Oxford: Clarendon Press, 1996), 367–387.

13 Gunnel Gustafsson and Jeremy J. Richardson, 'Concepts of rationality and the policy process,' *European Journal of Political Research,* 7(4) (1979): 415–436; Maurice Wright, 'Policy community, policy network and comparative industrial policies,' *Political Studies* 36(4) (1988): 593–612.

14 Grant Jordan and Jeremy Richardson, 'Policy communities: the British and European style,' *Policy Studies Journal* 11 (1983): 603–615; David Marsh and R. A. W. Rhodes,

'Policy communities and issue networks: beyond typology,' in *Policy Networks in British Government*, eds David Marsh and R. A. W. Rhodes (Oxford: Clarendon Press, 1992), 249–268.

15 Simon Bulmer, 'Domestic politics and European community policy–making,' *Journal of Common Market Studies* 21(4) (1983): 349–364; Jordan and Richardson, 'Policy communities: the British and European policy style.'

16 Martin Rhodes, *Understanding Governance*, 38; Tanja Börzel, 'Organizing Babylon—on the different conceptions of policy networks,' *Public Administration* 76 (1998): 253–273.

17 See for instance: Anthony R. Zito, 'Epistemic communities, collective entrepreneurship and European integration,' *Journal of European Public Policy* 8(4) (2001); Amy Verdun, 'The role of the Delors Committee in the creation of EMU: an epistemic community?' *Journal of European Public Policy* 6(2) (1999): 308–328.

18 Didier Georgakakis, 'Les métiers de l'Europe politique: acteurs et professionnalisations de l'Union européenne Presses,' Universitaires de Strasbourg, 2002.

19 For a more general approach to networks: Patrick Le Galès and Mark Thatcher, eds, *Les réseaux de politique publique. Débat autour des policy networks* (Paris: L'Harmattan, 1995); Rhodes, *Understanding Governance.*

20 John Peterson, 'Policy networks,' in *European Integration Theory*, eds Antje Wiener and Thomas Diez (Oxford: Oxford University Press, 2004), 117–135; Rod A. W. Rhodes et al., 'Policy networks and policy making in the European Union: a critical appraisal,' in *Cohesion Policy and European Integration: Building Multi-level Governance*, ed. Liesbet Hooghe (Oxford: Oxford University Press, 1996), 367–387.

21 See for instance: Martin J. Smith, 'From policy community to issue network: Salmonella in eggs and the new politics of food,' *Public Administration* 69(2) (1991): 235–255; John Peterson, 'Decision–making in the European Union: towards a framework for analysis,' *Journal of European Public Policy* 2(1) (1995): 69–93; Elizabeth Bomberg, 'Policy networks on the periphery: EU environmental policy and Scotland,' *Regional and Federal Studies* 4(1) (1994): 45–61; John Peterson, 'The European technology community: policy networks in a supranational setting,' in *Policy Networks in British Government*, eds David Marsh and R. A. W. Rhodes (Oxford: Clarendon Press, 1992).

22 Hussein Kassim, 'Policy networks, networks and European Union policy-making: a sceptical view,' *West European Politics* 14(7) (1994): 15–27; Keith Dowding, 'Model or metaphor? A critical review of the policy network approach,' *Political Studies* 43(1) (1995): 136–158.

23 Maria Green Cowles, James A. Caporaso and Thomas Risse-Kappen, eds, *Transforming Europe: Europeanization and Domestic Change* (Ithaca/London: Cornell University Press, 2001); Paolo Graziano and Maarten P. Vink, eds, *Europeanization. New Research Agendas* (Basingstoke: Palgrave Macmillan, 2008); Johan P. Olsen, *The many faces of Europeanization* (ARENA Working Paper 2/2002); Tanja A. Börzel and Thomas Risse, 'When Europe hits home: Europeanization and domestic change,' *European Integration online Papers* 4(15) (2003); Claudio M. Radaelli, 'Whiter Europeanization? Concept stretching and substantive change,' *European Integration online Papers* 4(8) (2000); Ramona Coman, Thomas Kostera and Luca Tomini, eds, *Europeanization and European Integration. From Incremental to Structural Change* (Palgrave MacMillan, 2013).

24 For a general discussion of this issue, see: Joop Koppenjan and Erik-Hans Klijn, *Managing Uncertainties in Networks. A Network Approach to Problem Solving and Decision Making* (London: Routledge, 2004); Yannis Papadopoulos, *Complexité sociale et politiques publiques* (Paris: Montchrestien, 1995). For a case study: Grace Skogstad, 'Legitimacy and/or policy effectiveness? Network governance and GMO regulation in the European Union,' *Journal of European Public Policy* 10(3) (2003): 321–338.

25 Stijn Smismans, 'European civil society: shaped by discourses and institutional interests,' *European Law Journal* 9(4) (2003): 473–495; Justin Greenwood, 'Organized civil society and democratic legitimacy in the European Union,' *British Journal of Political Science* 37(2) (2007): 333–357.

26 Marsh and R. A. W. Rhodes, 'Policy Communities and Issue Networks, 249–268; John Peterson and Elizabeth Bomberg, 'Decision making in the European Union: a policy networks approach' (paper prepared for presentation to the annual conference of the UK Political Studies Association, Leicester, 20–22 April 1993).

27 Greenwood, *Interest Representation in the European Union*; Andreas Dür, 'Interest groups in the European Union: how powerful are they?,' *West European Politics* 31(6) (2008): 1212–1230.

28 Paul A. Sabatier, *Theories of the Policy Process* (Boulder: Westview Press, 1999); Paul A. Sabatier and Hank Jenkins-Smith, *Policy Change and Learning: An Advocacy Coalition Approach* (Boulder: Westview Press, 1993).

29 Paul Sabatier and Hank Jenkins-Smith, *Policy Change and Learning, an Advocacy Coalition Approach* (Boulder: Westview Press, 1993), 5.

> An advocacy coalition consists of actors from a variety of public and private institutions at all levels of government who share a set of basic beliefs (policy goals plus causal and other perceptions) and who seek to manipulate the rules, budgets, and personnel of government institutions in order to achieve these goals over time.

30 Paul A. Sabatier, 'The advocacy-coalition framework: revisions and relevance for Europe,' *Journal of European Public Policy* 5(1) (1998): 98–130; Sabatier, *Theories of the Policy Process*.

31 This process was analysed in detail by Elisa Cencig: *Explaining EU credit rating agencies regulation: is the Commission back in the driving seat?* Master thesis, College of Europe, Bruges, May 2015.

32 Lucia Quaglia, 'Completing the single market in financial services: the politics of competing advocacy coalitions,' *Journal of European Public Policy* 17(7) (2010): 1007–1023.

33 Nadia Carboni, 'Advocacy groups in the multilevel system of the European Union: a case study in health policy-making,' *Open Journal of Political Science* 2(3) 2012: 32–33.

34 Olivier Costa, Renaud Dehousse and Aneta Trakalova, 'Codecision and "early agreements": an improvement or a subversion of the legislative procedure?' *Studies of the Foundation Notre Europe* 84 (2011); R. Karasheva, 'Codecision, Trialogues and the Legislative Influence of the European Parliament' (London School of Economics, 2009, unpublished manuscript).

35 Amandine Crespy, 'When "Bolkestein" is trapped by the French anti-liberal discourse: a discursive Institutionalist account of preference formation in the realm of EU multi-level politics,' *Journal of European Public Policy* 17(8) (2010): 1253–1270.

36 John W. Kingdon, *Agendas, Alternatives, and Public Policies* (New York: Longman, 2nd ed., 2003).

37 Sebastiaan Princen, 'Agenda-setting strategies in EU policy processes,' *Journal of European Public Policy* 18(7) (2011): 927–943.

38 Sebastiaan Princen and Mark Rhinard, 'Crashing and creeping: agenda-setting dynamics in the European Union,' *Journal of European Public Policy* 13(7) (2006): 1119–1132.

39 Frank R. Baumgartner and Bryan D. Jones, *Agendas and Instability in American Politics* (Chicago: University of Chicago Press, 1993); Sonia Mazey and Jeremy J. Richardson 'Interest groups and EU policy-making: organizational logic and venue shopping,' in *Europe Union: Power and Policy-Making*, ed. Jeremy J. Richardson, (London: Routledge, 2001), 217–237; Jeremy Richardson, 'Policy-making in the EU interests, ideas and garbage cans of primeval soup,' in *European Union: Power and Policy-Making*, ed. Jeremy J. Richardson (London: Routledge, 1996), 3–23.

40 Heather Field and Murray Fulton, 'Germany and the CAP: a bargaining model of EC 15 agricultural policy formation,' *American Journal of Agricultural Economics* 76 (1994): 15–25; Frans A. van der Zee, *Political Economy Models and Agricultural Policy Formation: Empirical Applicability and Relevance for the CAP* (Wageningen Agricultural University: Mansholt Studies 8, 1997).

41 George Tsebelis, 'The power of the European Parliament as a conditional agenda-setter,' *American Political Science Review* 88(1) (1994): 128–142.

42 See Chapter 5 for more information on the political role of the Court of Justice.

43 Nicola Lupo and Cristina Fasone eds, *Interparliamentary Cooperation in the Composite European Constitution* (Oxford: Hart, 2016).

44 Virginie Guiraudon, 'European integration and migration policy: vertical policymaking as venue shopping,' *Journal of Common Market Studies* 38(2) (2000): 251–271.

45 Elizabeth Bomberg and John Peterson, 'European Union decision making: the role of sub-national authorities,' *Political Studies* 46(2) (1998): 219–235; Liesbeth Hooghe, ed., *Cohesion Policy and European Integration: Building Multilevel Governance* (Oxford: Clarendon Press, 1996); Beate Kohler-Koch and Rainer Eising, eds, *The Transformation of Governance in the European Union* (London: Routledge, 1999).

46 Michael D. Cohen, James G. March and. Johan P. Olsen, 'A garbage can model of organizational choices,' *Administrative Science Quarterly* 17 (1972): 1–25; Jeremy Richardson, 'Policy-making in the EU: interests, ideas and garbage cans primeval soup,' in *European Union: Power and Policy-Making*, ed. Jeremy Richardson (London: Routledge, 1996), 3–23.

47 Fritz W. Scharpf, *Governing Europe, Efficient and Democratic?* (Oxford: Oxford University Press, 1998).

48 Giandomenico Majone, *Regulating Europe* (London: Routledge, 1996); Giandomenico Majone, 'The rise of the regulatory state in Europe,' *West European Politics* 14 (3) (1994): 77–101.

Conclusion

The European Union is a political system whose contours are uncertain. It is the product of dual inspirations: utilitarian and idealistic, international and state-based. This genetic code marks its institutional structure, its decision-making methods as well as their daily implementation. It also conditions its scientific and political interpretations. It is resistant to both reforms and crises and to this day debates on the future of the EU are structured around two antagonistic options: developing specific policies to demonstrate its capacity to meet citizens' expectations without challenging the nation state as a historical framework for democratic practice; or reforming the institutions and architecture of the Union, in order to increase their legibility and legitimacy, and revive the ideal of political integration. In the absence of a model, understanding the functioning of the Union thus implies maintaining the spirit of this ambivalence as its trademark.

A political system with structural difficulties of legitimation

This tension between utilitarianism and idealism is not without its many problems. The Union faces specific challenges to its legitimacy because it is a new political form, which does not fit the canons of democracy as understood at the national level, and questions the state as the classical framework for political action and legitimacy.

Euroscepticism is thus often only an extension of a form of populism and anti-system posture. Indeed, the scepticism expressed towards Europe is, in many respects, a more pronounced form of the distrust of political power in general. This misgiving stems from an observation of the centralization and elitist character of this system, as well as a framing of the representative principle as a masquerade devoid of influence on policy.[1] This comes with an anxiety-ridden discourse on the decline of the European socio-economic model, and even of European culture, under the triple threats of globalization, financial capitalism and human migrations. These criticisms have less impact on the Member States themselves than on the EU to the extent that there is a belief, often deeply rooted in the political culture of citizens, in the virtues of national political organization which the new institutional framework of the EU does not benefit from. In other words: aside from situations of extreme crisis, the criticism of their national political system, its institutions, actors and politicians are offset by the citizens' substantive attachment to this form of organization or to the nation which underlies it. For most citizens, the rejection of a national (or local) government or of its actions does not come with a challenge to the regime itself. This situation is very different at the EU level. For many citizens, criticism of EU policies, institutions and actors leads to an overall rejection of the project, as was the case in several Member States upon the ratification of the Treaties of Maastricht, Nice and Lisbon and especially of the European Constitutional Treaty. This is even more true in the case of the referendum on the membership of the United Kingdom in the EU.

Unlike the nation-state, the EU is not considered to be a legitimate holder of sovereignty by most citizens and therefore struggles to create broad support. The rejection of its institutions, its policies and its leaders can therefore easily lead to the questioning of its very existence – in the case of citizens who do not believe in the virtues of European integration or of those who are in favour of other approaches to integration.

Long-based on the rationale of legitimacy through results (output legitimacy) and on the relative indifference of its citizens, the Community has recently been faced with the emergence of public protests. To respond to these, often contradictory, demands and recriminations, several tools and procedures rooted in different logics of legitimation have been implemented. EU reforms have largely been guided by the need to provide citizens with more guarantees and increase their participation in the system. The supranational institutions have also developed strategies and discourses of legitimation which have paradoxically often yielded the opposite effect. The introduction of these new procedures has weakened EU legitimacy, while it has further increased both the reality and the perception of the complexity of its operations. The discourses of legitimation have not convinced their recipients and citizens have been expressing increasing discontent and distrust towards the EU.

The legitimation of the Union is handicapped by the absence of clear political objectives. The Treaty on European Union establishes a range of purposes (Article 3 TEU) and principles of government (Article 4 TEU and following) but does not prioritize them. In attempting to satisfy all parties, it is difficult to understand what the EU values most: is it the market, sustainable development, the fight against social exclusion? economic and social cohesion? territorial cohesion? or democracy and human rights? The period of European euphoria is over – maybe before it could ever extend beyond the circles of the political, administrative, economic and social elites. The austerity measures imposed at the European level in the past years in response to the sovereign debt crisis, the new constraints derived from the Fiscal Compact, as well as the growth of unemployment in Europe have contributed to strengthen the resistances to European integration, have fed populism and Euroscepticism, and led many national leaders (even within EU institutions) to denounce the EU diktats.

The lack of public support is complicated by a tendency to reject European integration because it affects state sovereignty. Not only is the EU accused by some citizens and politicians of violating the principles that founded democracy in Europe it is also accused of gradually undermining them by depriving national institutions of their competences and challenging the 'social contract' on which national political regimes are based.[2] In a context where European societies are marked by multiple fears (economic, social, industrial, environmental or cultural decline, migration, terrorism and the competition from emerging countries), and where populist and extremist parties constantly foster these fears and use them to challenge European integration, globalization and the opening of borders, the nationalist reflex is no longer perceived by a growing number of citizens as a historical regression but as a common-sense solution.[3]

More fundamentally, ever since Jean-Jacques Rousseau, national sovereignty is conceived as a precondition for the freedom of people. States should be sovereign within their territory (the government 'of the people, by the people, for the people') and sovereign outside their territory (the absence of domination in international relations and of any foreign interference). European integration and globalization both challenge this pattern and are perceived, in this context, as threats to freedom and democracy. These allegations are even more problematic because the EU's political system is not based on clear principles that answer the following question simply: in the name of what should citizens have to accept a European norm, especially when it is adopted against the advice of their national representatives in the Council and the European Parliament? What principle can justify such deprivation of liberty?

The European Union and sovereignty

So far, state sovereignty only accommodates three types of international arrangements.[4] The first is the classic international organization. It provides for the joint exercise of limited powers and respect for state sovereignty. The participating states have veto power over decisions taken in common or they may refuse to apply them in their territory: in both cases, the sovereignty of the state is preserved. The second form of collective organization of sovereign states is the confederation, a kind of international organization with broader powers. Here, the rule is unanimity so no state is obliged to implement decisions of which it disapproves. The third form is the federation whereby states form a union and abandon most of their sovereignty to a political system which follows the canons of parliamentary democracy. In a federation, state sovereignty is not preserved but changes in the level of exercise: citizens agree on the fact that there is, at the federal level, a sufficiently homogenous territory or population group to apply democratic principles to certain policies. The freedom of citizens is not compromised because the federation is a polity: it speaks directly to them and offers them the guarantees of a new social contract within that framework.

In classical political theory, there is no alternative to these three patterns. But after more than 60 years of developments and reforms, we must admit that the European Union – except for regarding it as fundamentally illegitimate – is a fourth mode of international accommodation of national sovereignty. The EU is a political system that makes decisions that bind states and their citizens and in which the authorities or national-elected officials are not required to agree with all of them. The problem with the EU is that it established itself as a method of integration but then also as a political system. This happened without prior theorization and did not lead to a clear model *a posteriori*. Of course, the Lisbon Treaty – which heavily drew its inspiration from the European Constitution in this regard – includes, for the first time, provisions for democracy at the European level and specifies some institutional logics for the EU. However, it does not elaborate the principles of a new type of regime and adheres to the finding of syncretism: the EU is a political system that borrows elements from a confederation, a federation, as well as from classic international organizations, all the while cultivating the original 'Community method' and functional logic. This situation satisfies national policy-makers, who have contrasting views of the finalities of European integration and prefer the status quo, but it complicates the EU's legitimacy as well as its analysis. After more than six decades of scientific debate, researchers only agree to recognize the complexity of this political system, described as an unfinished hybrid form[5] or a *sui generis* system which has lost its original characteristics. Various concepts have been proposed to describe the EU (federation of nation-states, consociation, multi-level system of governance, regional state, etc.)[6] but none has been accepted by the whole scientific community or found a place in treaties or everyday language.

The preserved influence of EU states

The fundamental specificity of the EU is that it was born from the integration of relatively old and powerful nation-states which, for the most part, have a strong national identity and want to preserve their sovereignty. In this sense, it has nothing in common with the United States of America (which federated 'young', sparsely populated states that were culturally not very differentiated) or even with the Federal Republic of Germany (which could, at least, rely on a common language). The EU's architecture and history were largely determined by this preoccupation: the need to respect the sovereignty of the nation-states and the weighting of their respective influence within the various institutions. This explains in part the complexity of the EU system, the difficulties in reforming it, the Byzantine nature of the division of powers between the states and the EU, as well as the multiplicity and complexity of its decision-making procedures. The issue of the balance of powers in the European integration process is a taboo for the Member States. For a long time (1952–2000), it was hardly ever addressed. Reforms mainly focused on the balance between the institutions and the vertical distribution of competences between Member States and the EU. The representation of the Member States within the institutions (voting procedures within the Council, number of Commissioners and MEPs, nationalities of senior political and administrative officials) was mentioned sporadically but was never at the heart of the negotiations because of the strong intergovernmental tensions it created. On the occasions of successive enlargements, the composition and functioning of the institutions were adapted in a simply mathematical manner which had the effect of freezing the institutional system and gradually depriving it of its original virtues. A thorough revision was regularly adjourned until better days, the Treaties of Maastricht and Amsterdam, in particular, having evaded the subject.

In view of the imminent EU enlargement to the East, institutional issues were finally addressed head on by the Intergovernmental Conference of 2000 and the European Council in Nice (December 2000). Not surprisingly, this issue raised national conflicts of unusual intensity and divisions between Member States that had been forgotten. These largely explain the unsatisfactory nature of the final compromise: incomprehensible voting rules in the Council, no facilitation of decision-making, the challenge of limiting the number of MEPs to 700. The refusal of some Member States to reconsider the hard-won agreement in Nice thwarted negotiations on the draft Constitutional Treaty developed by the Convention on the Future of the EU (Brussels Summit, December 2003) and made those on the Lisbon Treaty very delicate. Polish officials demanded and obtained multiple compensations to abandon the very favourable arrangement they had received in Nice regarding qualified majority voting. Similarly, in early 2009, the Irish government set the principle of one Commissioner per Member State as a prerequisite for the holding of a second referendum on the Lisbon Treaty although this principle had been called into question by the Treaty of Nice. Recently, the negotiations brought on by the Eurocrisis have once again revealed strong tensions between Member States and shown the reluctance of many national leaders to see the Union granted the legal means to monitor their budget and fiscal policies. Also, this crisis regarding the governance of the eurozone has highlighted the refusal of some states not part of the eurozone to let the members of the zone develop their own mechanisms of macroeconomic regulation, because they fear a decline of their own influence. The intensity of the conflicts raised by the question of state representation within the EU institutions and in the decision-making procedures illustrates well the ability Member States have preserved to control the process of European integration and the importance they attach to this issue. Since the entry into force of the Lisbon Treaty, this was also exemplified through the growing role played by the European Council in EU governance.

The history of European integration is characterized as well by the amount of attention paid to the division of powers between the national and European levels of government. Again, the treaties are particularly complex and obscure, and jurisdictional disputes and interpretations are frequent. Tensions between the two levels of government are strong, much more so than in classic federal systems. The national governments imposed the introduction of the principle of subsidiarity in the Maastricht Treaty for example. The Lisbon Treaty proposes a clarified typology of competences and gives detailed information on the principles of subsidiarity, proportionality and attribution (conferral), but if we look closely, it does not alter the previous situation. On the contrary, the new procedure, the so-called 'Early warning mechanism', that involves national parliaments in the monitoring of subsidiarity, has prompted a larger involvement of national MPs in the opportunity of EU legislative initiatives and given birth to an embryo of political dialogue between the national parliaments and the Commission.[7] Tensions are all the greater because the treaty recognizes – even if it fails to organize – the existence of differentiated integration, by granting several temporary or definitive exemptions to certain Member States. As we have seen since the financial crisis, the institutionalization of the European Council has also favoured the use of strictly intergovernmental procedures to solve problems outside the Union's legal framework.

The European Union: a sustainably ambiguous and ambivalent concept

Tensions between national and European institutions also arise from the uncertainties surrounding the EU's very nature. National and European policy-makers (as well as many academics) have differing views regarding the EU. It appears either as an international organization overseeing a single market supplemented with embryonic and subsidiary policies, or as a quasi-federal political entity with values and objectives distinct from the market, intended to act heavily on the international stage. The Convention on the Future of the Union opened an unprecedented debate on this issue but it failed to settle the question of the nature of the Union in the Constitutional Treaty. Moreover, the treaty itself was rejected. Thus, the uncertainty persists and has, among other factors, driven the citizens of the United Kingdom to vote in favour of an exit from the EU in June 2016.[8]

We will refrain from taking sides in the somewhat analytical, normative and political debate between the supporters of an intergovernmental approach (who place the states at the heart of the system and believe they remain the engine of integration provided it serves their interests) and those of a more federal or functional approach (who believe that integration takes place largely beyond the states and that it depends primarily on autonomous supranational institutions which enjoy a quasi-sovereignty). One can nevertheless consider that European integration was, originally, an enterprise driven by the agreement between national self-interests and a more idealistic integrationist discourse. National leaders, who sought above all to promote their respective economic, trade and security interests, agreed to participate in the European initiative providing that it would be limited to areas free of conflicts of interest and would not be an attack on the most symbolic elements of national sovereignty. European integration certainly owes much to the Federalists and the EU 'founding fathers', but they have mainly played a catalytic role. They failed to impose the federal and political European projects that had been discussed at the Congress of The Hague (1948), and had to deal with their countries' attachment to national sovereignty and its attributes. They were only able to promote the idea of a European economic construction by underlining the further interest that states would find there (peace, geopolitical stability and reconstruction). The European ideal certainly contributed to the mobilization of political, economic and social actors. It also helped to launch a process of integration on the European continent for which there is still no equivalent in terms of its ambitions, size and intensity. This ideal, however, should not obscure the rational determinants and the functional dimension of European integration. The same analysis holds true for the accession of Central and Eastern Europe countries, in the 2000s, or to currently pending applications. The citizens and officials of these states do not primarily wish to join the EU out of pure European idealism, but also and perhaps especially due to economic, budgetary and geostrategic calculations.

However, this rationalist and strategic vision of the EU's creation, strengthening and enlargement must accommodate its evolution over the past 60 years. The internal dynamics of the integration process alongside international and European historical events have created a European Union which is much more than an international organization designed to serve the interests of its Member States. Today, the EU has its own 'soul', which has at least three elements.

The first is the commitment of EU actors and institutions to goals and values such as democracy, human rights, sustainable development, or economic, social and territorial cohesion. This normative dimension, which was reinforced by the Treaty of Lisbon despite abandoning the constitutional ambition, is by no means necessary for a functional regional integration and proves that the EU is more than a collective arrangement aiming at pragmatically implementing a limited number of public policies. Second, we must underline the existence of independent supranational institutions such as the Commission, the European Parliament, the Court of Justice, the European Central Bank, the European executive agencies and the Ombudsman, which are largely beyond Member State control and tend to give the EU its own dynamic. Finally, we must consider the 'politicization' process, which has been underway in the EU since the early 1990s. It covers many aspects: the establishment of European citizenship and the recognition of the role of European political parties under the Treaty of Maastricht, the Charter of Fundamental Rights, the continued strengthening of the European Parliament powers by all the treaties adopted since 1970, the introduction of a procedure of European citizens' initiative, the references to representative democracy in the Treaty of Lisbon and the latest developments of the European elections, which determined de facto the appointment of the President of the Commission. Indeed, the organization of the 2014 European elections under the *Spitzenkandidaten* procedure was a new stage in the politicization and parliamentarization of the EU. It allowed the candidates of the five main European parties to present their views on European integration, established a link between the popular vote and the Commission President, and gave a more partisan approach to relations between the European Parliament and the Commission. Although the European Union system remains in many respects original, it can no longer be equated with the original intergovernmental project. Despite the challenges it has faced since the early 2000s (increasing Euroscepticism in public opinion, difficulties in treaty reform, the Commission's relative passivity, stagnation of several policies, tensions among national policy-makers, difficulties in handling the euro crisis, budgetary dispute, etc.), European integration has gained a degree of autonomy and normativity that reminds one more of a national political system than of a classic international organization.

We believe that the fundamental ambiguity between the normative and functional dimensions of the EU has rendered this political system very resistant to crises. Because the EU has its own goals, dynamics and supranational institutions, it does not suffer too much from the fluctuations of Member States' positions towards European integration and is not overly sensitive to the protectionist or nationalist tendencies that always emerge in periods of economic and social crisis. Also, because the EU is functional and focused above all on concrete matters, it can rally a wide spectrum of people, from true Federalists to pragmatic Eurosceptics who are attached to some European policies. Thanks to its hybrid nature and its underlying ambiguities, the EU has survived several deep crises over time and especially since the beginning of the 2000s.

Even if a majority of people and politicians do not wish for a federal Europe and are more attached to the nation-state than the Founding Fathers expected, most believe that European integration is necessary to address important contemporary challenges (sustainable development, competitiveness, climate change, regulation of globalization, security issues, migration, etc.). Therefore, more than 65 years after the creation of the ECSC, the tools of legitimization of the EU remain the same: first and foremost, it is still based on its capacity to fulfil efficiently a limited number of functions, i.e. on its 'output legitimacy'. Understanding how the EU really works and performs these functions is thus essential to grasp contemporary politics in Europe especially in a context where the interactions between the national political space and that of the EU is increasingly significant.

Notes

1   Olivier Costa and Paul Magnette, *Une Europe des Elites? Réflexions sur la Fracture Démocratique dans l'Union Européenne* (Brussels: Éditions de l'Université de Bruxelles, coll. 'Études européennes,' 2007).
2   Klaus Armingeon and Kai Guthmann, 'Democracy in crisis? The declining support for national democracy in European countries, 2007–2011,' *European Journal of Political Research*, 53(3) (2014): 423–442.
3   Dani Rodrik, *Straight Talk on Trade: Ideas for a Sane World Economy* (Princeton University Press, 2017).
4   Paul Magnette, *Le Souverain Apprivoisé. L'Europe, l'Etat et la Démocratie* (Brussels: Complexe, 2000).
5   Stefano Bartolini, *Restructuring Europe: Centre Formation, System Building and Political Structuring Between the Nation State and the European Union* (Oxford / New York: Oxford University Press, 2005).
6   Olivier Beaud, 'La souveraineté de l'État, le pouvoir constituant et le traité de Maastricht,' *Revue Française de Droit Administrative* 9(1) (1993): 1045–1068; Matthijs Bogaards, 'Consociational interpretations of the EU: a critical appraisal,' *European Union Politics* 3(3) (2002): 357–381; Olivier Costa and Paul Magnette, 'The European Union as a Consociation? A methodological assessment,' *West European Politics* 26(3) (2003): 118; Markus Jachtenfuchs, 'The governance approach to European Integration,' *Journal of Common Market Studies* 39(2) (2001): 245–264; Fritz W. Scharpf, 'The joint-decision trap: lessons from German federalism and European Integration,' *Public Administration* 66(3) (1988): 239–278; Vivien A. Schmidt, 'The European Union: democratic legitimacy in a regional state?,' *Journal of Common Market Studies* 42(5) (2004): 975–997.

7   Federico Fabbrini and Katarzyna Granat, '"Yellow card, but no foul": the role of the national parliaments under the subsidiarity protocol and the commission proposal for an EU regulation on the right to strike,' *Common Market Law Review* 50(1) (2013): 115–143.
8   Nathalie Brack and Olivier Costa, eds, *Euroscepticism within EU Institutions. Diverging Views of Europe* (London: Routledge, 2012).

Bibliography

The literature related to the EU, its history, institutions and operation is extremely rich. Most of the sources used in this book are cited in endnotes. Some essential and recent references are listed below.

A. General literature

Bache, I., Bulmer, S., George, S., Parker, O. (2014). *Politics in the European Union*. Oxford: Oxford University Press.

Bartolini, S. (2005). *Restructuring Europe: Centre Formation, System Building and Political Structuring between the Nation State and the European Union*. Oxford: Oxford University Press.

Christiansen, T., Piattoni, S. (2003). *Informal Governance in the European Union*. Cheltenham: Edward Elgar.

Dehousse, R. (2009). *Politiques Européennes*. Paris: Presses de Sciences Po.

Hix, S., Hoyland, B. (2011). *The Political System of the European Union*. 3rd edition. Basingstoke and London: Macmillan Press.

Hooghe, L., Marks, G. (2001). *Multi-Level Governance and European Integration*. Lanham: Rowman & Littlefield.

Jorgensen, K. E., Pollack, M. A., Rosamond, B. (2007). *Handbook of European Union Politics*. London: Sage.

Leuffen, D., Rittberger, B., Schimmelfennig, F. (2012). *Differentiated Integration: Explaining Variation in the European Union*. Basingstoke: Palgrave Macmillan.

Magnette, P. (2005). *What is the European Union? Nature and Prospects*. Basingstoke: Palgrave Macmillan.

Majone, G. (1996). *Regulating Europe*. London and New York: Routledge.

Majone, G. (2005). *Dilemmas of European Integration: The Ambiguities and Pitfalls of Integration by Stealth*. Oxford: Oxford University Press.

Nugent, N. (2010). *The Government and Politics of the European Union*. 7th edition. Basingstoke: Palgrave Macmillan.

Parsons, C. (2003). *A Certain Idea of Europe*. Ithaca: Cornell University Press.

Risse, T., Caporaso, J., Green Cowles, M. (2001). *Transforming Europe: Europeanization and Domestic Change*. Ithaca: Cornell University Press.

Schmidt, V. (2006). *Democracy in Europe: The EU and National Polities*. Oxford: Oxford University Press.

Schmitter, P. C. (2000). *How to Democratize the European Union ... and Why Bother?* Lanham: Rowman & Littlefield.

Stone Sweet, A., Sandholtz, W., Fligstein, N. (2001). *The Institutionalization of Europe*. Oxford: Oxford University Press.

Thomson, R. (2011). *Resolving Controversy in the European Union*. Cambridge: Cambridge University Press.

B. History of European integration

Dinan, D. (2006). *Origins and Evolution of the European Union*. Oxford: Oxford University Press.

Gillingham, J. (2003). *European Integration, 1950–2003, Superstate or New Market Economy*. Cambridge: Cambridge University Press.

Hoffman, S. (1995). *The European Sisyphus. Essays on Europe 1964–1994*. Boulder: Westview Press.

Milward, A. (1992). *The European Rescue of the Nation State*. London: Routledge.

Moravcsik, A. (1998). *The Choice for Europe: Social Purpose and State Power from Messina to Maastricht*. Ithaca: Cornell University Press.

C. Theories of European integration and the decision-making process

Bickerton, C., Hodson, D., Puetter, U. (2015). *The New Intergovernmentalism*. Oxford: Oxford University Press.

Bulmer, S., Lequesne, C. (eds) (2013). *The Member States of the European Union*. Oxford: Oxford University Press.

Christiansen, T., Jørgensen, K. E., Wiener, A. (2001). *The Social Construction of Europe*. London: Sage.

Cini, M., Borragán, N. P. S. (2016). *European Union Politics*. Oxford: Oxford University Press.

Coman, R., Kostera, T., Tomini, L. (eds) (2013). *Europeanization and European Integration: From Incremental to Structural Change*. Basingstoke: Palgrave Macmillan.

Costa, O., Magnette, P. (2003). 'The European Union as a consociation? A methodological assessment', *West European Politics*, vol. 26, n 3, pp. 1–18.

De la Porte, C., Pochet, P. (2002). *Building Social Europe Through the Open Method of Coordination*. Brussels: PIE Peter Lang.

Dehousse, R. (ed.) (2011). *The Community Method: Obstinate or Obsolete?* Basingstoke: Palgrave MacMillan.

Dunn, W. N. (2015). *Public Policy Analysis*. Routledge: London.

Farrell, H., Héritier, A. (2004). 'Interorganizational negotiation and intraorganizational power in shared decision-making. Early agreements under codecision and their impact on the European parliament and council', *Comparative Political Studies*, vol. 37, n 10, pp. 1184–1212.

Favell, A., Guiraudon, V. (eds) (2011). *Sociology of the European Union*. Houndmills: Palgrave MacMillan.

Featherstone, K., Radaelli, C. (eds) (2003). *The Politics of Europeanization*. Oxford: Oxford University Press.

Haas, E. (1958). *The Uniting of Europe, Political, Social and Economic Forces, 1950–1957*. London: Stevens & Sons.

Hooghe, L., Marks, G. (2009). 'A postfunctionalist theory of European integration: from permissive consensus to constraining dissensus', *British Journal of Political Science*, vol. 39, n 1, pp. 1–23.

Jachtenfuchs, M. (2001). 'The governance approach to European integration', *Journal of Common Market Studies*, vol. 39, n 2, pp. 245–264.

Keating, M. (2017). 'Europe as a multilevel federation', *Journal of European Public Policy*, vol. 24, n 4, pp. 615–632.

Lindberg, L. N. (1963). *The Political Dynamics of European Economic Integration*. Stanford: Stanford University Press.

Lindberg, L. N., Scheingold, S. A. (1991). *Europe's Would be Polity. Patterns of Change in the European Community*. New Jersey: Prentice Hall.

Pierson, P. (1996). 'The path to European integration: a historical institutionalist analysis', *Comparative Political Studies*, vol. 29, n 2, pp. 123–163.

Pierson, P. (2000). 'Path dependence, increasing return, and the study of politics', *American Political Science Review*, vol. 94, n 2, pp. 251–267.

Puchala, D. J. (1971). 'Of blind men, elephants and international integration', *Journal of Common Market Studies*, vol. 10, n 3, pp. 267–284.

Rosamond, B. (2000). *Theories of the European Integration*. Basingstoke: Palgrave.

Sandholtz, W., Stone Sweet, A. (1998). *European Integration and Supranational Governance*. New York: Oxford University Press.

Saurugger, S. (2013). *Theoretical Approaches to European Integration*. Basingstoke: Palgrave.

Scharpf, F. W. (1998). *Governing Europe, Efficient and Democratic?* Oxford: Oxford University Press.

Wallace, H., Pollack, M., Young, A. R. (eds) (2015). *Policy-Making in the European Union*. Oxford: Oxford University Press.

Wiener, A., Diez, T. (2009). *European Integration Theory*. 2nd edition. Oxford: Oxford University Press.

D. Institutional and non-institutional actors

Alter, K. (2001). *Establishing the Supremacy of European Law*. Oxford: Oxford University Press.

Auel, K., Benz, A. (eds) (2006). *The Europeanisation of Parliamentary Democracy*. Abingdon and New York: Routledge. coll. 'The library of legislative studies'.

Bergström, F. (2005). *Comitology: Delegation of Powers in the European Union and the Committee System*. Oxford: Oxford University Press.

Best, E., Christiansen, T., Settembri, P. (2008). *The Institutions of the Enlarged European Union*. Cheltenham: Edward Elgar.

Brack, N. (2017). *Opposing Europe in the European Parliament. Rebels and Radicals in the Chamber*. Basingstoke: Palgrave.

Busuioc, M., Groenleer, M., Trondal, J. (2012). *The Agency Phenomenon in the European Union: Emergence, Institutionalisation and Everyday Decision-Making*. Manchester: Manchester University Press.

Chang, M., Monar, J. (2013). *The European Commission in the Post-Lisbon Era of Crises. Between Political Leadership and Policy Management*. Brussels: PIE Peter Lang.

Christiansen, T., Larsson, T. (2007). *The Role of Committees in the European Union Policy Process*. Cheltenham: Edward Elgar.

Corbett, R., Jacobs, F., Shackleton, M. (2007). *The European Parliament*. London: John Harper.

Dimitrakopoulos, D. (2004). *The Changing European Commission*. Manchester: Manchester University Press.

Dür, A. (2008). 'Interest groups in the European Union: how powerful are they?', *West European Politics*, vol. 31, n 6, pp. 1212–1230.

Elgström, O. (2003). *European Union Council Presidencies: A Comparative Perspective*. London: Routledge.

Greenwood, J. (2011). *Interest Representation in the European Union*. 3rd edition. Basingstoke: Palgrave.

Hayes-Renshaw, F., Wallace, W. (2006). *The Council of Ministers*. London: Palgrave MacMillan.

Hix, S., Noury, A., Roland, G. (2007). *Democratic Politics in the European Parliament*. Cambridge: Cambridge University Press.

Hooghe, L. (2001). *The European Commission and the Integration of Europe. Images of Governance*. Cambridge: Cambridge University Press.

Judge, D., Earnshaw, D. (2008). *The European Parliament*. Basingstoke: Palgrave MacMillan.

Kassim, H., Peterson, J., Bauer, M. W., Connolly, S., Dehousse, R., Hooghe, L., Thompson, A. (2013). *The European Commission of the Twenty-First Century*. Oxford: Oxford University Press.

Kelemen, R. (2006). 'Suing for Europe', *Comparative Political Studies*, vol. 39, n 1, pp. 101–127.

Kluger-Rasmussen, M. (2016). *Lobbying in the European Parliament: The Battle for Influence*. Basingstoke: Palgrave.

Klüver, H. (2013). *Lobbying in the European Union: Interest Groups, Lobbying Coalitions, and Policy Change*. Oxford: Oxford University Press.

Kreppel, A. (2002). *The European Parliament and the Supranational Party System*. Cambridge: Cambridge University Press.

Martinsen, D. S. (2015). *An Ever More Powerful Court? The Political Constraints of Legal Integration in the European Union*. Oxford: Oxford University Press.

Mény, Y. (dir.) (2009). *La construction d'un parlement: 50 ans d'histoire du Parlement européen. 1958–2008*. Luxembourg: European Parliament.

Naurin, D., Wallace, H. (2008). *Unveiling the Council of the European Union*. Houndmills: Palgrave Macmillan.

Neuhold, C., Rozenberg, O., Smith, J., Hefftler, C. (eds) (2015). *The Palgrave Handbook of National Parliaments and the European Union*. Basingstoke: Palgrave.

Nugent, N. (ed.) (2016). *At the Heart of the Union: Studies of the European Commission*. Berlin: Springer.

Peterson, J., Schakelton, M. (2006). *The Institutions of the European Union*. Oxford: Oxford University Press.

Priestley, J., Schollgen, G., Penalver Garcia, N. (2015). *The Making of a European President*. Basingstoke: Palgrave.

Puetter, U. (2014). *The European Council and the Council: New Intergovernmentalism and Institutional Change*. Oxford: Oxford University Press.

Ripoll-Servent, A. (2017). *The European Parliament*. Basingstoke: Palgrave.

Rittberger, B. (2005). *Building Europe's Parliament. Democratic Representation Beyond the Nation State*. Oxford: Oxford University Press.

Schmidt, S., Kelemen, D. (2013). *The Power of the European Court of Justice*. London: Routledge.

Smith, A. (ed.) (2004). *Politics and the European Commission: Actors, Interdependence, Legitimacy*. London: Routledge.

Steunenberg, B., Thomassen, J. (2002). *The European Parliament: Moving Toward Democracy in the EU*. Lanham: Rowman & Littlefield.

Stevens, A., Stevens, H. (2001). *Brussels Bureaucrats? The Administration of the European Union*. Houndmills: Palgrave.

Stone Sweet, A. (2000). *Governing with Judges: Constitutional Politics in Europe*. Oxford: Oxford University Press.

Stone Sweet, A. (2004). *The Judicial Construction of Europe*. New York: Oxford University Press.

Tallberg, J. (2006). *Leadership and Negotiation in the European Union*. Cambridge: Cambridge University Press.

Tömmel, I. (2017). 'The standing president of the European Council: intergovernmental or supranational leadership?', *Journal of European Integration*, vol. 39, n 2, pp. 175–189.

Weiler, J. (1994). 'A quiet revolution: the European court of justice and its interlocutors', *Comparative Political Studies*, vol. 26, n 4, pp. 510–534.

Werts, J. (2008). *The European Council*. London: John Harper.

Westlake, M., Galloway, D. (2004). *The Council of the European Union*. London: John Harper.

Whitaker, R. (2011). *The European Parliament's Committees. National Party Influence and Legislative Empowerment*. London: Routledge.

Wonka, A. (2008). 'Decision making dynamics in the European Commission: partisan, national or sectoral?', *Journal of European Public Policy*, vol. 15, n 8, pp. 1145–1163.

E. Recent crises of the EU

Clarke, H., Goodwin, M., Whiteley, P. (2017). *Brexit: Why Britain Voted to Leave the European Union*. Cambridge: Cambridge University Press.

Copsey, N. (2015). *Rethinking the European Union*. London: Palgrave.

Crespy, A. (2016). *Welfare Markets in Europe, the Democratic Challenges of European Integration*. London: Palgrave.

Crum, B. (2013). 'Saving the euro at the cost of democracy?', *Journal of Common Market Studies*, vol. 51, n 4, pp. 614–630.

Dinan, D., Nugent, N., Patterson, W. (2017). *The European Union in Crisis*. Basingstoke: Palgrave.

Fabbrini, S. (2015). *Which European Union? Europe after the Euro Crisis*. Cambridge: Cambridge University Press.

Fossum, J.-E., Menendez, A. J. (dirs) (2014). *The European Union in Crises or the European Union as Crises*. Arena Report n 2.

Grimmel, A. (2017). *The Crisis of the European Union: Challenges, Analyses, Solutions*. London: Routledge.

Hobolt, S. B. (2016). 'The Brexit vote: a divided nation, a divided continent', *Journal of European Public Policy*, vol. 23, n 9, pp. 1259–1277.

Laffan, B. (2016). 'Europe's union in crisis: tested and contested', *West European Politics*, vol. 39, n 5, pp. 915–932.

Leruth, B., Startin, N., Usherwood, S. (2017). *The Routledge Handbook of Euroscepticism*. London: Routledge.

Lord, C. (2015). *A Different Kind of Democracy? Debates about Democracy and the European Union*. New York: Open Society Foundations.

Saurugger, S., Terpan, F. (2016). *Crisis and Institutional Change in Regional Integration*. London: Routledge.

Index